POSTMORTEM

Fieldwork Encounters and Discoveries

A series edited by Robert Emerson and Jack Katz

POSTMORTEM

How Medical Examiners Explain Suspicious Deaths

STEFAN TIMMERMANS

THE UNIVERSITY OF CHICAGO PRESS
CHICAGO AND LONDON

STEFAN TIMMERMANS is professor of sociology at the University of
California, Los Angeles. He is the author of two previous books,
including *Sudden Death and the Myth of CPR*.

The University of Chicago Press, Chicago 60637
The University of Chicago Press, Ltd., London
© 2006 by The University of Chicago
All rights reserved. Published 2006
Printed in the United States of America

15 14 13 12 11 10 09 08 07 06   1 2 3 4 5

ISBN: (cloth): 0-226-80398-8

Library of Congress Cataloging-in-Publication Data

Timmermans, Stefan, 1968–
    Postmortem : how medical examiners explain suspicious deaths /
Stefan Timmermans.
        p.   cm.
    Includes bibliographical references and index.
    ISBN 0-226-80398-8 (cloth : alk. paper)
    1. Autopsy. 2. Death—Causes. 3. Death—Proof and
certification. 4. Medical examiners (Law). I. Title.
    HV8073.T56 2006
    616.07'59—dc22   2005032147

♾The paper used in this publication meets the minimum requirements
of the American National Standard for Information Sciences—
Permanence of Paper for Printed Library Materials, ANSI Z39.48-1992.

CONTENTS

On November 14, 2003, the newspaper *USA Today* carried an unusual cover story. The title read "Grieving Coach Wages Fight for Son: Packer Ray Sherman Leads Charge to Have Self-Inflicted Shooting Death Ruled Accidental." The front page showed a large picture of Packers Assistant Coach Ray Sherman holding a photo of his son Raymond Glenn Sherman II, who died of a gunshot wound to the head at age fourteen. The story reflects the pain of a father who believes his son's death was misclassified as a suicide:

Deep down in his heavy heart, Sherman knows there is no way his son intentionally took his life. It *had* to be an accident, he says—a child playing with a gun that, Sherman acknowledges, was not properly locked up. It was one of three guns that the coach had received as a gift.

Sherman says he wants the record set straight, and only that will allow the family to properly grieve. Backed by a report from the Green Bay Police Department and independent opinions from three experts in forensics and/or suicide, the family filed a petition last week in Brown County Circuit Court to have the manner of death officially classified as an accident.

[Brown County Assistant Interim Medical Examiner] Klimek filed paperwork Monday to change the classification to "undetermined," which he says allows for the possibility that it was not suicide. This is unacceptable to the family, which says Klimek mishandled the case from the start and rushed to his initial conclusion. Only a judge can change the classification.

Sherman, who theorizes his son was role-playing a movie scene when the gun inadvertently fired, sees an accurate description of death as the last thing he could give Little Ray. He has spent "tens of thousands" of dollars on legal fees and is willing to spend more. The family gains nothing monetarily by a change in the ruling.[1]

This story is unusual because it reveals a conflict between relatives and a death investigator that more often remains hidden. A father is convinced that the classification of his son's death adds insult to grave injury, and a county official bases his decision for suicide on the undisputed fact that the fatal gunshot wound was self-inflicted. These stories rarely make the news or the courtroom. Instead, families fight these bitter battles out of the limelight.

This book is about forensic death investigators, about the difficult decisions of distinguishing among suicide, accident, homicide, and natural death. Death investigators are called when something goes seriously wrong. The deceased should have lived. Their death was either unexpected or premature, and the circumstances suggest violence, accident, destructive behavior, abuse, or simply ambiguity. These deaths are *suspicious* because they occurred out of the ordinary. Rumors swirl. Angry relatives call for justice and urge the police to take action. Devastated parents, hoping to save other families from similar tragedies, plead for more research. Suspicious deaths fall under the jurisdiction of a forensic death investigator charged with determining the identity of the deceased and the cause and manner of death.

For three years, I have shadowed the professionals who investigate such individual tragedies as the death of Ray Sherman II. In this book, I show how they reach their conclusions and explain why, in spite of protest, we often have no other choice than to believe them. My perspective is sociological; I am interested in how people in North American societies give meaning to deaths that seem unfathomable. Deaths that fall far outside the spectrum of dignified, normal dying raise many questions: existential questions about premature loss, political questions about pervasive violence in our society, medical questions about the causes of death, and moral questions about personal and societal responsibility. Most of these questions are not answered to the satisfaction of the people left behind, yet death investigation provides an official response.

Forensic investigators take bodies from the death scene, consult with police and physicians, read medical files, conduct autopsies, order laboratory tests, and then determine a cause of death. The information they

provide is useless for the deceased. Postmortem investigations are justified as a benefit for the living. The conflict following the death of Ray
Sherman II shows, however, that the benefit is not always clear. Conflicts can arise because relatives with deep existential questions find the
medical examiner's answers wanting. When family and friends reject the
moral implications of a suicide verdict, the death investigator may seem
heartless by insisting on a classification that needlessly agonizes relatives.
Reclassifying a suicide as an undetermined death after relatives protest and
no new evidence emerges, however, suggests that the initial classification
rested on shaky grounds—or, worse, that the investigation is vulnerable
to political influence. Such charges impugn death investigators' judgment
and professionalism. They undermine respect for the scientific expertise
that guides decision making. With their judgment subject to scrutiny, what
motivates the decisions of professional death investigators?

In popular media, the death investigator is often portrayed as a super-
detective who with a keen eye notices a small piece of evidence that reveals
the identity of a serial killer or other perpetrator. In the endless skirmish
between good and evil, the investigator's raison d'être is foiling the perfect crime. The reality of death investigation is less glamorous but no
less fascinating. Although death investigators rarely develop the intimate
relationships with law enforcement agencies that keep Dr. Quincy's or Dr.
Scarpetta's social life titillating, they define the boundaries of homicide,
suicide, accident, and natural death. While their role in criminal investigation is usually more limited than the fictional medical examiner's scuba
diving to check an underwater death scene (in Patricia Cornwell's *Cause of
Death*), they determine which deaths caused by others will be recorded as
homicides. Instead of diagnosing an individual patient with an infectious
disease, they aim to set a public health agenda by locating the dangers
of risky living. Their work takes place out of the public eye but greatly
influences how we make sense of suspicious deaths.

ACKNOWLEDGMENTS

This book could not have been written without the support of chief medical examiner "Dr. Cahill" and her staff in the medical examiner's office
where I was permitted to be an observer. I thank them for their availability,
trust, and encouragement. They work in what they describe as a "silent"
office, invisible until disaster or personal tragedy strikes. It took courage to
allow an outsider to observe death investigators when their work has often
been mystified, misunderstood, or contested. They shared their skills, humor, excitement, and frustration. I feel privileged and hope they recognize
themselves in this book.

While no colleagues cared to join me in the morgue, many offered suggestions on the evolving manuscript. Over the years, Peter Conrad has gone beyond the call of duty. He has gently shown me by example how to conceptualize and reach diverse audiences. I am grateful for his wonderful mentorship. I also thank Marc Berg, Charles Bosk, Allan Brandt, Wendy Cadge, Daniel Chambliss, Adele Clarke, David Cunningham, Steve Epstein, Humphrey Gardner, Emilie Gomart, Karen Hansen, Randy Hanzlick, Carol Heimer, Stefan Hirschauer, Sarah Lamb, Mike Lynch, Aaron Mauck, Kirsten Moe, Michael Nurok, Debra Osnowitz, Bernice Pescosolido, Lindsay Prior, Charles Rosenberg, Sara Shostak, Lucy Suchman, Meira Weiss, and Robert Zussman for their comments on parts of this manuscript. I thank Nancy Trotic for her meticulous copyediting. I benefited from a Mazer Faculty Research Grant from Brandeis University and finished the writing while I was a Robert Wood Johnson Health and Society fellow at Harvard University. Jack Katz and Bob Emerson not only provided a home for this book in their series but also welcomed me to their department. The legendary Chicago editor Doug Mitchell remained a wonderful supporter of this project. Anselm Strauss and Bruno Latour inspired by example.

A shorter version of chapter 2 has been published as "Suicide Determination and the Professional Authority of Medical Examiners," *American Sociological Review* 70, no. 2 (2005): 311–33; and an earlier version of chapter 6 was published as "Cause of Death vs. Gift of Life: Maintaining Jurisdiction in Death Investigation," *Sociology of Health and Illness* 24, no. 5 (2002): 550–74. Parts of the postscript have been published as "How Can You Watch Autopsies?" in *Reflections on Research: The Realities of Doing Research in the Social Sciences,* edited by N. Hallowell, J. Lawton, and S. Gregory (Berkshire, UK: Open University Press, 2005), 26–29.

Then there is the home front. While I was conducting this research, both my daughter Merel and my son Jasper were born. Attending autopsies of children contrasted with my deep love for them and constituted an incredibly painful reminder of the fragility of some lives and the uncomfortably fine line between good parenting and catastrophe. Ruth indulged my fascination with suspicious death with patience, humor, and occasional concern. I am not sure that dedicating a book about death to her honors her sunny vivacity. Then again, no book really could. So I dedicate this book to Ruth with love.

BROKERING SUSPICIOUS DEATHS

Death is not an individual but a social event. When, with a barely notice-able sigh, the last gasp of air is exhaled, the blood stops pulsating through arteries and veins, and neurons cease activating the brain, the life of a human organism has ended. Death is not official, however, until the com-munity takes notice. In modern societies, a physician—any physician will do—verifies that death has occurred, often by simply putting a stethoscope on the chest to listen for heart sounds and palpating for a pulse. Except in cases of organ procurement, the last medical act consists of filling out a death certificate, where the physician notes the time and cause of death.

Death work is routinized in three sequences, each with a different ori-entation: an implicit focus on death avoidance during life, a dignified dying experience, and a clean, quick disposal after death. As one of the first and most influential works of medical sociology explained, societies function on the premise that people do not get sick, and if they do get sick, it is their responsibility to get better.[1] Talcott Parsons's "sick role" could be extended to a "death role."[2] It is everyone's responsibility to keep on living. The health care system operates from a negative orientation: the traditional emphasis is not necessarily to promote wellness and health, but to minimize physical deterioration and complications among those al-ready ill. Death is the outcome to be avoided. Statistically, a country's bill of health is measured in infant mortality, life expectancy, leading causes of death, and potential productive years lost. The postponement of death permeates every aspect of health care but is particularly well manifested in the omnipresence of resuscitation technologies in intensive-care units and emergency departments.[3]

When in spite of all intentions and aggressive treatments death is inevitable, the interaction at the deathbed is reversed. With 75 percent of U.S. deaths taking place in hospitals or nursing homes,[4] most deaths occur as routines in well-prepared places, surrounded by specialized staff who manage culturally appropriate passings. The transition from cure to care might be made hours, days, or months before death occurs and is a consequence of an inoperable, incurable deterioration in an illness trajectory. Elisabeth Kübler-Ross's influential books on the psychodynamic acceptance of pending death paved the way for conformity in light of mortality and carved out a space for spiritual and religious guidance.[5] In near unison, patients, relatives, and health care providers report that they envision a "good" death as occurring with pain and symptoms under control, conscious decision making at the end, time to prepare for death, spiritual closure, an opportunity to reciprocate to others, and affirmation of the whole person.[6] New groups of specialists, including palliative-care physicians, cater to this cultural model by offering terminal care in hospices. Stringent right-to-die initiatives are gaining momentum. The emphasis is on maintaining autonomy for the patient while mining the medicine cabinet to ease pain and suffering.

Once death has occurred, medicine relinquishes any claims for further intervention (again, with the notable exception of organ and tissue procurement).[7] The attending physician certifies death by noting the time and a cause of death, which is usually the patient's primary diagnosis. The corpse is transferred to a funeral director, who takes care of embalming, wakes, and funerals according to laws and religious customs. A good disposal is a quick and clean event, celebrating the memory of the deceased.

The contradictory attitudes of death avoidance and acceptance are resolved in light of medical history and age. When old age has been reached or physicians have declared that a cure is unavailable, not only is death sanctioned, but one is also expected to accept death.[8] Even when it is unfathomable for relatives and friends, most deaths make medical sense: a diabetic patient was known to have had bad coronary arteries; a nursing home resident had been treated for advanced liver carcinomas; a child died after a lengthy bout with lymphoma; emergency-department staff noticed a heart attack in progress on the EKG monitor of a middle-aged woman and were unable to reverse the process. The medical history links an individual's death to the big natural killers: heart disease, cancer, stroke, and infectious diseases. The pattern softens the inevitability of the passing.

Death is not a random event but due to a chronic or progressive process that ravaged vital organs. For old people, a death of natural causes is tolerated in light of life's achievements and the physical decline and suffering associated with aging. Even without a strong medical history, the elderly are expected to live with the possibility of pending death.

When deaths fall outside this interpretive medical spectrum, however, the social order of dying is disturbed. About 20 percent of people die in suspicious circumstances, meaning out of place and time.[9] The social institutions and professionals taking care of the dying did not anticipate the death, which generates an anomalous, potentially threatening situation. Suspicious death raises the possibility of a public health danger. Did the itchy rash and flu-like symptoms mask an anthrax infection? Was a traumatic death due to criminal activity? After an unexpected death, rumors are rife about who might benefit financially or emotionally, casting doubt on the sincerity of the grievers. Sometimes it is not the manner of death that is questionable but the identity of the deceased. Who should be notified when an unidentified body is found? Because of the tight medical control surrounding most terminal events, death becomes suspicious not only when crime is involved, but also when the passing escapes a medical prognosis: when people die without medical records, when they die unexpectedly under medical care, or when they die because of trauma in a medical setting. The danger of a suspicious death resides in the possibility that more such victims will be claimed. To investigate the risk and uncertainty of suspicious death, another kind of death worker—a coroner or a medical examiner—toils in a morgue. These professionals are part of an invisible public health and criminal justice infrastructure whose sole task is to investigate suspicious deaths.

Social scientists, health care providers, and bioethicists have extensively studied the emergence of hospice care, right-to-die initiatives, and aggressive lifesaving interventions in order to evaluate the quality of the contemporary dying experience. Deaths that escape close medical management, however, have received attention only summarily.[10] The lack of critical scrutiny is remarkable, because death investigators enact a relationship to death different from that of the clinician. In contrast with common health care interventions, death investigators' work is guided not by cure or care—avoiding death or preparing for the final transition—but by the need to generate expert knowledge about life. Determining the cause and manner of suspicious deaths is highly technical work, dependent on scene investigation findings, autopsy observations, toxicology test values, and a close reading of medical files. This expert work necessarily has a strong cultural dimension, because it involves locating corpses in contested categories of death. This book, based on three years of observation in a medical examiner's office, looks at the daily work of death investigators as a cultural instance of managing lethal risk, uncertainty, and danger.

THE REPLACEMENT OF CORONERS WITH MEDICAL EXAMINERS

Coroners have traditionally conducted death investigations and still serve about half of the U.S. population. Their mandate dates back to the twelfth century, when officers collected money owed to the English Crown and were known as "crowners" or "keepers of the pleas of the crown." Coroners had broad powers to hold inquests, hear confessions in sanctuaries, grant pardons, seize treasure, confiscate royal fishes (whales, sturgeons, and porpoises), and investigate shipwrecks. Medieval coroners' rolls show, however, that they were engaged mostly with inquests into suicide and homicide.[11] The investigation of death carried consequences. Suicide was a crime against God and king that resulted in forfeiture of the victim's estate. Accidental deaths caused by an inanimate object with moving parts (e.g., a well, horse cart, or mill wheel) entailed forfeiture of the object. Coroners held inquests in public places after viewing the corpse and questioning witnesses so that the jury could render a verdict.

In the nineteenth century, the position of coroner in the United States was part of the patronage and spoils system of municipal government. Coroners were not judges but had the authority of committing magistrates, and they could make arrests and set bail for prisoners. In spite of their legal authority, coroners often had little legal knowledge; some lacked even basic literacy skills. Coroners initially operated on a fee-for-service basis, receiving payment at each inquest. In New York City, at the turn of the twentieth century, they first became salaried.[12] Regardless of the form of remuneration, bribes and embezzlement in coroners' offices were legion, because coroners had great leeway in presenting evidence and steering a verdict in a desired direction.[13] Politicians were put on the payroll of businesses attempting to avoid bad publicity or liability when deaths occurred because of safety violations. These politicians served as "fixers": for a fee, they tried to influence the coroner's court by picking the jury members, paying off the coroner or district attorney, condoning perjury, or sending key witnesses out of state. Similarly, well-connected families paid for suicides to be classified as accidents and unsavory details to be suppressed. George LeBrun, secretary to the New York coroner's and later medical examiner's office from 1898 until his retirement in the 1940s (and himself a political appointee) reported that the success of businesses and individuals depended on the corruption of the coroner: "A few of the coroners, and let me emphasize that it were only a few, were outrageous crooks who dispensed 'justice' for cash. Their only interest in each new case was to discover how they could extort money, and they used the power of their office for blackmail purposes."[14] Even uncorrupted coroners would manipulate the usual procedures of the death investigation system when a politician asked for a favor to protect a family against the stigma of suicide. When the determination of suicide was straightforward, for example, no inquest would be held, allowing the coroner to file the death certificate days later—escaping the attention of reporters, who checked only the new cases.

Coroners are now public officials, appointed or elected. They do not necessarily have medical backgrounds or training in death investigation. They may still, however, hold inquests before juries to determine the manner of death. For example, the coroner of McLean County, Illinois, may call an inquest in front of six citizens of the county. The inquest is open to the public, and the jurors determine the manner of death (suicide, accident, homicide, natural death, or undetermined death) on the basis of the information presented.[15] Coroners may employ physicians to perform autopsies and technicians to conduct toxicology testing. In some counties, anyone can become a coroner, so that the post has been held by tow-truck drivers, paramedics, plumbers, bar owners, nurses, carpenters, police officers, and funeral directors.[16] Coroners still run death investigations in counties and districts of eleven U.S. states. In an attempt to professionalize their trade, some counties have required coroners to meet stricter education requirements (including basic medical or legal training) and obtain certification in programs offered by the American Board of Medicolegal Death Investigators.[17] Eighteen states now have a mix of coroner and medical examiner systems, and medical examiners are the sole death investigators in twenty-two states, practicing on a state, county, or district level. Medical examiners began to replace coroners in 1877, in Massachusetts, but most systems switched between 1955 and 1985. The shift to a medical examiner then stalled in the mid-1980s.[18] At the beginning of the twenty-first century, about half of the U.S. population is served by coroners and the other half by medical examiners. There are more than two thousand death investigation jurisdictions, most at the county level.[19]

The switch to a medical examiner system entails an expansion of scientific power and a curtailing of political power. All states with medical examiners require them to be physicians, and most demand additional certification in anatomical and forensic pathology. Medical examiners do not preside over a jury inquest but base their conclusions largely on a scene investigation, medical files, an autopsy, and laboratory tests. All inquiries take place behind closed doors, out of the public eye. Although the police are in charge of the crime scene, medical examiners have jurisdiction over the corpse and can request paraphernalia found at the crime scene that might shed light on the death. Medical examiners are charged with identifying the body and determining the cause and manner of death. The cause of death is "a disease, abnormality, injury, or poisoning that contributed directly or indirectly to death,"[20] perhaps cerebral hemorrhage, asphyxiation, severe pulmonary congestion and edema, or sudden infant death syndrome. Five categories constitute the possibilities for the manner of death: natural, accident, suicide, homicide, and undetermined. The forensic manner of death is not legally binding for law enforcement or prosecution but is a crucial part of fact-finding in criminal investigations.

The replacement of coroners with medical examiners is a milestone in the long history of growing medical authority over death. George LeBrun, who witnessed the transition from the coroner's court to the medical examiner's office of New York City in 1918, noted the difference in the quality of the death investigation when the scrupulous Dr. Charles Norris, a professor of pathology at Columbia University medical school and director of the Bellevue Hospital laboratories, became the first medical examiner. Appalled by the lack of understanding of gunshot wounds, Dr. Norris and his assistants fired all kinds of guns into different materials from various ranges and angles, studied the gunpowder marks and shot patterns, and then applied this knowledge to cases. Dr. Norris's superior professional knowledge became apparent when he disagreed with a former coroner's physician (who was now working in law enforcement) and successfully established that a death previously considered a suicide was actually a homicide; in another case, Dr. Norris changed an apparent homicide to a suicide.

According to LeBrun, not only corruption but also legislative initiative disappeared with the coroner's court. When the coroner's inquest worked well, it was a perfect vehicle for bringing awareness of dangerous situations into the public realm and instituting reforms.[21] In the heyday of the New York City coroner's office, the politically savvy coroner's court was at the forefront in requiring elevator safety devices, advocating for the replacement of open streetcars discharging passengers in the middle of the street with buses that pulled up to the curb, requiring poisons to be labeled as such, fighting for driver's licenses, and spearheading one of the first gun-control laws, the Sullivan law.[22] LeBrun attributed the coroner's power to his privileged position and to the open character of the inquest, which led to well-cultivated contacts with politicians and reporters. The early New York City medical examiner's office still had the power to call public inquests, but Dr. Norris never used that privilege, preferring that the district attorney take the lead.

FORENSIC AUTHORITY

This book addresses the cultural trade-off created by placing suspicious death under the jurisdiction of the most professionalized of death investigators: medical examiners trained as forensic pathologists. Medical examiners fill out death certificates on the basis of scientific expertise, but their work is never simply about documenting the results from toxicology, histology, or pathology. Rather, they must reconcile deeply held moral values with the pathological signs of the body. Mediating between the corpse and the modern world, medical examiners make cultural connections for us. The work in the medical examiner's office starts from the assumption that the corpse harbors the secrets of its demise and that the death investigator's task is to reveal this knowledge for the public good. Much as we rely on insurance brokers to explain the arcane issues of insurance, we depend on medical examiners to be society's brokers of suspicious death: expert intermediaries who negotiate and establish the meaning of violent and suspicious deaths. Medical examiners determine what makes a death a suicide or what qualifies as abuse in the death of an infant. They aim to bring rational, scientific order by explaining the seemingly unexplainable. This cultural service, however, is far from obvious. Pathologists' expertise is based on the shape and function of diseased tissues and organs. Why would we expect these practitioners to solve the puzzle of suspicious mortality and to illuminate the risks of living in late modern societies? Why would we believe them?

Indeed, the cultural power of death investigators is often contested. Sociologist Eric Klinenberg, for example, gives an account of the conflict about documenting the number of heat-related deaths in Chicago during the scorching summer of 1995. Cook County's medical examiner began to classify deaths as heat-related. Chicago's mayor disagreed with the classification, arguing that a heat wave was a naturally recurring event in a city of extreme temperatures and that the vulnerable city dwellers in the morgue would have died anyway. When the tally of excess heat deaths grew to 739 within one week, several refrigerator trucks had to be brought in to store the bodies—dramatically underscoring the magnitude of this true disaster. Other forensic experts and public health officials then rallied around the medical examiner, and the mayor ceased to question the medical examiner's determinations.[23] Why had the mayor contested the classification? The political stakes of attributing deaths to a disaster are high for city leaders. A previous Chicago mayor had lost his job in part because of his administration's inability to handle a snowstorm. The public believes that if deaths can be attributed to severe weather, they might be preventable, and city government can be held accountable. Even where the circumstances are less dramatic, any death investigation might be contested, and previous allies might turn against medical examiners.

At the heart of this book is the question of the professional and cultural authority of medical examiners, which I will refer to as *forensic authority.* Professional authority is the legitimacy accorded to an occupational group to conduct professional work and have its judgments accepted by various audiences. The professional authority of clinicians, for example, lies in their ability to convince patients to follow recommended interventions based on a process of diagnosis and in their ability to receive reimbursement and recognition for their work from third parties. For medical examiners, professional authority encompasses the ways they investigate deaths and have each determination accepted as valid. Medical examiners' professional authority is reflected in the selection and investigation of cases, as well as the acceptance of their conclusions by relatives, public health officials, and law enforcement officers. As Paul Starr has pointed out, professional authority may involve cultural authority when professionals are also able to establish the definition of things. Cultural authority is the "probability that particular definitions of reality and judgments of meaning and value will prevail as valid and true."[24] For medical examiners, cultural authority lies in their ability to shape the understanding of relatives and other audiences about what suspicious death is. Forensic authority thus means not only establishing what caused a specific death according to professional standards (through professional authority), but also defining what suicide or homicide is about (through cultural authority). Medical examiners may have professional authority with little cultural authority if they conduct their investigations within the conceptions of death defined by others.

Forensic authority determines what medical examiners can and will decide. Scientific and lay notions of suspicious death are common understandings riddled with inconsistencies and exceptions. Take suicide. In an often-quoted formulation, the World Health Organization defines suicide as "a suicidal act with a fatal outcome" and a suicidal act as "self injury with varying degrees of lethal intent."[25] Working from this definition, the eminent suicide researcher Edwin Shneidman devoted an entire book to defining suicide and concluded, "Currently in the Western world, suicide is a conscious act of self-induced annihilation, best understood as a multidimensional malaise in a needful individual who defines an issue for which the suicide is perceived as the best solution."[26] Although useful for suicide prevention and scholarship, these definitions have little value for forensic investigations. How do you recognize "lethal intent," "a conscious act" resulting from "multidimensional malaise," "a needful individual," or "the best solution" in a corpse? When faced with a dead body and some traces of a spent life, how can a pathologist establish that a man intended to take his own life? Was the "I love you. Take care" scribbled on a gum wrapper a clumsy expression of love or a short suicide note? Did the fifteen-year-old girl miscount sleeping pills or intend to end her life? In spite of the ambiguity of suicide, forensic pathologists have to make definitive judgments about the value of evidence and intent.

Forensic authority consists in the reputation of the entire profession of medical examiners and reflects on individual practitioners' credibility, integrity, and legitimacy, their investigative procedures, and their conclusions drawn from forensic evidence. Every forensic pathologist in training gradually accumulates credibility from credentials, a broad variety of autopsy experiences, exchanges with others, and courtroom testimonies. The pathologist does not have to establish credibility from scratch: the authority invested in a community of medical examiners with similar training, credentials, and experiences serves as a reference for individual credibility. An individual medical examiner making blunders might lose credibility and so be unable to fulfill the task of death brokering, but the forensic authority of medical examiners need not be tarnished by a single wayward practitioner. Someone else will fill the position. Similarly, telegenic "star" medical examiners might develop reputations that surpass the authority of medical examiners as a group. Professional vulnerability would develop if the loss of forensic authority of medical examiners as a whole began to reduce the credibility of individual pathologists. In an example from another area of forensics, fingerprinting experts recently risked losing professional and cultural authority with legal challenges to their scientific credentials.[27] With authority lost, even the most skilled or experienced fingerprinting expert might as well be reading tea leaves; every individual fingerprint identification lacks credibility.

When medical examiners classify deaths as heat-related, they have forensic authority if the deaths are considered by relevant authorities to have been caused by excessive heat, which was indeed acknowledged in the Chicago heat wave of 1995. In the aftermath of the dispute between the mayor and the medical examiner, the Centers for Disease Control and Prevention (CDC) launched a study of the heat-wave victims in Chicago and alerted death investigators around the country about new facts on fatal heat exhaustion. These actions validated the authority of medical examiners as a professional group to recognize and classify these deaths. Maintaining forensic authority does not necessarily require that relatives and other parties agree with forensic classifications. Medical examiners lack coercive powers to enforce their determinations; instead, they offer official opinions. Forensic authority implies the surrender of private for expert judgment, even if forensic conclusions run counter to someone's financial interests, religious beliefs, or other deeply held values. A groundswell of criticism arising against medical examiners' classification of suicide, for example, might diminish cultural authority, especially if other parties (such as police officers or forensic psychiatrists) take over these investigations. When forensic authority is unquestioned, however, audiences are compelled to accept medical examiners' conclusions, and their determinations carry implications for courts, insurance agencies, and other institutions.

Forensic authority is a measure of successful death brokering, a gauge of medical examiners' ability to conduct their work and have their determinations accepted as true and valid. In our justice and public health systems, the forensic specialist's close scrutiny of corpses for signs of abuse and causes of death seems inevitable. How would we otherwise be able to detect the next lethal epidemic? How could we have homicide investigations without white-coated experts looking for signs of injury? Who would detect the next anthrax epidemic or alert us to the dangers of unsafe children's toys? The authority of death investigators seems rock-solid. A need for expertise, however, does not guarantee that forensic pathologists are or will remain the most appropriate specialists to inquire about death. The shaky fate of the once-authoritative fingerprinting experts is instructive here. And even if medical examiners are the preferred investigators, the deaths they investigate and the conclusions they draw may remain contested. Medical examiners could be reduced to technicians who simply process evidence for others to consider, exercising little or no cultural authority of their own. More often than disgruntled mayors, lawyers routinely contest medical examiners' forensic authority, especially when criminal cases hinge on the processing and interpretation of evidence. Rather than being rock-solid, the authority of a profession fluctuates and can decline suddenly.

THE THREE SOURCES OF LEGITIMACY FOR FORENSIC AUTHORITY

The forensic authority of medical examiners involves a mix of three sources of legitimacy: cultural need, legal mandates, and scientific expertise. Each of these sources comes with benefits and pitfalls for establishing and maintaining forensic authority; they may work to delegitimize as well as legitimize it.

The Cultural Need for Death Brokering

The forensic authority of medical examiners originates in part from the deep existential questions provoked by suspicious deaths. Cultural need, however, does not guarantee such authority. Influential philosophers, psychoanalysts, historians, and social scientists have argued that mortality ultimately limits modern societies because it constitutes the defeat of reason.[28] Reason cannot conceive of the reality of death and cannot conquer mortality. As sociologist Norbert Elias remarks, "It is not actually death, but the knowledge of death, that creates problems for human beings."[29] Awareness of mortality creates an existential ambivalence in individual and social life, generating cultural coping mechanisms.[30] According to historian Philippe Ariès, in premodern Europe "tamed death" was a coping mechanism; death was tame in the European Middle Ages not because of domestication but because it "was never wild before."[31] Death simply *was*. It could be bewailed or regretted but not manipulated. With this fatalistic perspective, the danse macabre gripped rich and poor, young and old alike; religious authorities explained death as a predetermined, egalitarian, cruel human fate.[32] In societies with more fluid boundaries between the earthly and spirit worlds, sudden death is explained by the actions of ancestral spirits.[33] With the Enlightenment, which emphasized mastery of nature and contingency, life expectancy increased, but mortality remained ultimately indifferent to instrumental human efforts. A medical, legal, and (later) therapeutic ethos gradually replaced religion as moral authority.[34] In the realm of death and dying, medicine prevailed, partly because it was preoccupied with determining the physical signs of death and thus could reduce the fear of live burial.[35]

While questioning the inevitability of death, modernity added anguish.[36] The security of small victories over acute, devastating diseases enhances insecurity over the ultimate demise, especially when people die suddenly. In modern societies, one common reaction to this frontier of reason is *seclusion and professional management:* hide death in institutions, disavowing its existence through spatial and social segregation under the supervision of medically trained experts.[37] Science might then provide answers. Mortality itself cannot be avoided, but individual *causes of death can be determined,* and then manipulated and postponed. The philosopher Zygmunt Bauman characterizes this frantic search for pertinent causes while losing sight of the ultimate futility of the endeavor as the "analytical deconstruction" of mortality, in which "fighting the causes of dying turns into the meaning of life."[38] Mortality is deconstructed in autopsies and reconstituted as mortality data in epidemiological health databases, which in turn form the basis of public health policies. The result of those twin death-brokering strategies is simultaneously a professionalization of the dying process and an "excessive preoccupation with the risk of death" in daily life,[39] leading to a society organized around the distribution of risk.[40]

If "societies are arrangements that permit humans to live with weaknesses that would otherwise render life impossible,"[41] medical examiners form a crucial professional group for mediating society's mortal anguish. Among all deaths, *suspicious* deaths most rattle a sense of security. Suspicion involves a surmise of disorder, something awry, unexpected, dangerous, out of the ordinary. Suspicion can be as ephemeral as an investigative hunch that something does not add up or as blatant as bullet wounds and ligature marks. The anxiety that suspicious deaths provoke resides in the possibility of foul play that may claim more victims. Suspicion resonates with concerns about the worst lethal faces of social disorder: unfettered violence; seemingly preventable deaths that occur at random; raging epidemics; deadly systemic problems in health care, justice, or politics; crippling poverty, famine, and other inequities.

With every disaster involving fatalities, the need to reassure and tuck death back into explanatory categories is renewed. In the past decade, death investigators faced massive hurricane fatalities, school shootings, terrorist attacks, gang violence, carjackings, police brutality, physicians who turned out to be serial killers, deaths due to backyard swimming pools, the danger of exploding tires and SUV (sport utility vehicle) safety, SARS (severe acute respiratory syndrome), fatal medication errors and surgical interventions,[42] suicide guidebooks, "preventable" deaths due to religious beliefs, and physician-assisted suicide. Also perennially present were childhood death, domestic violence, airplane and other transportation disasters, hundreds of shootings, new kinds of drug overdose, the emergence of new infectious diseases and the reemergence of old ones, various occupational hazards, and new forms of heart disease. The realization that the current death investigation system might be too fragmented and underfunded to identify and manage a bioterrorist attack has impelled the U.S. Department of Justice to review that system.[43]

Medical examiners state that they conduct postmortem investigations for the public good. The central value organizing their work is *hope.* By speaking to the living on behalf of the dead, they offer the hope of knowledge and justice. Their work asserts that the death was not in vain and that something can be learned to prevent similar deaths. The knowledge they generate may be used in public health, public safety, and prevention research. It offers the final "quality-control" check on countless institutions and people, including parents, employers, and government officials. The work of medical examiners may also hold others accountable for premature deaths and stimulate calls for justice and reform. The notion of hope acknowledges that while action is desirable, uncertainty remains over the outcome. It rises above the inevitability of death and appeals to a shift in perspective that emphasizes the possibility of a positive result. Hope is a condition for change, although it does not deliver change.

The need to explain violent, suspicious, or unexpected deaths and offer hope seems to provide a cultural guarantee for forensic investigations,
immunizing medical examiners against criticism. The same cultural demands, however, tend to cause medical examiners and their work to be
treated with distrust, even disgust. Indeed, the seclusion and professionalization of death reflect the cultural attitude toward death prevalent since
the Second World War: the "denial of death."[44] In a society where death
is covered up and hidden, medical examiners do the dirtiest of dirty work.
They do hands-on work with corpses and reveal unpopular truths about
life's finality. They face social pathologies daily—murder victims who were
themselves murderers, homicide victims who were in the wrong place
at the wrong time, the desperately suicidal, the hopeless and the homeless, the speeders and the drunk drivers, the unfortunate pedestrians, the
recluses, the battered children, and some "stupid" people who if they had
used simple common sense would still be alive.[45] Little dignified is found
on the stretchers in the morgue. To be a spokesperson for those who do not
vote, write letters to newspapers, testify before Congress, bring lawsuits,
or participate in civic life is to work at the margins of society. The stigma
of "that kind of death" rubs off on medical examiners' individual lives and
professional careers, and their social value is rarely recognized. Knowledge
extracted from the corpse comes too late to benefit the deceased. No happy
endings unfold in the medical examiner's office; at best, the ending might
be "grimly satisfying."[46] Bauman concludes that in late modernity, the
process of deconstructing mortality is still running its course but has lost
much of its interpretive value: "Little mileage has been left today in *the
old hope* of pushing back the frontiers of death."[47] This raises the question:
is the hope that medical examiners offer in explaining life and death still
culturally vital?

A Legal Mandate to Investigate Suspicious Deaths

The second source legitimizing medical examiners' forensic authority is
the institutionalization of cultural need as a legal priority.[48] Cultural demand is a necessary but not a sufficient condition to guarantee authority.
Medical examiners' opening up of corpses would be impossible if their
work were not oriented toward a substantive set of values. Death investigators contribute to the promotion of health and justice; but, more than that,
they aim to make sense of suspicious deaths and offer hope for the living.
Those cultural needs, however, could be fulfilled by other occupational
groups. Elected officials, journalists, religious leaders, law enforcement
personnel, clinicians, sociologists, neighbors, and relatives attend to the
same suspicious deaths and offer alternative explanations. But these other

parties lack death investigators' legal mandate to investigate suspicious deaths. Medical examiners have the statutory duty to take possession of well-defined categories of bodies and conduct a postmortem investigation, disregarding the objections of grieving relatives and other parties.

The property rights of the deceased to their bodies terminate at the moment of death. Over the past century, property rights to the dead body in the United States have remained with the surviving relatives or with death investigators, depending on the circumstances of the death. The next of kin has the legal right to dispose of the body unless the "demands of justice"[49] take precedence. Medical examiners and coroners have the legal prerogative to make such demands on behalf of the public. For example, Utah's Medical Examiner Act gives the medical examiner the mandate to investigate any suspicious or unusual death, including "deaths by violence, gunshot, suicide and accident,"[50] and to perform any examination necessary to determine the cause and manner of death, including requesting medical records. The statute supersedes a family's religious or social objections against autopsies.[51] It even interferes with law enforcement.

Sociologist Andrew Abbott argues that the most "durable"[52] jurisdictions are those encapsulated by legal means, especially when professions receive a legal monopoly over an area of expertise. When medical examiners received legal jurisdiction over suspicious dead bodies and the mandate to investigate them, they came to inhabit what sociologist Eliot Freidson calls a "professional market shelter"[53] protecting them against outside influences and competitors. Legal legitimation constitutes the most valuable protection for professions.

Yet a price is paid for such strong professional protection. The legal market shelter takes away the motivation for consolidating professional power. When they show up for work, medical examiners inevitably find autopsies to perform and reports to write. While each new body constitutes a unique scientific puzzle awaiting decipherment, the work of investigating suspicious deaths is valued by the same parties the medical examiner has been dealing with for decades. In spite of great variety across death investigation systems, offices have over time established durable relationships with local stakeholders. Without real competitors and with a guaranteed workload and well-established audiences, why would medical examiners worry about their authority? When a death fulfills legally defined criteria, an investigation is mandatory, and the conclusions of medical examiners are administratively binding. In addition, medical examiners are already the most professional of death investigators. If anyone should worry about redundancy, it is the local coroner vis-à-vis the more professional forensic pathologist.

Market shelters, however, weather. The once-durable protections can turn antiquated, precisely because they provide immunity against change. Over time, legal immunity can become a double-edged sword, as practitioners have little incentive to adapt to a changing world around them. Actually, medical examiners might be listed as an endangered profession, because few physicians join their ranks: there are more than 2,000 jurisdictions in the United States, but since 1959 only 1,150 forensic pathologists have been board certified. Many of the forty-one training programs have vacancies. In 2002, only thirty-four physicians received certification in forensic pathology (in that same year, more than fifteen thousand physicians graduated from medical school),[54] and there was a 38 percent failure rate on the American Board of Pathology examination in forensic pathology.[55] Anecdotal evidence suggests that chief medical examiners at the peak of their careers earn about the average salary of a physician recently graduating from residency.[56] Forensic pathologists likely would earn more money if they skipped the additional years of specialization in forensics and practiced as, for example, hospital pathologists. While medical examiners can earn extra income from consulting on court cases, few choose to do so, and some health departments ban medical examiners from taking these fees. In addition, there is little professional leadership in the field. The National Association of Medical Examiners offers accreditation of medical examiners' offices, but only forty-two offices, serving 23 percent of the U.S. population, are accredited, and accreditation has no effect on funding. No quality assurance is required by statute or regulation, and the profession is insufficiently organized to take disciplinary action against underperforming death investigators. One of the latest threats has been the replacement of forensic pathologists with pathology assistants as a cost-saving measure in some offices.[57] These problems are characteristic of a profession unable to close its ranks.

Medical examiners have few means of expanding or capitalizing on their jurisdiction. They are captives of a legal mandate that guarantees their workload. For more than a century, health professionals have bemoaned the corrupting influence of money in medicine. Here, we have a profession without financial incentives: no managed care attempting to curtail costs, no Medicare or Medicaid programs shifting priorities with spending policies, no drug firms spending millions on detailing, no lucrative outpatient-clinic spin-offs. The result: precious little innovation happens. Rather than growing stronger and more powerful, medical examiners, deprived of financial prospects, collectively diminish. As government officials, they have to fight at every budgetary cycle for resources, and they compete with teachers, police officers, social workers, hospitals, school nurses, and all other vocal constituencies. A statutory mandate guarantees a job but not the resources to fulfill tasks.

The Practice of Scientific Expertise

The legal prerogative to explain the cause of suspicious deaths belongs to either a medical examiner or a coroner. Medical examiners are convinced that their classifications and explanations are superior because they bring scientific expertise to the job of death investigation. The third basic source of legitimacy underlying medical examiners' professional authority is their promise to apply medically and scientifically validated skills that offer more accurate and objective knowledge. The Web site of the National Association of Medical Examiners makes this claim clear. Under the heading "So You Want to Be a Medical Detective?" the site explains the difference between coroner and forensic pathologist:

A coroner is a public official, appointed or elected, in a particular geographic jurisdiction, whose official duty is to make inquiry into deaths in certain categories. . . . The coroner may or may not be trained in the medical sciences. . . . In some jurisdictions, the coroner is a physician, but in many localities, the coroner is not required to be a physician nor be trained in medicine. *In the absence of medical expertise, the non-physician coroner may have difficulty in sorting out subtle non-violent and violent causes of death.*

Compare this summary of the coroner's position with the description of the forensic pathologist:

The forensic pathologist is a subspecialist in pathology whose area of special competence is the examination of persons who die sudden, unexpected or violent death. The forensic pathologist is an expert in determining cause and manner of death. The forensic pathologist is specially trained: to perform autopsies to determine the presence or absence of disease, injury or poisoning; to evaluate historical and law-enforcement investigative information relating to manner of death; to collect medical evidence, such as trace evidence and secretions, to document sexual assault; and to reconstruct how a person received injuries. Forensic pathologists are trained in multiple non medical sciences as well as traditional medicine. Other areas of science that the forensic pathologist must have a working knowledge of the applicability of are toxicology, firearms examination (wound ballistics), trace evidence, forensic serology and DNA technology. The forensic pathologist acts as the case coordinator for the medical and forensic scientific assessment of a given death, making sure that the appropriate procedures and evidence collection techniques are applied to the body. *When forensic pathologists are employed as death investigators they bring their expertise to bear upon the interpretation of the scene of death, in the assessment of the consistency of witnesses statements with injuries, and the interpretation of injury patterns or patterned injuries.* [58]

The difference between coroner and forensic pathologist lies in the latter's higher degree of professional knowledge. Yet the scientific expertise of medical examiners cannot guarantee forensic authority, because medical examiners' superior methodology relies on an outdated medical technique—the autopsy—and because their subject matter is inherently ambiguous.

★   ★   ★

Medical examiners' reliance on the postmortem investigation to produce knowledge about the causes of death is reminiscent of the high days of pathology and the birth of modern medicine. Philosopher Michel Foucault observed that the transition to scientific medicine in the eighteenth century rested on generating anatomical and pathological knowledge from the autopsy. He noted that "it is at death that disease and life speak their truth,"[59] meaning that the anatomical-pathological study of the corpse revealed the true nature of disease. To overcome life, diseases not only attacked the body from the outside, as previously thought in ancient Greek medicine, but also resided in the body and could be observed by systematically linking the physiological symptoms before death to the pathological conditions of dissected tissues and organs after death. Pathology emphasized localized lesions, physical diagnosis, and studies of normal and abnormal function that defined disease entities and explained specific causal mechanisms.[60] As Foucault noted, not only the autopsy but also the pathological paradigm, with the autopsy as investigative tool, ushered in the modern medical gaze. Physicians in the nineteenth century developed a cohesive set of causes based on the assumption that the truth about illness could indeed be found after death and distinguished from postmortem decomposition.

For most of the nineteenth and the first half of the twentieth century, the pathological paradigm constituted the authoritative touchstone of medical knowledge. From appendicitis to coronary artery disease to neuropathology, the postmortem investigation propelled an exponential accumulation of knowledge. Anomalies observed during an autopsy prompted hypotheses that could then be verified through comparisons in further postmortem investigations.

What were the achievements that assured such an important place for the autopsy? Among them were thousands of diseases discovered and described, numerous classifications of lesions, countless associations between diseases states and anatomical abnormalities, and innumerable ideas for medical and surgical treatment. . . . Virtually the whole of modern medical knowledge was created through study of autopsies, aided and supported by physiology, physical diagnosis and microbiology.[61]

Until recently, pathology's dominance was institutionalized in medical education. With strong support from the 1910 Flexner report on educational reform, a course in gross anatomy formed the first encounter with "real" medicine for medical students and was a preeminent educational experience.[62] Once familiar with the educational value of pathology, hospital physicians routinely verified the accuracy of their diagnoses after death had occurred, regularly detecting therapeutic errors and spinning off new research endeavors. The common admonition to "get the post" (i.e., obtain a postmortem examination) confirmed the authority of pathology. Several autopsy studies discovered clinical errors in 15 to 40 percent of cases. Misdiagnosis often led, and still leads, to errors in treatment, particularly for elderly patients.[63]

The prominent role of pathology and the autopsy in universities and hospitals declined after the surge in imaging technologies, emergence of biochemistry, growing reluctance of relatives to assent to autopsies, cost-consciousness due to the rise of managed care, fear of litigation if therapeutic mistakes are discovered, new hospital-based instruments of quality control, changes in the medical curriculum, and shifts in the discipline of pathology. The death knell came in 1971 when the Joint Commission on the Accreditation of Hospitals eliminated the autopsy requirement for hospital accreditation. An autopsy rate of 41 percent in 1961 had declined to 5–10 percent by the mid-1990s.[64] With the turn to evidence-based medicine, the autopsy also lost its prominent position in the realm of medical knowledge production. Advances in knowledge now occur in randomized clinical trials, test tubes, petri dishes, and laboratory animals. Hospital pathologists retreated from the corpse in favor of interpreting tissues and biopsies for abnormalities, and autopsy requirements have also been greatly relaxed for board certification in pathology.[65] The study of morphology has given way to immunology, bacteriology, and molecular genetics. The anxious clustering of first-year medical students in gross-anatomy courses has been partly replaced with an emphasis on advanced diagnostic technologies;[66] computed tomography (CT) and magnetic resonance imaging (MRI) enable physicians to view organs in the living body. The reluctance of managed-care companies and Medicaid to pay for autopsies and Medicare's policy of paying for autopsies without mandating that they actually be performed have hastened the demise of this former gold standard of medicine—a standard lauded by influential pathologist

Edward Gall as constituting "instruction, correction, discovery, investigation, storehouse and administration of the law."[67]

Only medical examiners still practice this modern form of knowing. In forensic pathology, the autopsy still promises to reveal the truth about the risks of living and the mechanisms of fatal disease. Forensic pathologists pursue their trade as they did fifty years ago. They have incorporated an impressive array of advances in biochemistry, microbiology, toxicology, serology, wound ballistics, and genetic tests into their medicolegal investigations, but the basic principle of conducting an autopsy to find the cause and manner of death still dominates forensic decision making. Innovative autopsy research in forensic pathology has been virtually nonexistent in recent decades. In spite of "a treasure trove of research assets," as a reviewer somberly noted,

only 11% of the nation's 125 medical schools have full-time faculty members who are forensic pathologists—39 total faculty members. Only two are principal investigators on research grants; one other forensic pathologist has some degree of research funding; and the field's research potential is curtailed by a shortage of future researchers. Only 38% of forensic pathology training programs offer any research opportunities to trainees.[68]

The anachronistic character of the profession becomes further apparent when one leafs through its flagship journal, the *American Journal of Forensic Medicine and Pathology*. Reflecting the dominance of epidemiological principles in the health care field, medical journals generally agree on a hierarchy of scientific medicine. For example, a meta-analysis of clinical trials trumps a large randomized, double-blind clinical trial, and a longitudinal prospective study yields better results than a cross-sectional study.[69] At the bottom of the knowledge hierarchy are clinical case studies. Because they represent a single observation rather than generalizable experimental knowledge, they are relegated in most journals to a cursory clinical-case-of-the-week column or to the letters section. In the *American Journal of Forensic Medicine and Pathology*, the overwhelming majority of articles consist of single or multiple case studies or culled retrospective reviews of similar cases.[70] The winners of the scientific-paper competition for residents organized by the National Association of Medical Examiners have usually written retrospective case reviews.[71] Furthermore, ten-year-old textbooks still teach the curriculum of forensic practice, even though a decade is an eternity in most life and behavioral sciences.[72]

With the decline of the pathological paradigm in general medicine and the turn to more experimental, clinical-trial-based knowledge, why do we trust that medical examiners can reveal the truth about suspicious death?

Under what kinds of circumstances does the autopsy still expose the secrets of mortality? What is the scientific authority of an autopsy? These questions gained urgency in 1993 when the U.S. Supreme Court, in *Daubert v. Merrell Dow Pharmaceuticals, Inc.,* redefined the criteria for admission of scientific evidence in court. The previous standard, the *Frye* test, dating back to 1923, stated that evidence could be introduced only if it was commonly accepted in the scientific field. The new Federal Rules for Evidence following the *Daubert* case require the trial judge to engage in a preliminary assessment of the scientific validity of the reasoning and methodology underlying the testimony and its application to the facts at issue. Several states have adopted the new standards for state trials. Legal observers have noted that *Daubert* turns the trial judge into a gatekeeper who will need to distinguish between accepted and "junk" science without usurping the jury's mandated role.[73] While forensic pathology has so far escaped the application of the *Daubert* criteria to its underlying scientific principles, observers are skeptical that the autopsy, in spite of centuries of experience and successes, would actually pass the new scientific test.[74] Legally, the autopsy might now be considered insufficiently scientific. Similarly, tissue and organ procurement organizations have questioned the necessity of the autopsy to reveal the cause of death; the routine slicing of organs prevents procurement in forensic cases. The heavy reliance on the autopsy, once the hallmark of medical acumen, might have become a liability for death investigators.

★ ★ ★

Another reason that medical examiners' scientific expertise does not guarantee forensic authority is the ambiguity involved in deciphering the cause of death from a corpse. Comparing themselves to basic scientists, medical examiners are fond of stating that a dead body does not lie. The corpse is presented as a layered palimpsest with impressions decipherable by those initiated in the science of forensics. Revealing the truth about suspicious death, as the chief medical examiner in my study repeatedly emphasized, is a matter of applying scientific methods and interpreting the evidence. A leading forensic textbook admonishes, "The medicolegal autopsy is stringently objective—allowing no leeway for speculation, bias, or emotional opinion or conclusion. The interpretation of the medicolegal autopsy requires specialized knowledge of patterns and causes of wounding and must be correlated with the circumstances of injury and death."[75] In this positivist framework, the expertise of the medical examiner consists of mastering the correct scientific methods and conducting a complete investigation to observe the causes of death. The claim for science is bolstered because forensic pathology does not have to deal with the subjective side of medicine—weighing the relevance of a patient's complaints—but strictly observes tissues and organs to coax out the secrets of death. This reliance on physiological parameters is often considered a great advantage: "Doctors take your blood so they don't have to take your word."[76] Starting from the indisputable fact that death has occurred and something must have caused it, the pathologist is free to formulate a hypothesis about immediate and underlying causes of death and verify it in situ.

Simultaneously, and unlike in other scientific disciplines, death investigators explicitly acknowledge that their expert work might not completely erase subjectivity. The death certificate requires the pathologist to document a *medical opinion* about the cause and manner of death, implying that determining the cause of death requires a lesser degree of certitude in forensics than in science, where causality is experimentally established and statistically verified. One of the reasons that pathologists' determinations are designated as opinions, rather than undisputed facts, might be that their raw material—the corpse—does not verbalize what went wrong. Death may be tricky to pin down in tissues and organs. The death of the human organism forms the beginning of a new life cycle of decay and decomposition, and the moments before death are often characterized by violent manipulation of the body during attempts at resuscitation. Decomposition and the trauma of resuscitation efforts are only some of the many ways that artifacts might be created, rendering subtle signs too subtle to indicate conclusively a cause of death. Deliberate deception requires forethought, so the body does not lie—but the cause of death can still remain ambiguous. A complete postmortem investigation might reveal nothing conclusive or might discover conflicting biological pathways.

A different reason for qualifying the cause of death in forensics is the social implication of the determination. Biologists routinely interpret the causes of death in laboratory animals—which, like corpses, do not talk—yet these scientists do not feel the need to qualify their findings. In forensics, unlike biology, the final designation matters because people are moral agents capable of self-knowledge. The death certificate is a legal document that casts the deceased—and by implication his or her life—in a particular light. The mouse community does not express concern when a scientist asserts that "onco-mouse" died of cancer, but relatives care deeply if the medical examiner decides that their loved one's death was a suicide while they are convinced that it was accidental. In fact, over the last three centuries, death investigations have been dogged by accusations of underreporting of suicide as well as other stigmatized deaths.[77] Death investigators are presumed to give in to pressure from relatives. For medical examiners, such accusations go to the heart of professionalism, because they imply a weak scientific base and insufficient independence. And as Klinenberg's discussion of heat deaths showed, the wider social community for whom the death matters might contest the death certificate, mobilizing law enforcement, media, and politicians if citizens disagree with the medical examiner.

If the body does not speak but others want to speak for it, how does a forensic pathologist know what story a corpse tells about life and death? During the investigation, the pathologist needs to establish a plausible connection between dead tissues and the moments of life leading up to death. When do such connections become plausible and credible? Medical examiners' claim that they are more objective than their competitors faces difficult challenges. Pathology is incompatible with retrieving the intent necessary to determine the manner of death. A gunshot wound might be self-inflicted, accidental, or caused by another person. No laboratory test, algorithm, or pathological examination can conclusively settle who pulled the trigger. In addition, the activity of opening corpses for the sake of knowledge always provokes a sense of apprehension. At best, relatives and religious leaders tolerate an autopsy for the public good. Medical examiners are looking for ways not necessarily to expand their jurisdiction, but to safeguard their expertise against claims of incompetence, random interpretation, voyeurism, unnecessary mutilation, and mistakes. Their promise of greater reliability and certainty also invites greater scrutiny. The inherent ambiguity in interpreting forensic evidence may render the medical examiner's forensic authority vulnerable.

WHAT IS AT STAKE?

In his account of the nineteenth-century English coroners' inquests, historian Ian Burney concludes that "the choice of medical witness at inquests . . . was ultimately as much about a choice between versions of inquests as between modes of reading bodies of evidence."[78] And one should add that the choice of death investigator is also about a choice between conclusions to be drawn from the evidence. Burney's observation points to the central argument of this book: death investigators' professional strengths and weaknesses will influence the detection, classification, and explanation of suspicious death. The most professional death investigations in the United States are conducted by medical examiners trained as forensic pathologists who have acquired legal protections and offer scientific expertise to fill cultural needs. Yet these sources of legitimacy do not safeguard authority, and the explanations medical examiners offer for suspicious death might be found wanting, especially when former strongholds of forensic power have become vulnerabilities. Every death investigation conducted by a medical examiner, every final autopsy report, every signed death certificate, reflects a claim for authority. When the work is routine, forensic authority follows unquestioned from institutionalized credentials, cultural needs, scientific methods, and legal mandates. Even in deeply sheltered professional outposts, however, routines may break down. When death classifications are challenged, new competitors emerge. Old doubts gain urgency when mistakes are publicized. The factors that legitimate the work become a hindrance when the field changes. At stake is not only the job of the medical examiner, but also the results of the investigation. At stake is who died of suicide, who was murdered, who died accidentally, who died of natural causes, and who died for unknown reasons. At stake is the modern truth about suspicious death: the notion that cold tissues reveal a causal sequence and that knowledge of this sequence can restore order in social life. At stake is how we conceive of suicide, homicide, accident, and natural death.

Following forensic pathologists at work, this book explores how the emergence of medical examiners as death investigators has affected the meanings of suspicious death. I take seriously the cultural charge of death brokering and analyze how the professional investigators and the process of investigating lead to specific expert knowledge. Where do medical examiners, with their scientific expertise and legal mandate, locate the risks of living? When do deaths become suspicious? How do death investigators satisfy audiences with conflicting expectations? How does pathology explain the finality of life? Who checks on the death brokers? What meanings do medical examiners give to hope? What do they tell us about our mortality? Why do we die too soon?

A MEDICAL SOCIOLOGY OF PRACTICE

A study of the forensic authority of death investigators is foremost a study of the process of generating and disseminating expert knowledge about suspicious death. Such a study connects these professionals with the kind of investigation they conduct and the knowledge they generate and provide. The theoretical relevance of this project goes beyond a group of rather odd professionals and how they make sense of suspicious death. This book is an answer to a powerful science-studies critique of medical sociology and, as such, offers a way of examining the practice, content, and norms of knowledge production.[79] Science-studies scholars have criticized medical sociologists for neglecting what is being done in medicine while focusing on the social environment of medicine or the social implications of medical encounters. In response, science scholars have proposed to look at how medicine is performed. In this turn to practice, however, there is a glaring omission: the reason for doing medicine. The normative content is explicitly ignored. A study of the forensic authority of medical examiners brings together who investigates, how they investigate, and what results their investigations reveal. Making the connection requires observations of forensic pathologists transforming bodies into expert knowledge about death. This study thus exemplifies a medical sociology of practice.

With several nineteenth-century precursors hinting at a similar division of scholarly labor, Talcott Parsons forcefully articulated the mandate for medical sociology in the 1950s, when he distinguished illness from disease and claimed illness as a topic for sociologists.[80] Disease constituted the territory of technically competent health care providers, while illness was understood as the socially defined management of the sick role. This separation of the social from the technical granted social scientists the ability to examine the social environment of health care, the interactions between care providers and patients, the medical professions, and the social distribution of health. Parsons analyzed physicians and patients for their functionality within a wider social system and saw care providers as gatekeepers maintaining order in society. Later sociologists took a more critical perspective, viewing medicine as an institution of social control and analyzing the inequities in health care. Functionalism gave way to critical and social constructivist theories. An early observer argued that a sociology of medicine runs the risk of losing its professional identity if it engages too closely with medicine itself.[81] Most medical sociologists thus kept, and still keep, their distance from what they call in shorthand the "technical" aspects of medicine. Instead, they add knowledge of the illnesses people live with to the knowledge of the diseases that plague their bodies, emphasizing that the two aspects are inevitably intertwined.

While Parsons delineated the subject matter for medical sociologists, other sociologists studied medicine as a kind of work. In the early Chicago Department of Sociology from the 1940s to the 1960s, Everett C. Hughes launched an influential program studying people at work. Observing and interviewing people doing their jobs, Hughes and his students were interested in how recurring work-related problems were managed across a variety of occupational settings, including how occupations transferred sets of tasks, how they handled mistakes at work, how they combined prestigious and less prestigious aspects of work, how workers restricted production to fair levels, how new tasks offered new career lines, and how one was socialized as a professional.[82] The premise of this literature was that workers in a particular occupation shared "bundles of activities," similar social roles, and positions in what Hughes referred to as "the social matrix," or larger system of occupations. Hughes articulated the mandate of the sociology of work as the study of whole settings in which particular occupations (professional and non-professional) occur, with attention to the shifting boundaries between them and the kind of cooperation required for any of them to perform effectively; to the shifting boundaries between the professional systems and the clienteles they serve; and finally, to the development of new definitions of [needs] growing out of constant social interaction and change.[83]

These interests lived on in the sociology of professions[84] and in a more narrow symbolic interactionist research tradition of work.[85] All these research endeavors emphasized how work was done; yet because they aimed to generalize across work settings, few addressed the substantive results of the work. Thus, Anselm Strauss and his coauthors asserted the conceptual value of different kinds of medical work—including safety, comfort, sentimental, and technological work—without elaborating how these tasks lead to particular health outcomes or relate to the broad values of health interventions.[86] Instead, they highlighted how tasks were socially organized.

For science-studies scholars, the genesis of medical sociology also contained its original sin. To demonstrate that medicine is a deeply social institution, medical sociologists tended to ignore what care providers actually did with patients: "the [social] investigator stood with his or her back to the heart of medicine and studied the 'social phenomena' surrounding it."[87] This division of scholarly labor led to a politically unsatisfactory solution. How could social scientists talk about changing medical hegemony or institutionalized inequities if they ignored medicine's intensely scientific knowledge base and granted physicians medical facts? At the same time, the specialized character of medical knowledge rendered it difficult for social scientists to penetrate. Social scientists are on shaky ground when evaluating how immunologists approach the physiology of childhood asthma. A much safer course is to take immunologists at their word and observe how they mobilize social and material resources in their interactions with patients.

One solution to the problem of ignoring the "technical" aspects of medicine came from the area of science studies in which social scientists had been analyzing the emergence of scientific facts. Rather than bracketing scientific knowledge as a technical attribute or as simply factual, social observers followed scientists at work to see how they establish the veracity of their findings.[88] The credibility of knowledge claims does not depend on innate rational qualities; rather, science-studies scholars asserted, rationality is itself an outcome of the process of knowledge production. A scientific fact is an accomplishment, produced after a process of testing its strength, anticipating and disarming criticism, and writing up research findings. This line of analysis allowed science-studies scholars to discuss rationality or objectivity not as universal norms that organize the work of scientists, but as qualities that are accomplished in practice and that may vary over time. The task of the science-studies scholar was to follow science in action: investigating how disparate epistemic elements are transformed into factual knowledge.

This turn to practice in science studies deeply challenged sociological scholarship. First, the interdisciplinary field of science studies constituted a radical break with the earlier institutional and normative sociology of science. Sociologist Robert K. Merton traced four institutional impera- tives or norms that, he argued, had governed a particular scientific ethos since the first French and English academies in the seventeenth century. These interrelated norms were universalism, communality, disinterested- ness, and organized skepticism; taken together, they shaped a communi- cation system aimed at producing true, reliable knowledge. Merton thus defined the aim for the sociology of science to be concerned with the social prerequisites of factual knowledge, the moral compulsions of meth- ods, and the institutional forms of scientific production rather than its technical content. His own work focused on the emergence of science, how scientists deal with the ambiguity of priority disputes, and conflicts between science and its social environment.[89] Breaking with Mertonian sociology, science-studies scholars, influenced by Thomas Kuhn, instead addressed the substantive content of scientific knowledge.[90]

Second, science studies called for "decentering of the subject," or a radical agnosticism about who or what actually does science. Agency was extended from people to things.[91] Scientists, their instruments, their re- sources, and their values are all intrinsically implicated in the process of knowledge creation, so that privileging human concerns—such as polit- ical interests or the group affiliation of scientists—over material factors became untenable.[92] Third, the science-studies analysis also extended to traditional explanatory sociological variables. Some science-studies schol- ars refused to grant a priori explanatory power to traditional social deter- minants, such as race, class, and gender.[93] They maintained that what constitutes race, class, or gender is continuously shaped and remade by new configurations of actors. For example, the decision to market a phar- maceutical against heart failure to African Americans may reinforce the notion that race is genetically or biologically determined.[94] In this case, the confluence of Food and Drug Administration (FDA) regulations, phar- maceutical companies' market decisions, and biological agents provides a particular interpretation of race that may be contested by others. What counts as "race" is itself an outcome of processes of knowledge production rather than a predetermined variable.

The most consistent extension of this turn by science-studies scholars to practice in medicine is empirical philosopher Annemarie Mol's book *The Body Multiple*.[95] On the basis of observations in a hospital, Mol explores what atherosclerosis of the leg vessels is. This is a radical step: a social scientist writing about what a disease—not just an illness experience—*is*. Mol shows that atherosclerosis is different from the unified disease physicians think it is. Surgeons and patients talking in windowless offices enact leg atherosclerosis as a disease that impedes mobility, renders legs colder, and slows palpitations. Atherosclerotic vessels might consequently need to be stripped, pushed aside, or circumvented with a bypass. For a clinical pathologist cracking a calcified artery of an amputated leg with a scalpel, atherosclerosis is a condition that can be inspected, even heard. Pathologists and vascular surgeons both work on atherosclerosis, but they never completely capture it. Instead, each specialty satisfies a different purpose. Although pathologists' findings are always too late to be clinically useful and their procedures are too cumbersome to comprehensively quantify the extent of atherosclerosis, the pathologist confirms the appropriateness of an amputation when examining a sample under the microscope. The surgeon, in contrast, is faced with diverse diagnostic technologies and therapeutic interventions, each of which produces different versions of atherosclerosis. The hospital thus harbors more than one leg atherosclerosis. This diversity, according to Mol, does not lead to fragmentation; she explores how atherosclerosis manages to accommodate different approaches without becoming a singular condition. Rather, atherosclerosis becomes a rallying point that coordinates different people, objects, and entities. Thus atherosclerosis is, she states, "a single disease that in practice appears to be more than one—without being fragmented into many."[96]

The Body Multiple offers social scientists a way into the scientific core of medicine. But once there, they find this venture somewhat disappointing. We learn a lot about how various practitioners enact atherosclerosis differently, but not the purpose of their enactment. As we might expect from someone rebelling against philosophers' traditional explanation of science as a normative endeavor,[97] Mol refuses to recommend any intervention, advocating instead for a politics of continuous doubt. According to Mol, we should always ask ourselves whether practices are good for subjects to live with, but she does not specify what qualifies as good, instead encouraging us—in reaction to the standardized end points of quality of life used in clinical trials—to approach quality of life creatively and comprehensively. The good is neither a singular standard nor the addition of more predetermined choices. This approach has a strange dehumanizing effect, because it ignores suffering, pain, healing, caring, and curing—the existential and normative dimensions that underlie health care interventions.[98] While de-centering human subjects and eschewing normativity, we lose track of the purpose of medicine. When patients suffer and care providers are trying to help, such politics of continuous doubt quickly turn hopeless.

The stakes of this debate are high, because they designate the coordinates for a sociological study of medicine. In turning to practice, science scholars have opened up disease for social analysis but have forfeited the normative content of medicine. A space has been created to write about disease, but not about the ends of interventions. The intellectual challenge is to avoid not only surrendering disease to a reactionary sociology of medicine, but also giving up on the reason for interventions. Especially in forensic medicine, a study of the practice of conducting autopsies must explore why someone would even try to deduce meaning about death from an inspection of organs. Cutting open bodies is itself an interesting activity, but it becomes even more interesting if we know that it might lead to the detection of a homicide. Attributing a broad normative mandate to forensic medicine is not a leap of imagination: normative aims are suggested in laws that specify medical examiners' jurisdiction. Yet how these purposes are implemented, managed, subverted, and achieved is an empirical question that can be answered ethnographically. Ethnography allows one to observe the process of death investigation, with all its uncertainties, before the result is encapsulated in a single cause of death. Medical examiners claim that they contribute to the public good, but we need not merely take them at their word. In their work, they will reveal how they rank various values that enact various public goods. Norms might clash, diverge, shift, or coexist in contradiction, collaboration, or tension. Like substantive outcomes, norms are entangled in everyday practice.[99]

A medical sociology of practice draws from the symbolic interactionist sociology of work, the turn to practice in science studies, and the focus on norms present in some of the earlier sociologies, without presuming normative universalism. The balancing act is to make sociological concepts earn their theoretical keep—using them without reifying them as explanations—and to not prematurely foreclose important aspects of medical work such as the substantive content of medical interventions or the normative goals they aim to convey. I envision four filaments of the medical sociology of practice as they pertain to this study of forensic medicine.

1. The touchstone of such an analysis is *practice:* the actual contingent, situated process of performing tasks, doing work together, and transforming something into something different. An analysis of practice concerns who does what, when, where, and with what consequences. In the case of medical examiners, practice consists of what they do in processing bodies from the moment they are notified of a new case to the time they close

the case. It may involve work in the morgue but also in courtrooms, where pathologists present evidence and offer expert opinions. Practice is thus apparent in real time, in the unfolding sequence of tasks to process a suspicious death; but it may also rewrite the past and foreshadow a particular future.

2. The *organizational context* comprises the structural elements, policies, and relationships that predate the actual tasks at hand but that are—and this is the important part—reestablished and reconstituted through work practices. The analytical question about the organizational context is which structural elements matter in practice. For example, some third parties may have a great stake in a death investigation. Their influence, however, cannot be presumed but needs to be tracked in forensic decision making. Thus, elements of the organizational context may influence forensic work, and policies and relationships may in turn be influenced by forensic work.

3. A medical sociology of practice examines the substantive *content* that is obtained through work. In forensics, the equivalent of clinical disease categories is causes and manners of death, as written on death certificates. The goal of a forensic inquiry is to present these categories as self-sufficient explanations of a death. Yet a focus on the process of classifying large numbers of deaths indicates the various conditions in work processes, evidence, relationships, and expertise that need to be met in order for a death to qualify for a particular outcome, along with the wide diversity of bodies that may be classified similarly.

4. *Norms* consist of an expectation of behavior that ought to occur or an attitude that one should have. In a medical sociology of practice, norms may relate to how practice should be performed; or they can be an outcome of practice. I use the idea of norms here in the second sense—as emerging out of practice. I am interested in how medical examiners enact a moral order of life and death through their work aimed at various audiences, sanctioning some kinds of behavior and ignoring others. Medical examiners work as what sociologist Howard Becker has called moral entrepreneurs.[100] The central question is how medical examiners give meaning to hope through their work.

A medical sociology of practice analytically orients this book. The question of forensic authority implies an interest in a particular outcome reflecting what medical examiners do and what they conclude about suspicious deaths, for whom such conclusions matter, and how medical examiners organize our understanding of the finality of life. The three sources of legitimacy undergirding medical examiners' forensic authority do not determine how a pathologist will classify a death. Several studies have shown that death investigators with similar backgrounds sometimes classify deaths differently.[101] The sources therefore need to be measured, mixed, blended, and balanced in the death investigation. To remain relevant, they need to be mobilized in practice. Forensic authority allows us to explore the content of medical work if we take it not as a fixed quality but as an achievement that fluctuates over time. A sociological focus on both the substantive content and the norms of forensic practice also provides new intervention points for social researchers. By investigating how processes relate to particular outcomes, we may find ways to favor some outcomes over others. Rather than letting all kinds of public goods flourish, we may want to stimulate some goods over others.

OBSERVING THE WORK OF FORENSIC PATHOLOGISTS

Because of the delicate legal nature of death investigation, access to a medical examiner's office as a living sociologist is not easy. At the first office that I contacted for this study, the acting chief medical examiner asked me only two questions: "How many people work above you? How many people work underneath you?" I was dumbfounded, and mumbled that as an academic I did not have many people working above or under me. He then told me, "We are not interested in your research." No explanation could change his mind. His questions crudely measured the political cost of ignoring my request. Having determined that the risk of political liability was low, he dismissed me. Soon after, this medical examiner's office was embroiled in a series of scandals. This encounter taught me a hard lesson about the contested nature of investigating suspicious deaths. An entire state was lost for this research.

I had more success in another jurisdiction where the chief medical examiner had worked as a university researcher before entering state government. While negotiating the terms of this research project, I explained to the chief medical examiner and the office's medicolegal administrator that my project would not be a sensationalist hatchet job but instead was guided by analytical questions. I entered the medical examiner's office with the intention of studying how social and pathological evidence is weighted in suicide but quickly expanded my scope to focus on other controversial manners of death. The dominant theme of forensic authority became apparent when I noticed the extensive anticipatory precautions that the entire medical examiner's staff took before closing an autopsy report. Staff members would mull over possible alternative explanations, check with their allies, and make sure that every interpretation and conclusion was backed with sufficient evidence. Every case was treated as if the reputation and survival of the medical examiner's office depended on it, and to some extent it did.

Given the suspicion of outsiders in forensic circles, the chief medical examiner of the office where I did my research took definite risks in giving me access to death investigations. The results of the death investigation—the autopsy report and death certificate—erase the deliberations, the differing opinions, and the weighing of uncertainties that characterize any death investigation. The reports are written in a strong, factual, and self-confident language. Yet I was interested in the discussions that take place before the reports are written, discussions through which medical examiners articulate their procedures and defend their reasoning. Sociological insights are, however, secondary to the value of forensic investigations for criminal proceedings. If my research notes were to be summoned in court, they could easily paint the medical examiner in an unprofessional light, because I wrote down issues that staff considered irrelevant; my notes might have insufficiently emphasized the factual outcome of the autopsy. To minimize the risk of even inadvertently undermining the medical examiner's credibility, therefore, the staff and I took several precautions. I agreed to a strict, layered confidence protocol: not only are all the names of staff and deceased persons pseudonyms, but I also changed some irrelevant identifying markers in case studies, even when writing field notes. For example, I might have written that someone jumped from a water tower rather than from an apartment building. I also do not identify the state where the research took place. To make sure that I have not inadvertently breached confidentiality, the chief medical examiner has read each chapter of this book. While she corrected some misinterpretations in pathology, she did not engage with the sociological analysis. In addition, no written record in the medical examiner's office documents that I attended autopsies. Every visitor has to sign in, but, like residents in training, I was allowed to neither sign in nor appear in police reports as an observer. The price for these extensive precautions is that independently confirming my findings will be difficult. I suspect, however, that this is the only way to conduct ethnographic research in such a guarded setting.

I observed medical examiners at work over a three-year period, during which I attended morning meetings and more than 225 autopsies, checked the files on many more cases, and repeatedly interviewed the staff informally, on an individual basis. The bulk of my research consisted of observing autopsies. I initially stood back in protective clothing while a pathologist and an assistant cut open the body, removed the organs, and analyzed what they found. Because I was a clean person in the autopsy room (in a morgue, "clean" means not contaminated with blood and other fluids; sterility plays a limited role during autopsies),[102] I was gradually invited to help out with taking pictures, holding and passing tools, and describing the contents of wallets and other personal effects.

After the body was opened, as the pathologists conducted the routine slicing of organs, a conversation would often develop among the staff and any others present. I would seize that time to ask the pathologist and the assistants about forensics. Eventually, as I gained greater familiarity with autopsy procedures and learned to look at a corpse pathologically, the interviews turned into conversations about various anomalies. After a couple of months, I occasionally took the position of assistant when staff shortages threatened to delay an autopsy.[103] My access was restricted more by my own time constraints than by limits set by the staff. A benefit of ethnographic research was that I was able to follow the closure of cases over time. After the autopsy, several months may ensue before a final death investigation report is written.

I did not observe autopsies continuously over the three-year period. I began this research in May 1999. Between May and September of that year, I conducted research intensively, visiting the medical examiner's office several times a week. From September 1999 until August 2000, I conducted research about once a week. By the end of that time, I had observed about 180 autopsies. From August 2000 until August 2001, I spent time analyzing the data, visiting the office occasionally. Then I conducted more research in the summer of 2001 but focused mostly on reviewing autopsy files. During the fall of that year, I mostly analyzed data. Between February and July 2002, I observed the remaining autopsies. I finished a first, rough draft of this manuscript by July 2003 and spent until May 2005 revising the various chapters. I estimate that for every day I spent in the medical examiner's office, I spent an additional three days analyzing data and writing.

Because of the open-ended nature of participant observation, ethnographers worry about whether they have spent enough time observing. I believe that I have reached what Barney Glaser and Anselm Strauss call "data saturation," for three reasons.[104] First, autopsies are repetitive events. The office has standard investigative procedures in place, and each pathologist removed and sliced organs in exactly the same sequence. After a couple of months, I understood the mechanics of an autopsy. I also felt that I had a good sense, from having observed earlier investigations, of how the pathologist was going to classify a death. Second, the chief medical examiner read over my chapters, and, considering her high standards, I anticipated her reaction as a test of verisimilitude. I felt reassured that I was on the right track when she made only some small corrections. Other pathologists also commented on the manuscript.[105] Third, early in 2004, when I had already finished the first draft of my book, I discovered two central documents—the proceedings of a workshop on death investigation in the United States and a booklet with guidelines to improve the manner-of-death classification approved by the National Association of Medical Examiners.[106] Both documents echoed the problems in professionalism that I had defined as the core issue of death investigation. The documents confirmed the tension between serving public health and criminal justice, the danger of missing some homicides, the equivocality of suicides, and the great variability among systems of death investigation.

The medical examiner's office in my study conducted forensic investigations for an area of about one million people living in one big city and several surrounding rural towns. In the same way that a comprehensive health care system is lacking in the United States, there is not only one system for death investigation. The office where I conducted my study, however, reflects the "gold standard" of death investigation: "a highly professional, well-endowed, medical examiner office with access to all necessary technical expertise."[107] Few offices in the United States are well-endowed. The office that I studied had to fight at every budget cycle for resources and personnel; it was at best adequately endowed and at some points struggled with understaffing. Technical expertise was limited, too, in part because a backlog of cases put pressure on the staff to complete investigations. In spite of these problems, the staff prided itself on a highly professional death investigation (for a while, the computers had a screen saver with the words "We're a cut above the rest" rolling down the screen). The office's excellence was apparent in the thoroughness of its forensic investigations, lack of mistakes or scandals, successful court testimony, good relationships with key stakeholders, and recognition by politicians, the media, and professional organizations. When a disaster hit the area, visiting forensic specialists praised the high-quality medicolegal investigations. The office fell under the jurisdiction of the state's department of public health and employed two to four forensic pathologists (staffing varied over the course of my research): the chief medical examiner, whom I will call Dr. Cahill; the deputy chief medical examiner, Dr. Douglas; and, at various times, Drs. Anthony, Brown, Egan, Franken, Gibran, and Hughes. Most of the pathologists moved to different jobs during my study, while others worked temporarily. Because the office that I studied used the terms *medical examiner* and *forensic pathologist* interchangeably, I will do so as well, even though in some jurisdictions, medical examiners are not board-certified forensic pathologists. I will use the term *death investigator* as a general term for medical examiners, coroners, and their staff.

The office also employed three pathology assistants (called *dieners* or *agents* in the office): Zachary Sharpe, Vanessa Atwood, and David Dings (also pseudonyms). Their main task was to help the pathologist during autopsies, but they also picked up bodies from hospitals and nursing homes. The staff further consisted of five scene investigators, often retired police officers or forensic assistants who had moved up the hierarchy. They screened phone calls, conducted scene investigations, requested medical files, and helped retrieve bodies from death scenes. At the end of my research, one of the assistants became a scene investigator. The remaining personnel were administrative staff and included case managers, who kept track of the paperwork regarding individual cases and transcribed autopsy dictations; and front-office personnel not involved in death investigation but responsible for processing burial and cremation requests, maintaining records, and answering phones. They were supervised by the medicolegal administrator, who also communicated with relatives, journalists, politicians, and police. The office conducted about six hundred autopsies a year. In the medical examiner's office, physicians were called "doctor" with their last name, while other staff members were addressed on a first-name basis; I will follow that practice in this book. The deceased were referred to by their last names and, more generally, were designated as "cases" or "bodies."

Not all chapters in this book depend on the ethnographic data. An incident I observed between organ procurers and medical examiners, recounted in chapter 6, stimulated an exploration of the tensions between medical examiners and the organ and tissue procurement community. The empirical material of that chapter consists mainly of a review of medical and media accounts. The material used for the discussion of the Louise Woodward case in chapter 3 consists of archival material available at the Middlesex County Superior Court and the Massachusetts Supreme Court, media reports, and articles in the medical and legal literature on "shaken-baby/impact syndrome." Because this material is publicly available, I use real names in that chapter.

★   ★   ★

Medical examiners justify their work by citing the benefits it provides for the public good. Let's examine how they detect, classify, and explain suspicious death for our benefit.

CHAPTER ONE

MAKING THE CASE FOR HEART DISEASE

Playwright John Webster wrote in the seventeenth century, "Death hath ten thousand several doors, for men to take their exits."[1] Yet as contemporary mortality statistics show, heart disease, in its myriad variations, has been the leading cause of death in industrialized societies since the 1930s. Heart disease accounted for 29 percent of deaths in the United States in 2001.[2] Every year, more than half a million people die from heart disease, and 4.5 million are newly diagnosed with the condition. Autopsy reports confirm the lethal character of cardiac disease. Even when investigating suspicious and violent deaths, the medical examiners I observed most often wrote "arteriosclerotic cardiovascular disease" (ASCVD) on a death certificate. This postmortem diagnosis implies that a hardening and narrowing of the arteries around the heart has caused or contributed to the death.[3] As a leading forensic pathology textbook notes, "In medical examiners' offices, coronary artery disease accounts for approximately 75% of all sudden deaths, depending upon the population handled by the office."[4]

For social scientists, the predominance of heart disease on death certificates indicates the unnecessary "pathologization" that forensic pathologists inflict on death.[5] Pathologization represents the far-reaching professional medicalization that has replaced the extensive personal experience with death common in earlier times. In the early nineteenth century, British coroners held inquests in public spaces, usually in taverns. Coroners exhibited bodies, often in various stages of putrefaction, in the tavern's shed, because legal mandates required the jury to view the corpse before rendering a verdict.[6] Taverns were also the places where physicians met their patients, government officials collected taxes, and authorities kept prisoners. Concern for public health, however, eventually separated the coroner's work from daily activities. Tavern owners objected that smelly bodies were a health hazard and bad for business. Medical reformers argued that the solemn task of rendering a verdict should not be conducted in an alcohol-suffused atmosphere. The 1875 Public Health Act in Britain allowed communities to use public funds to construct mortuaries with separate viewing rooms, but even then the location of dead bodies in the midst of a community was considered morally unhealthy, because such buildings provided insufficient privacy and sanitation. Death and death investigation were becoming increasingly segregated activities.

An attack on public viewing created a second barrier between the public and the inquest. Viewing the body had long been an inviolate feature of the inquest. Before hearing any testimony, the coroner and the jury personally examined the body; neglecting this procedure could render the verdict invalid. By the turn of the twentieth century, however, critics regarded viewing as a "residual barbarity out of place in the modern world, . . . and the source of profane interference with the efficient and purposeful production of scientific knowledge."[7] Viewing thus became both an invitation to infection and an act incompatible with the effort to advance pathological knowledge. As science developed more sophisticated means to explain death, experts also deemed jury verdicts unreliable. Civilized means of murder, such as poisonings, did not necessarily leave external traces, so that lay juries would be profoundly misled by their impressions. The Coroners Act of 1926 in Britain rendered public viewing discretionary and allowed non-jury inquests under some circumstances. By 1938, about half of coroners' cases were decided on postmortem examination alone.[8] Still, medicalization of the inquest was not absolute: the coroner was not required to have either medical or legal credentials, general practitioners were allowed to conduct postmortems, and "the act appeared to leave intact the proposition that publicity was the inquest's underlying principle, with the public's involvement in the apparatus of death inquiry to be limited only in cases construed as publicly 'uninteresting.' "[9]

With the introduction of the current model of the medical examiner system in the United States in 1918, the move toward the professionalization of death investigation, medicalization, and seclusion was complete.[10] Not only do autopsies now take place behind closed doors in windowless rooms without representatives of the public present, but the public also has no role as final decision maker. In medical examiner systems, all suspicious deaths—from the uninteresting to the controversial—are now classified solely by forensic pathologists. Determining the cause of death no longer depends primarily on the narratives elicited from witnesses, but on tissues and medical histories. The turn to seclusion is apparent even in the morgue's architecture. The medical examiner's office that I studied was tucked away on the ground floor of a nondescript brick office building and marked only by a small sign stating "Medical examiner deliveries, use back entrance." Out of sight, at the side of the building, was a sign identifying the medical examiner's office and reserved parking spots.[11] Relatives entering the office met an administrator behind a glass partition and a locked door, and they could view the body only when visual identification was required; even then, most saw pictures of a washed body or, occasionally, a carefully draped, cleaned-up corpse.

Not surprisingly, observers of death investigation have associated this increased medicalization with "alienation" and "loss," and social scientists studying mortality statistics and coroner's records have consistently noted a reduction in socially situated death. Removed from a community context, death is an anatomical-pathological phenomenon. Lindsay Prior, who studied death in Belfast, summarizes the history of locating death in the human body: "Thus, step by step a thousand deaths came to replace a single death and the signs of death were sought in tissues and cells as well as in bodily organs and specific anatomical signs."[12] Prior deplores the loss of community and social life as "placing the active subject(s) in parenthesis," "dehumanization," "a myopic somatization," "anatomy-pathologization," "medicalization," "clinicalization," "decontextualization," "normalization," "naturalization"—in short, "dethematization" of death.[13] Cross-cultural comparisons draw similar conclusions about impoverished mortuary rituals. Prior compares death investigators to the Azande studied by the British anthropologist Evans-Pritchard in colonial times, while Clive Seale notes Alexander Spoehr's 1949 study of a community in the Marshall Islands. Seale summarizes the effect of medicalization by pathology and other modern means: "All of these, then, can be understood as similar in their function to the mortuary rites described by anthropologists studying tribal or traditional societies. The task of the living is to enclose and explain death, reduce its polluting effects, and symbolically to place individual deaths in a context which helps survivors turn away from death and towards continuing life."[14]

*　*　*

"Well," said Dr. Brown when I asked him early in my research about how he knew that heart disease caused death, "let me show you." Always helpful and eager to explain, this forensic pathologist went into the case manager's office and came back with a manila folder full of forms and pictures. He flipped through the pictures until he found a photo of one part of the heart. In the picture, a blue-gloved hand held a small set of forceps, which in turn lifted a piece of the left anterior ascending coronary artery. The pathologist pointed to the cross-section of the artery at the end of the forceps. "See how the artery is partly occluded by yellow plaque," he explained. "That decreases the diameter of the vessel, depriving the downstream tissue of oxygen and leading to death. It is basic physics: if you halve the diameter of a pipe, the volume is reduced four times. The picture is taken with what we call a 1:1 camera, meaning that it offers no scale distortions. One inch of photo corresponds with one inch of the photographed area." I saw indeed a small vessel, about two to three millimeters in diameter, partly blocked by a white-yellow substance. Later that morning, during the autopsy of a young car-accident victim, Dr. Brown showed how he "discovered" coronary artery disease. He took the heart in his left hand close to his face and with a scalpel in his right hand made small transversal incisions about one-eighth of an inch apart. He cut with the edge of the scalpel, then used the scalpel blade to push the soft tissue back and reveal the diameter of the artery. In this case, a coronary artery showed a small amount of crusted plaque. "Cholesterol at work," he observed.

Dr. Brown emphasized the straightforward use of pathological techniques to reveal the cause of death. He applied basic physiology, even basic physics, following the realist notion that "the body does not lie" and that death is the outcome of predictable, uniform breaches in biochemical communication. Death leaves pathological changes in the body that can be retrieved from a careful study of the corpse's anatomy, histology, and toxicology. Coronary arteries supply the heart with oxygen-rich blood. Coronary artery disease is due to deposition of plaque (atheromas) in the large and medium-sized arteries serving the heart. The buildup of the deposits can abruptly interfere with the blood flow. Physiologically, fatally obstructed circulation means that oxygenated blood cannot reach the vital organs, the oxygen-poor (ischemic) heart enters a fatal arrhythmia or experiences pump failure, and without immediate, aggressive intervention, death follows.[15]

Social scientists and forensic pathologists thus seem to agree on the primacy of tissues as the manifestation of death, albeit for different reasons. What social scientists consider unduly reductionist is for pathologists simply an observable, scientific explanation. Yet singling out anatomy, histology, and physics as providing a full explanation of the work of medical examiners in a death investigation quickly becomes unsatisfactory. Every discussion of new forensic cases during the staff's morning meeting indicated the multiple feedback loops between pathology and the deceased's life circumstances. For example, one Tuesday morning a ship's engineer was airlifted to a hospital by the Coast Guard after he complained of chest pains and collapsed. The staff wondered whether engine fumes might have contributed to the man's death, and they decided to conduct a carbon monoxide reading. A pathologist cannot run this test indiscriminately; it would be too costly and time-consuming. Faced with a corpse, forensic experts need to apply distinctions in order to know when a test might shed light on the cause of death. To reduce to pathological parameters the knowledge that pathologists generate about death misses the complexities and ambiguities of their work. Yes, pathologists focus on findings in tissues, but they need to extract historical relevance from the past and select socially relevant characteristics. The forensic pathologist needs to draw a connection between life—not the whole of a life, but some aspects of it—and death, that is, some of the factors that initiated the lethal cascade of events.

I will argue that, rather than practicing mechanistic reduction, forensic pathologists transform. While pathologists undoubtedly reduce the social world, their reductions add value to the body, allowing measurements, calculations, temporal ordering, and causal explanations. As they transform the organic stuff of bodies into numbers and descriptions, the causes of death that they determine are never purely pathological, but are necessarily socially informed. Beyond reductionism, medical examiners' work also generates social contributions. The critique of pathological reductionism is one manifestation of the age-old humanitarian argument that modernity involves a loss of community and the connections that sustain social life.[16] Regardless of the empirical accuracy of such an analysis, the more interesting issue is how contemporary society still maintains and transmits an understanding of the social world. It is in the actual work of medical examiners as it unfolds in the morgue that we can observe one contemporary way of tying individuals to collectivities.

TRIAGING DEATH

The death-alert line in the investigator's office has a distinctive ring to make sure that it is not mistaken for any of the other phone lines in the office. While picking up the phone, investigator Don Barthes grabs a clipboard with a worksheet covering a number of questions. The case I will be following in this chapter is one of the most routine encountered by death investigators. A police officer has called to notify the medical examiner's office that a corpse was discovered by a building manager in a third-floor apartment. Neighbors complained about an odor, and when the landlord's knock on the door went unanswered, he let himself in and discovered the corpse, lying on a bed.

Don writes down the name of the police officer making the call and asks whether the deceased has been identified. The police officer replies that they are still sorting out the identity but that the building manager thinks it is the body of his tenant, a single man in his mid-forties. The investigator asks about signs of foul play. The officer reports that the apartment was messy, with clothes and bottles strewn on the floor, but with no sign of forced entry on either the door or the windows. The investigator zeroes in on the bottles: were they medicine bottles or beverage bottles? The police officer replies that she found an empty vodka bottle and several empty beer cans on the floor and the bed, but no indication of drug use and no medication bottles. The officer had not looked very closely at the body because of the overpowering stench but did not think the body had any obvious signs of trauma.

The major decision Don has to make, on the basis of the phone call, is whether the reported death falls under the jurisdiction of the medical examiner—that is, whether this death is suspicious. This decision determines the trajectory the corpse will follow: Is this a body that can be disposed of by relatives or guardians, or will it become a case in the medical examiner's office? And if it becomes a case, what investigative procedure will need to be followed? The investigators are notified, usually by law enforcement or medical personnel, whenever a questionable death occurs in the geographical area they cover. By statutory law, death is suspicious when it involves violence; when it happens on the job, in jail, or within twenty-four hours of admission to a hospital; when it involves drugs or addictive substances; or when the physician has no reasonable explanation for the sudden passing.[17] Even with these legally specified criteria, however, the scene investigator still judges whether he will need to bring the case in.

Whether a death requires a forensic inquiry depends not only on the presence of bodily trauma, but also on the ties the deceased had developed with others. If the man found in the apartment had had relatives, roommates, or friends who witnessed how he died or who had found him shortly after death, they might have been able to account for the sudden passing and alert his physician. Deaths of people living alone or in isolation are likely to be discovered only after someone notices an absence from social life or after a corpse begins to smell. By then, the death has become suspicious because of the decomposition and lack of a ready explanation. Another path to the morgue is the absence of a recent medical record. Regular doctor visits and a personal relationship with a physician can obviate the need for a forensic investigation. An attending physician might be able to explain the sudden demise and volunteer to fill out the death certificate. Some people end up in the morgue because their physician was on vacation and the physician on call was unwilling to sign the death certificate. Even before an investigator sees the body, the degree of suspiciousness about a death reflects social values such as regular medical attention and community ties.

More generally, death investigation assumes that dying people either take action to stop or slow the dying process or, at a minimum, alert relatives and visit doctors to confirm their concerns. Suspiciousness thus implies a lack of preventive action. A suspicious death might mean that a person deliberately sought to die—as in suicide—or that the deceased was unable to act, or was unaware of the factors that precipitated death. The very notion of suspiciousness directs the death investigation to particular explanatory factors while excluding entire areas of life. Suicide complicates suspicion tremendously, because medical examiners have to relate the mechanism of death to the intention of the deceased, who has often tried to hide this intent and is certainly unable to report it. In all other cases, however, medical examiners presume that dying people rationally seek medical attention or take other precautions to avoid death.

When cases fall under the jurisdiction of the medical examiner's office, the investigator probes to determine the condition and location of the body and the events preceding death. As the investigator asks questions based on experience and a checklist, however, the clock is ticking: the longer the investigator waits, the more likely it is that the scene or the body will be disturbed. Some police officers do not know what to look for in a dead body or do not want to check out a corpse. For example, in the case of a woman who exsanguinated from her dialysis shunt, the police failed to mention the blood covering the walls. In a different case, the police assured the scene investigator that they had turned the corpse after they were explicitly asked how close they had come to the body. They reported no sign of foul play or even seeped fluids. Yet only an hour later, the scene investigator found the body so severely decomposed that it fell apart when moved. The staff's wry joke—covering up frustration with the unwillingness of police officers to take a close look at the body—was that the police thought the deceased "looked ugly" instead of decomposed. After the phone call, Don drives to the place of death for a scene investigation and body retrieval.[18]

SCENE INVESTIGATION

Most scene investigators have collaborated closely with law enforcement or worked previously as law enforcement officers and are therefore familiar with both scene investigations and the procedures of other authorities.

Once a person is declared dead and the case falls under the authority of the medical examiner's office, the police remain in charge of the scene, but the forensic investigators have jurisdiction over the body and anything possibly related to the cause of death, including weapons, ammunition, clothing, suicide notes, and drug paraphernalia. Usually, the scene investigator introduces himself to the officer in charge of the scene and asks what has happened. In the case of the man found dead in his apartment, the police officers are waiting outside for the scene investigator to arrive.

After opening the windows and turning on a ceiling fan in the small apartment, Don Barthes enters the bedroom with a notebook, a Polaroid camera, and a 35 mm camera. He takes pictures of the body on the bed and the pile of empty alcohol containers next to the body. Wearing rubber gloves, Don carefully looks over the man's body without seeing any obvious signs of injury. He checks the bedside table and the bathroom for medication but spots only the usual Band-Aids, antihistamine pills, and over-the-counter painkillers. Looking in the man's refrigerator, Don finds to his surprise no food, not even a jar of mayonnaise or a bottle of ketchup, but only packs of cheap American beer. He takes a picture of the refrigerator's contents. Returning to the bedroom, Don notices a sheet of paper on the floor. It contains some handwritten words, the beginning of a letter stating only "Dear Mary, I am not sure how to tell you this." After some hesitation, he decides to include the sheet in his file. He identifies a pair of pants in the pile of clothes next to the bed and finds a wallet in the back pocket. The wallet contains a picture ID card. Checking the man's face against the ID, Don thinks he has a match, but because of the decomposition, he is not entirely sure. Later, the landlord confirms that the deceased was indeed his tenant, and he provides the same name as on the ID card, Steve Albom. The landlord also supplies Don with the name of the man's brother, who is living several thousand miles away. The building manager does not know when Albom last visited a primary-care physician or whether he even had one. With the help of a worker from a specialized delivery service, Don moves the body into a body bag and then loads it onto a stretcher and into the van. He takes the sheet of paper and Albom's wallet with him. The police officer signs off on the removal of the body and the evidence from the scene. Don asks the police officer in charge whether she wants to attend the autopsy, but she declines. She promises to fax her police report by the next morning. Don closes the van and drives off.

The purpose of the scene investigation is to provide information about the deceased's life and circumstances of death. Even when a body is found in an apartment without signs of trauma, the origin of death could be in the food, the air, the plants, or even toxic mold in the building. It could relate to the last phone call, a relationship from long ago, a childhood trauma, or a recent setback. As Virginia Woolf illustrated in *Mrs. Dalloway*, a death might appertain to war trauma or someone's furtive kiss decades ago. While in theory any aspect of life might lead to death—and the cause would therefore be overdetermined—scene investigators focus on deindividualizing the deceased by picking out clues that might lead to generalizable knowledge. Their death investigation entails an inversion of what matters in life and in grieving. "As far as the bereaved are concerned, the corpse is first and foremost a site of personhood; a point at which persona, social existence and the idiomatic soul interconnect. It is therefore a site over which people weep, express sentiments of love and loss; over which they pray and eulogise."[19] Fulfilling relationships, job skills, a healthy body, a quick wit, great compassion for animals, or a love for food—all the life-enriching aspects that will be commemorated during a memorial service and in condolence notes are largely ignored in the death investigation. Such characteristics might add drama to the death, as when a police officer noted that a young woman in a car accident had just graduated with a degree in environmental ecology, or when a man with a large pendant of Santa Barbara (the patron saint who protects against sudden death, fire, lightning, and artillery) died from gunshot wounds. But they do not help explain the death. It is through ignoring most of social life that death investigators cultivate knowledge about death. The investigator asks about a sequence of events or a limited number of salient risk behaviors that from a forensic perspective are unhealthy. Depending on the circumstances of the death, heavy alcohol or illegal-drug use, gun ownership, a checkered driving record, convictions for assault or abuse, a fondness for risky sports such as rock climbing or snowboarding, or even emotions such as jealousy or anger might become relevant.

The investigator's queries reflect the open-ended questions for preliminary research that will eventually result in the deceased's *thanatography*, the written account of a person's death—analogous to a biography, which forms the narrative record of an individual's life.[20] A thanatography selectively relates aspects of life that set a deadly sequence into motion. Like a biography, a thanatography is ordered chronologically, with the death constituting the plot line. A thanatography is purposeful. The open-ended questions at the scene are narrowed down first by the pathological postmortem investigation that will follow and later by the legal and administrative determination of the cause of death. The scene investigator is therefore attentive to information that can be captured on film, has a factual character (such as age), or relates to medical issues (e.g., complaints about chest pain).

The removal of the body further underscores the death investigation's focus. By transporting the body with the sheet of paper and the wallet, Don physically separated the corpse from the scrapbook with sports articles, the journalistic award above the TV cabinet, and the dusty piles of pictures in the nightstand drawer, all of which he considered irrelevant. Philosopher of science Bruno Latour has emphasized the importance of relocating evidence to turn it into factual knowledge. Latour followed a number of botanists and soil scientists on a field expedition in Brazil, trying to figure out whether the rain forest advances on the savanna or the other way around.[21] Instead of carrying the entire forest home with them, the biologists removed carefully measured samples of soil and plants, substituting the sounds, smells, heat, and biotope of the forest with the samples. The transportation preserved scientifically pertinent features, allowing patterns to be discerned when the samples were spread out on a table in an air-conditioned office. "In losing the forest, we win knowledge of it," Latour explained.[22] Decontextualization is not simply a loss of information, but a necessary condition for the professional transformation of evidence. Similarly, by moving the corpse out of its "natural habitat" and losing most of the connections that are celebrated in life, pathologists can extract histology and toxicology specimens, manipulate them in labs, and correlate them into explanatory frameworks to shed light on the cause of death. Losing most of the body's individuality allows the application of generalizing scientific disciplines on the corpse. As sociologist Andrew Abbott noted, "Diagnosis not only seeks the right professional category for a client, but also removes the client's extraneous qualities."[23]

Once removed from the scene of death, the body's transformation has begun. The transported corpse is not only less but also more than an ordinary dead body. It is a registered corpse, and as such it is a medical examiner's case. Registering it singles out aspects pertinent to establishing the identity of the corpse and draws attention to clues that might explain the cause and manner of death. At the medical examiner's office, the body is entered in a census log and receives a case number. Don logs the letter and the wallet as pieces of evidence and opens a manila folder containing his report and some empty forms to be filled in as the inquiry progresses. He arranges the Polaroid pictures in a narrative format, circling the vodka and beer bottles in the picture in order to draw the pathologist's attention to them. Before leaving the scene, Don had placed the body in a pouch and locked it. Every plastic lock has a number, recorded both by police officers and by the investigator. If the lock is broken, someone might have tampered with the body. The lock not only secures the body in the bag but links law enforcement with forensic pathology. When the officer and the scene investigator sign off on the number of the lock, they establish that the corpse is now forensic *evidence* and subject to rules determining who can handle and manipulate the remains. From a dead body, the corpse has now become a medicolegal case to be explained and now constitutes, in part, its own evidence.

MORNING MEETING

Around 8:30 a.m. the next day, Dr. Cahill, the chief medical examiner, announces over the office intercom that the morning meeting will take place. Pathologists, case managers, assistants, scene investigators, and the medicolegal administrator convene around the big mahogany table in Dr. Cahill's office. Case manager Noreen Carey follows a routine in discussing the cases. She starts the meeting with the previous day's finished cases, providing a short summary of each case and noting whether the pathologist has determined a cause and manner of death. Then she reads the case numbers of the new cases, states whether the deceased has been identified, spells out the name of the deceased, and gives his or her age and race: "Case 2405–01. Steve Albom, a 43-year-old white male."[24] This first notice provides a number of signifiers for the death investigation. If the name of the deceased is mentioned, the body has been officially identified, and further identification efforts are not necessary. Giving a specific race for the person—if there is any ambiguity, the race will be left undetermined— might indicate whether religious objections against autopsies are likely, as they are for Native Americans. Age and gender might correlate broadly with possible causes and manners of death. The case manager hands any available medical records to Dr. Cahill and passes around the pictures of the scene investigation. The case manager then reads the investigator's report aloud. Don had written:

Police reported the death of this 43-year-old white male found in a third-floor apartment on 17 Broad Street in Juliaheim. Neighbors reported a foul odor coming from the apartment for the last two days. The building manager found the deceased after gaining entrance in the locked apartment. Door and windows did not show any signs of forced entry. Police did not find any signs of foul play. Rescue pronounced him dead at 2:40 p.m. The deceased was laying on a bed with empty alcohol containers and papers. He had a history of ETOH [ethanol] abuse, attended AA [Alcoholics Anonymous]. No signs of obvious trauma on the body besides decomposition. According to the building manager, the deceased had moved in two months previously. No known medical history. Deceased was identified from drivers license in wallet and by building manager. Wallet contained $12.48. A note was found next to the body. Police will not attend post mortem investigation. Jurisdiction accepted.

Don received the information about Alcoholics Anonymous from Albom's brother, whom he had called. The brother also told him that Steve occasionally worked as a freelance sports journalist. Don did not include this information in his report. The brother did not know whether Steve Albom had a regular physician, suffered from any ailments, took medication, or had recently undergone surgery. He guessed that the deceased had not seen a physician in years.

The investigator's report forms a first, short, incomplete draft of the deceased's thanatography. Forensic pathologists will triangulate laboratory tests and postmortem findings with the condensed narrative about Albom's life to generate an account that mixes history and medicine. Because history and medicine each bring a different orientation to life and death, striking the correct balance is not always an easy task. Sometimes a beautifully clear pathology does not make sense in light of a history, or the deceased's history suggests too many alternatives while pathology remains mute. During the morning meeting, forensic pathologists envision ways in which the history described by the scene investigator can be integrated with possible postmortem findings.

Albom's case does not spark a lengthy discussion. The repeated references to alcohol consumption suggest an ethanol-related death. The sheet of paper does not appear to be a strong indicator of a self-inflicted death. The scene investigator was unable to identify the Mary to whom the note was addressed. Only if the postmortem investigation suggests suicide might the letter become relevant.

The next case generates a longer discussion: a self-employed mechanic was crushed when the car he was working on fell off its jack. Dr. Cahill is concerned that the jack might have been faulty, in which case the manufacturer might be held responsible for the death. Discussion with the investigator and a review of the scene pictures show that the decedent was repairing the car on a sloping street and that the asphalt had softened with unusually warm spring weather. The jack likely shifted under the weight of the car and then fell over. The investigator adds that several bystanders had asked the man whether he knew what he was doing, and one passerby had told him outright that it did not look like a safe setup. The decedent had brushed their concerns aside. Because of this discussion, the pathologist performing the autopsy will likely focus on the crush wounds and only cursorily check the jack. If the jack were considered faulty, it might need to be brought to a specialized tool-testing shop and would become the center of the investigation. Scene investigators select aspects of life in anticipation of the pathological postmortem, while pathologists cull investigative strategies based on the elements offered to them by scene investigators.

Although most of a scene investigator's report remains tentative, the account maps out a limited number of possible death scenarios, continuously foretelling a possible deadly sequence.[25] Scene investigators do not access all available data sources: they will not, for example, seek Internal Revenue Service (IRS) records or read through occupational records. The information in their reports consists largely of a description of the body at the scene, medical records, and police files. The anguish of unemployment, loves lost or gained, immigration status, or financial duress will be known only if the information was included in a medical record or volunteered by relatives or acquaintances. The pathologists further restrict the number of plots available for the thanatography by discussing forensic procedures. Every decision about an investigation might make some causes of death more likely to show up than others. Pathologists are active participants in death investigations not only because they interpret pathological findings but, more important, because their expertise determines what can become a cause of death.

While death abruptly severs most relationships, the medical examiner's staff will be most interested in two specific ones: the deceased's relationship with an attending physician and with the next of kin. In the medical examiner's office, the deceased's relationship with a physician is authoritative and privileged. If the person had regular checkups, the medical file might narrow down possible causes of death or suggest avenues that should not be considered. Of course, the patient's medical record might also show the attending physician's lack of clinical accuracy; verifying clinical acumen was once a quality-control function of hospital pathology. The medical examiner's office, however, has no institutionalized way of providing feedback to clinicians other than by notifying the state physicians' board.

During a case discussion, a staff member is bound to ask whether the office has located the next of kin. A next of kin stands in a specific legal relationship to the deceased, a relationship newly created by death. The next of kin, usually the nearest blood relative, is expected to claim the body and make arrangements for its disposition. The medical examiner's office follows a relationships chain to determine who is the next of kin. The first person to qualify is the spouse, followed by parents, children, and siblings. Once identified, that relative needs to either assume responsibility or designate someone else. The next of kin is responsible for final arrangements, receives the possessions retrieved with the deceased, and provides permission for the autopsy report to be shared with third parties, such as insurance agents. When a corpse remains in the office's freezer long after the autopsy, the reason is usually a dispute over who qualifies or should qualify as next of kin. In one case, for example, a rabbi filed a restraining order against the sister of the deceased, whom the medical examiner's office considered the legal next of kin. According to the rabbi, the deceased was a deeply religious man who would have wanted to be buried according to Jewish customs, while the sister was going to have him cremated without a religious service.

IDENTIFICATION

If the deceased has not been identified, the staff will discuss during the morning meeting how best to proceed with identification. For the identification to be successful, the medical examiner needs to trace embodiment, the connection between physical presence and an identity. Naming occurs at birth and is a sign of life, not of death. Forensic pathologists therefore work with case managers, scene investigators, police officers, and dentists to establish the deceased's identity. While DNA technologies have received much media attention for providing objective and foolproof identification, the medical examiner's office relies on well-established administrative linkages.[26] Most dead bodies are identified from pictures, such as on a driver's license. If these are not available, the corpse might be visually identified by friends, roommates, landlords, or family members on the scene, in the hospital, or in the medical examiner's office. If it is badly decomposed, the body might be identified from tattoos or scars. If there are no identifiers but the deceased might have a criminal record, police will fingerprint the corpse and check the results against fingerprint files. If no fingerprints are on file but authorities suspect an identity, the office will check mouth X-rays against dental records, or chest X-rays against premortem hospital records. The identification of one decomposed body was facilitated by initials engraved on a tooth. These standard procedures resolve about 99 percent of the identifications. During my research, the office used DNA technologies only when a plane had crashed and the remains were small and scattered.[27]

One of the most difficult identifications I observed was a headless, handless, largely decomposed body that had washed up on a beach (a tourist from the Midwest reported a big turtle to the coastal authorities). Discussing this case during the morning meeting, Dr. Douglas thought he would be able to identify the body from a missing-persons report. In the end, no missing person matched the body's characteristics. The deceased did, however, have a previously broken bone that had been set with a pin and six screws, over which was an atypical growth of bone marrow. Observing the atypical growth, Dr. Douglas suspected that the surgery had probably been performed three to six months earlier. He asked the chief orthopedic surgeon of the local university hospital whether anyone remembered a similar surgery. Indeed, a resident surgeon had set the man's bone three months earlier and provided positive identification. Here, the postsurgical growth linked the damaged corpse to an identity. The man had last been seen walking along a cliff, but when he failed to return, his relatives did not report him missing.

Because people are entangled in multiple bureaucracies during their lives, databases often contain authoritative proof of identity. It is difficult to die anonymously. Only newborns abandoned in public places and completely skeletal remains routinely lack identification.[28] Anonymity, however, can also stem from too many identities. For example, wallets may contain picture IDs with different names. In one such case, the medical examiner's staff decided to use the name provided by the deceased's brother and let the police sort out the person's identity.

THE POSTMORTEM INVESTIGATION

Around 9:30 a.m., after the morning meeting, pathology assistant Zachary Sharpe takes Albom's body out of the morgue and rolls the stretcher into the autopsy room. Visitors entering the autopsy room almost inevitably gravitate to the right side of the room. The right side contains the tools of documentation: desks, cabinets, forms, pens, cameras, evidence bags, even a plastic skeleton. The opposing wall contains three bays, each with a large stainless-steel sink, hoses, bowls, cutting boards, saws, knives, scalpels, needles, soap, bleach, formaldehyde solutions, and other tools to manipulate the corpse. One might most associate forensic expertise with the left side of the autopsy room, but the right side, with its paperwork, is important in establishing the authority of forensic pathology. In the autopsy room, the transformation of the corpse into a cause and manner of death depends on the methodical removal of blood and tissues on the room's left side and the gradual addition of figures and observations on the right side. In some cases, the cause of death is clear; a body riddled with bullet wounds, for example, leaves little ambiguity. Yet the autopsy reports of homicides—likely to be scrutinized in court by adversarial lawyers—are the cases that confirm the forensic expertise of medical examiners. Forensic expertise consists not only of revealing or discovering a cause of death, but also of backing up or proving what all involved suspect. Without documentation, a "cause" remains merely a circumstantial association. An imaginative defense lawyer might, for example, argue that the deceased had a heart attack before being shot or that the corpse was only accidentally hit during target practice. Medical examiners help arguments meet legal standards of proof.

Biologically, the change from life to death is the cessation of electrochemical intercellular communication in the brain and heart.[29] From the outset, therefore, the forensic pathologist is at a disadvantage: once a corpse is ready for a postmortem inspection, all functional communication has ceased, and clues that point to a cause of death might be fragmentary. A leading forensic pathologist explains the dilemma.

Since the fundamental difference between living and dead organisms is functional rather than structural, the pathologist who focuses exclusively on anatomic causes of death is doomed to fail. The autopsy provides morphologic evidence of disease and injury, and it sometimes provides clues to the temporal course of disease and injury. However, the autopsy cannot provide a record, in real time, of the electrophysiological disturbances culminating in electrical silence of the brain and heart.[30]

In other words, if the dying process were a movie, the pathologist would walk in, at the earliest, when the credits were rolling. At that point, an observer might extrapolate something about the movie from the cast. A certain combination of actors might suggest a comedy or an action film. If the credits were finished, the actors unknown, or the film unusual, identifying the genre would be more difficult. Similarly, even if pathologists know that death is a multiorgan, electrophysiological process, the autopsy will provide only morphological and anatomical indicators. Pathology substitutes for physiology, and structure subsumes function. If these indicators constitute the only positive evidence, they are most likely to explain the cause of death. Because forensic pathology lies at the intersection of law and medicine, pathologists have more stringent standards of evidence than do clinicians. A psychiatrist might prescribe medications for schizophrenia without a complete understanding of neurology; medical examiners, however, are unable to write down a suspected cause of death without pathological proof. To have medicolegal standing, the cause needs to be documented appropriately and comprehensively, following legally admissible, standard procedures.

Dr. Douglas starts his postmortem investigation on the right side of the autopsy room, glancing over the report from the scene investigation and scanning the police report. He then takes a template with an outline of a male body out of the manila folder and fastens the form on a metal clipboard. He walks over to the corpse. Zachary has already attached the stretcher perpendicular to the sink to create a sloping, lime-green autopsy table. He has taken the body out of the pouch—recording the time that he broke the plastic lock—to weigh and measure it. The pathologist systematically observes the external condition of the body. Dr. Douglas makes note of the tattoos on Steve Albom's shoulder and right ankle, a small abrasion on his head, the yellow metal band at his left third finger, the presence of livor mortis (body discoloration after death), the bloated face and torso with patches of skin coming loose. All is recorded on the form and photographed with Polaroid and 35 mm cameras.

Why would the pathologist write "yellow metal band" to indicate the ring on Albom's finger? To most observers, the ring would not be yellow but gold, and would not be a simple "metal band" but most likely a wedding ring. In Western societies, solid golden rings worn on the third finger of the left hand are usually wedding rings. To see a yellow band as a gold wedding ring seems a small interpretative step that provides more detailed information. For pathologists, however, a legally defensible description is more important. If the pathologist's note appears in court, how can Dr. Douglas prove that the ring was really gold without having had it examined in a lab? How did he know that the band was a wedding ring without validating testimony from others? Describing a piece of metal as a gold wedding ring on a piece of paper that will most likely remain in a file folder might seem inconsequential, but exactly such small interpretations can invalidate the pathologist's inferences. A lawyer might question such procedures, suggesting that careless descriptions imply a sloppy death investigation. Therefore, no one examined by pathologists dies with an engagement or wedding ring or with a silver, gold, or platinum diamond ring, but with a yellow or white "metal band," set with or without "a stone." Here, legal validity is substituted for precision.[31]

Zachary turns the body to allow the pathologist to inspect the back. The clipboard now becomes a tool to check the lividity (livor mortis), as Dr. Douglas pushes a corner of the clipboard into a discolored area. He needs to know whether the reddish purple color indicating livor mortis blanches when pressed. Livor mortis is said to be *fixed,* meaning that the body has been marked by a steady discoloration of the skin. Yet as time passes, decomposition will dissipate the fixed livor mortis. The breakdown of blood vessels and then of the overall cell structure will cause blood liquid to leak into the surrounding soft tissue. Similarly, the medical examiner's description and photographs of the corpse fix its condition as a moment during an ongoing biological process. A corpse is teeming with life; as a Dutch proverb puts it, "Death for one is bread for another."[32] During putrefaction, the corpse is a fertile and virulent microhabitat of sprawling vitality as bacteria, maggots, ants, cockroaches, and—if the corpse was immersed in the ocean—lobsters or starfish devour the body, making it part of countless new life cycles. Some of this process is observable. As bacteria start to liquify internal organs, for example, released gases inflate bellies to look like balloons.

The pathologist's task, however, is to relate the fixed death to courses of action that could have caused it. Decomposition and the new life that it generates are the adversaries of the primary forensic objective, confounding the deadly sequence that the pathologist wants to retrieve. The continuous nibbling and microscopic transformation of the body can obscure evidence of biochemical processes that might have caused death, and they can generate artifacts that make postmortem changes indistinguishable from premortem ones. Medical examiners have to compensate for this vibrant process of putrefaction. They try to slow down life by putting the body in the walk-in cooler, spraying the maggots that fall off the dissection table with an insecticide, and preserving organ parts in a formaldehyde solution. During the autopsy of a decomposed man found in a pond, the pathologist warned before making his incision, "If something jumps out, kill it." But some life remains necessary for the autopsy to proceed. Stopping life altogether, by freezing the body, renders opening the corpse difficult and alters the sight and feel of the organs. Even maggots can be useful and should not all be killed. Some specimens will be picked off the corpse and fed a piece of raw cow's liver to identify their species and stage of development. The presence of various species of insects, combined with information about temperature, weather conditions, and location of the body, provides forensic entomologists with clues about when the corpse was exposed to insect life.[33] Entomologists also use maggots to detect cocaine and other drugs. To explain death, some forms of life—albeit not necessarily social life—might thus be cultivated.

In the bay next to Albom, Dr. Anthony is struggling with a different set of artifacts, caused not by insect life but by the wish to extend human life. She is performing an external examination of the man crushed under the car when the jack collapsed. After fire and rescue workers freed the man, he was transported to the hospital. Paramedics claimed to detect a pulse and began resuscitation protocols: chest compressions, intubation, ventilation with a mechanical device, defibrillation with electric countershocks, and the administration of drugs. In the emergency department, a zealous trauma surgeon resorted to open-chest cardiac massage, making an incision in the chest and pumping the heart with his own hand. Because these lifesaving efforts created injuries and bruises while death was settling in, Dr. Anthony has difficulty reconstructing the crush wounds over the marks of the resuscitation efforts. She thinks she knows where the crush wound starts but, because of the opened chest, is not sure where it ends. She also wonders whether the broken ribs are a consequence of the car falling or of aggressive CPR (cardiopulmonary resuscitation). Vanessa Atwood, her assistant, shakes her head at what she considers unnecessary lifesaving efforts. She notes that luckily, the deceased was not shot, because then the incision made for open-heart massage might have covered up an entrance or exit wound. In lifesaving efforts, the exigencies of life and death clash. Attempts to revive a person often create premortem artifacts and can void an explanation of death. The fact that futile efforts to resuscitate—survival rates after CPR remain in the low single digits[34]—undermine the purpose of a death investigation, however, matters little to the hospital staff. Medical examiners have urged emergency departments to document the condition of a body before initiating lifesaving efforts, but as long as the body is not officially a corpse, such documentation remains a violation of life.

Zachary and Dr. Douglas have now changed into protective clothing in a dressing and supply room off the autopsy room. They both wear protective suits, shoe covers, hairnets, two pairs of gloves, and arm protectors. Zachary also wears a mouth mask. In the autopsy room, they each don a helmet with a protective vision shield. Zachary begins to fill about eight tubes with femoral blood and takes the vitreous fluid out of the eyes. Dr. Douglas walks to the counter and picks up a scalpel. The actual opening up of the corpse goes quickly. Zachary puts a wooden block under the shoulders to prop up the body, and Dr. Douglas swiftly makes the universal Y incision—two cuts from the left and right shoulders to the middle of the chest and then down to the belly button. The doctor removes the flaps of skin and two-inch layer of fat from the rib cage, and Zachary cuts out a large triangle of ribs with an electric bone saw. Dr. Douglas turns away to avoid inhaling the flying bone dust. Their quick efficiency belies the centuries of excommunication, imprisonment, repugnance, ridicule, and wrangling that had to be overcome before it was possible to open bodies.[35] The Y incision is so much the routine that even if the death is obviously caused by bleeding after accidental leg amputation, most of the autopsy will still consist of an examination of the internal organs. When Dr. Cahill was autopsying the organs of a twenty-two-year-old Hispanic man shot in the head, she referred to the organs as those of a "normally healthy dead."

Opening the corpse turns the body into a pathological object. Medical commentators have used the term *objectification* loosely, arguing that most medical actions reify a patient, to be acted upon as a thing and not as a whole human being. Surgery and anesthesia, for example, are said to objectify patients, reducing them to organs to be cut instead of fully constituted, acting and thinking subjects.[36] This humanist critique of medicine points to the narrow focus of medical action. I use the word *object*, however, more descriptively, to mean a thing displayed for observation. No equivalent manipulation of the body—either in surgery or in funeral sciences—produces the same visual effect as an autopsy. The pathological body is objectified for instrumental reasons: it provides pathologists access to anatomy and morphology. Although a secondary meaning of *object* is something that excites a particular emotion—and the emotion most often associated with viewing dead bodies is horror and shock—forensic pathologists proceed with detachment. They anticipate the scientific puzzle to be solved. They express occasional excitement or frustration, but their excitement is usually prompted by discovering the ravages inflicted by an unusual cause of death.[37] Frustration comes from a lack of significant findings; it rarely has to do with death itself. Pathologists tend to manage their emotions in order to avoid personal transformations.[38]

The opened rib cage provides information about the level of fluids in the body, broken ribs or lacerated organs, and the color and texture of the prominent liver. In Albom's case, the protruding liver looks not smooth and brown, as it should, but yellowish orange and granular. Now Dr. Douglas needs to decide how to disturb the organs: is he going to remove them one by one and thus focus on the shape, texture, and morphological condition of each, or is he interested in investigating the organs in situ, concentrating on their location in relation to each other? His decision will determine which pathological processes will be observed. In the case of a laceration caused by a knife stab wound, the pathologist will first trace the knife's deadly path through the organs in situ, tracking how the injury disturbed the relationship between them. For most death investigations, however, the body's own space is too economical; the organs fit too tightly over and around each other to be easily examined. Organs are therefore usually removed.

Dr. Douglas waits a couple of seconds to let some of the methane gas escape from the bloated body. Then he removes more thick and increasingly liquid fat layers and starts eviscerating. First he disembowels the body, pulling hard to remove the entire mass of entrails. They slide down the sloping green autopsy table and are put in a red hazardous-waste bag. He locates the appendix and saves it in an open container of a formaldehyde solution sitting next to the sink on his right. Then he detaches the aorta and takes out all the organs at once, putting them in front of him on a large cork cutting board.[39] One by one the organs are freed and put in a metal surgical bowl. The left kidney is marked with an incised X to distinguish it from the right.

As when the body was transported from the death scene to the morgue, extracting the organs both removes from and adds to the corpse. What the pathologist loses in the overall view through successive reductions of the body parts is regained in the measurements and calculations that such reductions make possible. Zachary lifts each organ with his left hand, weighs it, writes the weights down on a white board with a pen in his right hand, and then puts the organ back in the metal bowl between the ankles of the corpse. Dr. Douglas picks up the organs to dissect them, following the same sequence in every autopsy. In Albom's case, the liver and heart are the most important. The pathologist positions the liver on the corkboard and cuts it into three-quarter-inch slices with a large knife. Leaning over the corkboard, he scrapes the knife across each slice, and round yellow fat globules color the silver metal. He holds a piece of the liver between his gloved fingers and can easily push a finger through it. This is obviously a cirrhotic liver; it does not have the smooth, firm feel and dark color of a healthy liver. Steve Albom was likely a long-term alcohol user. The condition of his liver retrieves one of his identities during life, but we do not know whether he was a *lethal* drinker. Alcohol does not have the same effects in all bodies. Some long-term, heavy drinkers have pristine livers, while others have advanced liver disease. The coronary arteries of alcoholics are often remarkably well preserved. The doctor will need further laboratory tests to determine the havoc that excessive alcohol consumption wreaked in Albom's body and will need to know the blood ethanol level at his death.

Dr. Douglas picks up the heart in his left hand and holds it up near his chest. With a scalpel, he makes small incisions in the heart's coronary arteries. He is in luck. Albom was one alcoholic with both liver disease and heart disease. One of the coronary arteries is about 75 percent obstructed, while a second one has a segment that is 90 percent obstructed. The bad news for Albom is good news for Dr. Douglas—another inversion between life and death that the autopsy makes possible. Although at the end Dr. Douglas will write "pending toxicology" in the space allowed for the cause of death, he decides that death could have resulted from one of only two scenarios. If the toxicology results show a very high ethanol level at the time of death, then the advanced liver disease will be the immediate cause of death and heart disease will be an underlying cause. If toxicology comes up with low ethanol levels (which Dr. Douglas doubts, considering the many empty alcohol containers on and near Albom's death bed), then arteriosclerotic cardiovascular disease will be the immediate cause of death and cirrhosis will be a significant condition, indicating chronic alcoholism. With an eye to possible future skeptics, Dr. Douglas takes pictures of the obstructed coronary arteries with the 1:1 Polaroid camera and saves a piece of heart tissue in formaldehyde.

At this point in the postmortem investigation, the unfinished letter loses all explanatory relevance. The sheet of paper has become background noise, as irrelevant as the sheets and pillows on the deceased's bed and the people he loved and left behind. Albom's death was not a suicide but a natural death, due to either excessive ethanol consumption or a diseased heart. Yet even if Steve Albom, like Nicholas Cage's character in the movie *Leaving Las Vegas,* had deliberately set out to drink himself to death, proving his death a suicide would be difficult without an explicit written statement. Substances are associated with intentions.[40] Alcohol is a substance with addictive qualities presumed to take precedence over the intent to kill oneself. An alcohol-related death will often therefore be classified as a natural death (unless guns or cars interact with the alcohol). If Albom's last drink had consisted of window-washing liquid, a substance considered not addictive but poisonous, his death would have a better chance of being considered a suicide.

MATTERS OF THE HEART

When Dr. Douglas looked at the transversal incisions in the heart, something important happened. He claimed to have found a possible cause of death. How did he make the transition from calcified circles of tissue to such an abstract concept as the cause of death? At this point in the autopsy, the step from physical matter to abstraction was minimal, because the entire medical examiner's office had been closing the gap all along—by excluding other explanations and creating a context that allowed the coronary arteries to emerge as the cause of death. During the postmortem investigation, life lost features, while death was made compatible with the discipline of pathology. At every stage, with every procedure and discussion, the staff removed clutter, the elements of life that localized and individualized Steve Albom, while the pathologist isolated and magnified possible causes of death.[41] When the doctor points to the pictures of the obstructed coronary arteries and states, "This is the cause of death—straightforward heart physiology and pathology," the obvious step from coronary obstruction to cause of death has required having the legal authority to remove a corpse from its death scene, entering it in several logbooks and records, following standardized autopsy procedures with the help of an assistant, noticing the calcified circles, and applying a notion of causality that singles out a pathological factor.[42] Only if all those elements are in place is the conclusion inevitable. And only within the discipline of pathology and after a forensic death investigation is the difference between life and death attributable to small pieces of plaque.

Still, these efforts fail to explain why forensic pathologists find coronary artery disease to be the leading cause of death in modern societies. The reason lies in the fact that many pathological pathways lead to obstructed coronary arteries, and the disease category is conceptually versatile, connecting a variety of very diverse elements: the discipline of pathology, with its emphasis on visible causes; the heart as the primary seat of life and death; the positive proof required in death investigation; the balancing of the deceased's history with the medical orientation of forensic pathologists; and the death certificate, with its sequential and etiological ordering of death. Coronary artery disease has even come to stand almost as a synonym for death itself.

The Greek root of *autopsy* means "seeing with one's own eyes," and the emphasis on visible abnormalities lends itself well to finding obstructed coronary arteries—which is not difficult even after decomposition has set in. For example, in the case of a man discovered a week after his death in a closed-up trailer during a sweltering summer, Dr. Brown found most of the internal organs decomposed, dissolved into a grayish red mush. He could still pick out the heart, however, and could feel the calcified coronary occlusion. He took off his second layer of heavy rubber gloves and, while staring at the ceiling and concentrating on the path of one of the arteries on his cutting board, did indeed find calcified obstructions. Opening a body and slicing organs is a procedure designed to discover abnormalities such as coronary artery obstructions, thromboses, a burst aneurysm, or internal exsanguination. An autopsy is far less effective for identifying complicated multiorgan interactions or invisible biochemical and metabolic processes.[43] Dr. Brown told me how he once did an autopsy on a person whose liver looked fine. A hospital pathologist, however, had performed a biopsy of the man's liver right before his death, and the sample showed that enzymes had reached levels that could have killed the man. The forensic pathologist is less attuned to enzyme, hormone, or electrolyte imbalances and is unable to retrieve them post mortem. If a cause of death cannot be observed or proven with laboratory test results, it cannot manifest itself in the forensic context.

Coronary artery disease has a further advantage: it does not require extensive triangulation with findings from the scene investigation and medical history. The self-sufficiency of coronary artery disease as a cause of death is physiologically and clinically supported. A forensic textbook observes that "sudden death is in fact the initial [and only] symptom in approximately 25% of individuals dying of coronary arteriosclerosis."[44] Sometimes people complain of shoulder, neck, or abdominal pain before dying; or antacids in a pocket might suggest heart disease, because heartburn is frequently mistaken for heart problems. Often, however, there are no previous complaints. Forensic pathologists Charles Hirsch and Vernard Adams note that pain symptoms are regularly overlooked, particularly in mental health settings. Even outside the hospital, stoicism, a high pain tolerance, or chronic alcoholism might mask any signs of impending death. Neither the medical file nor interviews with relatives and friends might predict the significance of the obstruction: "This is an example of the great discrepancy that may exist between the gravity of an organic lesion and the comparatively trivial clinical manifestations associated with it."[45] Coronary artery disease has become the pathologists' cause of death. Pathologists can determine it by themselves and are often the first to establish it. The finding obviates the need to evaluate ambiguous letters or notes, vague opinions about what the deceased might have meant by staring out the window much longer than usual, or the meaning of scratches on an arm, the position of the body, or the significance of the date of death. The scene investigation and past medical history function primarily to exclude other possible causes and to frame the plausibility of positive findings for this condition.

Coronary artery disease also fits nicely on the lines of the death certificate: it is sufficient as an immediate cause of death and is associated with many other conditions for which it can function as an underlying cause of death. The model death certificate used in the United States asks the pathologist to note an immediate cause of death but offers the possibility of listing up to two intermediate causes of death and one underlying cause.[46] A separate section allows the pathologist to write down other significant conditions. An immediate cause of death is defined as "the final disease or complication directly causing the death." The underlying cause of death is "the disease or condition that initiated the train of morbid events leading directly to death"[47] and is considered the more important piece of information on the death certificate. Read from bottom to top, the death certificate orders the terminal events chronologically (from remote to most immediate cause) and etiologically (from underlying condition to subsequent tissue damage or impairments).[48] If the only positive finding during a death investigation is coronary artery disease, the pathologist can simply write "severe ASCVD" as cause of death, and the death certificate is considered complete. The pathologist need not specify any additional factors; coronary artery disease is a sufficient, lethal condition. Yet heart disease is associated with a host of other conditions prevalent in the medical examiner's office, particularly drug use, hypertension, hypothyroidism, and diabetes. The coronary obstructions might thus be a more immediate lethal consequence of underlying diseases. On the other hand, coronary artery disease might be the underlying cause of thrombosis, stroke, myocardial infarction, or congestive heart disease. The logic of the death certificate accommodates the versatility of heart disease. The primacy of cardiac disease was supported as long ago as 1912, when the *Manual of the International Statistical Classification of Disease, Injuries, and Causes of Death* introduced the rule that cardiac causes of death take precedence over diseases of the respiratory system. Lindsay Prior notes, "It was a rule which, in the twinkling of an eye, altered our image of the human condition at death."[49]

Another reason for the persistent leading role of coronary artery disease in the drama of death is the marginal significance of other organs.

Few other organs provide a decisive lethal alternative as the cause of death. Many deceased people show congested lungs, for example, at autopsy, but this finding is often considered nonspecific and not necessarily lethal. Unless the circumstances surrounding the death suggest that lung congestion might be significant (as in drownings) or unless advanced lung disease is documented in a medical file (as in tuberculosis), congested lungs do not constitute a significant finding. The second most common cause of death in the United States, cancer, is also rarely identified in the medical examiner's office, because most cancer-related deaths are certified by a hospital physician who has followed the patient over a lengthy period. Early in my research, I asked Dr. Douglas why he did not routinely check for breast or prostate cancer. He answered that medical examiners had difficulty establishing that breast cancer had caused death, that only metastasis to vital organs would suggest that a lethal breast or prostate cancer required the pathologist's attention.[50] Patients dying from cancer rarely come to forensic attention, because clinicians will sign death certificates based on an extensive, lethal medical history. Such is the prominence of the heart that pathologists have adapted their dissection procedure to focus on this organ. Some pathologists autopsy the heart first, in order to make sure they have at least a backup cause of death if they find nothing else significant. Others keep the heart as the last organ to be dissected, to force themselves to pay careful attention to the other organs. Either way, the heart becomes the defining organ.

The heart and circulatory system harbor most of death's "natural" origins. Besides coronary artery disease, people might die of hypertension, valve disease, cardiomyopathy, myocarditis, cerebrovascular accidents (strokes), hemorrhaging, or berry aneurysms. Forensic pathologists have not supported "brain death" as a sufficient criterion of death. The lack of electric brain activity in "beating-heart organ donors" is useful for organ-transplantation purposes and indicates the time of death for forensic pathologists,[51] but it is not the starting point of the postmortem investigation. Surprisingly, the deceased who arrives at the medical examiner's office after a first heart attack will rarely be found to have died of it, because fresh heart attacks do not leave pathological traces. In other words, it is virtually impossible to see with an autopsy or even histology whether the decedent had a fresh heart attack or whether the heart malfunctioned. When a myocardial infarction is suspected, the pathologist will look attentively for scar tissue from previous heart attacks. To make a determination of myocardial infarction stick, the doctor would have to find a heart with telltale white lightning patterns, indicating an earlier heart attack.

Another important advantage of coronary artery disease for forensic pathologists is that almost every elderly person will have some artery occlusion,[52] so that an incision of the heart's arteries will usually provide a cause of death. In addition, the criteria for establishing that a coronary narrowing caused death are flexible. Forensic pathology textbooks state that occlusion of about 75 percent of the diameter of the artery with plaque or calcium deposits is sufficient to qualify as a cause of death. The 75 percent is estimated; there is no real measurement besides "eyeballing" the arteries. I observed that under some circumstances, lesser obstructions could qualify as underlying causes of death. Some decedents had only small obstructions of about 50 percent in one artery and almost nothing in the other arteries, yet the doctor would still explain the death with coronary artery disease. The significance of such obstructions depended upon an interpretation of other factors, such as an elevated blood pressure, irritation of the heart by caffeine, cocaine, or epinephrine, and the emotional state of the person before death. Emotional stress and strong emotional surges can destabilize the electric functioning of the heart; one can thus be literally scared to death.[53] Even when such factors were lacking, heart disease might prevail because it constituted the only positive finding of a full death investigation.

Of course, not every case of coronary artery disease has a primary role on the death certificate. Many victims of shootings and plane crashes also have occluded coronary arteries. I observed countless diseased heart valves, an aorta full of plaque and malformations, an aneurysm that had not yet burst, and one obstruction after another in coronary arteries, sometimes leaving only a pin-sized opening in the left descending coronary artery. Those with a 95 percent obstruction had obviously not died when they had a 75 percent occlusion. The longevity of those who have a bad heart but die from a car accident or a self-inflicted gunshot wound is puzzling. When I asked the physicians for an explanation, they admitted that occlusion was not always deadly but depended on the size of the arteries, the ability of other arteries to take over from the diseased artery (collateral revascularization), other diseases, stress levels, and a variety of unknown factors. Dr. Egan speculated that for some people, the transition from 40 to 50 percent occlusion could be lethal, while for others the gradual slippage to 80 percent would lead to death. He could not point to more specific factors. The pathologists did not consider such findings contradictory evidence for the primacy of the heart. If a gunshot killed the person, then the cause of death was obviously not heart disease, regardless of the obstructions detected in the heart. Immediate lethal trauma supersedes lethal chronic disease.

The ubiquity of coronary artery disease as a cause of death creates the impression that instead of using it to explain death, pathologists use it to attest to death. A manual on cause of death published by the College of American Pathologists warns that instead of describing the mechanism of death, the pathologist should explain the etiology and chronology of death.[54] For that reason, terms such as *cardiac arrest, cardiopulmonary arrest,* and *electromechanical dissociation* are unacceptable, because they are the means by which the underlying cause exerted its lethal effect (the mechanism of death). The pathologist is interested in finding out not about death itself but about the conditions that initiated the deadly cascade. The handling of "in absentia" cases by the medical examiner's office, however, showed that the line between cause of death and attesting to death becomes blurry. In some cases, the pathologist would determine the cause of death after a review of the medical file but without autopsy. If the deceased (usually an elderly person who had experienced a fall without any other positive findings at the scene, the trauma qualifying the death for the medical examiner's jurisdiction) had died suddenly and had not seen a doctor in the past year, the pathologist would give coronary artery disease as the cause of death. The medical reasoning was that an elderly person with a life-threatening condition would have gone to a doctor and received treatment for it. The diagnosis would have been included in the medical file, or the attending physician would have been able to provide a more specific cause of death. An autopsy was unnecessary because the pathologist was likely to find obstructed coronary arteries. Anyone over about age 60 was assumed to have occluded blood vessels. The cutoff point dropped to about 55 if the deceased was a heavy smoker, to 50 if diabetes was present, and to 45 if it was a man who had complained about chest pain. Coronary artery disease thus became a synonym for death by old age. We can call it the "coronization" of old age.[55]

CLOSING UP

Let's return to Zachary and Dr. Douglas. Even though he has determined a possible cause of death, Dr. Douglas dissects the other organs and saves small samples in formaldehyde. At this point, he does not expect to find anything pathologically abnormal, but he still needs to confirm the lack of agency of the other organs. An autopsy not only reveals but also excludes. Negative findings make the positive findings stand out and confirm the strength of the causal connection. In principle, excluding causes of death could require the doctor to cover every possible contingency that might have caused death. In the same way that proving the cause of death consists of observations on a pathological level, excluding causes of death remains on the level of organ morphology and pathology. Dr. Douglas quickly slices through the other internal organs. Albom's lungs show small bubblelike extensions (called dilated airspaces) on the ends of the upper lobes, a sign of emphysema. Dr. Douglas does not consider these to be lethal signs. He guesses that Albom might have been a little short of breath because of smoking. The body does not have any other observable and lethal disease patterns. In the meantime, Zachary has peeled back the scalp and opened the skull for Dr. Douglas to inspect for signs of injury. After the doctor gives the go-ahead, Zachary lifts the brain and removes it after swiftly cutting through the optic nerves, the carotid arteries, and finally the spinal cord. He then weighs the brain. Dr. Douglas remarks in frustration on the softness of the brain, comparing its consistency to mayonnaise; this is due to decomposition (autolysis).[56] When dissecting it, he looks for brown spots, indicating hemorrhage, but finds nothing remarkable in the brain slices spread out on the cutting board. He nevertheless saves a piece in a small formaldehyde container. The last step of the autopsy consists of taking out the neck organs, upper airways, and tongue—a tricky procedure, because the pathologist does not want to make an incision high up in the neck. The doctor saves the thyroid glands, larynx, and hyoid bone; slices the tongue to check for bite marks; and then cuts open the upper part of the esophagus and trachea to look for hemorrhaging, strangulation, and foreign matter. As expected, those body parts are pathologically normal.

Then Dr. Douglas leaves Zachary to sew up the body, takes off his bloodied gloves and arm protectors, and goes to the desk on the other side of the room to fill out the paperwork. Zachary takes the bright red plastic hazardous-waste bag and adds the sliced organs and brain matter to the bowels. He lifts the bag into the body cavity. Then he sews up the Y incision with rough threads and wraps the head in a towel. One of the other assistants turns the sewing up of the incision into fine handiwork, using regular, close stitches. Zachary, who previously worked in a funeral home, rolls his eyes at such needlework. He knows that fine stitches create unnecessary work for the funeral workers when they embalm the body. As Jessica Mitford so evocatively described, in North America funeral personnel enact an aesthetic relationship to the corpse.[57] They do not care about the knowledge of life and death hidden in the vital organs but aim to represent the corpse in a lifelike, peaceful condition resembling sleep. Zachary and Dr. Douglas take this future transformation of the body into consideration. To allow the embalming fluid to circulate freely to the head and facial areas, the pathologist was careful not to sever the carotid neck arteries when he removed the tongue and larynx. Pathologists also minimize incisions to the face, to avoid interfering with funeral-home viewing. Such courtesies help reconcile the sometimes opposing interests of funeral directors and forensic pathologists processing the same corpse. Zachary puts the remains in a new body pouch, attaches a name tag to the left big toe, and wheels the stretcher back to the cooler. The body pouch is no longer locked. After the autopsy, the body becomes a corpse waiting for final arrangements, not a piece of evidence in a death investigation.

THANATOGRAPHY

Bent over the desk in the morgue, still in his protective suit, Dr. Douglas fills out a stack of forms. First he copies down the weight of the organs and any pathological abnormal findings from the white board onto a draft sheet with small drawings of the organs; then he completes the personal-evidence sheet and orders laboratory tests on a request form. It is easy to overlook the importance of the paperwork the doctor fills out. Pathologists—and particularly the scene investigators and assistants—do not consider it "real" work. While observers of the medical field have noticed the increase in required paperwork over the years, few analysts have looked at what purpose forms serve in health care.[58] Yet, much as the death certificate imposes a particular logic about the sequence of causes of death, forms are crucial to the knowledge production of forensic expertise. The medicolegal administrator explained that they do not hire pathologists if they are good at conducting autopsies but lack writing skills. "Writing is 75 percent of the work," he said. When Dr. Douglas fills out the laboratory request forms, every test he marks constitutes its own postmortem investigation. If the toxicologist does not check for cocaine, there might as well be no cocaine in the body. If a toxicology request form is incomplete, an opportunity is missed to include this information with the other findings from the autopsy, possibly misleading the pathologists by omission; and because heart disease has been strongly linked with cocaine in the medical literature, the knowledge about the cause of death would be incomplete.

Recording the deceased's personal effects is similarly important to the success of the death investigation. The signed and dated forms track who possessed the personal effects, creating a chain of custody for the evidence. If a wallet contained $350 when the police signed it over to the scene investigator and at the autopsy the pathologist finds only some nickels and dimes, the paper trail can be followed in reverse to determine who was responsible for the loss of the money. These recordings have primarily legal value, to prove that evidence was not tampered with and to be used when conflicts arise. A deceased's personal effects have sentimental value as well. The medicolegal administrator repeatedly told the cautionary tale of a funeral director who cremated a body without taking it out of the pouch. The medical examiner's staff had been unable to remove the deceased's "yellow metal band" and left it on her swollen finger, and it was turned into ashes along with the body. Because the funeral director had signed a form stating that the medical examiner's office had released the body with the ring attached, the medical examiner's office was legally off the hook. The funeral director was held liable for the sentimental as well as the monetary value of the wedding band. In some versions of the story, the lawsuit led to the funeral director's bankruptcy.

The two most important forms in a death investigation are the death certificate and the autopsy report. The final product of the investigation is not the Polaroid pictures of the coronary obstructions. The pictures only support the pathologist's conclusion; they will be shown during the next day's morning meeting to demonstrate the extent of the occlusion and prove that coronary artery disease was warranted as the cause of death. If relatives disagree with the conclusion or if the case goes to court, the pathologist might show the pictures again. The final product of the death investigation is, instead, the few lines on the death certificate and the lengthier narrative of the autopsy report, written after the autopsy and when the toxicology and additional laboratory results are available. The report needs to be complete, accurate, definitive, and self-sufficient. Without reliance on other documents, it must contain a complete description of the medical examiner's investigation and conclusions. Every word in the autopsy report counts. To some extent, the documentation of evidence is more important than designating the "correct" cause and manner of death, because contesting a cause of death is very difficult when the documentation is watertight. In contrast, an outsider can relatively easily discredit even the most obvious cause of death if mistakes or oversights occurred in the documentation and recording process.[59] A forensic investigation stands or falls with the completeness and internal consistency of its records.

The autopsy report does not contain a sequential description of the pathologist's postmortem investigation, retracing procedures, and investigative steps, but a purposeful ordering of the death investigation with a final result in mind.[60] At this point, the pathologist knows what caused the death, and the final report needs to convey the lethality of this single process. The report begins with the results of the external examination, evidence of recent medical therapy, and evidence of injury. It then discusses the internal organs by organ group or system. The investigation is summarized in an anatomical diagnosis and a synopsis of the case with a cause and manner of death. In the case of Steve Albom, the sections on the internal investigation of the hepatobiliary system and the cardiovascular system are the most relevant.

Hepatobiliary system: The liver weighs 2650 grams and is yellow in color. Its capsule is smooth. The cut surface is markedly firm and friable with a nodular architectural pattern throughout.

Here, the weight of the liver is more than one would expect for a man of Albom's size; a normal liver weighs about 1,500 grams. The abnormal condition is further confirmed by the color. The liver of a "normally healthy dead" person is supposed to look brown red or tan red. Diseased livers look anywhere from tan orange to yellow orange to yellow and fatty with green peribiliary discoloration. These descriptions are not calibrated; they do not correspond to clear disease patterns but reflect the interaction of disease and decomposition. Indeed, depending on the level of decomposition, the color of the liver might become meaningless. The softness of the liver could also be explained by decomposition, but the "nodular architectural pattern"—that is, the granular consistency of the organ—is a clear sign of cirrhosis.

Cardiovascular system: The pericardial surfaces are smooth, glistening and unremarkable; the pericardial sac is free of significant fluid or adhesions. The heart weighs 358 grams and has a normal external configuration with a glistening epicardial surface and a normal amount of epicardial fat. The myocardium is firm, red brown, and shows no focal lesions. The cardiac chambers are of normal size and contain clotted blood. The atria and their appendages are normal. The right and left ventricles are of normal thickness. The cardiac valves are normally formed and appear in good functioning condition with thin pliable valve leaflets and thin discrete chordae. The endocardium is smooth and glistening and shows no fibrosis or petechiae. The coronary arteries arise normally through unobstructed ostia and pursue their normal anatomic course. Serial sections at 2-mm. intervals show approximately 90% stenosis of the proximal one-third of the left anterior descending coronary artery and 75% stenosis of the proximal two-thirds of the right coronary artery by atherosclerotic plaque. The ascending aorta is of normal caliber and branching distribution and shows no obstruction and insignificant atherosclerosis. The superior and inferior vena cava are unremarkable.

Every word or phrase of this description could point to a pathologically abnormal condition and indicate a cause of death. For example, instead of pursuing their "normal anatomic course," the coronary arteries can disappear into the heart muscle, a potentially lethal phenomenon called tunneling. I was struck by the repeated references to "glistening" surfaces in the description. When a corpse is opened, everything seems to glisten, because of a thin coating of blood. Dr. Hughes explained that in the context of the report, glistening is the opposite of a dullness that might indicate bacterial heart disease. By extensively describing how normal the heart was, the pathologist allows the abnormalities to stand out: the 90 percent and 75 percent stenosis (narrowing). The entire investigation has been condensed into the stenosis as a sign of mortality in the autopsy report. While the picture of the vessel allowed the pathologist to ignore the materiality of the heart, the percentage of stenosis ignores even the visual representation. In theory, a skeptic could go back from the percentage to the picture, then from the picture to the heart tissue preserved in formaldehyde, and then from that piece of tissue to an exhumation of the corpse. But in reality, the percentage will stand for the difference between life and death as long as the steps from body to picture and picture to percentage remain accepted as legally valid, standard pathological practice.

The words on the death certificate form the final link in a chain of transformation from life into death. Seemingly minor observations such as "Both testes are palpable and of normal size in the scrotal sacs; they are not removed" could topple the entire death investigation if medical records showed that the man had had a testicle removed during life. Even if the missing testicle had nothing to do with the cause of death, a failure to notice it would cast great doubt on any statements made by the medical examiner and might invalidate not only the postmortem investigation but also the office's handling of the chain of evidence. The oversight could be the small crack that makes a carefully crafted dam burst, washing out medicolegal credibility. No wonder the office instituted several layers of oversight and cross-checking mechanisms for the writing of these reports, with the chief medical examiner overseeing the process. No wonder, too, that pathologists tend to worry more about writing their reports than about postmortem investigations.

In the autopsy report for Steve Albom, the role of the stenosis is further emphasized in the anatomic-diagnosis section. There the pathologist lists the positive findings of the autopsy.

Anatomic diagnosis
I. Atherosclerotic coronary artery disease
    A. Severe stenosis, proximal left anterior descending coronary artery
    B. Severe stenosis, proximal and mid right coronary artery
II. Hepatitis steatosis, cirrhosis
III. Hepatomegaly

The positive findings include coronary obstructions and a fatty, enlarged, cirrhotic liver. What happened to the alcohol consumption? The toxicology investigation found a level of 141 mg/dl (milligrams per deciliter) in the postmortem femoral blood and 282 mg/dl in the postmortem vitreous fluids, indicating that Albom did indeed have ethanol in his body. Even with empty beer cans on and near the bed, the origin of the ethanol was not completely clear. Decomposition sometimes elevates ethanol levels and thus offers an alternative, internal source for the finding. While the higher level of ethanol in the vitreous fluids than in the femoral blood suggests that Albom had been drinking for a while and had metabolized some alcohol, the pathologist cannot attribute with certainty all the ethanol levels to alcohol consumption. In addition, while the ethanol levels are higher than the legal limit for driving, they are not lethal. For a man of Albom's size with a history of alcohol consumption, the pathologist would need to see a level of at least 300 mg/dl in order for alcohol consumption to be considered the cause of death. If Albom had been a driver in a fatal car crash, the office would have included his ethanol levels as significant findings, because they were higher than the legal limit. But because he was found in bed, they were not included.[61] The autopsy report reads like a straightforward descriptive medical file, but what appears and what is left out—even if it constitutes a positive finding—depends upon the circumstances of the death, the history, and the scene investigation. The final cause of death is situated in the pathology and anatomy of the corpse, but its location is ultimately forensic—a legally valid mix of medicine and history, sociology, and laboratory pathology.

The synopsis of the autopsy report at the end of the document renders a sudden and unexpected death meaningful and explainable. This part of the report is written with lay readers in mind.

Summary: On March 25, 2001, at approximately 12:10 p.m., this 43-year-old white male, Steve Albom, was reportedly found unresponsive in bed by his landlord who was checking on his well-being after other tenants informed him of an odor coming from the apartment. The apartment had been secure, and Mr. Albom had reportedly last been seen alive approximately one week before. Mr. Albom was identified by his landlord and from picture identification.

Postmortem examination revealed marked to moderate decompositional changes, severe atherosclerosis (hardening of the arteries) of the left anterior descending and right coronary arteries. In addition, Mr. Albom had a markedly enlarged and fatty liver. No lethal injuries were noted. The low level of ethanol (alcohol) detected in postmortem toxicology is consistent with postmortem changes. He had been consuming ethanol beverages prior to death.

Cause of death: atherosclerotic coronary artery disease
Other significant findings: hepatic cirrhosis
Manner of death: natural
Circumstances: found unresponsive in home

In contrast to the tentative tone of the scene investigation report, no uncertainty remains at the end of the death investigation. Even if the manner

of death is left undetermined, the nonspecific designation is stated with
certainty. At this point, with the final autopsy report, every statement
has one of three referents. A statement can be based on the pathologist's
observation or on laboratory tests, in which case it is presented factually
as "detected" or "revealed." If it is based on what people told the scene
investigator or medical examiner, it is qualified as "reported." Finally, it
can be extracted from a medical file and represented as "clinical history."
Thus, if relatives say that the deceased had been drinking heavily for years,
the summary might state, "Mr. Johnson was reportedly a long-term alcohol user"; but if the medical file shows that he received treatment for
alcoholism, the summary would state, "Mr. Johnson had a clinical history of alcohol use." When several potential causes of death are detected,
the pathologist will order them in the summary and designate one cause
as immediate and one as underlying. Occasionally, some more-tentative
observations will be included because they are consistent with the cause
of death. Thus, in the report on a car-accident death that the medical
examiner determined was due to a heart attack, the pathologist wrote that
the driver had "reportedly grabbed his chest." Finally, the factual findings
are again given more credibility by the negative results. In the summary,
the negative results do not include details about other organs but refer to
broad areas of the investigation: "He had no significant medical history"
or "No lethal injuries were detected."

When cross-checked and signed by Dr. Cahill, the cause-of-death sheet
and the autopsy report become the official version of the deceased's thanatography. The documents are a legally binding and factual record of how
this person died.[62] From community presence, multiple identities, and
lifetime medical history to death scene, clothing, organs, tissues, blood
volatiles, and histology slides, the forensic pathologists have pared down
the specificity and particularity of Steve Albom. At the end of the autopsy,
little is left besides some tissue fragments in a bowl of formaldehyde and
some tubes of blood. And when the file is closed, even less material is left:
a neatly typed report, a couple of pages with numbers from the lab, a body
drawing scribbled with numbers and notes, and some pictures. No wonder
this strikes some observers as an undue reduction of person to pathological
entity. At each stage of the dwindling of Albom's life, however, we have
gained calculations, interpretations, and knowledge about him and his
death. His individuality has morphed into generalizability. By removing
properties of life, the pathologist has made the corpse compatible with
the discipline of pathology and the legal requirements for determining a
cause of death. The added value could be considered minor—discovering
the color and texture of the liver and small calcium deposits in arteries; but those small abnormalities make the difference between life and

death. They ultimately explain why Steve Albom died. Transforming bits of tissue into causes allows medical examiners more knowledge than they took away.

PATHOLOGISTS AS CREATORS OF LIFE AND DEATH

In the context of forensic pathology, life and death are not binary opposites separated by an unbridgeable gap. Life is not the self-contained whole of an individual's animated existence, and death is not its opposite, an insentient "absolute nothingness." In the morgue, life and death flow into each other. Life as it is commonly understood contains the seeds of one's demise, and the death of a biological organism takes on a regenerated, soulless life of its own. Forensic pathologists separate the life of death from the life of living in order to explain retrospectively a specific death. They reveal a causal sequence that the deceased might have been unaware of, might have tried to keep from others, or might have found unavoidable. The typical cause of death that emerges from the work of forensic pathologists is some disruption in ongoing biological processes that manifests itself in the internal organs by abnormalities, deformations, or foreign matter. These abnormalities might be observed by the eye or the microscope, or they might require further calculations in laboratory tests in order to show their deviation from normal ranges. They create a disturbance of the blood flow with a cessation of the heartbeat and respiration. Acute disturbances are more significant than chronic conditions, and organs are ranked in a hierarchy of vitality. As a consequence, the essence of life depends on keeping the blood and oxygen flowing and free from obstructions. To find the cause of death, the forensic pathologist tries to come as close as possible to the moments preceding death and from there reconstructs a deadly cascade, dissecting the corpse on the basis of clues from the death scene and from the deceased's life as recounted in medical and police files, working toward the findings that will eventually be used in public health statistics and criminal investigations. Through an active engagement with the corpse, medical examiners transform messy deaths into specific knowledge about life.

Because the medical professions have been redefining disease, birth, and death for several centuries in Western societies, to characterize the "medicalization" of death as a "reduction to pathology" is misleading, for two reasons. First, a comparison with idealized historical and anthropological "social" dying can distract the observer from the multiple impure "social" entities that medical professionals bring into being. Paradoxically, such comparisons tend to overemphasize the role of pathology in death investigations. On the basis of an analysis of the cause-of-death sequence in written death certificates, Lindsay Prior concluded, "At no stage was the causal process deemed to be other than a medical process and at no stage was death ever perceived in other than physiological terms."[63] Compared to the richness of lived life, a death certificate might indeed reflect an unnecessary pathological reductionism. Yet this plausible conclusion overlooks the multiple decisions, complexities, and ambiguities that make possible the authoritative tone of the autopsy report. Death brokering is itself a complex process. Death investigators work hard to make their writing self-sufficient. To say that pathologists pathologize is to compliment them, to say they successfully flushed out all messy uncertainty, including social life, from their determinations. When we open the carefully black-boxed death certificate and autopsy report, forensic pathology is not limited to interpreting tissues and pathological samples. When I asked Dr. Douglas whether he knew of a blind experiment in which a pathologist had only a corpse to determine the cause and manner of death, he answered categorically, "Without scene investigation and medical history, I am lost. I can't do my job."

The social decontextualization that some critics deplore ultimately allows medical examiners to explain death by reconnecting the pathology of the corpse with diverse attributes of life—medical, social, legal, and administrative. Instead of comparing death investigators to the Azande, a more appropriate comparison might be with Evans-Pritchard, who in a colonial context ascribed particular values, kinship relationships, culture, and religion to this African people. Besides interpreting tissues, forensic pathologists weigh the credibility of relatives, wonder about the lethality of "social problems" such as alcoholism and drug abuse, try to retrieve the interactional sequences preceding gunshots, anticipate the reaction of adversarial lawyers, question or collaborate with law enforcement authorities, worry about the relevance of religion and other values. They spin an intricate network of diverse elements into various lethal sequences. John Webster's ten thousand doors of death are not reduced to one mega-portal of cardiac disease, but the door of cardiac disease encompasses multiple entrances, back alleys, passwords, and keys.

Second, the "pathologization" critique overstates the humanistic message about the loss of community, social solidarity, and shared values. Forensic pathologists, personifying the most scientific and professionalized approach to death, seem to hammer one more nail in the coffin of skill-based, holistic, humanitarian medicine. There is truth in such criticism: the procedures of forensic pathologists differ greatly from the eighteenth-century British coroners' public involvement. Medical examiners purposefully employ scientific rationality to illuminate a specific cause of death.

They objectify the corpse, and their inevitable reductionism creates mis-alignments, disappointment, and resentment when their categorization does not fit lived experience or fails to reveal the deep social structures that allow "accidents" to recur. The forensic autopsy is a far cry from a social autopsy, in which the social scientist uses death as an occasion to interrogate social inequities. But again, such a critique overlooks the ways in which medical examiners' categories help connect individuals to the broader collective, privilege kin and care relationships, and legitimate institutions. The lost individuality and sociality is replaced by generaliz-ability over locality, subjectivity, and idiosyncracy. Such generalizability is meaningful, even for individuals, when the determination of the cause of death allows a rationale to emerge from the unexplainable, to be articulated or, paradoxically, contested. In this sense, the death categories conceptu-alize experience as well as document it. The causes of death accumulate in death registries and allow the formulation and evaluation of health and safety policies. The words written on the death certificate offer a language for communication between the state bureaucracy, legal institutions, and medicine. Historian Charles Rosenberg noted that "disease entities are social realities, actors in complex and multidimensional negotiations that configure and reconfigure the lives of real men and women."[64] Similar conclusions can be drawn about death categories: their power does not re-side in their abstracting quality, but in their ability to acquire social texture and to legitimate actions of others. This chapter thus illustrates a general mechanism through which forensic authority operates: claims gain author-ity when they are transformed into factual knowledge and integrated into new organizational configurations. The work of medical examiners lays the basis for forensic authority.

This chapter also exemplifies some of the added value of a medical sociology of practice. Rather than examining how the organization of medical work impacts and mediates social relationships, we learn about the specific knowledge that forensic pathologists generate about death. What is cardiac disease when a forensic pathologist writes "ASCVD" on a death certificate? Medical examiners' work procedures—from the mo-ment the office is alerted to a potential suspicious death to the time of final signature on the death certificate—favor a particular set of causes of death. In numerous people, heart disease exists; some may be unaware of it, others may suspect it, still others may have a documented history and receive treatment. Heart disease may be embedded in practices of ignorance, denial, stress reduction, dietary changes, exercise, medication regimes of statin drugs, beta-blockers, aspirin, thrombolytic agents, even internal pacemakers. The heart disease of medical examiners, however, is different. Medical examiners actively create heart disease as a cause of death by revealing it in a postmortem investigation. Their cardiac disease has a unique compatibility with the expertise of pathology, which is aimed at visual lesions, the collection of evidence at the scene, the deceased's medical history, a history of pathology, and the organization of the death certificate. Their heart disease glosses over some unknowns in physiology but still prevails authoritatively on the death certificate.

Why does it matter that medical examiners reveal heart disease as the leading cause of death and not, say, cancer? Medical examiners aim to bring an order to suspicious death, and it matters where they locate danger. If most of us will die of heart disease, we may seek medical attention when we experience pangs in the chest, watch our cholesterol levels attentively, and avoid recognized cardiac risk factors.[65] Status as the leading cause of death may translate into awareness, angst, and urgency, research priority and funding. Eventually, it contributes to a particular worldview about life's finality. Also, heart disease implies a natural manner of death. How does medical examiners' proclivity to discover natural disease affect their interpretation of trauma—especially when the lethality of both the trauma and the natural disease remains somewhat ambiguous? In the following chapters, I will show how forensic pathologists qualify deaths as suicide, homicide, and child abuse. There, the social, legal, political, and moral implications of the link between forensic knowledge and practice will become self-evident. In those more traumatic deaths, the lethality of injuries needs to trump the lethality of natural disease. Forensic pathologists' expertise, however, may not always offer such a nice fit with an intent to die or kill as it does with heart disease.

The work of brokering the boundaries of natural death reflects the expertise of forensic pathologists. Dissection not only disconnects the deceased from life but also establishes new relationships. The removal of the tongue preserves the arteries in the neck and a working relationship with funeral directors, who need the arteries to circulate embalming fluid. The dissection procedure enacts the ties between law enforcement officers and medical examiners, between death investigators and tissue procurement organizations, between seemingly individual events and the social fact of cardiac mortality. Every cut in the body—both those aimed at revealing and those aimed at excluding causes of death—and every word on the death certificate and autopsy report constitute forensic expertise, because death investigators link the internal organs with forensic allies such as clinicians or law enforcement personnel. Medical examiners proactively advance relationships with allies through their practice. Forensic pathologists have, however, no absolute power; they still depend on the corpse to show pathological obstructions and on their allies to go along with their determination. For various reasons, any connection the pathologist fosters with allies might not hold.[66] Suicide, the topic of the next chapter, remains the most troublesome category in the knowledge networks that pathologists establish. Critics have been arguing for centuries that coroners and medical examiners either over- or underestimate the incidence of suicide, but no agreement exists on alternatives or correction factors.

CHAPTER TWO

THE FIFTY-ONE PERCENT RULE OF SUICIDE

*Pilot (commander): Excuse me, Jimmy, while I take a quick trip to the
toilet. . . .*
[whirring sound similar to electric seat motor operating]
[sound of click]
[sound similar to cockpit door opening]
Co-pilot: go ahead please (go ahead please).
[sound of several clicks]
Pilot: . . . before it gets crowded. While they are eating, and I'll be back to you.
[sound similar to cockpit door operating]
[sound of thunk, clink]
Co-pilot: I rely on God. [heard faintly]
*[series of thumps and clicks starts and continues for approximately seventeen
seconds]*
*[whirring sound similar to electric seat motor operating, also heard through the
first officer's hot microphone system]*
[sound of two faint thumps, one louder thump, two clicks, and two thumps]
Co-pilot: I rely on God
Co-pilot: I rely on God
[four tones similar to Master Caution aural beeper]
Co-pilot: I rely on God
Co-pilot: I rely on God

Co-pilot: I rely on God
Co-pilot: I rely on God
[sound of loud thump]
Co-pilot: I rely on God
Pilot: What's happening? What's happening?
Co-pilot: I rely on God
[sound of numerous thumps and clinks continue for approximately fifteen
seconds]
[repeating hi-low tone similar to Master Warning aural starts and continues to
the end of recording]
Co-pilot: I rely on God
Pilot: What's happening?
Pilot: What's happening, Gamil? What's happening?
[four tones similar to Master Caution aural beeper]
Pilot: What is this? What is this? Did you shut the engine(s)?
[change and increase in sound, heard only through first officer's hot
microphone system]
Pilot: Get away in the engines.
Pilot: Shut the engines.
Co-pilot: It's shut.
Pilot: Pull.
Pilot: Pull with me.
Pilot: Pull with me.
Pilot: Pull with me.
End of recording.
End of transcript. [1]

On October 31, 1999, EgyptAir Flight 990 plunged into the Atlantic Ocean
about sixty miles south of Nantucket Island, Massachusetts, killing all
217 passengers and crew aboard. During the last minutes of the flight,
the pilot left the cockpit to go to the restroom, leaving the co-pilot in
charge. The latter's mantra-like repetition of "Tawakilt ala Allah" (I rely
on God) gave National Transportation Safety Board (NTSB) investigators and the U.S. media the strong impression that the EgyptAir plane
was crashed intentionally. Investigators pointed out the co-pilot's calm,
determined demeanor, the pilot's frantic questioning, and the fact that
earlier, at takeoff, the co-pilot had used his seniority to oust the flight's
originally designated co-pilot. In addition, leaked FBI files suggested that
the co-pilot was a religious man overwhelmed by Western sexual norms.
The lack of clear mechanical failure strengthened the suspicion of suicide.
The investigators insinuated that the co-pilot took his own life and in the
process killed 216 others. The NTSB decided to forgo a public hearing,

because its investigation did not leave any "unresolved safety issues." In 2002, the NTSB issued its final report and concluded, rather ambiguously, that the disaster was due to "the relief first officer's flight control inputs. The reason for the relief first officer's actions was not determined."[2]

During the investigation, Egyptian government officials and the co-pilot's relatives strongly objected to even the suspicion of suicide. Looking over the same transcripts, Egyptian officials noted that the co-pilot had cooperated with the pilot and did not prevent the commander from trying to save the plane. Uttering the *shahada*, the Muslim prayer of faith, was considered an almost instinctive recourse in times of danger and did not indicate suicide. In one explanation of the *shahada*, those who speak the first part—"I rely on God"—are cast into an endless ocean. Stating the second part is what saves people from drowning in the infinite depths of the absolute. If the co-pilot had intended his own death, Muslims would have expected him to add the second part. Relatives claimed that the co-pilot was a pious, stable, and happy family man. EgyptAir officials and the Egyptian pilots' association instead questioned the plane's elevator-control system. They felt vindicated when Boeing urged all airlines flying the 767, the model of the plane that crashed, to make special checks on the hydraulic controls of the elevator flaps. NTSB officials noted, however, that in simulations all test pilots were able to correct a failed elevator flap. Such findings did not deter Egyptian co-investigators. They alternately suggested a ghost plane, a stray missile, a terrorist bomb, strange weather, and a range of possible mechanical failures—anything short of "human error"—to explain the crash.[3] When Egyptian officials charged that the investigation fit with a conspiracy against Muslims and a cover-up for Boeing's mechanical failures, the U.S. media countered that Egyptian religious and cultural pride stood in the way of a rational judgment, that is, accepting suicide as the manner of death.[4]

In the EgyptAir crash we have some of the best evidence available after a suspicious death, but the painstakingly transcribed cockpit recording might as well have been a Rorschach inkblot. The crash caused a charged international debate over the meaning of suicide in Western and Egyptian societies. NTSB investigators attempted to settle the dispute with more evidence and more information. The diplomatic polemic over the possible suicide provides a public glimpse of an impassioned debate that has been simmering for the past 150 years.[5] Simply put: When is a suspicious death a suicide? How do we know that someone intentionally took their life when we have only some secondary evidence—a lifeless body, some scraps of paper, or a tape recording? And who has the ability to make authoritative suicide judgments: relatives who knew the deceased intimately, or professionals who impute intentions? As the high-level diplomatic involvement and passionate pleas of the co-pilot's relatives underscore, these are not trivial questions.

Medical examiners do not only establish a medical cause of death; U.S. death investigators also determine the *manner* of death. The manner-of-death classification appeared in 1910 as a box to be checked on U.S. death certificates and consists of five categories: natural, suicide, homicide, accident, or undetermined.[6] Little is known about the initial reasons for asking about the manner of death, but "the assumption of those now working in the National Center for Health Statistics is that the manner box was added as a means of gathering more information on the death certificate regarding the circumstances surrounding death."[7] Its purpose was to help nosologists in coding and classifying cause-of-death information for statistical purposes. The manner of death is administratively binding and has great social relevance. The standard for death classification is the *ICD-10*, the tenth revision of the *International Statistical Classification of Diseases* developed by the World Health Organization and used worldwide to create mortality statistics. In contrast to U.S. death certificates, the *ICD-10* has the manners of death implied in its cause-of-death codes. For example, code E865.1 is used for "accidental poisoning by shellfish." Early in the twentieth century, pathologists involved in creating the international classification system complained that terms such as *accident* and *suicide* had "no preventive value" and therefore fell outside the purview of the death investigator.[8] Statisticians, however, insisted that these details be included in cause-of-death certificates "for their sociological interest and for the police."[9] Although public health interests mandated a manner-of-death classification, no guidelines were provided to distinguish manners. The most ambiguous and contested manner of death was, and still remains, suicide.

Sociologists have been interested in the determination of suicide ever since Emile Durkheim, one of the founders of sociology, used suicide to demonstrate that social phenomena have a factual character beyond their individual, clinical manifestation. In the nineteenth century, suicide was seen as the most individual of acts, reflecting an individual psychopathology.[10] To pave the way for a sociological study of social phenomena, Durkheim showed that isolated deadly actions can be causally explained by social factors. He assumed that a healthy society integrates and regulates humans, yet too little or too much of either of these functions pushes people to self-destruction. Relying on a statistical analysis of mortality figures, Durkheim distinguished the social causes of suicide according to the presence of social integration and regulation.[11]

Durkheim's study not only established a sociological perspective for studying apparently individualistic phenomena but also situated suicide as a mainstream sociological topic. Although during the first decades of the twentieth century few sociologists engaged in suicide research, and those who did merely replicated Durkheim, his status as founding father guaranteed continued attention to suicide. Suicide turned into a mainstream research topic during the 1960s when several researchers attempted to expand Durkheim's theory from a psychological and stratification perspective.[12] Like Durkheim's work, most of these research endeavors relied on the correlation of mortality statistics to discover the social causes of suicide, taking the quality and uniformity of mortality data for granted. Durkheim discussed some possible objections against the use of mortality statistics—particularly the fact that motives imputed to suicide should not be confused with social causes—but assumed that the numbers were sufficiently approximate for his analysis.[13] Researchers working outside the Durkheimian tradition, however, questioned the accuracy of suicide rates. Psychiatrist Gregory Zilboorg, for example, set out to debunk the belief that suicide rates increase in modernized societies.[14] He noted that suicide statistics are unreliable because they underreport the true suicide rate.

Since Durkheim, the literature on suicide accuracy has fallen into two camps: a minority position argues that suicide determination is biased, and a majority view states that while suicide might be underreported, the data are sufficiently accurate. During the 1960s, the radical, minority critique of suicide statistics emerged from researchers studying deviance and subcultures.[15] Sociologist Jack Douglas translated this critical-interpretive agenda into the area of suicide research.[16] He argued that Durkheim and his followers had uncritically accepted the accuracy of suicide rates of different populations. Douglas countered that the notion of suicide in mortality statistics reflects how government bureaucracies define suicide and reveals assumptions made in the process of gathering statistics but does not necessarily indicate the phenomenon of suicide.[17] Among the many problems he saw in gathering suicide data were culturally varying official definitions of suicide, the difficulty of deciphering in a dead body an intent to kill, different organizational structures for collecting statistics, and the problem of concealment of suicide because of the shame attached to self-killing.[18] Instead of assuming that people across the Western world have a similar notion of suicide, Douglas made the social meanings of suicide the topic of study. He envisioned a social science that would map the meanings of suicide within the lifeworld of the deceased, look for interpretive patterns, and relate those patterns to broader cultural values and institutional practices.[19]

Inspired by Douglas, British sociologist Maxwell Atkinson was the first social scientist to study—by reviewing coroners' records and observing their decision making—how official death certifiers determine suicide.[20]

Atkinson argued that some deaths are obviously suicides while others are unlikely to be designated as such. If a suicide note was available, a relative reported a suicide threat, or the mechanism of death was hanging or gassing by a tube attached to a car exhaust, a suicide verdict gained credibility. During the inquest, the coroner focused on clues in the deceased's biography and in the hours preceding death that rendered suicide more likely, looking for underlying crises, erosive mental illness, or relationship problems that might have pushed a despondent person over the edge. The coroner reached a suicide verdict on the basis of a variety of sources, none of which provided sufficient certainty in itself but which, taken together, made suicide more likely than an accident, homicide, or death due to natural causes. Atkinson's analysis highlighted that coroners generate and order the evidence according to assumptions about a typical suicide. "By defining certain deaths as suicides, they are in effect saying to others in the society: 'These kinds of deaths are suicides, these are the kinds of situations in which people commit suicide and these are the types of people who commit suicide.' "[21] He considered the coroners "moral entrepreneurs"[22] whose notions of suicide diffuse in society, influencing the general public and suicide research.

The majority perspective—that suicide is underreported but the data are unbiased—is reflected in the search for "hidden" suicides in other death classifications: single-vehicle accidents, pedestrian deaths, natural deaths, accidental poisonings, drownings, and undetermined deaths.[23] This literature also analyzes specific demographic groups in which suicide is more likely to be misclassified, namely, African Americans, Native Americans, women, adolescents, and the elderly.[24] Most studies confirm underreporting; estimates vary between 1 and 99 percent.[25] Some researchers, however, claim that official suicide statistics might overestimate the "true" suicide rate.[26] Despite this extensive literature, sociologists and social epidemiologists have concluded that suicide underreporting is randomly distributed and minimal, and that mortality figures are sufficiently accurate for statistical analysis.[27] Other researchers, however, warn that complacent use of official mortality rates might skew research findings, particularly international or historical comparisons.[28]

The lingering uncertainties regarding suicide accuracy cause any controversial finding to be questioned. For example, when President Eisenhower stated that the elevated suicide rate in Sweden was a consequence of too many years of socialist government, social scientists asserted that the difference in suicide rates between Scandinavian countries and other countries was a result of varying recording practices.[29] More recently, cross-comparative researchers attributed an apparent increase in Irish suicide rates over the past three decades to more accurate reporting.[30] Their analysis drew a sharp rebuke from Irish suicide researchers arguing that the increase in suicide rates was genuine—due to demographic and social changes—and that Irish suicide rates were actually more accurate than those of England and Wales.[31] Similar doubts have arisen about the relatively low suicide rates of African Americans and women.[32] Because the official suicide rate indicates that suicide is the eighth leading cause of death in the United States and the third leading cause of death for people between the ages of 15 and 24, public health officials have joined the debate. The surgeon general issued a call to action to prevent suicide in 1999, in order to generate awareness of suicide as a preventable public health problem. The surgeon general's national suicide-prevention strategy contained measures to improve the "surveillance system" for suicide, including the development of standardized protocols for death-scene investigations.[33] A 2002 Institute of Medicine report on reducing suicide qualified its findings with the statement that "official suicide statistics are fraught with inaccuracies."[34] An accurate certification of suicide forms the foundation for social science and public health scholarship based on mortality statistics, provides the basic parameters to evaluate suicide-prevention initiatives, and informs health policy.

Researchers generally offer three reasons for possible inaccuracies in suicide determination: (1) the equivocality of suicide; (2) legal, administrative, and procedural variations across geographic regions; and (3) pressure from relatives who wish to avoid the stigma of suicide. The equivocality of suicide has been identified through vignette studies documenting the variability of death classification, in which deaths that might have the characteristics of suicide generate the greatest variability.[35] Several studies have found negligible the effects of differences in legal, administrative, and procedural guidelines and the background of death investigators on the accuracy of suicide reporting,[36] but other studies have hypothesized that these factors must have an explanatory role.[37] Although researchers have claimed for more than a century that relatives influence death investigators, no one has documented, beyond anecdotal accounts, whether and how relatives achieve this effect.[38] The presumption is that relatives either conceal evidence or pressure death investigators to classify a death differently, to avoid the social and religious stigma and the legal and financial consequences.[39]

The stalemate over the accuracy of suicide statistics may be resolved if we examine suicide classifications from the perspective of the professionals making the determination. With the exception of Atkinson's study of coroners, no research has looked at how death investigators actually determine suicides. For medical examiners, the allegation of inaccurate suicide determination tarnishes the nature of their authority, because it presumes scientific incompetence and a preoccupation with private rather than public needs.[40] Medical examiners face two sets of suicide critics: public health officials allege underreporting, in part because medical examiners cave in to the pressure from relatives; and relatives accuse medical examiners of overzealous suicide reporting. Changing suicide determinations because relatives fear the moral, religious, or legal stigma of suicide makes death investigators look softhearted and needlessly empathic at best, but more often it makes them appear to be biased, manipulated, or even corrupt experts.

Suicide determinations thus not only form a barometer of a country's ability to respond to serious public health problems but also gauge medical examiners' forensic authority: their ability to convince others that their findings are valid and true and do in fact define suicide. Such authority depends on (1) whether death investigators can classify deaths according to their professional standards; (2) who constitutes the audiences for their determinations; (3) what impact these audiences—particularly relatives and public health officials—have on the detection of suicide; and (4) whether medical examiners' definition of suicide prevails in the outside world. Medical examiners promise to bring a more scientific approach than other death investigators to suicide classifications. The increase in scientific expertise, however, does not necessarily produce more accurate suicide data. Suicide determinations depend on how medical examiners' work allows suicide evidence to emerge and be positively classified using a local medicolegal standard. Medical examiners might not offer the best tools for the job, but they nevertheless have the last word on what qualifies as a suicide.

EVIDENCE OF SUICIDE

Medical examiners do not work with aggregate statistics; they face individual corpses that come with dispersed pieces of information. The first task of forensic pathologists contemplating a possible suicide is to find evidence that might indicate suicide. The case of Barbara Morris, which came into the medical examiner's office early in my research, shows the difficulty of locating suicide evidence through autopsies.

In this case, two fishermen found the body of an unidentified white female in a lake. The body was resting among some rocks and was partly decomposed. During morning meeting, the case manager relates that the investigators have a good idea of who the deceased is, because a young woman was reported missing six months ago in that area and her car was found near the lake. She adds that the car's windshield was broken and the glass was scattered inside the car. Dr.

Douglas asks for police records of this incident and requests that the police attend the autopsy. He turns to Dr. Brown and wonders whether he has any ideas. Dr. Brown has already checked the X-rays and noticed that she was missing four teeth. There might have been a hole at the back of her head, but he did not see any foreign objects in the skull.

Because this is the first autopsy of a decomposed body I will observe, Dr. Douglas teases me, saying, "This is the case that will separate the men from the boys." Bodies that have been immersed in water, or "floaters," are "corpses at their worst—their smelliest and slimiest."[41] In a more serious voice, he explains the biological postmortem changes we are likely to encounter in the body. In the decomp room, the assistant, Vanessa Atwood, burns incense in anticipation of the overwhelming odor of a body immersed in water.[42] When she opens the body pouch, there is a distinct, penetrating stench. The woman's skull is visible, with some flaps of decomposed skin and muscle hanging over the face. Her shoulder bones stick out. A disintegrated shirt and sweater are pulled up, showing a pinkish bra. The deceased was wearing black bell-bottom pants. Her shoes are partly disintegrated, but we can clearly see that she had blue socks. While the assistant takes pictures, the doctor carefully notes the condition of the body. The assistant photographs a tattoo of two interlocked hearts for identification; the skin is a pale greenish black but nicely preserved under the socks. She puts a towel around the tattoo to cover up the advanced decomposition further up the leg. She also takes out the jawbone to compare to dental records.

The police officers arrive and identify the woman as Barbara Morris, a missing person. They explain that they had searched the lake after she disappeared but did not find anything. Dr. Douglas makes the Y incision. A malodorous smell of decomposed tissue and methane gas escapes from the body. I move to a corner to get used to the odor. Noting that there are no body fluids, the doctor decides to submit pieces of tissue to the laboratory. He explains that an autopsy cannot reveal whether she fell, was pushed, or jumped off a rock into the lake. He does not find any obvious signs of trauma or foul play in the chest. The arteries of the heart are small but non-occluded. The neck is mostly disintegrated; he cannot check for strangulation marks. The brain is completely putrefied. The doctor prods it with his scalpel for brown spots, signs of hemorrhaging, but does not find anything. He locates some dirt in the trachea, but the body has been in the water too long for him to assign much significance to it.

With an essentially negative autopsy, the pathologist now questions the police officers who had spoken with the woman's friends and relatives. He asks whether she had a boyfriend.

"Yes, she lived with her boyfriend, but she did not have any trouble with him."

"Did she know the area?"

"Her aunt used to live close by, and she visited as a child."

"Any signs of depression?"

"She used to take rides for hours, listening to music in her car. She liked the band Tool."

The doctor asks what kind of music that is. The officers exchange uncomfortable glances. They had listened to a tape; the music, they say, sounds very angry, almost satanical, containing obscenities and rants against authorities. The young woman also thought that the musicians spoke directly to her. She had posters of the band in her room, but when she thought the lead singer was upset with her, she took the posters down. Right before her death, she put them back up. The physician is very interested in this information. The police officers explain that she thought that if she died, she would be reincarnated as a baby. The pathologist pauses and reflects that she sounds a lot like an undiagnosed schizophrenic. He seems to lean closer to a classification of suicide. He tells me that listening to such bands is something for fourteen-year-olds, not for people in their early twenties. Such a death does not come out of the blue. He wonders whether she walked into the water to be reincarnated as a baby. He asks the police officers whether she was a heavy drinker. Apparently, she only drunk socially and occasionally smoked marijuana. When the doctor states that he leans toward a suicide, the police officers confirm that this is also their impression.

Still, there is the car with its smashed window. The senior officer thinks that her car struck a telephone pole, because there is yellow paint on the car from a curb and a dent from a pole. The physician asks whether he could have a forensic psychiatrist talk to her friends and relatives to check whether she was suicidal (i.e., conduct a psychological autopsy). The police officers will give him the list of names and addresses. The doctor looks at a picture of the young woman at a high school prom and comments that she does not look like a person likely to listen to satanic music. Before closing up the body, the pathologist checks her fingernails. He repeats that he did not find any evidence of foul play, no chest or abdominal injury. The assistant points to the scarred eyes and asks what that means. The doctor says that water insects ate her eyes post mortem. For now, the case is pending and undetermined.

The forensic psychiatrist talks with the police detectives and Barbara's mother, brother, and best friend. He reports that the young woman was well-liked, kept journals, and was interested in astrology and poetry. She had a job in a supermarket but had been denied a promotion not long before her death. According to the mother, Barbara stated that she was "drowning in sin and maybe I should drown too." Her father died a couple of years ago. She also had gone to a very significant concert exactly a year previous to the day of her disappearance. Her mother described her as sad and depressed. In her last conversation, Barbara felt apologetic about "not being a good child." Her diary was filled with symbols, observations, and poems featuring violent themes, such as "One word wrong, one wrong action. To follow on a path to self destruction." She had a strong personal identification with Maynard James Keenan, the lead singer of Tool. Her diary contained a draft of a letter in which she thanked the band for all they had shown her.

A surprising revelation of the psychological investigation was that immediately after the car was discovered but before it was impounded, the woman's mother and boyfriend had gone to the vehicle and removed several journals. One of them contained an apparent suicide note, written on a notepad and left in the car. The psychiatrist concludes: "To a reasonable degree of medical psychiatric certainty, psychiatric and behavioral evidence strongly suggest motive for suicide, and I believe the mode of death was, in fact, a completed suicide." Dr. Douglas signs out the case as a suicide, citing the findings of the psychiatrist.

The case of Barbara Morris reveals the process to establish a suicide. A body submerged in water could indicate a homicide, suicide, natural death, or accident. The car with a broken window raised the suspicion that someone had robbed or attacked the young woman and then drowned her. After six months in the water, many signs of violence would have dissipated. Even if such signs were present, it would be difficult to decipher whether they were self-inflicted or not. Even without the added difficulties of interpreting decomposed bodies, an autopsy alone rarely provides sufficient evidence for suicide. A study of 185 forensic cases in which the medical examiner initially decided the manner of death based on an external examination showed that in only one case did a later autopsy result in a change of the manner of death.[43]

What guidance do death investigators have for recognizing suicide in a corpse? The U.S. Centers for Disease Control and Prevention (CDC) circulates a set of guidelines known as "Operational Criteria for Determining Suicide," specifically aimed at medical examiners and coroners.[44] To classify a death as a suicide, the investigator needs to establish that the death is *self-inflicted* and *intentional*. The first criterion is ascertained from autopsy findings, witness reports, toxicology, and scene information, although bodies rarely reveal conclusively whether injuries were caused by the deceased or by another person. A single, deadly shot could have been fired by the deceased or by a perpetrator. Even if it was fired by the deceased, the gun might have gone off accidentally, as in the ubiquitous gun-cleaning accidents.[45] The second criterion poses even more problems. Intentionality can be established explicitly from verbal or nonverbal expressions of a wish to kill oneself, or it can be inferred from implicit evidence, including preparations for death, signs of farewell, expressions of hopelessness or great physical pain, previous suicide attempts, precautions to avoid rescue, and serious mental disorder. According to medical examiners, the heavy weight of establishing intentionality renders the criterion inoperable, because the death investigator must second-guess the deceased's mind, inviting rather than resolving ambiguity.[46] Whether an elderly woman's mention of killing herself was done in jest or whether she reached a breaking point and deliberately took too many sleeping pills needs to be carefully scrutinized. To further complicate the matter, last-minute changes of intent are common in suicides.[47]

To determine conclusively whether the deceased intended to commit suicide, the death investigator would need to question the dead person. Because this is impossible, the investigation needs to establish an intent to kill oneself from secondary evidence. As Atkinson noted, a single source of secondary evidence is not definitive. Rather, different pieces of evidence need to be triangulated. Generally, medical examiners provide support for a suicide determination from seven sources.

1. *Witness reports.* The most direct indication of suicide is several independent witness reports. As in the case of Barbara Morris, however, suicides are usually solitary acts. Only occasionally do people have the misfortune to witness the event. Girlfriends, wives—and in one case, a four-year-old daughter—of several young men in my study witnessed self-inflicted shootings. A witness report constitutes a rare stroke of luck in a suicide investigation; but even then, alternative explanations might be readily offered, as for the indirect witness report of the EgyptAir recording. Eyewitnesses' recall of what they saw is also notoriously unreliable and often at odds with other evidence.[48]

2. *Suicide notes.* Suicide notes are the second most direct indication of intent that the dead leave for the living. Only 20 to 35 percent of presumed suicides, however, involve notes.[49] Although a note might be conclusive for a suicide determination, it is insufficient in itself, and a suicide verdict will need corroborating evidence, such as the circumstances of death and biographical factors. The portability of suicide notes also renders them vulnerable. Scene investigators suspect that in the same way drug paraphernalia tend to disappear from a crime scene, suicide notes regularly vanish as well, as happened in Morris's case.

3. *Use of suicide guidelines.* A clear indication of suicidal intent is a death that corresponds to the suicide directions in Derek Humphry's book *Final Exit.*[50] In three cases during my research, the deceased had overdosed on prescription medicine and taped a plastic bag around their head, as advised by Humphry.[51] In one of these suicides, the book was found next to the body, opened to the "how-to" pages. The pathologist merely checked for signs of struggle and for moisture in the bag to verify that the man was breathing before the bag was placed over his head. In earlier times, suicidal people would collect newspaper clippings of successful suicides, often carrying them with them when they took their lives.[52]

4. *Previous suicide attempts.* A history of unsuccessful suicide attempts is also a strong indication that the death was intentional. Such history may be apparent from the medical file or from physical signs such as scars on

the wrists. In many situations, however, knowledge of the history depends on accounts from relatives.

5. *Testimonials.* The fifth best witnesses for suicidal intent are relatives and health care professionals who knew the deceased intimately and report suicide threats. These people, however, might have reasons to want to make the death appear not to be a suicide. Relatives and friends are assumed to be concerned not with an accurate death investigation, but with preserving the best possible memory of the deceased. "The families seek answers to their questions as to how the death could have occurred. They also require details of the lost time before death in order to compose the last stages of the deceased's biography and to map that narrative onto their own continuing biographies. In contrast, the coroner seeks closure. With an eye to a future existence without the deceased, bereaved people look for explanation, understanding and even compassion, but not necessarily closure."[53] Because relatives and friends are assumed to engage in "deliberate deception and concealment," their information is considered unreliable, especially if it cannot be corroborated with medical clues.[54]

In addition, when relatives recall statements of the deceased that could be taken as signs of depression or cries for help, they often add qualifiers that dismiss the gravity of these statements. If they had really thought the signs were serious, they say, they would have done something. A similar, routinized qualification occurs in psychiatric and psychological records. One psychiatrist had two patients who committed suicide in the span of a week. Looking over the patients' records, I noticed that the psychiatrist had written at the end of each weekly session "no suicidal ideation" or "client denies suicidal ideation." When I questioned this psychiatrist's skills, Dr. Douglas explained that he had a good reputation, but that psychiatrists often simply cannot recognize suicidal ideation; some patients might be upbeat exactly because they have decided to take their lives.[55] When psychiatrists expect patients to kill themselves, they are supposed to take preventive measures.

6. *Life crises.* Pathologists dismiss the "no suicidal ideation" qualifiers and read the psychiatric report for signs of chronic depression, previous suicide attempts, and any indication of a recent crisis.[56] They check the few clues of biographical information in the investigator's report and consider whether there are enough problems that someone might want to take their own life. Medical examiners look for disturbances in the rhythms of life. Prime suspects are relationship problems. In the case of a student who overdosed on over-the-counter sleeping pills, Dr. Douglas immediately asked whether she had boyfriend troubles. Next, investigators look for serious problems at work. When an investigator found out that a dead farmer had worked for a farm cooperative at which layoffs had been occurring, this

factor became a possible reason for depression. A third type of disruption is the death of a loved one. One man shot himself shortly after his wife died from cervical cancer; earlier that day, he had expressed to his parents that life had become meaningless. Finally, worsening chronic health problems might lead to suicide, although bad health might also indicate a natural death. When a cancer patient who had repeatedly expressed a wish to die was found dead, Dr. Brown wondered whether the terminal cancer had followed its course to the end or whether the man had hastened his death. The date of the death might also be symbolically meaningful, as in the case of a prisoner who hanged himself a year after his grandmother died. For every one of these disturbances, the pathologist wonders whether the decedent could have considered them sufficient to choose a stigmatized, self-inflicted death.

If biographical clues do not indicate suicidal ideation, suicide is not necessarily ruled out, because the staff believe that some people are reluctant to talk about their problems and might just snap and kill themselves. One of the most surprising suicides during my study was carried out by a successful businessman who was supposed to join his wife for a vacation. Instead, he bought a handgun, waited the required seven-day period before picking up his pistol, and shot himself in the head after firing a practice shot in the yard. The entire family was in shock, and the death was treated as a possible homicide until records revealed that the man had great financial debts. No one interviewed by police or the scene investigator seemed to have a clue that the businessman had even contemplated suicide.

7. *Mode of dying.* Suicidal intent can also be inferred from the mode of dying or precautions taken to avoid rescue. Medical examiners evaluate the mechanism of death in light of the extent to which it reflects desperation, painlessness, deadliness, aesthetics, symbolism, and cultural appropriateness. Death investigators presume that hangings, for example, are difficult to disguise as anything other than suicide, because one needs a more or less willing victim. Even in hangings, however, some kind of additional investigation is required. The medical examiner checks for defense wounds and sex tools around the body. Defense wounds would suggest foul play, while sex paraphernalia might indicate an accidental asphyxiation as part of sexual arousal. The same reasoning is followed for people annihilated by a passing train. If the scene investigation does not suggest an accident, these situations will generally be interpreted as suicides. Other modes of death are more ambiguous. A single gunshot wound to the head, the most common mode of suicide in my study, is also the most common way homicides are committed and might occur accidentally as well. Drownings, such as in Morris's case, are also equivocal and require further evidence to make the suicide classification stick.

While the categories of evidence indicating suicidal intent are similar for coroners and medical examiners, it is not the evidence in itself but the fit between evidence and scientific expertise that determines a suicide. Evidence is not a given entity; it can indicate suicidal intent only if the professional perspective allows one to look for such evidence, find it, and interpret it. The information about Barbara Morris's life crises, for example, required that a scene investigator ask the right questions, because few people volunteer such information after a loved one has died. Asking such sensitive questions necessitates having an uncontested legal jurisdiction with incentives for volunteering this information. In the case of Morris, the retrieval of evidence required reconstructing the last days of her life from her diaries and from in-depth interviews with relatives and friends, as well as an extensive examination of her body, clothing, and car. None of these steps was obvious, and their relevance became apparent only after suicide emerged as the likely manner of death. Medical examiners must thus have an active engagement with the corpse and the circumstances of the death in order to identify a correspondence with suicide. For medical examiners, whose primary focus is on pathological evidence, suicide constitutes somewhat of a mismatch with their skills. As the investigation of Morris's death demonstrates, the autopsy did not clarify the situation, because it could not exclude or confirm any manner of death. The extensive questioning of her relatives and friends, however, revealed a likely biomedical indication of suicide when signs of unaddressed mental illness appeared.

Even when information is available, its relevance for a classification of suicide is not self-evident. Considered in isolation, the biographical evidence, scene evidence, or mechanism of death revealed in Barbara Morris's death could be considered "normal." If listening to the rock band Tool qualifies as suicidal behavior, many youths must be at risk, because the group's debut album, *Undertow*, went platinum, and the group had one of the most financially successful tours of 2001. And although some of the diary entries indeed sounded depressed and violent, the diary also contained hopeful, future-oriented entries. Indeed, another observer could look at the same darker elements and consider them innocuous, typical for a young person going through emotional growing pains. Morris had been passed over for a job before and coped well with it the first time. She also had a stable relationship with her boyfriend and her mother. To walk into the water, as the investigators presumed she had done, is not an obvious way for a young woman to kill herself—especially without using weights.[57] The damage to the car remained unexplained.

Relatives are generally at a disadvantage for influencing the generation of evidence for suicide, because they are rarely prepared for a medicolegal death investigation. Morris's mother and boyfriend initially succeeded in hiding the suicide note, but the note only confirmed an already growing opinion; even without the note, the verdict likely would have been suicide. The first rescue person to enter a death scene—usually a paramedic or police officer—is required to describe the scene in detail, and their report is a key document in the death investigation. When homicide is suspected, as it was in Morris's case, another disadvantage for relatives attempting to hide a suicide is that police detectives launch a parallel investigation. Homicide detectives generally interview a number of relatives and friends and are particularly attentive to inconsistencies and contradictions in the emerging story. The general impression of a disturbed young woman was confirmed independently in several interviews by the police. The forensic psychiatrist that Dr. Douglas called also interviewed relatives and friends, making it even more unlikely that hiding the note would leave the suicide undetected. Medical examiners and law enforcement officials assume that relatives and friends are rarely able to sustain a unified front under repeated interrogation, particularly when strained by grieving. Mourning friends and relatives sometimes volunteer their own theories of why secondary evidence, such as the place and time of death, might make sense. Even if relatives and friends vehemently argue against a suicide verdict, their denials are suspect, because death investigators assume that relatives have an interest in making that point.

In the case of Morris, there was little disagreement among the staff that this was indeed a suicide. What matters for a suicide determination, then, is an evidentiary "gestalt" that emerges retrospectively out of disparate elements retrieved by the staff—a cumulative pattern of "unusual" behavior that remained, for a young woman in her situation, unexplainable except by suicide.[58] The police officers, pathologist, and psychiatrist work backward, starting from the indisputable fact of a dead body, and then selectively pick through aspects of the self to gather a consistent pattern of evidence indicating that taking one's life was indeed a meaningful act for the deceased. Sociologist Jack Douglas wrote that suicide should be situated within a person's biography as a wish for a radical transformation of the self.[59] The death investigators collaborate with such a self-transformation. They selectively build up a particular image in their collecting of evidence. While the deceased often hopes for redemption or an end to pain and suffering, the picture that emerged through the medicolegal investigation of Morris's death was that of a deeply unhappy young woman with unaddressed psychiatric problems. Whatever memories her friends and relatives hold of her, the official closure of her life emphasized the "abnormal" that normalized a suicide. Even when withholding the suicide note, Morris's immediate relatives were unable to stop her self-transformation.

THE FIFTY-ONE PERCENT RULE

And I
am the arrow,
The dew that flies
Suicidal, at one with the drive
Into the Red
Eye, the cauldron of the morning.

SYLVIA PLATH, *Ariel*

The question remains: How do medical examiners determine that disparate pieces of evidence conclusively amount to suicidal intent? When does the gestalt of suicide emerge? As with medical examiners' active engagement with evidence, their decision making in suicide cases shows certain patterns based on professional reasons. Medical examiners work not deductively—determining a suicide on the basis of a checklist of evidence—but inductively, building a case for suicide from diverse pieces of evidence. The regularity of suicide determinations consists of results from a probabilistic decision-making process in which the evidence of the entire investigation needs to meet a certain threshold. The decision-making rule—the fifty-one percent rule of suicide—underscores how medical examiners' scientific expertise is mediated by their twin roots in the areas of medicine and criminal justice.

The chief medical examiner articulated the decision-making process in the investigation of the death of Guy Dubos, which had many characteristics of a suicide but was classified differently.

Guy Dubos, a white man in his late thirties, was found dead in his apartment. The scene investigator treated the case as an obvious suicide, stating that the deceased "left 3 suicide notes and indicated he overdosed." He had been drinking and was argumentative toward his girlfriend. The girlfriend reported that Guy was jealous of one of her male co-workers with whom she had had lunch. He had also recently filed for bankruptcy after a previous divorce. He was diabetic and had a white insulin pump inserted via a catheter into his lower abdomen. Near the body, the investigator found an empty bottle that had contained sixty antidepressant pills, and an empty beer can.

After being notified of the death, Dubos's relatives fly into town and vehemently state that they do not believe that he caused his own death. His brother, a former defense attorney, argues that Guy's death was due to alcohol, diabetes, high blood pressure, and emotional distress. The relatives dismiss the apparent suicide notes as "amateurish dabblings in poetry." The police officer who was present at the scene and is now attending the autopsy tells us that Dubos was a recovering alcoholic. He seems to agree with the relatives, because in his opinion no one would kill himself over a fight with a girlfriend. Dr. Brown, who conducts the autopsy, dismisses the likelihood that the notes are suicide notes, adding that "poets tend to be a morbid kind." While I help with taking pictures, I remark that cemeteries are filled with famous poets and writers who have killed themselves.

The deceased carries a medical-alert bracelet indicating insulin-dependent diabetes and an allergy to penicillin. While cutting the heart, Dr. Brown observes that the man has a pretty good vascular system for a diabetic; there is only mild arteriosclerotic disease. The pathologist sighs, saying that it would have been relatively easy for Dubos to overdose on insulin. He had only to turn up his pump too high or inject himself with an extra dose. An insulin overdose is almost impossible to prove, because insulin breaks down in the body post mortem, and this man had been dead for four days. Even the vitreous fluids will not reveal the insulin rate, unless he used a massive dose. The autopsy does not uncover anything pathologically abnormal. At the end of the autopsy I ask Dr. Brown what the verdict is. He answers, "Hell if I know." The case is left pending laboratory studies. If the toxicology tests detect that he overdosed on antidepressants, it will be a suicide case.

The toxicology results come back negative. Dubos apparently did not overdose on the antidepressants. When Dr. Brown discusses the case and how to interpret the three notes with Dr. Cahill, she moves the debate away from the intent behind the notes and focuses instead on whether the insulin pump malfunctioned. The relatives, who now blame the pump, claim that the manufacturer had recalled the device. The manufacturer denies ever recalling the pump and states that the pump worked properly. The relatives mail in the glucose meter, and the lab downloads the glucose readings of Dubos's last days. The readings neither reveal nor eliminate the possibility of an overdose.

In the case summary of the autopsy report, Dr. Brown simply states that they found "3 pages of lyrics and poems of a depressive nature" and that in these pages the decedent "asked his girlfriend to pray for him."[60] He notes that "the possibility of an insulin overdose either accidental or deliberate cannot be excluded. As insulin rapidly breaks down in the body, insulin levels could not be measured following death. Toxicology revealed a low level of ethanol and no toxic or lethal levels of medications or drugs. The possibility of hypoglycemia or a cardiac arrhythmia as a cause of death is most probable. However, neither can be proven or disproved. Cause of death: undetermined following complete autopsy and toxicologic evaluation. Manner of death: undetermined." Over the next months, the relatives call several times demanding a more conclusive ending to the investigation. They now believe that the deceased was a "brittle" diabetic and alcoholic who experienced a fatal alcohol relapse.

A year after the death, Dr. Brown has left the office, and two new young pathologists have been hired. When closing Dr. Brown's cases, Dr. Cahill asks the new hires to review and comment on Guy Dubos's death. Everyone goes over the file carefully. These pathologists point out that in the scene pictures, Dubos lies dressed as if he were about to leave the house. If he had really wanted to commit suicide, they would have expected him to make himself comfortable and lie on a bed. They also note that the syringe and glucose bottle found next to Dubos's body are used to fill the insulin pump and not to inject oneself with an extra dose. The pathologists decide that the death is natural.

The final autopsy report dismisses the significance of the notes: "The decedent had been under financial distress and had filed for bankruptcy. In his home, they found three pages of lyrics and/or poems of a depressive nature. There were no straight forward sentences indicating that he was taking his own life, and his family indicates it was his custom to compose such lyrics." Instead, the report centers on the possibility of pathological causes of death. The cause of death is changed to "cardiac arrhythmia associated with moderate atherosclerotic coronary artery disease and diabetes mellitus." The manner of death is natural.

Because of Guy Dubos's young age, a natural death initially seemed unlikely. His diabetes might still have made him a candidate for a natural death, but when the coronary arteries turned out to look relatively good, Dr. Brown leaned toward either accident or suicide. Because Dubos's relatives argued against a suicide verdict, it seems as if the staff caved in to them. In the medical examiner's opinion, this case was not classified as a suicide because crucial pieces of evidence were questionable. The scene investigation produced some of the strongest indication of suicide: written notes. In addition, he had multiple life crises and an easy opportunity to kill himself by overdosing on insulin or antidepressants. Still, the death was classified as natural. How did the staff reach this conclusion?

When I reviewed Dubos's death with Dr. Cahill, she laid out the professional interpretive frame that guided her decision making. Referring to "the fifty-one percent rule of suicide," she explained that when she looks over all the evidence her office has gathered in a case, she imagines herself defending the manner of death to the deceased's relatives. Her ultimate criterion is whether she can conclude from the evidence with 51 percent certainty that this is indeed a suicide. If in her opinion the evidence provides a pattern that points more than 50 percent to suicidal intent, she will call it a suicide. A suicide classification is therefore neither a matter of elimination nor a default option. Rather, it is a manner of death that must be positively demonstrated. In fact, Dr. Cahill interpreted the fifty-one percent rule as requiring a preponderance of evidence.

In the death of Dubos, the pathologists found the evidence lacking for demonstration of suicidal intent. Researchers have closely scrutinized suicide notes in the hope that their content or linguistic structures might reveal an underlying suicidal etiology.[61] Expecting grand revelations about the end of life, observers have been struck by the disappointing flatness of the notes: "Suicide notes often seem like parodies of the postcards sent home from the Grand Canyon, the catacombs or the pyramids—essentially *pro forma,* not at all reflecting the grandeur of the scene being described or the depth of human emotion that one might expect to be engendered by the situation."[62] Suicidologists have noticed the multiple references to concrete situations and people, the often-commanding instructions, and the recurrent themes of loss, abandonment, and rejection with regard to significant relationships. Although suicide notes express feelings of hate, self-hatred, and revenge, studies suggest that they commonly also express regret and love. "In fact, the person in the suicide note appears to be strikingly ambivalent (i.e., affectionate *and* hostile), toward the same lost or rejecting person. It is this ambivalence and the emotions of aggression, hopelessness, and helplessness that appear to be most critical in the emotional state of the suicide."[63] In addition, suicide notes apparently seem rational to the person writing the note. The writers note the inconsistencies in other people but fail to critically question their own premises. Notes by younger writers (under forty) tend to be harsher and center more often on relationships. People over sixty note more illness, pain, and loneliness, while the groups in between express a sense of disappointment with life.[64]

In this largely psychological research on suicide notes, the researchers seem to be confident that the notes they analyze are actually suicide notes. Yet as Atkinson pointed out, the obviousness of suicide notes needs to be inferred, because few notes are titled "Suicide Note," and few allude to the suicidal act or to death. The difference between a distressed letter, an upset diary entry, a love letter, "morbid poetry," and a suicide note is therefore in the eye of the reader.

In the case of Dubos, we have several notes, but do they add up to a suicide note? The first page of writings consists of four statements separated by a drawn line and initials. The page begins:

I can't find my way.
I can't find my way in those who surround me.
I can't find my way within my own self.
The strength of friendship is stranger than that of love.
No matter who that friend might be.

———————————————————————GD

I was meant to fly alone.
Thou I long for that one with another to be
I fly alone in sorrow for the rest of my life
it shall be

———————————————————————GD

I long for the understanding of why I am here but maybe it is because it is there.

———————————————————————GD

I wait for the phone call that shall never be . . .
All I can say is that I am sorry though that shall never be
All I can say that I love you and that shall always be.

The second page seems to be a draft of the first, because after three lines repeating "I can't find my way," there is a scribble down the page. The third page starts with "I have a line drawn in the sand," followed by several unreadable lines; then "who is right, who is wrong, though we both know it"; and then, halfway down the page, "The reason why I die is [presumably male name] is greater than N + Y." A little lower on the page, the note says, "It is [name of current girlfriend] unto I curse, [other female name] PRAY FOR ME." Under these lines is a time and a day of the week. The time is half-erased, but the day corresponds to the day Dubos quarreled with his girlfriend and was last seen alive.

Suicidologist Edwin Shneidman has argued that notes become meaningful within the context of the individual's life story.[65] Putting the note in the context of Guy Dubos's cascade of failing relationships and financial crises, his alcoholism, and his reported history of depression, the scene investigator felt that a suicide determination was appropriate. He saw a difference between the first and last notes. The first notes were indeed lyrical but still expressed depression, loneliness, despair, and a longing to be with a significant other. The last note lacked the poetic element and was more direct in expressing suicidal intent. In his opinion, Dubos explicitly anticipated his death and asked a woman to pray for him. The CDC's operational criteria for determining suicide consider an acknowledgment of impending death and expression of hopelessness as a sufficient indicator of intent to die. Researchers from the United States, Europe, and Asia have also shown that suicide is more common in highly creative or successful people: "Eminent scientists, composers, and top businessmen were five times more likely to kill themselves than the general population; writers, especially poets, showed considerably higher rates."[66] Literary critic Alfred Alvarez surmised that poets and other artists, particularly in the modernism of the late twentieth century, take their own lives because their creative tendency to innovate, destroy, and surpass accepted styles forces them to explore their inner state and their position in the world. According to Alvarez, the higher rate of suicides among artists reflects the ultimate expression of their art: "Under the energy, appetite, and constant diversity of the modern arts is this obdurate core of blankness and insentience which no amount of creative optimism and effort can wholly break down or remove. It is like, for a believer, the final, unbudgeable illumination that God is not good."[67]

The consensus among the pathologists who reexamined the case, however, was that the notes found with Dubos were insufficiently explicit.
They lost relevance in light of medical examiners' orientation to pathological evidence. Dr. Cahill noted that many poets thrive on writing about
death. Some famous poems even contain suicidal threats in every stanza,
but their authors die a natural death in old age. The notes were not meaningful in themselves but would have gained significance in light of medical
findings. Medical examiners are more oriented toward officially recorded
medical clues than are coroners, who, as Atkinson showed in his study
of how suicide is determined, tend to rely more on biographical information provided by relatives and friends during an inquest. Even if the
manner of death cannot be medically established, forensic pathologists
privilege medically authorized information over clues from other sources.
A recorded history of depression in a psychiatric file and bodily signs of
a previous suicide attempt (such as scars on the wrists) confirm suicide
in a way that biographical factors cannot. In this case, the ambiguity in
the medical information actually undermined the more solid nonmedi-
cal indications of suicide. Similarly, sociologists Bernice Pescosolido and
Robert Mendelsohn note that "the dependence on 'hard' evidence and
objective proof called for by the scientific method may actually decrease
the suicide rate."[68]

Instead of fishing for possible suicidal intentions in the biography, the
doctors reoriented the investigation toward a straightforward mechanical
and medical question: did the insulin pump fail? If the insulin pump was
malfunctioning, the death would be an accident. Unfortunately, an investigation of the pump did not provide the expected conclusive evidence.
Because the pathologists explicitly looked for signs of an overdose but
did not find any, suicide was not simply unsupported; it was disproved.
Next, they zeroed in on the medical complications that they were sure
about. The one positive finding from Guy Dubos's autopsy was the heart
disease. It was too moderate to qualify as a cause of death in itself, but
because it occurred in a diabetic body, it gained importance. Diabetics
often have fatally compromised cardiovascular systems. Taking into consideration the position of the body, the clothes the deceased was wearing,
and the kind of syringe lying next to the body, the pathologists backed off
from a determination of suicide.

The activism and pressure on the part of the relatives, one of whom
mentioned in every interaction his credentials as a lawyer, might have
made the classification of suicide more unlikely. While the family's resistance reinforced the negative morality of a suicide determination, it was
insufficient for the relatives to simply state their opposition to a suicide

verdict. They worked within the investigative frame of the medical examiner, questioning the strength of the medicolegal evidence and offering
alternative explanations. They did not merely offer biographical reasons
why Dubos was an unlikely candidate for suicide but focused on invalidat-
ing the most damning evidence. The doctors' opinion that poetry is full
of ambiguity was augmented by the interpretations of others: the police
officer's reasoning that a fight about jealousy was insufficient reason to
kill oneself, and the relatives' repeated claim that the deceased had been
writing morbid poetry for years. The medicolegal administrator compared
deciding between different manners of death to balancing on a teeter-
totter. The evidence would weigh the seesaw down to one side, but in a
case filled with ambiguity, the suicide side was more difficult to reach. He
concluded, "When it's not a simple black or white case but one full of gray
values, we never end up in the suicide range. You owe that to the family
and to the decedent."

The fifty-one percent rule reflects medical examiners' professional position in the legal and medical world. The probabilistic decision-making
rule retains a strong presumption against suicide that is refutable only by
evidence. Following a process of differential diagnosis, clinicians usually
treat the most plausible cause of illness, even when clinical uncertainty prevails.[69] Pathologists are board-certified physicians, but they are required
to follow a more stringent legal standard in death determinations than the
guidelines orienting their clinical colleagues. Legally, suicide is considered
an act against human nature, and any death is presumed to be natural unless demonstrated otherwise.[70] Suspicious deaths are thus suicides not because they resemble suicides, but only because the accumulated evidence
indicates a likely suicide. The legal standard is further confirmed by Dr.
Cahill's imagining a defense of her conclusion to hostile relatives who are
bound to disagree. Rather than an indication of the power of relatives,
her imagined confrontation reflects the standard of certainty needed to
defend one's opinion in an adversarial criminal cross-examination. Other
pathologists also mentioned that they pictured being "assailed in court"
when writing "suicide" as the manner of death. Medical examiners testify regularly in criminal court, where their pathological descriptions and
findings are crucial in prosecuting cases of suspected violent or suspicious
deaths and where their procedures and opinions are closely scrutinized by
opposing counsel.

In the case of Dubos, although Drs. Brown and Cahill relied on the
same evidence and decision-making rule, they still disagreed about the
classification of the death. When disagreements between pathologists occurred, Dr. Cahill's determination prevailed, because she was the chief
medical examiner and ultimately responsible for safeguarding the office's

reputation. She decided when the evidence justified a specific classification. After conducting an autopsy or reviewing laboratory tests, the other
pathologists had to defend their conclusions to her. In addition, she proof-
read and cosigned every autopsy report and every death certificate. She
was adamant that no information about an ongoing investigation be shared
with the media or third parties. As in sociologist Renée Anspach's study of
decision making in the neonatal intensive-care unit,[71] the staff presented
a united front to the outside, smoothing out differences in opinion and
making it difficult for relatives to contest a conclusion.

PRESSURE FROM RELATIVES

The relatives of Andy Williams also contested a suicide determination,
but they were unsuccessful, as relatives dissatisfied with a suicide determination more typically are. These family members did not engage with the
professional perspective of medical examiners but offered biographical
reasons for eliminating a decision for suicide. British sociologist Glennys Howarth observed, in her study of a coroners' court, how relatives
might attempt to confound a suicide determination by offering biographical reasons: "In the modern coroners' court, in the case of suicide, the
biography of the deceased may be consciously written in a way which
raises considerable doubt as to the nature of death; so much doubt, in
fact, that the classification becomes one of accident or misadventure. The
actions, behaviour and voice of the dead person may not simply be silent
but may be drowned out in the desire to recreate a good death—one which
stigmatises neither the dead, nor the living."[72] Andy Williams's relatives,
however, were shut out of the decision-making process and were left to
protest after the decision for suicide was already made.

The case of Andy Williams, a tall white man in his early thirties, is discussed
during morning meeting, along with a hanging, three victims of a small-plane
crash, and two apparent natural deaths. Williams was a patient in a mental health
facility who was on weekend release with relatives. He was found at the bottom
of the parking garage of the city's new rock-and-roll museum. When Dr. Brown
hears the case description, he turns to the assistants and exclaims, "What did
I tell you?" Indeed, when the museum had opened a couple of weeks earlier,
the pathologist predicted that it would not take long before someone jumped
off the building. The case report, in fact, mentions that Williams's therapist
had warned his relatives that taking him to the museum was not a good idea.
When Dr. Douglas hears this, he urges the police to get a statement from the
therapist right away, because he predicts the family will claim it was a fall and
sue the museum for a lack of safety. An emergency-room physician wrote that
Williams had suffered broken leg and arm bones and a broken skull. During

the autopsy, Dr. Brown remarks dryly that most of these fractures must have miraculously healed, because he sees only a broken femur. Most of the damage is internal. The spleen sticks through the diaphragm, the liver and left kidney are lacerated. The vena cava burst on impact and filled the chest cavity with blood. Surprisingly, the skull is intact. The cause of death is crystal clear. The only question that remains is whether Williams fell or jumped off the garage.

A thick pile of psychiatric records arrives later that day. Andy Williams had been diagnosed with bipolar disorder. In his manic phases he acted as if he were the Antichrist, but his brooding, sad, and depressed moods most worried his therapists. Williams confided to them his anxiety about never getting well and his fear of living. He told his therapist that he liked to harm himself and often had suicidal thoughts, particularly a wish to jump off a tower. When his illness took an increasing toll, Williams had to give up his job as a plumber, his wife divorced him, and he became a resident in a state mental health facility. His family remained supportive and involved in his treatment. His parents and sister would take him out for a weekend whenever the staff decided that his suicidal ideation had sufficiently subsided. But there had been a couple of near misses. Williams once cut the gas line in an apartment and narrowly escaped death. His latest residency was prompted by his compulsion to jump from the roof of a board-and-care house. He had also climbed the water tower on the grounds of the mental health facility and threatened to jump but was coaxed down, ironically, with the promise of a McDonald's Happy Meal. The lengthy mental health records stated repeatedly that Williams's long-term goal was the elimination of suicidal ideation, thoughts, and attempts.

According to the notes of a staff meeting, the week before Williams's death the therapists were unsure about letting him go on his next weekend release, because he seemed very sad. They decided to hold a team meeting with his relatives on Thursday and monitor him closely. Williams seemed to improve that week. Some of the clouds in his head lifted after he was named most valuable player in the weekly basketball game, and on Wednesday he went on an exciting fishing trip. During the team meeting with his parents, the staff supported the weekend release. Williams's mother casually mentioned that she planned to take him to the recently opened rock-and-roll museum in the city. The staff's group leader tried to dissuade her. The notes of the meeting reported the exchange: "I explained that with son's attempts to jump off of the water tower, that taking him to that new museum, a five-story open area, might not be in son's best interest. She said that Andy would never jump when he was with her. I then explained that I would be remiss if I did not warn her." The group therapist added that an acquaintance of Williams had jumped to her death from a bridge a month earlier and that this might still be fresh in his memory. On Saturday morning, Williams left with a weekend supply of medication.

The police report details what happened at the museum. When Williams and his parents, sister, and brother-in-law went to retrieve the car from the fifth floor of the parking garage, Williams said that he wanted to smoke a cigarette next to a side wall. His sister and brother-in-law walked to the car, and when the sister looked back, she saw in a split second the last of his legs and shoes disappear over the wall. According to the police report, she screamed, "Andy jumped. Andy jumped." The family ran downstairs, where Williams was spread out dead on the sidewalk.

When talking to the scene investigator, Williams's sister changes her account. She now reports that she saw Andy "become dizzy and roll off the edge." The investigator goes to the parking garage, takes extensive pictures and measurements of the wall, and notes the garage's safety measures. According to the police and scene investigator, someone standing on the floor of the garage would likely be unable to fall off. The relatives call the office at weekly intervals and, frustrated by the slow pace of the investigation, request a formal hearing with the department of health services. During an informal meeting with the family, Dr. Cahill explains her office's procedures and presents the investigation as ongoing. She decides to go all out on this case and asks the forensic psychiatrist to conduct a psychological autopsy. The family is satisfied with this promise and retracts their request. The psychiatrist reviews the records and interviews the mental health institution's staff and Williams's friends and relatives. In his opinion, Williams committed suicide. In addition to the psychiatrist's findings, the final autopsy report puts the most weight on the adequacy of the parking garage's safety measures: "The decedent was 75 inches in height, and the safety bar at the top of the wall was 3 feet 11 inches above the floor. According to the police investigation, there is also a safety wire, which is 2 feet 2 inches above the floor and 1 foot 1 inch inside the wall. If a person were standing on the floor of the garage adjacent to the lower safety wire, if he were to fall forward, his center of gravity would be well below the top of the safety bar and he would not fall out of the garage."

The manner of death is, finally, determined to be suicide. The relatives request another meeting with the medical examiner's staff. They dismiss the information presented by the pathologists and the psychiatrist. They repeat, "You didn't know Andy. He would never jump if we were around. It was unlike him to jump." While the medical examiner's staff had looked at the mental health records and found validation there for suicide, Williams's father and sister detect instead the signs promising a recovery. They assert that he was getting much better and that climbing a tower was insignificant if he would come down when offered a hamburger. The father, previously well-dressed, looks more disheveled and desperate. He states pleadingly that he simply cannot live with a suicide determination. The relatives offer to sign a form that they will never sue anyone if the pathologist changes the classification to undetermined. They wonder, "What's the big deal? Why can't you just change it?" The medical examiner's staff expresses sympathy but does not change the suicide determination.

In light of Andy Williams's history of threatening to jump off buildings to commit suicide, his repeated suicide threats and fantasies, and the circumstances of his death, a suicide classification seemed inevitable. To the medical examiner's staff, however, the case was not at first that straightforward. Even people with death wishes might accidentally fall off buildings. If Williams had left a suicide note or if a passerby had seen him dive off the building, the case would have been much clearer. The sister's changed story rendered her witness report suspect. The evidence that clinched the case was the information about safety in the garage. The wall and safety wire were interpreted as positive proof that this death was not an accident. Williams needed to make a deliberate effort to get over the wall and so established an intent to die. All the other mental health and biographical information pushed the evidence for suicide over the 51 percent likelihood that Dr. Cahill had set as the standard for her office. Because she thought the family would not accept a suicide classification, she enrolled the help of the forensic psychiatrist.

According to the suicide literature, relatives are presumed to steer the verdict away from the stigma of suicide, whereas medical examiners are expected to rely on objective criteria.[73] But the relationship between medical examiners and the stigma of suicide is more complicated. Forensic pathologists are well aware of the stigma of a suicide classification and consider it when they weigh the possibility of suicide. They may occasionally argue against a suicide determination because of the stigma, but they nevertheless apply the category and even reinforce the stigmatizing connotations of suicide to convince dissenters. Thus, the stigma of suicide motivates not only relatives but also professionals; the distinction is a difference in the power to act on a concern about stigma.

First, medical examiners are conscious of their moral-entrepreneurial role as "labelers" of suicide.[74] Because their patients cannot be injured or harmed, they are rarely sued, but any lawsuit will most likely involve a suicide case.[75] Williams's relatives had mentioned their willingness to sign a waiver if the pathologist changed the death certificate, so the staff anticipated that they might file a lawsuit. The pathologists were also confronted with the ongoing situation of a father distraught by the suicide classification of his son's death; this father had contacted state and federal officials in a fruitless attempt to change his son's death certificate. The pathologists expressed some sympathy for relatives unhappy with suicide classifications and even understanding for family members who angrily argued with them or hid suicide notes. Dr. Douglas acknowledged the gravity of a suicide classification when he noted that it would "ostracize" a family, creating a "heavy burden" and a more difficult grieving process. Suicide becomes a marker of deep, possibly hereditary mental health issues, an "immoral act," or even a crime.[76] The pathologists also pointed out to me that suicide classifications might void double-indemnity insurance payments and influence civil litigation.[77]

Second, as members of society, pathologists share the general notions about the stigma of suicide and consider them central to suicide deliberations. Yet not only do they have a better opportunity than relatives to act upon those notions, they also need to apply those norms in deciding about suicidal intent. When evaluating evidence, medical examiners ponder whether the deceased could have intended to commit suicide *in spite of* the stigma. The level of desperation thus needs to be high enough to overcome any hesitance due to the stigma. Medical examiners consider the stigma a demotivating factor. In a society where suicide constitutes an honorable death (as with kamikaze pilots during the Second World War, for example, or suicide bombers in the Middle East) or is apparently routinized (as in Inuit and Samoan cultures),[78] officials might be more likely to classify suspicious deaths as suicides. At this particular historical moment, however, the stigma of suicide in most cultures necessarily affects every aspect of suicide determination.

The medical examiners' active evaluation of the stigma when establishing intent was most apparent in the deaths of two teenagers. In both cases, a boy died an apparently self-inflicted death, but the medical examiner did not deem the death a suicide. In the first case, a young boy was found partially suspended by a dog leash in a bathroom; in the second case, an older teen jumped off a bridge. In both cases, much evidence pointed to suicide: the boy found hanging had a classmate who had killed himself the previous year in a similar manner, and the teen who jumped from the bridge had repeatedly engaged in risk-taking behavior that skirted the edge of suicide. The discussions in the medical examiner's office, however, turned on whether these teens fully grasped the lethal consequences of their actions and whether the stigma of suicide would have deterred them. The staff concluded that the young men recognized neither the stigma of suicide nor the consequences of their acts. In the case of the young man who jumped from the bridge, the medical examiners agreed that the death was self-inflicted and reckless but not intentional; it was classified as accidental. In the other case, the staff had no idea why the boy had hanged himself, and they left the death undetermined.

Third, medical examiners invoke stigma both to confirm and to negate suicide. Depending on the strength of the evidence, similar kinds and levels of family involvement in possible suicide cases are evaluated differently. In Dubos's case the evidence was considered weak, and the pathologists acknowledged the negative moral implications of labeling the death a suicide and the heavy load the label might place on a grieving family. The medical examiners instead emphasized the heart disease complicated by diabetes and the ambiguity of the poetry. A death investigator explained: "When in doubt, don't use [suicide]. This is the consensus of medical and forensic examiners."[79] In Williams's case, however, the medical examiners regarded *suicide* not as a moral term but as a medicolegal description grounded in an inductive examination of the evidence. Suicide was not a mere stigmatizing label but a substantiated entity, a legally defensible, professionally established fact. The morality that surrounds the official suicide classification is the morality of scientific proof, legal objectivity, and neutral expert knowledge. This morality supersedes the stigma attached to suicide. Suicide has become an officially validated truth. To convince Williams's relatives, the medical examiner fell back on forensic evidence but acknowledged that the family would not be satisfied with the information.

Fourth, medical examiners rely on the stigmatizing connotations of suicide to justify their classification: the stigma of the manner of death becomes a self-fulling prophecy. For Williams's relatives, suicide would never become a scientific or legal descriptor but would always indicate a moral stigma that could not apply to their son and brother. Andy's parents and sister seemed to see the suicide classification as a personal affront: how could Andy have killed himself, they argued, when the people who loved him most and knew him best were around? They countered every past indication of suicide with a story of small victories, attempting to sweep away medicolegal evidence with biographical information. In light of the identity pollution implied in suicide, they argued that no public health benefit could justify their immense suffering. Their fears were realized. Ironically, their objections further confirmed the stigma of suicide and turned them into *deniers* who *refused* to accept suicide. The mental health terms that surrounded Williams's life (such as "compulsive" and "obsessive") thus slipped into the medical examiners' references to his relatives.

The medicolegal interpretive frame turns disparate pieces of evidence into the gestalt of suicide. Williams's relatives were unable to make the "gestalt switch": the medical examiners' foreground remained for the family an unperceivable background. Relatives and death investigators present two different standards, moralities, and truths grounded in a common cultural notion of suicide as a stigmatized category. Here, incommensurability does not lead to a paradigm shift, a new way of thinking about suicide. Nor does the voice of medicine overwhelm the voice of the lifeworld.[80] When ambiguity prevails, medical examiners apply arguments against suicide similar to those of relatives. The difference in implementation stems from the institutionalization of professional power. As stigma researchers point out, "it takes power to stigmatize," and medical examiners' power resides in their legal mandate as professionals to classify suspicious deaths.[81] The course of Andy Williams's death investigation clearly shows that relatives have little or no recourse against medical examiners' determination. Once a death is officially validated, dissatisfied relatives run up against the cautiously crafted nature of professional work.

The medical examiner's staff did not believe that they caved in to external pressure. They noted that sometimes they happened to go with what the family wanted, but that simply indicated that the evidence did not support a suicide determination. The main effect of pressure from relatives was that the staff would perform an in-depth investigation. Yet any case threatened with the cloud of liability or lingering questions from relatives required an extensive investigation, not just suicide cases. In the staff's opinion, the legal principle of a preponderance of evidence prevailed. To underscore this point, Dr. Cahill told me a cautionary tale about a colleague who was chief medical examiner in a midwestern county.

This old lady was in the hospital and her family wanted to put her in a nursing home. She didn't want to go, and she hung herself with her hospital bathrobe. The hospital nurses put her in bed and when the family came, they told them, "Grandma has died. Her heart stopped." They did not mention anything about the suicide. But when the hospital called the medical examiner, they explained how they had found her. The medical examiner conducts a thorough investigation and calls it a suicide and mentions hanging as circumstances. The family goes ballistic. For the next two years they call him every week. He has several meetings with them to explain his findings. Nothing helps. Then after two years, he has another meeting with them and asks them, "What would make you happy?" They say that they don't like suicide. That's when he makes his mistake. He says, "Okay, I can't make it a natural death, but I can leave the death undetermined." So he changes the death certificate. About two weeks later, he is contacted by the sheriff. The family has gone to the sheriff and says that he was incompetent because he missed a homicide. The medical examiner explains to the sheriff what has happened, and the sheriff tells the family that he will not investigate. The family accuses the medical examiner of manipulating the sheriff and goes to the attorney general. He in turn checks with the medical examiner and decides not to pursue the case. The family now accuses the attorney general of covering up the examiner's mistakes. They take their case to the board of medical licensure, and the medical examiner almost lost his license.

The moral of the story was crystal clear: allowing relatives to dictate the results of a death investigation torpedoes a medical examiner's credibility.

PRESSURE FROM PUBLIC HEALTH

If relatives have few opportunities to influence death investigations, how do other stakeholders fare? Social epidemiologists and sociologists have long suspected that death investigators underreport suicide. Have their critiques directly or indirectly changed forensic practice?

On a frosty October afternoon, Dahlia Schweingruber, a fifty-eight-year-old retired white woman, was extracted from her car without a pulse. She had apparently driven her new Ford Explorer over two concrete medians and hit a telephone pole. The collision occurred at about 2:00 p.m. while the weather and road conditions were clear. The event was unwitnessed. The first people who drove past the site mentioned a cloud of dust and smoke. Dahlia had eaten lunch and was on her way to a hairdresser's appointment. Right before an intersection, her car veered off the road and hit the wooden pole. She was not wearing a seat belt, but both front air bags deployed. She was transferred to the state hospital and was declared dead on arrival. The medical examiner's office picked up the body, and during morning meeting, the investigator notes that there is not much medical history because she had not seen a physician in years. Dr. Cahill wonders whether the woman experienced a cardiac event.

She does the autopsy with a state police official present. On the X-rays, she notes that all the ribs on the right side are broken. She wonders whether the bones might be osteoporotic. The arms are covered with bruises. Dr. Cahill explains the bruises as air-bag injuries. The deceased also has a broken neck and a ruptured vena cava. Her lungs are collapsed, and the heart is bruised. The autopsy provides enough elements to explain the woman's death, but the pathologist looks for a medical indication for driving off the road. Dr. Cahill expects a bad heart, but the coronaries are fine. This finding poses a problem, and the pathologist does not know what she will do with it. In the end, with the precipitating event unresolved, Dr. Cahill writes "massive internal bleeding due to vena cava and heart injuries" for cause of death and "accident" for manner of death. Before sending the body back to the storage refrigerator, she informs the attending police officer of her main findings.

What is remarkable about this case is that the suspicion of suicide was never raised, although it may have explained a seemingly preventable accident. Over the period of my study, I observed six single-vehicle accident cases in which people went off the road, hit something, and died. In four cases, the driver's blood alcohol level exceeded legal limits. In all these accidents, determining the cause of death was straightforward: there were lacerated organs, torn vessels, or cerebral injuries. From the outset, these cases fit with accident as the manner of death, and the determination went unchallenged.

Public health officials have long suspected that single-vehicle accidents are one of the major sources of suicide underreporting.[82] According to pathologists, however, the lack of motor vehicle suicides indicates not oversight but the strength of their scientific investigative process. A similar situation would be with, say, a bench biochemist who is convinced that a particular protein plays a role in breast cancer but is unable to prove it with the customary DNA technology. No journal would publish the biochemist's paper if it was only based on a hunch and not backed up with experimental research. The unproven results would be dismissed as a mere artifact. Similarly, a suicide hunch would not hold up in court; depressed people might have fatal car accidents, accidentally overdose on pills, or die young from natural causes.

With respect to the search for evidence confirming suicide, a standard forensics textbook explains that evidence of braking before impact can help distinguish accident from suicide. If witnesses did not observe braking, if the tire tracks do not indicate any swerving to avoid the obstacle, or if the sole of the driver's shoe shows the pattern of the gas pedal instead of the brake pedal, then the deceased was accelerating, or at least not braking, at the time of impact. Yet the brakes provide only "confirmatory evidence of a suicide."[83] The more important evidence is a history of previous suicide attempts or psychiatric treatment. Because scene investigators do not check the deceased's home for a suicide note, this kind of evidence is not taken into consideration unless relatives voluntarily turn over a note. Relatives will be only cursorily interviewed by scene investigators, and police officers or a forensic psychologist will not interrogate relatives and friends. Few people will come forward with a suspicion of suicide. Because major evidence that could suggest suicide is thus routinely unavailable,[84] a suicide determination in a single-vehicle accident or pedestrian death is unlikely.[85]

Why have decades-long suspicions by epidemiologists that single-car accidents harbor undetected suicides been unable to alter medical examiners' investigative procedures? Epidemiologists' limited success in changing forensic practice is due to their peripheral role in death investigation. If the "organizational ecology" of the medical examiner's office comprises the institutional arrangements necessary to fulfill its professional tasks,[86] the office is most vulnerable in needing particular kinds of information from several sources in order to classify suspicious deaths. Forensic pathologists receive information from various agencies and process it into data useful for state bureaucracies. Medical examiners gather information from health care providers and rely heavily on the scene descriptions provided by first responders—paramedics, emergency medical technicians (EMTs), and police officers. The parallel investigation by law enforcement in cases of suspicious death intensifies the medical examiner's relationship with police officers. Law enforcement officials not only bring additional evidence to autopsies (and are the only outsiders permitted to attend them); they also have an opportunity to confirm or dispute preliminary interpretations. In complicated, equivocal cases involving the possibility of foul play, Dr. Cahill often called a meeting with district attorneys and law enforcement officials to review the evidence and consulted with these parties before the cause and manner of death were determined. The organizational ecology further includes the parties to whom the medical examiner communicates the determination: the office of vital records, the legal next of kin or authorized representative thereof, health and law enforcement agencies involved in the investigation, and occasionally consumer-protection or professional gatekeeping organizations.

Death investigators help provide the raw material for mortality statistics, but epidemiologists rarely interact directly or indirectly with them during the postmortem investigation. Medical examiners give the death certificate to the funeral director, who files it with city administrators, who in turn send it to the state's office of vital records. Only at that point do mortality data come under the purview of public health officials. During my research, the pathologists mentioned receiving only one letter from the CDC, urging them to be aware of heat-related deaths during the summer months. Communication was formalized through the office of vital records, and if unusual deaths merited public health attention, the medical examiner's office would take the initiative to inform public health officials. Medical examiners did not receive funding or resources specifically for suicide detection. As one pathologist put it, "We don't play the numbers game," meaning that there was no yearly "quota" of suicides to meet. Medical examiners are less concerned with identifying every possible suicide than they are with proving that every death determined to be a suicide meets their evidentiary standard. A false negative—a suicidal death classified as natural or accidental—does not tarnish their credibility. A false positive—classifying a nonsuicidal death as a suicide—might, however, challenge their professional authority. Even entertaining the possibility of other manners of death in "obvious" car accidents could lead to an escalation of ungrounded suspicions. And why stop at suicide? Every sudden or unexpected death could conceivably become a full-blown homicide investigation. Maybe someone altered the brakes of Schweingruber's car, or another car drove her off the road? Possible lethal conspiracies are infinite, but they must remain speculative. Citing epidemiological and safety research, medical examiners point out that car crashes are less likely to be caused by suicide or homicide than by driving under the influence of alcohol or drugs, speed, reckless driving, falling asleep at the wheel, or environmental hazards such as slick roads, construction, or poor road markings.

The lack of external pressure to accurately define suicides carries one important exception, but it is the proverbial exception that confirms the rule. The forensic pathology literature is attuned to resolving ambiguity in violent deaths with characteristics of either suicide or homicide, such as in the Barbara Morris case. In these situations, the medicolegal stakes are very high: a false suicide certification might provide the perfect cover for a homicide, and a false determination of homicide might implicate innocent people in a criminal investigation. In such ambiguous cases, the medical examiner's closest allies in the organizational ecology, law enforcement officials, interact directly and closely with the medical examiner from the time the body is discovered to the moment the death certificate is signed.

WHEN IS A SUSPICIOUS DEATH A SUICIDE?

An interesting Tower of Babel grows around the meaning of suicide. Public health officials and epidemiologists using statistical tools discover hidden suicides where medical examiners working with physical and documentary evidence see accidents or undetermined deaths. Relatives situating death in the life course of their loved one see even less suicide than the medical examiners. We seem to have discovered a rule of proximity in suicide: the closer one is to the deceased, the less likely one is to consider the death a suicide.[87] Thus three groups, each using its own criteria, develop different notions of suicide: biographical suicide, suicide as a statistical rate, and medicolegal suicide.

A *biographical suicide* is grounded in the long-term memories and personal experiences of relatives and friends. After people die, relatives and friends usually do not dwell on the corrosive mental illness and signs of looming self-destruction, but rather on the joys, pleasures, victories, promises, and accomplishments. The comprehensive memories render pointless the classification of a personal death in some category or another. Suicide is often too final and too stigmatized to capture accurately a life that ended prematurely. At stake is the personal identity of the deceased, not pieces of evidence. A biographical suicide arises in a context of closure, grieving, memorialization, suffering, and pain.

The *statistical suicide rate* constructed by sociological and public health criteria is far removed from either the smell of death or the memories of the living. It is a profile grounded in mortality statistics and centered on a limited number of quantifiable demographic characteristics. Statisticians view their methods not as opinions but as proof of significance, causality, control for biases, and correction for errors. Theirs is an objective science that can detect underreporting. At stake in suicide classification are the prediction, correlations, and prevention of premature death.

A *medicolegal suicide* is a professional classification made according to investigative criteria. It is inductively constructed from pieces of evidence, and it functions under the aura of empirical sciences and legal authority. The death certificate that the medical examiner fills out states, "In my *opinion* as certifying physician, this death is due to . . ." (my italics). A professional suicide classification is partly a medical opinion, a *judgment,* based on the available evidence. The medical aspect of the medicolegal suicide is further reflected in the pathologists' inductive approach when evaluating evidence, an approach based on patient-assessment procedures and medical history taking. Forensic pathologists prefer evidence from a medical authority (such as a psychiatrist), from the autopsy, and from biochemical tests. The importance of "subjective" biographical information pales in comparison with the "objective" results of biochemical tests. In order for the evidence to add up to a suicide verdict, the investigators must selectively sift through notes, medical files, biographical information, circumstances of the death, and the corpse itself. Yet it is difficult to predetermine the number of sources or amount of evidence that will be needed to come to a consensus of suicide. No piece of information constitutes evidence in itself, but the pieces become meaningful when triangulated with other elements. Pathologists' procedures, organization, and approach to classifying death follow the diagnostic process that physicians typically use. Suicide is not a mere diagnosis, however; it becomes an official and legally sanctioned classification.

The legal aspects of medicolegal suicide refer to the preponderance of evidence needed for a suicide determination and the judicial status of the final classification. The suspicious death needs to be *positively proven* to have been self-inflicted and intentional; suicide is not a default or residual option. In other words, when a suspicious death is not a homicide, accident, or natural death, it does not automatically become a suicide. Once a medical examiner writes "suicide" on the death certificate, his or her expert authority prevails, and the term is official and legally binding. Parties who disagree with it have few means to appeal the verdict. In medicolegal suicide determinations, medical opinions are thus turned into legal facts. To minimize dissent in cases of equivocal death and to decide when the evidence for suicide fulfills the fifty-one percent rule, the chief medical examiner double-checks the classification, and medical examiners exchange information with key law enforcement allies in the organizational ecology of the investigative system.

The three notions of suicide do not differ with respect to the stigma of self-inflicted deaths. The pathologists consider the history of suicide as a stigmatized way of dying in their work practices and, in turn, confirm the stigma when triangulating evidence, applying a high decision threshold and drawing conclusions conservatively. Philosopher Ian Hacking notes the "looping effect" of concepts such as suicide: they "may be made and molded by attempts at knowledge and intervention, [to the extent] that there is no stable object to have knowledge about."[88] Medical examiners are not passive observers but active and privileged parties in the hermeneutic loop of suicide; their classifications will influence how others understand suicide.

The coexistence of three notions of suicide means that suicide as an entity independent of claims makers does not exist. Whatever phenomenon we classify as "suicide" reflects the criteria and work practices of the classifier. When relatives or epidemiologists disagree with the official medicolegal classification, discord may erupt, but they are at a disadvantage when it comes to directly influencing the outcome of the death investigation. A concerned relative might hide a suicide note but cannot guarantee that everyone interviewed will maintain the united front. Relatives are usually unprepared for a death investigation and have little knowledge of the details that matter. They have few opportunities to offer their interpretation directly, and whatever they say is presumed to be biased and is screened by police officers, psychiatrists, or scene investigators. If relatives disagree after the death certificate has been filed, they have little chance to prevail in a lawsuit if the medical examiner has followed standard procedures. Public health officials have even less opportunity and inclination to directly influence suicide determinations. The presumption in the many statistical reports noting "hidden pockets" of suicide seems to be that the best solution for dealing with the problem is not changing the recording practices of death investigators but to find a statistical measure to correct for alleged errors. Because of the insoluble problems of premortem intent and self-infliction, no alternative method can establish the validity of suicide statistics (in contrast, cancer death certificates filled out by clinicians can be compared to autopsy data),[89] making it impossible to determine conclusively the size of a possible statistical correction. Sociologists and epidemiologists therefore continue to rely on the classifications of death investigators.[90]

Contrary to common wisdom, relatives' lack of opportunity to influence the death investigation might actually stifle suicide detection.[91] In comparison to the coroners that Atkinson studied, medical examiners have incorporated a stronger medical orientation in their deliberations. The growing power of science in medicine raised the bar for suicide detection.[92] Increasingly, toxicology results and autopsy findings have become the determining evidence in death investigation. Yet those research procedures rarely indicate suicide. The standardized toxicology screen does not check for most lethal poisons, unless the pathologist explicitly requests it. An autopsy might rule out other manners of death, but it almost never proves suicide. As we saw in the case of Guy Dubos, the attention paid to scientific proof increased the ambiguity instead of bringing the case to a close. Although the medical examiner's investigation puts great emphasis on biomedical information, it is biographical clues that often alert them to the likelihood of suicide.

In contrast, most of the inquest exchanges reported by Atkinson centered on a lengthy and detailed discussion of the clues in the biography and the death scene. The coroner asked witnesses at length about the habits of the deceased, the person's mental health, and previous suicide attempts. The pathologist was an important expert witness, but not the ultimate decision maker. The character information provided by witnesses formed a detailed portrait of the deceased's disposition toward living and often clinched the case. In the medical examiner's office that I observed, however, the usual procedure was to have the scene investigator ask questions at the scene and maybe call the relatives again if issues remained unaddressed. Suicide rates were likely lower because relatives and friends did not have the opportunity to formally voice their opinion and relate the biography of the deceased in the many car accidents, pedestrian deaths, and sudden deaths of the elderly where suicide was not initially suspected. Lower or higher suicide figures, however, do not necessarily imply less accuracy but, rather, reflect a shift in the criteria for suicide evidence with the medical professionalization of death investigations.[93]

One occasionally hears anecdotal stories of suicides that remained officially undetected, which seems to confirm that broader inquiries by medical examiners involving interviews with relatives might reveal deaths that were self-inflicted. On different occasions, two of my colleagues provided me with touching examples of "hidden suicides" involving elderly parents. One colleague's stepfather, a retired professor, was in his late seventies when his wife was institutionalized with severe dementia. He had been diagnosed with Parkinson's disease. He finished his last manuscript and summoned his stepdaughter. He told her about his intention to take his own life with pills on a particular day. They talked for a long time and had their last meal in a favorite restaurant, and then he asked her to leave. She left the city but booked a return ticket. Exactly on the day he told her he would die, she received a call that he had passed away. His death was not investigated but was signed out as a natural death due to Parkinson's disease with complications from pneumonia. My colleague was never contacted by the medical examiner's office. Instead of presuming that the local medical examiner "covered up" the suicide, I think it more likely that the death of a man in his late seventies with a diagnosed terminal illness and without any signs of foul play did not warrant a forensic investigation. This suicide slipped through the cracks because of the assumptions in the medicolegal system about who is allowed to die, when, and for what reason. A routine questioning of relatives might have revealed that a suicide had taken place.

Differences in reporting between coroners and medical examiners are not necessarily problematic for epidemiological research if suicide determination remains systematic. Geographical variation suggests otherwise, however. Medical examiners readily admit that suicide determinations differ from jurisdiction to jurisdiction.[94] My research suggests two reasons for geographical variation. First, medical examiners employ internal oversight procedures to make sure that determinations meet the evidentiary standard of the chief medical examiner. Second, the chief consults with law enforcement and district attorneys to ascertain the legal validity of the determinations. The medicolegal standard is thus locally based, dependent on shifts in jurisprudence and personnel.

If social epidemiologists wanted to standardize suicide determinations, they would need to play a more prominent role in the organizational ecology of death investigation, requiring an intensive commitment of resources and time. Death investigators have also been criticized for underreporting child homicide.[95] For that reason, child advocates supported by federal and state laws and professional organizations have set up interdisciplinary child-death review teams to collaborate with medical examiners and coroners.[96] These death investigation teams combine the expertise of public health officials, physicians, and personnel from agencies for child welfare, education, social services, law enforcement, the judicial system, and mental health. Most observers are satisfied that, after interdisciplinary review, few child-abuse deaths remain misclassified.[97] In my research site, a team of child death and injury reviewers co-chaired by one of the medical examiners discussed cases quarterly and issued biannual reports that highlighted preventable deaths. Compared to suicides, child deaths are relatively rare and well-defined by age, and abusive child deaths are considered major criminal transgressions. In spite of its stigma, suicide does not seem to mobilize the same resources. Instead, forensic professional organizations echoing the recommendations of the surgeon general have attempted to standardize suicide determinations with operational criteria,[98] even though these tools constitute some of the weakest means to change professional behavior.[99] Psychological autopsies might also provide more accurate suicide determinations,[100] but only two jurisdictions use them routinely.[101]

In sum, when medical examiners write "suicide" on a death certificate, the death was, in their professional perspective, a true suicide even if relatives and public health officials disagree with them. The medicolegal criteria and the investigative process render their determination appropriate. Their forensic authority is organizationally, legally, medically, and scientifically anchored. Because medical examiners are the officially sanctioned gatekeepers of suicide, their notions of suicide weigh heavier than those of relatives and statisticians. "Around every core of 'expert' knowledge is a penumbra, a domain in which core competence is helpful but not definitive, in which competent experts may disagree, and disagree because the questions in this domain cannot be decided in terms of the core issues that define competence."[102] Suicide belongs to the penumbra of death investigation. Medical examiners have the official mandate to detect, document, and classify suicides, but suicides are not easily determined by pathologists.

CHAPTER THREE

FORENSIC CREDIBILITY AT THE "NANNY TRIAL"

Dr. Cahill kneels beside a cut and bloodied yellow muscle T-shirt, spread out on a white sheet on the floor of the autopsy room. She earlier counted four bullet holes in the torso of the young man lying on the stretcher. She easily finds three holes in the T-shirt but is not sure where to locate the fourth. Paramedics at the scene had cut open the shirt to attach defibrillator leads. It looks to me as if they cut through the missing bullet hole, because the jagged cut seems to open up a little. I point it out to the pathologist. She looks at it intently and answers, "Maybe this is the fourth hole, but I would not want to testify about it in court."

When medical examiners determine that a suspicious death is a suicide, the decision is virtually incontestable. Protected by legal statutes, forensic pathologists autonomously issue binding determinations. Such enormous powers, however, raise the specter of abuse: what keeps medical examiners from engaging in corrupt practices? On a broader level, philosopher Stephen Turner wondered: when a liberal state sponsors experts working outside the public sphere with expertise aimed at other state workers, where are the checks and balances on the knowledge they create? Is their discretionary power not a threat to democratic accountability? Unlike those who dismiss expertise as ideology, Turner says no. He redefines the conflict between power and accountability on theoretical grounds. Leaving some questions to experts, he argues, is not to grant them absolute power. Ultimately, he says, the public has the last word, deciding whether claims to authority are to be honored. Turner does not, however, explore the process of legitimation and delegitimation. Instead, he suggests that "what counts as 'expert' is conventional, mutable and shifting."[1] He elaborates, "My thought is that we need to think of experts more or less game-theoretically as active players in the task of legitimation, in which they impose self-limitations, put themselves under new, unbiased masters, certify one another's competence, and so forth. They are held accountable indirectly through these devices, and if they fail, the game has to begin again."[2] Turner thus proposes that experts actively monitor the legitimacy of their claims. In the case of medical examiners, I will argue, self-restraint in the morgue is greatly disciplined by courtroom testimonies.

The determination of forensic homicide represents the gold standard for conducting death investigations. Medical examiners will likely be asked to defend their autopsy findings publicly in an adversarial court setting, where counterexperts will cast doubt on their findings. Forensic investigations serve many audiences, but the court is by far the most critical. Public health officials might be concerned about the underreporting of suicide, but they do not routinely ask forensic experts to justify why a particular death was not classified as a suicide. And while next of kin might disagree with a forensic finding, they have little recourse. In homicide investigations, however, lawyers will pore over every word of an autopsy report and death certificate to make sure that forensic procedures have been followed and that the conclusions are supported with sufficient evidence. References to possible future court appearances, similar to Dr. Cahill's comment about the fourth bullet hole, abound in the everyday conversations of medical examiners. As I conducted my research, several pathologists mentioned that they mentally rehearsed their defense of a suicide determination in court before filling in the death certificate. In homicides, such a rehearsal is not an academic exercise. Anything pertaining to the legal case is open for scrutiny in cross-examination: what the medical examiners did and what they did not do, how they gathered evidence and what conclusions they drew from it—even their professional experience and their familiarity with the scientific literature.

The possibility of having to give court testimony informs the procedures and political scope of death brokering. Medical examiners do not simply anticipate a court examination. Rather, the close, adversarial scrutiny at a trial offers a *professional script* for conducting their work. Court proceedings provide a legally admissible standard. The likely questions on direct and cross-examination determine how forensic pathologists gather and handle evidence and what conclusions they reach. Dr. Douglas told me that he was once asked in court how many steps he took between the autopsy gurney and the table where he wrote his notes, indicating that the most minute details might gain importance in a trial.[3] The relevance of such particulars lies in the adversarial nature of a trial. Often, the prosecution bases the criminal charges on forensic findings. A criminal case might be won or lost over doubt cast on the chain of custody. Medically trained forensic pathologists, therefore, learn to practice their profession in legally appropriate ways.

At stake in criminal and civil trials is one of the most important assets of forensic pathologists: their professional credibility. Credibility is achieved when an audience accepts a claim.[4] In court, a forensic expert witness is credible when juries and judges accept a description of body trauma as evidence and an alleged mechanism of death as the way the deceased died.[5] Medical examiners claim that they alone have the professional expertise that allows them to draw conclusions about the identity of the deceased and the time, manner, and cause of death. Yet they do not have the final word in the courtroom: the defense will introduce counterexperts with similar credentials who will, drawing from the same resources, offer alternative explanations. Sociologist Sheila Jasanoff succinctly explained the importance of credibility and its relationship to truth and plausibility: "A common-law trial is not purely and simply a search for the truth: it is, more accurately, a contest of credibility between two carefully packaged, competing accounts of the 'same' reality. Plausibility is what carries the day: by trial's end, the winning story is the one that strikes the fact-finder as the more believable."[6] Indeed, all efforts to establish credibility are funneled toward the issue at stake during the trial, and neither party needs to establish an absolute truth. Instead, each attempts to present the most plausible account. Plausibility is the extent to which the proffered opinion is consistent with prevailing cultures of belief.

The credibility of forensic pathologists is firmly tied to five broad areas: (1) who the experts are; (2) on whose behalf they speak; (3) what they did; (4) what they concluded; and (5) how their conclusions fit with the scope of their discipline. Credibility stems from expert opinions grounded in the evidence, but such opinions lose all persuasive power if the evidence was mishandled, the expert did not come to a conclusion independently, the expert was not credentialed, or the opinion contradicts fundamental premises of the field. Through courtroom interaction, therefore, credibility emerges as a situationally specific achievement: the experts' actions on the witness stand document professional credibility in the eyes of fact finders.[7] The court explicitly confirms expertise. Except in cases of mistrial or hung jury, the judge or jury separates winners from losers in a criminal trial. Although it may be difficult to identify which expert has made the stronger case, forensic specialists find it professionally advantageous to be part of the winning team. When an attorney invokes an expert's track record at trial, a history of losses works cumulatively to erode professional credibility. A loss of credibility at a high-profile trial can spell the end of a career—as happened to Florida medical examiner Joan Wood, who revised her opinion about the manner of death in the 2000 trial involving a Church of Scientology member who died from a blood clot. Dr. Wood changed her opinion from "undetermined" to "accidental," leading to a dismissal of the charges against the church. The medical examiner resigned shortly after the revision; prosecutors and defense lawyers argued that her "error" would weaken any future court testimony she might give.[8]

A particularly controversial forensic category is "shaken-baby syndrome." The condition was first described in 1974 by a pediatric radiologist to define the constellation of signs and symptoms resulting from either violent shaking alone or from shaking with impact (an important point of contention) of the head of an infant or small child. While internal trauma is necessary for the diagnosis, external evidence of trauma is not necessary (this remains another point of controversy). The presumed scenario in a shaken-baby syndrome is a caregiver vigorously shaking an inconsolable crying infant for a period of as little as twenty seconds (again, a point of contention), causing permanent damage and possibly death because of the baby's underdeveloped neck muscles and skull. The contentious history of shaken-baby syndrome has prompted some legal analysts to dismiss the condition as a "crime du jour,"[9] and a review of the medical literature prior to 1998 summarized the state of the field as "an inverted pyramid with a small database spreading to a broad body of somewhat diverging opinions."[10] While shaken-baby syndrome has received some legal standing, influencing prosecution and defense strategies in court, the controversies surrounding it have also been used to raise "reasonable doubt." Of all trials involving shaken-baby syndrome, the landmark case has been the trial of nanny Louise Woodward.[11]

In October 1997, Louise Woodward went to trial for the first-degree murder of eight-month-old Matthew Eappen. The twenty-one-year-old British au pair had been employed as the nanny for Matthew and his older brother, Brendan, in the household of Sunil and Deborah Eappen, both physicians. On February 4, 1997, Woodward placed an emergency call to Newton Rescue in Newton, Massachusetts, telling the operator that Matthew was having difficulty breathing. The responding paramedics initiated resuscitation and transported Matthew to Children's Hospital in Boston. The infant's condition deteriorated, and he died on February 9 after being removed from life support. Suspicion of child abuse and shaken-baby syndrome emerged almost immediately, and Louise Woodward was accused of violently shaking the baby and slamming his head against the floor to silence his crying. The defense argued that Matthew had suffered an undetected traumatic brain injury three weeks earlier, which re-bled on February 4, causing the baby's death. Televised on Court TV, the unfolding trial drew a large audience—partly because Woodward was being defended by celebrity lawyer Barry Scheck, who had been credited with helping to acquit O. J. Simpson of murder in the 1995 "trial of the century." The "nanny trial" quickly became symbolic of issues in British-American relations, differing justice systems, and social class, in which well-to-do parents pay those of lower status for the daily care of their children. The trial produced a torrent of letters to the editors of various British and U.S. newspapers and the creation of several Web sites touting the innocence of Louise Woodward or the victimization of Matthew Eappen.

For the media, the high point of the trial was the testimony of the defendant, but most of the proceedings were devoted to scientific and forensic issues. Unlike in many trials, the Woodward defense team had the resources to hire counterexperts. During jury selection, both the defense and prosecution chose jurors they deemed able to comprehend the scientific complexities of the case. Of thirty-eight witnesses, fifteen possessed scientific expertise spanning the fields of emergency medicine, neurosurgery, neurology, neuroradiology, neuropathology, forensic pathology, ophthalmology, pediatrics, child abuse, and biomechanics. The prosecution presented Dr. Gerald Feigin, a medical examiner from Massachusetts who had conducted the autopsy of Matthew Eappen; and Dr. Umberto DeGirolami, a consulting neuropathologist to the medical examiner's office. The defense offered expert testimony from Dr. Jan Leestma, a pathologist and author of a neuropathology textbook; and Dr. Michael Baden, a former chief medical examiner of New York City and at the time of the trial director of medicolegal investigations for the New York state police.

In the courtroom of Middlesex County Superior Court Judge Hiller B. Zobel, the jury's charge was to determine whether the government had established beyond a reasonable doubt that Louise Woodward killed Matthew Eappen.[12] To that end, the prosecution presented the shaken-baby/impact theory in its opening statement: "This case is about Matthew Eappen being violently slammed against a hard object and severely shaken, causing massive injuries. This violent shaking and this severe slamming being done by the defendant Louise Woodward in a frustrated, unhappy, resentful rage, based on her attitude toward her job and a crying Matthew Eappen on February 4th of 1997."[13] Before the trial, the defense hypothesized that Matthew had a preexisting neurological condition or had been harmed by his brother. At trial, however, the defense presented the "bleed-rebleed" theory—the argument that what happened here, ladies and gentlemen of the jury, is that this child, Matthew Eappen, unfortunately, suffered an injury earlier. And it caused this fracture from much less force. You'll hear that it might well have been an accident. You've heard mention of this forearm fracture, both of this child's physician parents will tell you that they didn't know that this child had suffered a fracture. And they didn't know he suffered a skull fracture either. And that he suffered a head injury either. That's what they'll tell you. Well, ladies and gentlemen, we are going to present evidence that they did. That it took far less force to do that. And that it caused initially a leak in the bridging blood vessels between his brain and his skull. And that this eventually built up to the point where it stopped and it started again. And at one point, this situation gets to the point where even a slight jarring, a trivial impact, even spontaneously, this can start again. And the unfortunate and horrible thing is that it didn't stop the last time, and it caused Matthew Eappen to die.[14]

Both parties agreed that Matthew died of massive intracranial bleeding due to blunt trauma and that he had an undiagnosed, three-week-old wrist fracture, but they differ on the cause and timing of these injuries. In the trial's opening statements, the prosecution anticipated the importance of the forensic investigation: "The best evidence of what happened to Matthew Eappen that day," stated lead prosecutor Gerald Leone Jr., "is Matthew Eappen's bruised, broken, and battered body."[15] Leone elaborated the prosecution's theory that on February 4 Matthew was suffering from a two-and-a-half-inch skull fracture, a massively swollen brain, and bloody retinal hemorrhaging. In his opening statement, defense counsel Andrew Good also emphasized the condition of the body, noting that "this child came to the emergency room with absolutely no, none, not a mark on him—no swelling, no bruising, no abrasion, no bumps, no lumps—nothing on his head. Nothing on his body. Clean. No external sign of trauma at all."[16] Foreshadowing the line of witness interrogation to follow, Good pointed to problems with the evidence.

We have been hampered to some degree by the lack of care in preserving, and gathering the specimens and the evidence that one needs, in fact some of the best evidence. You'll hear evidence that Louise Woodward's lawyers sought a second autopsy, and that, under law, the Eappen family could prevent that from happening, and they did. We got a court order preserving, ordering the autopsy people, the medical examiner's office, to preserve whatever they took from this autopsy. But the best evidence, many pieces of the best evidence, were not preserved, and not gathered. First of all, the clot that was inside Matthew Eappen's head, in violation of hospital rules, was thrown away. They took samples of this forearm fracture in order to attempt to date it by microscopic means. They didn't do that with the skull fracture. During the course of our investigation, the neuroradiologist, Dr. Gean, who looked at the C-T scans and said, "Let's look at, I think I see old injury here. Let's get the section of the brain that still remains and verify it microscopically." When we went, we found that it was either missing, or destroyed, it's not there. Other parts of the brain are there, but those parts are not there. And you'll hear how the story changed by way of an explanation of why they're not there.[17]

In addition, the defense promised that "the medical examiner, their own medical examiner, the Government's medical examiner, will disagree to a significant degree with Dr. Newberger."[18] Dr. Eli Newberger was the director of child-protection services of Children's Hospital in Boston, the first to diagnose the death as a potential shaken baby.

Both sides vowed that Matthew's body could reveal the truth about the case. But in light of insufficient preparation of evidence, differences among the prosecution witnesses, and disagreements over the interpretation of the physical body, the trial rested on the credibility of the experts and the plausibility of their theory of how Matthew Eappen died. My purpose, however, is to analyze forensic professional credibility as it is established and questioned within the institutional context of a court trial. I will argue that the script of professional credibility emerging from the "dos and don'ts" of handling and interpreting forensic evidence transcends the courtroom to constitute a professional standard for *all* positive death determinations. Importantly, the anticipated court performance explains why medical examiners rarely take an activist role but remain conservative in imputing intent from pathological specimens and other trace evidence. Adversarial court testimony thus buttresses medical examiners' forensic authority by defining culturally appropriate interpretations of forensic evidence.

CREDIBILITY FROM PROFESSIONAL CREDENTIALS

Testifying begins with an investigation of the witness's credentials. This procedure involves admitting an expert witness in a specific area of expertise, entering a CV (curriculum vitae) as an exhibit, and a question-and-answer review of any additional experience pertinent to the case. For pathologists and neuropathologists, this additional questioning consists of asking about board certifications, number of autopsies performed, and experience with potential child-abuse cases. In a bench conference, defense counsel Barry Scheck expressed concern to the judge that because the prosecution's clinical witnesses were employed in world-renowned Boston hospitals, their institutional affiliation exuded credibility. To compensate, he selected expert testimony from national authorities in certain fields (e.g., a contributor to the development of MRI and a leading textbook author) and began direct examination with a more detailed review of their accomplishments.

Through accreditation, medical professions have instituted formal warrants of credibility. Professional candidates must fulfill education and practice requirements and pass an accreditation exam. [19] Further expertise then flows linearly from the accumulation of accomplishments. Job candidates, for example, are compared on the basis of research and clinical experience, ability to attract patients and research funding, and reputation in their respective fields. Established professionals gain additional credibility from institutional affiliations and membership in professional organizations. Viewed from the outside, the expert witnesses at a trial are all accredited authorities with lengthy lists of relevant experience. In the courtroom, however, the relationship between expertise and accomplishments is not straightforward. Indeed, "legal inquiry has the power to redefine the very parameters of professionalism from one case to another." [20] Professional reputation, publishing record, and experience mean little if these accomplishments do not directly relate to the issues contested during the trial. Strong credentials outside the courtroom can quickly be inverted to question the professional credibility of courtroom witnesses.

As national authorities, several defense expert witnesses had written textbooks. Dr. Leestma, for example, was introduced as the author of the only forensic neuropathology text in print. [21] Prosecution experts confirmed the authority of this book. Dr. Feigin based one of his opinions on it, and Dr. DeGirolami noted that it was absolutely authoritative. Unfortunately for Dr. Leestma, some of the book's statements contradicted the opinions of the defense experts, including his own opinions, leading to a vigorous cross-examination by prosecution counsel Martha Coakley. Dr. Leestma became flustered when confronted with his writing of a decade earlier that stated that "one of the most common forms of head injury observed in victims of fatal child abuse is a subdural hematoma with or without a skull fracture" [22] and "it is an inescapable fact that the vast majority of seriously head-injured infants and children, when automobile and other major accidental trauma can be ruled out, acquired their injuries as a result of abuse." [23] A fragment of a different text he published in 1996—one year before the trial—contained a particularly damning passage, discrediting the doctor's own testimony.

Q: Doctor, in that book you wrote, did you not, "Under a skull, from which the brain has been removed, illustrates the common pattern of rather diffuse or widely spaced subdural hemorrhages in child abuse victims. Often, there are older membranes beneath the fresh hematomas that signal prior head trauma episodes. Such older membranes are often invoked," quote— I'm sorry—parenthesis, "by defense attorneys," unparenthesis, "to explain recent subdural hematomas on the basis of spontaneous re-bleeding. Such explanations do not take into consideration the brain swelling, which is invariably present, and the fatal outcome which cannot be accounted for on the basis of subdural hematoma mass effect, but rather are caused by a new episode of trauma."

Did I read that correctly, Doctor?

A: Yes, you did.

Q: And that was your opinion in 1996?

A: Particularly relevant to that illustrated case, yes.

Q: And are you telling us today that your opinion has changed, that you believe now that a mass effect as a result of a subdural hematoma can cause a fatal outcome in a child?

A: Yes, I have had subsequent case material and instances in which I think that's too narrow an interpretation. [24]

Dr. Leestma was not only forced to concede that the clinical diagnosis of child abuse in Matthew Eappen's case was "a good working hypothesis and a reasonable conclusion to draw at the time" on the basis of his earlier writing; he was also compelled to qualify publicly—even retract—his recent and older writings: "I suppose I used a bad choice of words there." [25] His testimony implied that either his previous opinion was inaccurate or his current opinion was—as his writings suggested—a far-fetched theory by defense attorneys unwilling to acknowledge the obvious source of trauma. When Coakley repeated the same procedure during her cross-examination of Dr. Alisa Gean, a neuroradiologist and textbook author, Scheck fumed to the judge that it is "fundamentally unfair" to take quotes out of context. The judge reminded him of "an old saying: 'Oh, that mine enemy had written a book.' Now, people write books and they get cross-examined on them." [26] Indeed, "the practice of cross-examination in American courts respects no preordained limits on the kind of questions asked to undermine an expert's credibility." [27]

Dr. Baden encountered similar trouble. [28] He was probably the country's best-known forensic pathologist and had testified at numerous highly publicized trials. Claiming to have conducted about twenty thousand autopsies (compared to four thousand for Dr. Feigin), he had been the chairman of a forensic pathology committee appointed by Congress to investigate the assassinations of President John F. Kennedy and Dr. Martin Luther King Jr. [29] He thus enjoyed much experience and prestige, other traditional hallmarks of credibility. [30] When Dr. Baden's qualifications were being discussed, the judge asked via defense counsel Scheck whether the pathologist had testified in Middlesex County, the place of the trial. Dr. Baden answered negatively. On cross-examination, prosecution counsel Coakley asked him whether a good working hypothesis would assert that an injured child without a documented history of any accident would be regarded as a potential shaken-baby/impact syndrome victim. Dr. Baden replied: "Shaken doesn't explain anything about the autopsy or pathology. That is just a speculation. An impact would cause all those findings." He defined shaken-baby syndrome as "an unusual occurrence today," one in which "a baby is shaken hard enough to cause injury to the neck area, to the shoulder area, and to produce some intracranial hemorrhage, whether it's a subdural or subarachnoid hemorrhage, without any impact or external injury to the head. It can happen, but it's very unusual."[31]

Unfortunately for the credibility of Dr. Baden's memory, he had previously testified in front of the same judge (who deadpanned, "I didn't take it as an insult")[32] in a similar child-abuse case, for the prosecution.[33] There he had given a much broader definition of shaken-baby syndrome, with greater emphasis on hemorrhaging. Coakley read Dr. Baden's earlier testimony:

It refers to the concept that an individual can take a baby in his or her hands, holding the baby around the chest or abdomen, and shake the baby so violently that hemorrhages occur around the brain or behind the eyes, or in the back of the eyes, because the baby's head is heavy compared to the rest of the body, heavier than an adult, and the head acts, the neck acts as a fulcrum, and the head whips back and forth at a great enough speed and force to cause blood vessels to rupture in the eye and brain region. And that's the concept of the shaken-baby syndrome.

He added in the earlier trial that "from a medical examiner–pathology point of view, it was the hemorrhaging about the brain and eyes that are characteristic and pathognomonic of shaken-baby syndrome."[34] At the Woodward trial, however, he claimed that an infant could experience retinal hemorrhaging for many different reasons and that the eye injuries are atypical of shaken-baby syndrome. These contradictions undermined his credibility: whom should we believe, the old Dr. Baden or the new? The contrast created the impression that Dr. Baden had selectively tailored his opinions to the side for which he was testifying.

As these exchanges indicated, those who are experts in their respective fields might not be the best experts at a particular trial. Even for an expert who has contributed to Nobel Prize–winning research (as had Dr. Ayub Khan Ommaya, a biomechanical expert testifying for the defense), a few questions can reveal that at least twenty years have elapsed since the expert investigated a possible child-abuse case. In the courtroom, credibility is not an ascribed characteristic, flowing from the acronyms after a name or the entries on a CV. As the judge reminded jury members, juries should base their judgment on the evidence presented in court and should not conduct their own research, as did Henry Fonda's character in the movie *Twelve Angry Men*. This blank-slate approach applies as well to the credibility of experts and their areas of expertise. The adversarial tone of the interrogation and the seemingly peripheral issues it raises can dim even the brightest academic star.[35]

CREDIBILITY BY ASSOCIATION

Opposing attorneys further try to discredit court testimony as partisan, suggesting that the scientific expert did not really consider all available evidence but, motivated by external factors, jumped to a commonsensical conclusion (as the prosecution witnesses in the Woodward case were portrayed as having done) or a far-fetched one (in the case of the defense witnesses). This set of questions aims to undermine the independence, integrity, and objectivity of expert witnesses. During cross-examination, the counsels suggest a strong alliance between the other side's expert witnesses or between the witness and the side to which the witness belongs. Medical examiners in Massachusetts are state employees, and because this case pitted the Commonwealth of Massachusetts against Louise Woodward, the pathologists testifying for the prosecution could have easily been presented as cronies of the prosecutors. The impression of independent expertise was further complicated by the multiple consultations between district attorneys and medical examiners during the forensic investigation.[36] I watched medical examiners at my research site meet with law enforcement officers and officials from the attorney general's office to discuss preliminary findings and generate a consensus about the evidence. Before consulting with defense attorneys, the medical examiners notified the attorney general's office. Strict rules determine which parts of the autopsy file can be turned over to defense attorneys (even if everything was subpoenaed). One common defense strategy, therefore, is to undermine medical examiners by tying them to the prosecution.

Interestingly, while occasionally questioning Dr. Feigin's conclusions, Scheck treated the pathologist as a supportive witness on cross-examination. Dr. Feigin denied that he had met with prosecutors to discuss the case, and Scheck acknowledged that he had met with the "gracious and kind" pathologist at an earlier time.[37] Although Scheck pointed out in his cross-examination of Dr. Feigin and others that the defense had been unable to conduct a second autopsy and referred to the pictures Dr. Feigin had taken as "prosecution pictures,"[38] he relied on the forensic pathologist's testimony to weaken the prosecution's case. The medical examiner (Feigin) and the consulting neuropathologist (DeGirolami) did not believe that Matthew had been shaken. They asserted that he died from impact alone. Scheck emphasized the discrepancy between the opinion of the medical examiner and those of other prosecution witnesses.

Q: Now, I notice, Doctor, that in your autopsy report, and in your testimony here today, you did not give as a mechanism here, or a contributing cause of death, shaken-baby, is that correct?

A: That's correct.

Q: And you know Dr. Eli Newberger, do you not?

A: I met him for the first time on another case last week.

. . .

Q: And so you do have disagreements with Dr. Newberger about this so-called shaken-baby syndrome, or shaken impact baby syndrome.

. . .

A: I had some disagreements with him, yes.

Q: Now, with respect to this case, and your findings, from the autopsy of Matthew Eappen, would your findings be consistent with this baby being taken and shaken back and forth violently for about a minute, its head moving uncontrollably back and forth?

A: No.

Q: And I take it the reason for that is that you don't see any evidence of any injuries to the neck or the spinal cord that would be consistent with such a violent shaking.

A: That's just part of it. The other part is there was a skull fracture which you don't get just from shaking.

. . .

Q: But I'm only asking you about whether or not the autopsy evidence is consistent with violent shaking back and forth for the minute, are you with me?

A: No, it isn't consistent with that. [39]

Scheck elicited here the impression that even the state's medical examiner doubted the prosecution's theory. The pathologist saw no evidence indicating shaking. To bolster his allegation that the clinicians had jumped to conclusions, Scheck emphasized the difference of opinion between Drs. Feigin and Newberger. Dr. Feigin countered the impression of conspiring with defense counsel, however, by detailing the extent of his postmortem investigation and relating his opinions to forensic findings. In other parts of the cross-examination, Scheck suggested that Dr. Feigin drew the wrong conclusions from the evidence and mistook artifacts for significant findings. In the argument phases of the trial, however, he cast doubt not on the credibility of Dr. Feigin, but on Dr. Newberger and the prosecutors, whom he scathingly characterized as overzealous witch hunters.

The prosecution attorneys also employed discursive means to suggest that defense witnesses were biased partisans. Coakley, for example, began her cross-examinations with questions about how much each witness was billing the defense (the amounts varied from $250 to $900 per hour) and how many hours they had spent on the case. Her goal was to create the impression that the defense experts were simply hired guns. In addition, she asked these experts whether they testified only for defendants, and she spent much of the cross-examination disentangling which opinions were originally formulated by the expert and which were developed in collaboration with other defense experts. Such questions portray an expert witness as a mouthpiece for the defense rather than an independent specialist.

THE SCIENTIFIC AUTHORITY OF FORENSIC PATHOLOGY

The court system has formal procedures for admitting scientific evidence. Based on the 1993 U.S. Supreme Court ruling in *Daubert v. Merrell Dow Pharmaceuticals, Inc.* and two subsequent cases,[40] four criteria determine the admissibility of scientific evidence: (1) Is the science based on a testable hypothesis? (2) Was it peer-reviewed? (3) Did it have a known or potential error rate? (4) Was it generally accepted within the relevant scientific community? In an article discussing the application of the *Daubert* criteria to forensic identification sciences, legal scholar Michael Saks distinguishes between forensic sciences drawn from basic sciences (e.g., forensic chemistry, derived from chemistry) and the identification sciences aimed at connecting an object or subject to a crime scene (such as the analysis of fingerprints, tire, firearms, and bite wounds). Saks concludes that the latter sciences would have great difficulty meeting the *Daubert* criteria.[41] Forensic pathology draws from both the basic sciences and the identification sciences, but the base of its knowledge is the autopsy—which, in spite of its century-long history, does not meet the criteria for testability and error rates. Instead, its science is based on accumulated experience. Because of its inclusive and normative character, several observers argue that forensic pathology should be held to a high evidentiary standard that it might not pass.[42] Forensic pathologists absorb advances in adjoining fields, but little new knowledge supports the science of the autopsy. Surprisingly, considering the adversarial character of trials, defense lawyers have not consistently applied the *Daubert* criteria to forensic pathology.[43] The Woodward trial was no exception. There, the attorneys limited themselves to circumscribing the scientific power of forensic pathology, identifying the questions pathologists can and cannot answer.

The main struggle during the trial occurred between bench scientists—particularly the defense experts in biomechanics, who on the basis of theoretical models questioned whether shaking could lead to lethal injuries—and the clinicians who treated Matthew Eappen and claimed that he had died from shaken-baby syndrome. In closing arguments, the prosecution referred to the biomechanical experts as "arrogant" "back-seat-drivers, Monday-morning-quarterbacks" who relied on "guinea pigs" to explain the case,[44] while the defense painted the clinicians as people who made a "snap judgment, . . . who abandoned careful, critical, objective scientific scrutiny of these facts."[45] Underlying this major divide were countless smaller fissures about disciplinary boundaries and domains of expertise, two of which pertained to forensic pathology.

One point of contention related to the inclusiveness of forensic pathology; here, Dr. Baden differed from the other pathologists. Drs. Feigin, DeGirolami, and Leestma viewed forensic pathology *conservatively*, emphasizing the specialized subject matter of the discipline. Dr. Feigin described his specialty as drawing inferences from pathological data. Dr. Leestma distinguished objective evidence from circumstantial evidence and emphasized that his expertise lay with the former. He added, "Ultimately, I have to go to the material to see whether the supposition A matches up with the evidence and the material that I look at."[46] Dr. Baden, in contrast, embraced a more *expansive* view of forensic pathology. He defined it as a "horizontal specialty,"[47] incorporating information from other specialties and experts in order to explain injuries. He saw forensic pathology as an overarching discipline, integrating evidence in a final interpretation. This difference affected the opinions the experts were willing to offer. Dr. Feigin and the neuropathologist remained close to the forensic evidence. Dr. Feigin, for example, refused to interpret CT (computed tomography) scans and brain X-rays. Dr. Baden, in contrast, readily repeated the neuroradiology and neuropathology opinions of other expert witnesses.

This open-ended strategy backfired, however, when Dr. Baden was asked to explain the evidence on which he based his opinion that the forearm and skull fractures were weeks old. He had initially stated that the injuries were at least twenty-four hours old. But only weeks before the trial, along with all the other defense witnesses, he changed his opinion and decided that they were weeks old. On cross-examination, he explained the expanded time frame by the argument that he had lacked sufficient information. Because Dr. Baden claimed expertise in neuropathology and neuroradiology, Coakley reviewed the visual evidence in detail. After a lengthy cross-examination, Dr. Baden admitted that he had not reached this opinion independently but instead had followed the interpretive lead of Drs. Leestma and Gean. This admission cast doubt on Dr. Baden's independence. According to the rules of evidence, a witness can testify only to issues of which that witness has personal knowledge. An expansive view of forensic pathology has a great potential payoff for the defense, because it helps integrate diverse pieces of evidence, but it carries a greater risk to credibility.[48]

The second point of contention about the jurisdiction of forensic pathology also emerged in cross-examination of Dr. Baden. The pathologist's major contribution to undermining the prosecution's theory was his claim that the skull fracture and the underlying membrane known as the dura mater, or dura, showed signs of healing and so could not have been days old but must have existed for weeks. Coakley confronted Dr. Baden's testimony with neuroradiological principles about aging fractures and subdural hematoma expounded in Dr. Gean's book. After Dr. Baden identified calcium deposits in one of the CT images of Matthew's skull, Coakley stated that, according to Dr. Gean's book, calcium deposits are visible only after six months to a year. The assertion challenged Dr. Baden's ability to offer such precise dating. Coakley here touched on a sore point relating to forensic pathologists' authority. Which are more objective in dating injuries: imaging technologies or autopsies? In hospitals, imaging technologies have contributed to the decline of autopsies, and radiologists have usurped much of the traditional clinical jurisdiction of pathologists. Dr. Baden, following the line of forensic pathologists, adamantly asserted that forensic pathology allows investigators to see things that might not be visible on X-rays, MRIs, or CT scans. He repeatedly corrected Coakley, who suggested that pathologists take X-rays to confirm fractures: "No, you're going backwards. I do a microscopic slide, as it was done here, to confirm what has happened to the bone. The X-ray is much more general than the autopsy and a microscopic slide. If we see something that looks like a fracture on an X-ray, we want to confirm it by autopsy. And oftentimes at an autopsy we find fractures that are not picked up on X-rays."[49] In fact, at my research site, pathologists first looked at X-rays for a general orientation, then conducted an autopsy, and finally took sections for microscopic evaluation. By slightly twisting the sides of the ribs and moving over them with gloved fingers, they often discovered fractures in bones that looked pristine on X-rays.

To what extent can the discipline of forensic pathology reveal the truth about past events? This trial does not discredit the scientific authority of forensic pathology. A major area of contention could have been whether pathologists can date injuries at all. After admission to the hospital, Matthew Eappen spent several days in intensive care on a ventilator, potentially creating pathological artifacts. Furthermore, little is empirically known about dating injuries in eight-month-old infants. Rather than exploring these uncertainties in forensic pathology's stock of knowledge, the prosecution and defense teams circumvented the uncertainty around dating because both theories relied on analysis of fractures, and a too-radical skepticism would have quickly turned counterproductive.[50] None of the attorneys or expert witnesses assailed forensic pathology as a scientific discipline in order to reveal a medicolegal truth. Instead, Scheck repeatedly stated that the defense should have had an opportunity to conduct a second autopsy. Dr. Leestma emphasized the importance of documenting autopsy findings for independent verification. Nonpathologists also stressed the importance of pathology in resolving controversies about dating of injuries. For example, Dr. Ommaya, a neurosurgeon and biomechanical specialist, stated in reference to the blood clot, "The pathology is always the final answer in terms of taking all the clinical information and making the sequence of events and the mechanism complete."[51] The authority of forensic pathology as a medicolegal discipline thus emerged from the trial largely unharmed. The same cannot be said of the credibility of individual pathologists and neuropathologists.

CREDIBILITY OF EVIDENCE FOUND AND NOT FOUND

At the beginning of the trial, the court clerk instructed the members of the jury to "harken to the evidence."[52] Most of the examinations by Leone, Coakley, and Scheck consisted of a review of clinical and pathological evidence leading to a solicited expert opinion about its meaning. Several categories of pathological evidence mattered at the trial: evidence available (fractures observed, tissues collected, and test results obtained); evidence unavailable because it was allegedly missing or because a test was not performed; and evidence critical in light of the defense or prosecution theory. The latter category is less about evidence itself than about the plausibility of an entire theory.

Evidence occupies the domain of what forensic pathologists *do* rather than who they are, whom they associate with, or what discipline certifies them. As hours of testimony explain how pathologists conduct their work, attorneys ask leading questions, insinuating that an investigation failed to follow appropriate procedures or that the chain of custody was not maintained. The law stipulates that forensic facts can be entered in evidence only if they can be proven to have come from the corpse. Because a trial follows postmortem investigations, however, anticipating which evidence will matter is difficult. Evidence often becomes significant only in light of a proposed theory. Even if the pathologist has an obsessive eye for detail, one more test could probably have been done or one more section taken. Evidence is indeterminate.[53] The task for forensic pathologists is to conform to their field's standard operating procedures. Even then, expertise is reconstructed de novo in the context of a trial. Inevitably, the lengthy interrogations that forensic pathologists face in court inform and influence the conduct of their investigations.

The Hands-On Expertise of Drs. Feigin and DeGirolami

Q: Sir, could you describe what an autopsy is, in general, for the ladies and gentlemen of the jury.

A: An autopsy is an examination of a deceased body where you do an external examination, which is looking at the skin for the presence or absence of injuries, and other normal and abnormal findings. Then I would do an internal examination where I look at all of the organs from the brain down through the pelvis. Sometimes special things, like examining the skeleton, and then try to determine trauma or lack of trauma, disease, lack of disease, and then come up with cause of death.[54]

Dr. Feigin explained what an autopsy is without offering much detail about conducting an external or internal examination. His audience accepted his account of an autopsy as a standard forensic procedure consisting of consecutive steps. His explanation achieved what historians Steven Shapin and Simon Schaffer call "virtual witnessing": he invoked scientific procedures to secure his credibility.[55] None of his forensic findings were disputed, but questions arose instead about the meaning of the evidence.

Dr. Feigin did not perform the autopsy on the brain and dura of Matthew Eappen. When he noticed the soft condition of the brain and its neuropathological relevance, he fixed it in formalin (a formaldehyde solution) and asked a consulting neuropathologist to examine the brain materials. The brain was examined by Dr. DeGirolami, Dr. Douglas Anthony, and Dr. Matthew Frosch. Dr. DeGirolami testified. In anticipation of an adversarial cross-examination, the prosecution asked him to describe his procedures in detail.

Q: I'd like to ask you some questions regarding your procedure, observations, and findings during the course of that examination, Doctor. How did you conduct the microscopic examination, how was it done?

A: The way it's done is, samples—at the time of the gross examination, samples of tissue are removed and are put into small cassettes.

Q: And how were those samples removed in this case?

A: In this case, they were removed by our team, one of the members of our team.

Q: And which member was that?

A: Dr. Anthony.

Q: And how is it done? Specifically, what do you do to take these sections?

A: You, with a scalpel, you take a little bit, you take a sample, a little bit of brain tissue, and you put the sample into a little cassette. And then you take this cassette and you process it for, embed the tissue in a wax, and then you cut the sections on a microtome, stain them, and then examine them under a microscope.

Q: And what do these little—was that a paraffin block, those wax blocks?

A: Yes, a paraffin block. I have a sample of it here if you'd like to see it.

Q: Well, is what you've brought with you today, is that—well, what is it?

A: It shows a cassette, and it shows paraffin, and it shows a, you know, a piece of gauze that has been put in there. It's just a sample. . . .

Q: Now, what is the table, if you will, what are you doing these cuts, what did you do the cuttings on? Where does it take place?

A: It takes place at the medical examiner's office. There is a board, so-called "cork board," I believe it's made out of cork. And upon this board, with a scalpel, individual little samples of tissue are taken and then put into one of these cassettes.

Q: So on this board, the brain is placed, and the brain is cut on this board.

A: That's right.[56]

In contrast to Dr. Feigin's quick summary of an autopsy, Dr. DeGirolami described routine neuropathological work, seemingly too banal to require reflection. How could it matter to Louise Woodward's guilt or innocence that the neuropathologist cut the sections on a corkboard? "Virtual witnessing" works as a means of persuasion only if a relevant community is willing to accept the disciplinary conventions of routine work. In light of the allegation of tampering with neuropathological evidence, routine work becomes extraordinary. The prosecution hoped that spelling out the steps of gathering samples would create trust through transparency. Yet having to describe mundane work drew attention. The neuropathologist was in a defensive position, the transparency inevitably clouded over. Why did the pathologist decide to cut here and not there, to take a sample from this part of the dura but not that part? The answers come from years of experience, from knowing where the interesting issues might lie. Yet those answers were unsatisfactory. Scheck insinuated that what was interesting also stemmed from Dr. DeGirolami's association with the prosecution.

A: . . . But the experienced neuropathologist, that's what we do all the time, we judge the, on gross, when we cut the sections, we judge where the microscopic sections should be taken on the basis of our experience. It would be very impractical to actually serially section through the entire brain for microscopic sections. So that we choose, at the time of gross examination, to the best of our ability and knowledge, which ones are the areas that are worthy of examination. And in this particular case, what you've shown me there looks like an acute lesion.

Q: All right. The point is, I think as you've just testified, that you do not obviously take sections of every piece of the brain, right?

A: Yes.

Q: One takes sections of the pieces that you think are of particular interest, right?

A: Yes, that's correct.

    . . .

Q: Well, Doctor, there are biases that enter into scientific examination that come from expectation, true?

A: Well, that's just the nature of our practice.

Q: Well, isn't it a well known scientific principle that there's something called an "expectation bias"?

A: I don't know.

. . .

Q: Would it be fair to say, Doctor, that sometimes, if you have an expectation that you're going to see one thing, that might bias you in your selection of materials, and you fail to see another?

A: Well, I can't comment on that.

Q: Never happened to you?

A: I don't know if it "never" happened to me, but I cannot comment on that supposition.[57]

Highlighting untested assumptions about forensic work, assumptions that tacitly inform the production of knowledge, challenges forensic credibility. The professional solution is to routinize practice by formulating a set of rules and standards. Dr. Feigin, for example, implied that his autopsy followed standard procedures. As Dr. DeGirolami experienced here, rules and procedures are prime targets when credibility is being challenged. The new issue becomes whether the practice corresponds to the rule. As philosophers and sociologists of science and technology long ago established, formal guidelines can never capture the full spectrum of activities and skills needed to execute even the simplest task.[58] Inevitably, discrepancies and shortcuts can be accentuated in cross-examination.

Dr. DeGirolami's credibility was thus tainted by the allegation that he biased his data to support the prosecution's theory. After Dr. DeGirolami described the trauma to the brain,[59] Scheck showed him an enlargement of Dr. Leestma's dura slides and asked him to interpret them. Dr. DeGirolami stated that they all represented acute lesions, adding, "I would doubt that Dr. Leestma and I would disagree on this issue." Scheck replied ominously, "That remains to be seen."[60] The next assault on Dr. DeGirolami's credibility came from Dr. Leestma, who not only disputed all of Dr. DeGirolami's conclusions but also cast doubt on the selection and preparation of the dura sections.

What we have here is, if you can visualize the dura as a thin piece of paper, thin piece of cardboard, maybe like an index card. And if we want to look at it, the proper way to examine this is to make a slice of it and embed it on edge. So that when we make our paraffin sections, we're looking at both sides of the specimen. . . . What has happened here is that this cross section has then flopped over, so that we're making a plane section, that is, instead of looking at the edge of the dura, we're looking at the dura cut on its flat side. And that makes examination and analysis extremely difficult with a thin structure because you can't see the other side, you're only seeing something in the middle.[61]

This is the nightmare scenario for expert witnesses. That Dr. DeGirolami did not actually prepare the dura section himself (one laboratory technician processed all the samples) mattered little. Counterexperts gain credibility by correcting and casting doubt on their colleagues. Those who did the original work were at a disadvantage, because the other party can impose a high standard and conclude that the work was insufficient.

Dr. Leestma had an opportunity to conduct his own neuropathological investigation of the brain. In anticipation of Dr. Leestma's review of his findings, Scheck asked him about good pathological practice in selecting dura slides.

Q: Now, Dr. Leestma, in working in forensic neuropathology, when examining the dura as depicted in this photograph in the center, what kind of practice is good practice in terms of your observations of discolorations and the process of sectioning? How should that be done?

A: Well, in selecting these areas and making the proper sections, virtually anything that's discolored on the dura is a suspect lesion. That is, it could be abnormal. The dura normally has a parchment-like quality and is egg white, egg-shell white. So if one sees any area of discoloration, such as I'm pointing to in the photograph, these dark areas (indicating), those should be sampled.

Q: Now, Dr. Leestma, is it a good practice for a neuropathologist to just look at dura that looks brown and make an eyeball judgment that it's acute and not older?

A: Well, you can do that in the gross examination, I mean that's perfectly appropriate, but these areas should be sampled for histologic examination. And by that I mean, make slides like these, look at them under the microscope, because you can miss many things by just leaving it after gross observation.[62]

While this principle of selecting sections is similar to the account provided by Dr. DeGirolami, the question-and-answer session established Dr. Leestma as an expert who follows standard neuropathological practice by taking multiple samples of potentially interesting findings in the dura.[63] Dr. Leestma took a swipe at Dr. DeGirolami, who selected only one dura sample and seemed to have missed several potentially interesting parts of the brain. An impromptu question by the judge, however, forced Dr. Leestma to acknowledge that his own slides contained preparation artifacts.

JUDGE: Doctor, what is that sort of Y-shaped?

DR. LEESTMA: This is what you're referring to, Your Honor? This is an artifact of preparation, because these pieces of tissue—you can see it right here in the 90–1, where these specimens are prepared, they're sliced very thin with a razor-blade-like knife on a microfilm, paraffin material. And when they put them down on a hot-water bath to cause them to flake out so they can pick them up with a glass slide, frequently pieces of tissue fold over one another.

JUDGE: So that has nothing, that's not of any significance to any issue before this jury, am I correct?

DR. LEESTMA: Of no significance at all.[64]

The major offensive against Dr. DeGirolami's credibility, however, came with the allegation that evidence had been lost on his watch. Scheck had made his legal reputation in the acquittal of O. J. Simpson, where he argued, in part, that forensic evidence was mishandled by racist agencies out to frame the former football star.[65] At the Woodward trial, the defense team argued that both the blood clot removed during surgery and the skull fracture should have been preserved and that crucial pieces of the brain and the dura were missing, despite a court order to preserve them. The defense had also asked to conduct a second autopsy but was denied that opportunity by the parents of Matthew Eappen.[66] The defense then filed a pretrial admissibility motion asking for the charges to be dismissed because of prejudice due to missing pieces of dura and brain tissue. This motion was denied, but the judge allowed the defense to raise the possibility of missing tissue during the trial. The prosecution therefore preemptively asked the pathologist and neuropathologist whether any brain tissue had been discarded after the cutting. Dr. Feigin answered categorically, "No, none whatsoever," and stated that documentation of the evidence had been adequate. Dr. DeGirolami agreed that no tissue was missing.

On cross-examination of the neuropathologist, Scheck engaged him in a lengthy discussion about the missing dura pieces. At a pretrial hearing in September, Dr. DeGirolami had testified that when making a section of the dura, he cut out a square of three to four centimeters and then took a smaller section for the paraffin block to make the slide. Dr. DeGirolami, who at the time of his examination of the dura had not known about the court order to save every scrap of material, added that the remainders had been "discarded." Before the trial started, however, he contacted the prosecution counsel and told them that he had consulted with the other neuropathologists and that nothing of the dura had been discarded. This discrepancy, recorded in various documents, became the target of the examination.

Q: Okay. And did you then testify that, "the remaining section from the right parietal area of the dura was," to use your words, "discarded"?

. . .

A: Yes, I did say it.

Q: And when you said it, you were sworn to tell the truth, and you were testifying at that time to what you thought was the truth.

A: That's right.

Q: And did you also testify at that hearing, that the left parietal three by four centimeter squarish section that you took, you cut, "was then also discarded"?

A: I believe that was my testimony.

Q: And that was discarded without even a small section being taken from it and preserved in a paraffin block. That was your testimony.

A: It was.

Q: And, in fact, as far as you know as you sit here today, no small section at all remains from that squarish cut from the left parietal section of the dura.

A: If my recollection was correct at the time.[67]

In these drawn-out questions, Scheck added a nuance to each phrase, emphasizing Dr. DeGirolami's earlier testimony about "discarding" evidence. Confronted with his changed testimony, the neuropathologist offered the only reconciliation possible: he was originally wrong.

Q: Did you then conclude, after talking with Dr. Anthony, that whatever missing sections of dura existed, were put back in the bucket?

A: After speaking with Dr. Anthony and Frosch, they both were emphatic that no tissue is ever discarded in these cases.

Q: Well, are you—

A: So my recollection was wrong.

Q: Did you—

A: My recollection was wrong.[68]

Dr. DeGirolami had to admit not only that his previous testimony was wrong, but also that when he later looked in the bucket in which the tissue was supposed to have been saved, he failed to find the scraps of dura and did not measure the entire dura. These admissions were dramatic because the defense elicited them gradually, in front of the jury. Dr. DeGirolami was attempting, seemingly for the first time, to reconcile a discrepancy. Instead of virtual witnessing, the jury was present at the actual interpretation of evidence. The admission followed the format of a confession, a powerful legal trope. In re-cross-examination, the neuropathologist repeated that his testimony at the pretrial hearing was due to "erroneous recollection."[69] His admission capped the confession of sloppiness and undermined his professional credibility. The jury then had to decide whether it was the neuropathologist's memory or his evidence gathering that was faulty.

Having undermined Dr. DeGirolami's credibility with allegations of selection bias and incompetence in tissue selection and preparation, and with an admission of "erroneous recollection," Scheck used a leading question to suggest that the doctor had not adequately documented the chain of custody for evidence.

Q: So, in other words, there aren't any documents in existence that indicates who went, where they went, what they did, when they went in and out of the medical examiner's office, cut sections of the brain, put them in the bottle; there is no paper trail or documentation that shows who did what to what sections of the brain, right?

A: Well, there is a record that, when the additional sections, the additional five sections arrived and were logged in by the technician, there is a record of that. And I have, you know, checked that.

Q: Well, there's a record that somebody logged something in, but it doesn't identify what, or whom, or—

A: It does, it does. It identifies it very clearly. It identifies the four, how many— the four additional sections that were put through. It does identify it.

Q: Well, just so that we have no more confusion about any of this, Dr. DeGirolami—

A: Yes.

Q: —if it hasn't been clear before, and with leave of the Court, could I ask you to produce—

A: Yes.

Q: —every piece of paper—

A: Yes.

Q: —that could be used to reconstruct and document what happened.

A: Yes, yes, I can do that this afternoon.

Q: Well, please. As a matter of fact, Dr. DeGirolami, arrangements have been made for you and Dr. Leestma this afternoon to go back and look at the brain.

A: Yes, I'll give it to you, yes.[70]

When Scheck suggested that notes should document who physically put the brain in a bottle, he offered an idealized standard for a chain of custody that few forensic practitioners could meet.[71] Documenting such details goes beyond the customary handling of evidence in the medical examiner's office, where written records are required only when evidence changes hands. Again, by playing on the discrepancy between idealized and actual practice, Scheck set Dr. DeGirolami up to go wrong, suggesting that he failed even to understand a "true" chain of custody. Dr. DeGirolami thus made another potentially damaging acknowledgment that facilitated Scheck's admonition, in a tone like a parent dealing with a recalcitrant child, to produce all necessary paperwork. Dr. DeGirolami's assent confirmed his failure to meet the legal standard. Dr. Leestma then reinforced the impression of sloppiness in neuropathological procedures when he described the missing dura pieces as "really the bull's-eye of the medical problem that was going on."[72]

At no point did Dr. Leestma or Scheck suggest that Dr. DeGirolami was intentionally mishandling evidence. Instead, they drew a picture of untrustworthiness in this legal case. Dr. DeGirolami might be a well-respected neuropathologist at Brigham and Women's Hospital—but he was, they implied, in this case guilty of selection bias, violating a court order by discarding evidence, bad tissue preparation, and "erroneous recollection." His work did not meet the standard of a medicolegal investigation. Therefore, in this case, he was not a credible witness.

The Hands-On Expertise of Dr. Leestma

Although Scheck and Dr. Leestma devastated Dr. DeGirolami's credibility, Dr. Leestma's claims to expertise were also tarnished on cross-examination. Dr. Leestma created his own evidence when he took additional dura samples, and his gathering and handling of this evidence also received scrutiny. Coakley, who entered the trial as the local underdog and lacked Scheck's national reputation, proved to be his equal in tenacity of cross-examination. Not only did she back Dr. Leestma into a defensive position with quotations from his own book, but she also questioned his credibility as a practicing pathologist.

Coakley initially followed a strategy different from Scheck's. Rather than suggesting incompetence, she questioned the significance of the evidence itself, drawing attention to small pieces of dura tissue with important implications for the case. She first pointed out that Dr. Leestma's entire theory—and by implication the defense's theory—was based solely on four slides of dura and disregarded other evidence from credentialed experts.

That opinion is based upon the information that you derived from taking the four slides of dura and saying, "Ah ha, I have found something now that is different from what the surgeons saw at Children's, from what the autopsy report showed, from what the neuropathologist saw, from what the child abuse specialist saw, and I think that it's an old subdural," and that's what you've come here today to tell us.

The neuropathologist replied, "That's right."[73] Later in the cross-examination, Dr. Leestma admitted that only two sections conclusively showed evidence of an older injury. Coakley then questioned the preparation of the slides and highlighted the order of magnification: "You're looking at this little tiny section, you're telling us that on this tiny, tiny, tiny fragment is evidence of an old subdural hematoma, is that correct?"[74]

Coakley further isolated Dr. Leestma's evidence by asking whether an untrained eye would notice the neomembrane. Dr. Leestma answered, "Probably not, unless I point it out." The judge interjected, "Then it becomes a trained eye."[75]

Here the step from forensic evidence to expert opinion appears to be a leap. Coakley contrasted a lay perception of the world with the authoritative vision of the expert witness, opposing two cultures of belief. The prosecution theory relied on what would be common sense to an educated lay audience: if a caretaker was alone with a child and that child died of severe head trauma, any layperson could see that the caretaker carried responsibility for the death. In contrast, Coakley portrayed the defense theory as far-fetched, based on minute, nearly invisible pieces of evidence that contradicted the opinions of clinicians and other scientists. She raised the ante for credibility. The prosecution thus depended not only on the words of its experts, but also on the jury members' experience. In contrast, the credibility of the defense theory depended completely on an expert's seeing something in "tiny, tiny, tiny" pieces of tissue.

Coakley also managed to highlight some weaknesses in Dr. Leestma's allegation of missing dura and brain matter. The neuropathologist granted that in his first examination of the brain, he did not know that brain pieces were missing. Only when Dr. Gean asked him for a specific piece of brain tissue did he recognize that brain pieces were missing. Similarly, when he looked at the dura, he saw only "fragments of dura" and so acknowledged that he did not know what pieces of dura were present before the autopsy. Coakley further pointed out that the dura tends to adhere to a child's brain, making sections difficult to remove. She asked Dr. Leestma to identify on a three-dimensional model the places from which he had taken dura samples; she noted that he could not point out the location of one of the specimens he had attributed to the area of the skull fracture. Dr. Leestma conceded, "I didn't know it when I took the section, but now my inference is that's where it came from."[76] Coakley thus demonstrated that Dr. Leestma's reconstruction came from memory and some notes jotted on a napkin. She implied that because he failed to record physical movement of the evidence on the appropriate forms, his documentation of the chain of custody also failed to follow standard protocols. Again, an attorney's cross-examination introduced a standard for the chain of custody that exceeded the reality of daily practice, setting up the witness to fall short.

Coakley also turned the tables on Dr. Leestma by asking why he did not order particular tests. For example, when discussing siderophages (a natural iron-binding compound) in the hematoma membrane, he mentioned, "I didn't have iron stains provided to me."[77] Picking up on this comment, Coakley asked for elaboration. Dr. Leestma answered that he did not receive the tests he had requested. Coakley could then insinuate that the defense had countered the request. By suggesting that the defense feared test results that would refute its theory, Coakley could question the doctor's objectivity and independence.

Witnessing the Drama of the Pictures

Of all the experts, the neuropathologists' credibility was most contested. Both sides presented allegations that impugned credibility: sloppiness in evidence gathering and handling, memory lapses, and defensiveness. After Dr. DeGirolami's acknowledgment of "erroneous recollection," Coakley managed to cast doubt on Dr. Leestma's claims about missing dura pieces and sloppy evidentiary procedures. The prosecution might have lost the case on the last day of the trial, however, when a forensic anthropologist in the medical examiner's office discovered pictures of Matthew's brain that had not been available to counsel on either side.[78] The belated discovery of the pictures was a bad day for the Massachusetts medical examiner's office. It represented a situation that all staff in any medical examiner's office, from administrators to forensic pathologists, try to avoid. They know that even an inadvertent mistake can allow the defense to allege manipulation or deliberate concealment of evidence. Prior to this incident, Scheck had repeatedly emphasized that the medical examiners had neglected to inform the consulting neuropathologist (Dr. DeGirolami) about the court order to preserve all evidence, and he expressed concern to the judge about being "sandbagged" with "something from a bucket."[79]

The pictures were material proof that evidence had been missing and that record keeping in the medical examiner's office was questionable. The emergence of the pictures amounted to a "real-time" enactment of lack of credibility—much stronger than Dr. DeGirolami's confession, because such "hard" evidence did not depend on other people's testimony.[80] Indeed, as soon as the pictures became available, the defense argued that they showed definite signs of healing in the skull fracture. The prosecution argued that the pictures were similar to those already in evidence, but Judge Zobel was not convinced. He allowed the defense to call Dr. Baden back to interpret the skull fracture. The pathologist remarked:

On the margins of the fracture is a little rounding and lipping of the fracture line on either side. That would indicate that there's part of a healing process in process, going on. It takes a few weeks to develop. These are not the sharp edges of a fresh fracture as if a plate is broken, and one gets sharp edges on the edge of a plate, is what happens to the skull when it breaks. But over the period of a few weeks, the edges become a little rounded as here (indicating), and there's a little lipping, and little excrescences form at the top that are apparent on the photograph. . . . When I say "lipping," as the healing process goes on, there's a little bit of calcium, where the bone tissue grows slightly above the margin in the healing process.[81]

On cross-examination, Coakley wondered why Dr. Baden had been unable to interpret the age of the tissue from other pictures, thus trying to downplay the importance of this new evidence. Still, because of the late analysis of evidence, a recalled witness, and hypersensitivity about expert credibility, the new pictures must have damaged the prosecutor's case.

The lengthy discussion of missing evidence during the trial had three legal purposes. First and most important, it fueled the claim for dismissal of charges due to prejudice. The defense had sought to establish conclusively that evidence had been lost and mishandled. Indeed, after the jury found Louise Woodward guilty of second-degree murder, the defense argued that the case should have been dismissed because the prosecution had deprived the defense's experts of access to crucial physical evidence, including pieces of dura and the skull fracture. In their motion for dismissal, they also listed the late appearance of the pictures. Second, the questioning of how evidence was gathered was aimed at undermining the trustworthiness of the experts in the eyes of the jury. Such discussions become personal, because they directly address the professional expertise of witnesses. Experts' independence, selection bias, and professional competence, as well as the relevance of evidence, are directly linked to a witness's credibility. Every action can thus become questionable. Third, missing data became legally the most important evidence. In a bench conference, for example, Scheck referred to the missing dura pieces as "extraordinarily powerful evidence, neuropathological evidence, with respect to the existence of this old subdural bleed."[82] Speculating about definitive tests that could have been conducted supports or undermines a theory.[83]

★ ★ ★

Taken together, the discussions of evidence in the Woodward trial reflect the core principles of professional, forensic expertise and provide a public lesson about how medical examiners should do their job. The adversarial discussion of evidence explains, first, why postmortem investigations are such comprehensive efforts with seemingly unnecessary procedures—why, for example, pathologists will conduct an extensive autopsy on a young boy who has obviously drowned in a pond. The cause of death of asphyxia due to drowning would become indefensible in court if the pathologists could not testify that they had checked for natural causes, such as disease, and that no unauthorized people had had access to the body. Without exploring what might be missing, pathologists' positive findings remain vulnerable. Second, courtroom interrogations also explain an obsession with paperwork. Testimony depends on written records. One mislabeled blood tube, one forgotten picture, can destroy years of professional credibility. Paperwork is thus closely scrutinized, checked, and rechecked before it leaves the medical examiner's office.

Third, the adversarial nature of courtroom exchanges explains why medical examiners might conclude that some attorneys and their clients are out to nail them. Their distrust can become a mentality; this is why medical examiners keep relatives and other outsiders at a distance during the investigative process. The same mentality accounts for why medical examiners routinely consult with law enforcement and district attorneys to make sure that everyone agrees about the evidence. As the medicolegal administrator at my research site explained, differences of opinion are possible, but they should be known in advance. A trial should have no surprises. Fourth, the courtroom interaction even explains medical examiners' tardiness in issuing autopsy reports. The medical examiners in the short-staffed office in my study preferred to be behind in filing autopsy reports if the alternative was issuing timely but slipshod reports that could haunt them if shortcomings were discovered.

CREDIBILITY AND PLAUSIBILITY OF OPINION: WHAT DOES IT ALL MEAN?

Opinionating constitutes the true battle of the experts and the core of cultural authority. When there are opposing opinions, scientific experts are called to educate the jury. In the Woodward case, the debates about experts' credibility were aimed at undermining opinions about the timing of Matthew Eappen's injuries and the plausibility of the other side's theories. The forensic experts all offered a broad variety of opinions. At the Woodward trial, they contested two issues: the age of the injuries and the broader controversy of shaken-baby syndrome. Dr. Feigin was instrumental in dating the lethal injuries as having occurred on February 4, while Drs. Leestma and Baden argued that the injuries were weeks old. All parties invoked various aspects of credibility and scientific and cultural authority in order to lodge or dislodge an opinion.

Sociological studies of controversy have documented how groups of experts appeal to nature (in this case, forensic evidence) in order to advance different theoretical accounts. In his work on scientific controversies, sociologist Harry Collins offers a variation of the Duhem-Quine thesis and emphasizes the "interpretative flexibility" of scientific data: evidence is never in itself sufficient to bring a controversy to closure. Instead, evidence can be infinitely interpreted in light of different theories by adjusting the overall conceptual or instrumental framework.[84] Closure of scientific controversies depends on social processes: the broader macrosocial interests of scientists,[85] negotiation about the rules of observing evidence and the interpretation of facts,[86] and the institutional politics through which scientific controversies are played out.[87] Resolving controversies, this reasoning suggests, requires reaching a tipping point—when one set of interests has become more powerful than the others.

In the courtroom, the mechanism of closure is ultimately prestructured: in determining whether the prosecution proved its case beyond a reasonable doubt, the jury and judge decide which side they believe. The two sides appropriate social closure mechanisms of scientific controversies in order to undermine the plausibility of the expert opinion. Opposing attorneys might, for example, try to undermine credibility by linking an expert's opinion to broader interests that suggest bias; the expert witnesses might explain their standards of practice to the jury and contest the other party's standards as insufficient. In the Woodward trial, the two alternative interpretations of the evidence were based on Louise Woodward's implied guilt or innocence and on existing medical theories. Expert opinions aim not to close a controversy—indeed, the adversarial nature of courtroom proceedings makes every qualification a point scored for the opposition— but to forge the strongest possible link between the evidence and a given interpretation.

Courtroom proceedings resemble as much a scientific contest as a controversy. The question-and-answer sequence constitutes a display of expertise in which coherence, consistency, and clarity are as important as the actual interpretation of evidence. The goal is not only to reconcile scientific evidence with a social agenda, but also to win the contest by transforming expertise into plausible persuasion. An expert opinion depends, therefore, on upgrading some evidence by defining it as solid and crucial while downgrading other evidence by declaring it irrelevant or artificial.[88] Applying forensic principles, experts articulate links that promote a position that simultaneously undermines the opponent's position. Locally established credibility becomes a precondition for the veracity of expert opinion and for the plausibility of the defense or the prosecution.

Opinions about the Age of the Injuries

For all his skepticism over whether shaking contributed to Matthew's death, Dr. Feigin was adamant that the lethal injuries occurred on February 4. The key piece of evidence for dating the injury consisted of "subgaleal swelling and hemorrhaging" that Feigin noticed in the scalp under the skull fracture. In redirect examination, prosecution counsel gave the pathologist an opportunity to explain the dating procedure, allowing him to expand on observations he had made during the autopsy:

The other part was that there was a large subdural associated with it. And when I see a skull fracture that's away from the parietal bone or the side of the head, when I see one that big with a subdural, and the subdural when it's removed is unclotted, and the residual portion I have is not really clotted either, a small piece had basically dissolved, I look at that, the sequelae, meaning the subdural, or the complications of the fracture. Then I look at the color of the bruise as well, and what color it is. Is it purple? If it's purple, it's fresh. If it turns yellow and green and brown, the way bruises heal, it's older. There was no color change, it was fresh.

One can try to age it under a microscope, but the reports were done on rabbit aging, and they're not very precise. Usually, an eyeball method works as well or better than anything else in the color change one would see with healing bruises. And there were no color changes at all associated with this skull fracture and the bruise over it. And I know the bruise is from the skull fracture because it came from the blood vessels by the skull fracture, not from outside of the scalp, but from the blood vessels immediately above the fractured bone.[89]

Dr. Feigin explained his reasoning by upgrading the importance of the subgaleal hematoma (swelling filled with blood). He based his judgment on his inspection of the size of the hematoma, its consistency and constitution, its relationship to the skull fracture and the other subdural hematoma, and, most important, its color. Then he justified the fact that he had not conducted a microscopic analysis by citing the lack of precise and presumably validated scales to date subdural hematomas. Finally, he explained how he knew that the subdural was related to the skull fracture. Dr. Feigin thus retraced his inference by relating characteristics of the evidence and standard methodological practices and minimizing the step from forensic evidence to expert opinion. He inserted a number of benchmarks[90]—forensically approved properties of the world—to argue for the validity of his conclusion.

The link that Dr. Feigin made between the hematoma and the skull fracture came under attack from defense experts. With CT scans from the surgery and photographs taken during the autopsy, Scheck suggested to Dr. Feigin that the subgaleal hemorrhage was an iatrogenic artifact of the surgery. He ran into difficulty, however, because Dr. Feigin did not feel qualified to interpret surgical CT scans and because the pictures alone were inadequate for distinguishing among injuries. Although Dr. Feigin's conservative strategy paid off, Scheck repeated the question sequence with other expert witnesses. Bone window 38 on a CT scan taken before the surgery became a crucial exhibit.[91] According to the defense witnesses, the bone window did not reveal the subgaleal hemorrhage; if it had been a fresh injury, it should have been visible on the scan. Dr. Leestma stated, "Just by cutting through these tissues, you break open blood vessels, and tissue is exposed to the air as the surgeon goes about his business; retractors, other instruments, are frequently in contact with the reflected scalp. There's all sorts of manipulations in it which have their own pathology, I guess if you will, and evolution, from which, through which it may be difficult to see what a preexisting injury might be."[92] Dr. Leestma concluded that the hemorrhaging was likely an artifact of the surgery; he thus neutralized a crucial piece of evidence, much as Coakley would do with his own data.

Dr. Baden not only reached the same conclusion as Dr. Leestma but also, under direct examination, criticized Dr. Feigin for failing to conduct an additional procedure that could have conclusively dated the subdural hematoma. He thus suggested that Dr. Feigin may not have been applying up-to-date forensic procedures.

Q: Now, Doctor, is there a procedure that could have been employed even at autopsy, beyond just examination of the C-T scans, to determine whether or not these hematomas were related?

A: Yes, to see if they were one continuous hematoma, yes.

Q: Aside from just visually looking.

A: Yes.

Q: And what would that procedure be?

A: To make incisions into the scalp tissue itself, to see if there was a connection between the top hemorrhage and the bottom hemorrhage.

Q: That's between the hematomas.

A: That's right. Because there's a space between the hematomas where there's no blood, but incisions would clarify whether or not there was a connection on the other side of that space, of the exposed soft tissues.

Q: That's blood flowing through tissue planes.

A: Through different tissue planes. So you have to look at all the different tissue planes.

Q: And, Doctor, do you have an opinion to a reasonable degree of scientific certainty whether the subgaleal hematoma in the area of the fracture site identified by Dr. Feigin was what is known as "iatrogenic" or caused by subsequent therapy?

A: Yes, it was not present when the child came into the, when the child came into the hospital, and it developed while in the hospital, so they call it "iatrogenic," as a natural consequence of the surgery.[93]

In this exchange, Dr. Baden challenged Dr. Feigin's appeal to standard forensic procedures while leaving forensic pathology's ability to settle controversial dating issues intact. This instance remained an isolated challenge to Dr. Feigin's credibility. Most important for the defense, Dr. Baden dismissed the significance of the evidence.

Dr. Baden's, however, was not the last word on the meaning of the subgaleal hemorrhage. By questioning Dr. Baden's basis for dismissing Dr. Feigin's opinion, Coakley undermined the defense pathologist's credibility. Questions about Dr. Baden's credibility emerged principally from the many opinions he formulated during a short direct examination. In a much longer cross-examination, Coakley created a classic "witness dilemma," in which she asked the doctor to agree to a number of "reasonable" statements that led to a conclusion he would likely reject.[94] The result was an apparent contradiction. In effect, Dr. Baden was "enjoined to adhere to elementary norms of consistency and coherence, while being led step-by-step to admit contradiction and yield to the interrogator's position."[95] In the first part of the exchange, Coakley summarized Dr. Baden's direct testimony in absolute terms:

Q: Doctor, you told us today that you didn't believe, besides the evidence about Dr. Leestma and the aging of the skull fracture, you said that you didn't believe there was a recent skull fracture because you didn't see anything on the C-T scan; you didn't see any subgaleal swelling on the C-T scans, is that correct?
A: That's, I did say that, yes, and that's an important aspect.

She then played on Dr. Baden's expansive approach to forensic pathology by pointing out that he reviewed CT scans even though he lacked formal training in neuroradiology.

Q: And you reviewed the C-T scans, correct?
A: Yes.
Q: Although I know you look at C-T scans in your work, but you are not a neuroradiologist, are you, Doctor?
A: That's correct, I am not a neuroradiologist.
Q: And you're not a pediatric neuroradiologist, are you?
A: That's correct, I'm not.

Although Dr. Baden acknowledged that he was not a trained neuroradiologist, Coakley initiated questions about the difference between the skulls of children and those of adults. She was allowed to pursue such questions because Dr. Baden claimed expertise in reading CT scans. Cautiously, Dr. Baden agreed to her "reasonable" general statement but qualified his response to minimize the effect, offering only provisional agreement.[96]

Q: But you are aware, are you not, based on your training and experience, that children's skulls, particularly in the area of the occiput, are very different in some respects from adult skulls, isn't that true?

A: Slightly different, yes.

Q: They're "slightly different" by your words. And one of the reasons that they're slightly different is because there's a greater material of fatty tissue that a child has in that area of the occiput, isn't that true?

A: Yes, yes.

Q: So that if there is an impact in that area, even if it causes a fracture, there's going to be a greater percentage of the impact or trauma that gets absorbed by that tissue, is that fair to say, Doctor?

A: I think that's fair, yes.

In the next sequence, Dr. Baden seemed to sense the trap and asked for a repetition of the question. Coakley suggested that the difference between the skulls of adults and children might offer an alternative explanation for the lack of subgaleal swelling on the bone scan done before the surgery. Dr. Baden again minimized the possible effect.

Q: And that would affect the time and degree to which you would see any evidence of that kind of swelling on a C-T scan, isn't that fair to say?

A: Can you repeat that? I'm sorry.

Q: Sure. Because of the way the child's head is at that age, at eight months, and because of that fatty tissue, that factor will affect both the timing and the degree to which you could expect to see swelling on a bone scan that's taken after an acute fracture in that area, isn't that true, Doctor?

A: I think it would have a minimal effect, a minimal effect.

Q: That's your opinion?

A: Yes.

Q: It would have some effect, do you agree?

A: It could. But the more important thing is the degree of trauma, but it could have a slight effect.

To counter the minimization, Coakley confronted Dr. Baden with his testimony given only an hour earlier. In response, the pathologist slightly revised his earlier testimony. Coakley emphasized Dr. Baden's revision to again portray him as someone who easily changes opinions. She then asked him to define the time frame.

Q: Well, you've already told us that you believe skull fractures can happen with some slight trauma, is that your testimony?

A: Yes.

Q: And so if that trauma on the skull fracture—strike that. Doctor, you indicated that, when you were asked by Mr. Scheck, that you would expect to see that kind of swelling a few hours later, did you not on direct testimony?

A: Yes, in less than a few hours.

Q: I'm sorry, what—

A: My opinion is, there would be swelling in less than a few hours.

Q: Didn't you say "in a few hours" when Mr. Scheck asked you that?

A: I may have, but I would—

Q: You want to change that now?

A: No. I mean within a few hours, within a few hours, is I believe what I said.

Q: Okay. Within two hours?

A: Sure, absolutely.

In the next sequence, the reason for the questioning becomes clear. Coakley argued that because of the difference between the skulls of adults and those of children, the subgaleal swelling might not have been apparent on the CT scan; the scan had been performed before the swelling took place, rendering the lack of swelling on the bone window meaningless. With this alternative spelled out, Scheck objected, and Dr. Baden refused to agree with Coakley. He was in a tough spot, however, because he had tentatively agreed with all the assumptions but refused to commit to their logical conclusion. He tried to return to the timing of the injury, but Coakley focused instead on the importance of the bone window. Their exchange thus became a struggle between prosecutor and witness, with Coakley attempting to lead Dr. Baden to an unfavorable conclusion and portray him as evasive.

Q: But you would agree that if this impact happened at 3:15 or 3:30, that when a child has a C-T scan at 5:10, which is under two hours, you wouldn't necessarily see any swelling, isn't that fair to say?

MR. SCHECK: Objection, vague, as to which impact and severity.

MS. COAKLEY: I'll ask it in a hypothetical then if you wish.

Q: Dr. Baden, if a child had an impact that caused a two-and-a-half inch fracture in his occiput at 3:30 in the afternoon, by your own testimony, you wouldn't necessarily expect to see swelling in that area by 5:00 or 5:10, would you?

A: I would expect to see swelling, yes.

Q: But the fact that you didn't, could not rule out that that child had a fracture in that area, could it, Doctor?

A: It wouldn't rule out that there was a fracture there, but it would rule out that it was a recent fracture.

Q: Well, that wasn't my question. You couldn't rule out, with that time frame, under two hours, that the child did not have a fracture at 3:30, could you, based on that one factor alone, that you didn't see any swelling on the C-T scan.

A: It would speak strongly against it.

Q: Let me ask the question again, Doctor: You couldn't rule it out, could you?

A: You're saying is it possible? Anything is possible. It's possible.

Coakley recapitulated the exchange, emphasizing Dr. Baden's apparent contradiction. He defended himself with a legal move: he is required to offer opinions with medical certainty, yet the scenario described was only a possibility. His conclusion then contradicted his earlier statements, suggesting that *in this case* the time frame for swelling did not apply.

Q: But you came and told this jury that you believe that that fracture could not have happened at that time, at least for one reason, because you saw no swelling.
A: That's correct.
Q: Is that fair to say?
A: I said it to a reasonable degree of medical certainty, not to all possibility.
Q: So my question to you is: Based upon what you know about the child's anatomy, and based upon your years of experience, the fact that you didn't see it on the bone scan says you can't rule out that it happened at 3:30, can you?
A: In my opinion, to a reasonable degree of medical certainty, it didn't happen within two hours.
Q: Okay, thanks, Doctor.[97]

Coakley's strategy was to depict Dr. Baden as someone who reaches conclusions quickly and draws inferences beyond the evidence presented. She undermined his credibility by drawing him into discussions of evidence that lay outside the narrow area of forensic pathology. Coakley not only managed to show that Dr. Baden might be expressing opinions about evidence he did not completely grasp but also allowed him to contradict himself and others. She lacked advantages such as a written testimony of "discarded" evidence, which Scheck had with Dr. DeGirolami; she lacked a witness who collected his own evidence, as Dr. Leestma did; but she had an expert eager to offer opinions. As cross-examination progressed, Coakley did not elaborate on the contradictions. Having compromised Dr. Baden's credibility with several witness's dilemmas and with his testimony at a previous child-abuse case in front of the same judge, she let the contradictory statements stand as verbal exhibits of a witness lacking credibility. She also returned to Dr. Baden's claim that Dr. Feigin should have used an extra procedure to date the subgaleal hemorrhage.

Q: Okay. So when you give us your opinion that you believe it was from these other things, you're just saying, "Gee, it would be nice if we had taken incisions, because that would show us definitively." But because that wasn't done, you can't say either way whether that bleeding was from surgery or something else. Isn't that true, Doctor?
A: No, that's not true.
Q: Okay, thank you.[98]

Dr. Baden's answer did not make sense. If, as he claimed, Dr. Feigin would have needed the additional procedure in order to properly date the hematoma at February 4, Dr. Baden would also have needed it to date the injury at three weeks. Coakley did not allow Dr. Baden to explain this contradiction. Having shown that the pathologist seemed prone to contradictions, she moved on to the next topic. Because it was understated, this exchange was devastating to Dr. Baden's credibility. Coakley so reduced his credibility that any difference of opinion he might have with a colleague would reflect not superior knowledge but idiosyncracy. Dr. Baden was isolated.

★   ★   ★

Expert opinion forms the summit of the credibility pyramid. Opinions gain credibility from the base of evidence from which they are drawn, the professional qualifications of the expert, the expert's independence, and the broader scientific authority of the discipline. In addition, expert opinions reinforce one another through consistency, clarity, and coherence over the course of a trial. The goal is adequate truthfulness, beyond a reasonable doubt.

The questioning of experts in direct and cross-examination provides a part of the professional script that guides the daily work of medical examiners. Courtroom exchanges determine the political scope of medical examiners' decision making. As a professional group, medical examiners tend to be conservative. Rarely do they assert far-fetched inferences or break new ground with death classifications. They tend to tie their opinions about the cause of death closely to the evidence, and when ambiguity prevails, they give the deceased the benefit of the doubt. Because attorneys scrutinize every statement for unwarranted inferences, the message to medical examiners is that they should stay very close to the evidence if they want to survive in the courtroom. Every opinion needs to be backed with a preponderance of evidence on which the pathologist is willing to testify. Dr. Baden's expansive approach invited an adversarial cross-examination. His advantage for the defense, besides his name familiarity and star quality as an expert, was his ability to make connections between dispersed opinions and pieces of evidence. Yet an experienced child-abuse prosecutor such as Martha Coakley could quickly show that these connections were not convincing.[99] Even without the media attention surrounding the Woodward trial, the message of courtroom testimony for medical examiners is to offer opinions cautiously and to ground them in evidence.

Medical examiners might become subjects of external investigation if they venture beyond the conservative limits of evidence interpretation. For example, Dr. Thomas Bennett, a former medical examiner in Iowa, relied predominantly on microscopic tearing and leakage in the brain to diagnose shaken-baby syndrome. In one case, he based the allegation on four specks of blood. Several of his cases did not show retinal hemorrhaging, skull fractures, or visible brain hemorrhaging. According to the majority opinion in the pathology community—including staunch advocates of shaken-baby syndrome—such minor leakage should be considered an artifact of removing the skull during autopsy. In several cases diagnosed by Dr. Bennett, prosecutors did not file charges or had to drop charges because no medical expert would support the pathologist. Once the lack of credibility became known, most of Dr. Bennett's seventeen cases of shaken-baby syndrome, diagnosed between 1989 and 1997, were reopened for independent review. Parents sentenced to jail were subsequently released. One pathologist-reviewer wrote: "I am reluctant to believe that Dr. Thomas Bennett would risk the credibility of his office as the Iowa state medical examiner by drawing the serious and far-reaching conclusions of 'shaken-baby syndrome' and 'homicide' based on these meager findings."[100] While Dr. Bennett considered himself to be at the forefront of an evolving field, his critics offered what is a grave epithet for a medical examiner: they called him an "advocate."

Opinions about the Shaken-Baby and "Bleed-Rebleed" Controversies

Expert opinions offered in a trial correspond to opposing sides in larger controversies about the plausibility of various proposed theories. At the Woodward trial, controversies that had been going on since shaken-baby syndrome was first described were revisited. The major issue was whether shaking is sufficient to kill an infant or whether an impact is also necessary. Most of these discussions took place during the testimony of Dr. Lawrence Thibault, the author of a paper describing experimental work that initiated the controversy. Drs. Feigin and DeGirolami supported the view that shaking, if it had occurred, was incidental to the death of Matthew Eappen. Instead, they asserted, he died of a deadly impact. Dr. Feigin explained the mechanism of death.

The mechanism is that the blunt trauma to the head caused a subdural hematoma, a large one, which is blood around the membranes of the brain, surrounding the brain. And when that was removed to preserve Matthew's life, there was a resultant rebound edema or swelling of the brain called "hydrostatic brain edema," where the brain immediately swells up rapidly and uncontrollably, and that caused the rest of the brain to swell up with it, the entire brain swells up, some more than others, and that causes the inability to breathe and maintain bodily functions. And that's the mechanism of death.[101]

The clinicians, on the other hand, based their opinion that shaking was a cause of death on the characteristic retinal hemorrhaging found in

Matthew's eyes upon his admission to the hospital and on other injuries consistent with child abuse. A dramatic point of the trial was when Dr. Newberger of Children's Hospital demonstrated one minute of shaking, the minimum time he claimed was necessary to have produced Matthew's injuries.

The defense proposed that the broader problem with shaken-baby syndrome is overzealous child advocates who, in spite of contradictory evidence, conclude that shaking must have caused a death. Shaking in itself is not lethal, the defense claimed, and shaken-baby syndrome unfairly blames caregivers for the deaths of children. Several defense witnesses hinted at this broader conspiracy, but prosecution counsel objected, arguing that it was not pertinent to the case at hand. For example, Dr. Leestma began to formulate the conspiracy but was stymied.

A: The issue of the so-called shaken-baby is a very complex one, it's one that has many problems for a lot of people involved in their contact and analysis of these cases. In conjunction with my medical examiner work, I have seen a number of cases that I think truly represent the so-called "shaken-baby syndrome." There are many instances in which this term is applied to fatally injured infants, I think incorrectly or without sufficient information. And in a sense, it is almost, to my chagrin and disappointment—

MS. COAKLEY: Judge, I'd move to strike as unresponsive to the question, the answer at this stage. It asks for a very specific opinion.

THE COURT: Well, it's discursively responsive. I think it would probably be a good idea, Doctor, to get to the point.[102]

The bleed-rebleed theory was also controversial. Coakley had already quoted Dr. Leestma's writings to suggest that it was a far-fetched defense theory that disregarded obvious evidence of trauma. When she cross-examined Dr. Leestma, she insinuated that the "talk-deteriorate-die" phenomenon, on which the bleed-rebleed theory is based, pertains principally to elderly institutionalized patients. Here, too, an objection was raised that such discussions were not relevant to the trial.

Q: Doctor, this notion that a subdural bleeds and re-bleeds, that we know mostly from looking at what happens in chronic subdurals in older people, isn't that fair to say?

A: In anyone.

Q: But what happens in older people particularly is, people get older and the brain shrinks, you get those bridging veins, you get a slight jostle or a jar, you get a slow venous bleed, and you get a small hematoma that builds up and builds up, is that correct?

A: Sure, that's often what happens.

Q: Common. And that happens with a re-bleed because people can get bounced going in and out of their wheel chairs, or a fall, or a slight re-bleed, or even a spontaneous re-bleed can happen, is that right?

A: That can happen that way.

Q: And we think there may be no symptoms of that, isn't that fair to say, people may have this with no symptoms.

A: Exactly, it can be silent.

Q: But it's also fair to say that often, those people are asymptomatic or appear to be, because their caretakers aren't attentive, or they're on medication, or some of the symptoms also appear to be those of aging—Alzheimer's, for instance.

A: Well, that's some of the explanation. The fact is that they—

THE COURT: Well, we're getting away from this case.

MS. COAKLEY: Okay.

THE COURT: Let's get back.[103]

In closing statements, the prosecution ridiculed the defense theory as the "exploding brain and rebleed" theory.[104] Lead prosecutor Gerald Leone Jr. argued that children simply do not die of small injuries sustained three weeks earlier. Actually, Coakley's "harbor question"—the last and most important question she asked expert witnesses—was whether they had ever seen another case in which a child suffered a greenstick wrist fracture, skull fracture, and subdural hematoma and died three weeks later. Except for Dr. Baden, the expert witnesses all answered negatively.

The preference for conservative interpretation of forensic evidence explains why the forensic experts at this trial were unwilling to put their professional credibility on the line by claiming that Matthew Eappen had been shaken. They were uncomfortable with the fact that there were no broken ribs and no hemorrhaging on the arms and neck. For them, the evidence did not warrant a determination of shaken-baby syndrome. The skull fracture and resulting brain swelling were not only a sufficient but also a provable cause of death. In general, clinicians use a different approach to evidence. In clinical practice, few patients present with textbook cases of symptoms, but physicians still need to act on what they consider the most likely diagnosis. Physicians rely on differential diagnosis, a model of elimination that leads to the more likely clinical pathway. Learning to handle clinical uncertainty is the hallmark of learning to be a doctor, and even experienced clinicians are often baffled by symptoms. Interprofessional disagreements are common.[105] In the clinical setting, inferences are readily made and unmade, because time will tell whether the clinician is right. If the symptoms begin to point in a different direction, the treatment can always be corrected. That Matthew did not exhibit all the telltale signs of shaken-baby/impact syndrome therefore does not rule out this diagnosis. The circumstantial evidence of a caregiver solely responsible for a fussy infant points to child abuse. The diagnosis gained credibility when Dr. Newberger correctly predicted that Matthew had broken bones in addition to the skull fracture. Moreover, clinicians, especially emergency physicians, are more attuned to abuse, because they witness a broad range of children with broken bones and other injuries due to abuse. When charging Louise Woodward, the prosecution listened more to the clinicians than to the medical examiner. If forensic experts had prevailed, Woodward might have been charged with manslaughter instead of murder.

THE LEGACY OF THE "NANNY TRIAL"

In a controversial legal twist, Louise Woodward gambled at the end of her trial with an all-or-nothing strategy: guilty of first/second-degree murder or acquittal. The jury found her guilty of second-degree murder. After the trial, the jury members did not identify the expert witnesses they considered most credible. A trial offers closure of interpretative flexibility but no final explanation, only a terse separation of winners and losers. The guilty verdict might have meant that the jury bought the entire shaken-baby/impact theory or thought, as Dr. Feigin suggested, that shaking was irrelevant to the fatal impact. When Judge Zobel decided to reduce the verdict to manslaughter and sentence Louise Woodward to time served, he wrote that "the jury spurned, as not worthy of belief, professional opinions emanating from a corps of highly-qualified, authoritative experts."[106] He was careful not to indicate his own opinion of the evidence.

In the aftermath, the defense blamed the inability of a jury trial to sort out scientific issues.[107] In a guest editorial in the *Wall Street Journal*, defense attorney Harvey Silverglate summed up the stumbling block.

The central problem in the case arose when the jury was faced with one group of expert witnesses relying on hard data interpreted according to accepted scientific principles, vs. another group of seemingly well-credentialed experts who placed themselves wholly at odds with data that they simply refused to acknowledge. Ludicrous though it might seem to a true scientist, to a lay jury the specter of credentialed and seemingly respected experts refusing to change their opinions in the face of hard data might well result in questioning the validity or relevance of the data.[108]

A close reading of the trial transcripts shows that all the experts, including Drs. Leestma and Baden, persisted in opinions that contradicted some of the evidence, even when confronted with plausible alternative explanations. Evidence alone is never automatically convincing. As Silverglate also suggested, the reputation of Children's Hospital ("a local institution virtually enshrined in holy writ") helped win the case for the prosecution. Reputation, he suggested, provided ascribed credentialing, unlike the credibility achieved during the trial. Curiously, his remedy consisted of further institutionalizing ascribed credibility: professional organizations should accredit independent, objective experts, unspoiled by a political agenda.

The debate over shaken-baby/impact syndrome moved to the pages of professional journals when a group of seventy-two pediatricians, with only one forensic pathologist among them, published a petition noting that "many in the media and the public have failed to credit the jury in this case with having had the intelligence to understand that the prosecution put forward well-established medical evidence that overwhelmingly supported a violent shaking/impact episode on the day in question, when Matthew was in the sole custody of Ms. Woodward."[109] A forensic pathologist then countered that the prosecution in the Woodward case had not met the *Daubert* standard for admissible scientific evidence.[110] At the 1998 annual meeting of the American Academy of Forensic Sciences, eminent forensic pathologist Dr. Vincent DiMaio stated that while shaking may be lethal, he had never, in nearly thirty years of practice, seen a baby who had been shaken to death.[111] A position paper of the National Association of Medical Examiners settled upon "abusive head injuries in young children" as a diagnosis, rather than the "controversial" shaken-baby syndrome.[112]

Regardless of the outcome for Louise Woodward, the trial has been generally credited with bringing shaken-baby syndrome into the public realm as an acceptable clinical entity. Shaken-baby syndrome, rather than the bleed-rebleed theory, is now well known. At the trial, however, the media, not the forensic pathologists, established the diagnosis. Medical examiners can be instrumental in advancing new causes of death; but, consistent with their conservative interpretive approach, such advancements more typically depend on stimulating public health and medical research.[113]

Stephen Turner writes that "the expert who is a threat [to liberal democracy] is the expert who exerts influence through the back door of training and validating the confidence of professionals, and whose advice is regarded as authoritative by other bureaucrats but not by the public at large."[114] Courtroom proceedings open the back door of the morgue to public scrutiny. They hold medical examiners accountable and circumscribe their discretionary powers. Medical examiners practice self-restraint not primarily because of a higher professional duty, but because they know they will be hammered in court if they stray from standard forensic practice. They could even be recalled or replaced if their practice deviates. Such deviation rarely occurs, because medical examiners tend to be conservative practitioners, anticipating courtroom interrogations before finalizing their reports. The clearest indication of a loss of credibility comes when law enforcement agencies express distrust in the medical examiner.

Constituted in the framework of each trial, forensic professional credibility flows back to the workplace and circumscribes medical examiners' forensic authority by defining what inferences from forensic evidence are legally acceptable. Clinicians or research scientists, who are reluctant to be engaged as expert witnesses and for whom court testimony is a side project, are less influenced by the exigencies of court testimony. Pathologists, who are certified in medicine, learn the legal aspects of their job under fire, in the adversarial courtroom.[115] Trials instruct medical examiners better than could any written directive that their conclusions require checking for alternative explanations, that nothing counts unless it is documented, that everyday practices need to follow written guidelines closely, and that they must be careful about consultations. Adversarial questioning impresses upon forensic pathologists the need to remain cautious and conservative in drawing inferences from evidence, because every inference will likely be challenged. Trials also show, however, that following all precautions provides no guarantee of one's credibility remaining intact—and that failing to follow these legally relevant principles inevitably leads to self-destruction. At my research site, the privileged position of the forensic homicide investigation was confirmed by the practice of rechecking the corpse the day after the autopsy was conducted and before the body was released to the funeral director. The pathologist who had conducted the autopsy would convene colleagues and show all pertinent findings, allowing everyone to ask questions and make sure that nothing had been missed. In other cases, the morning meeting sufficed as a method for quality control. In every case, "Can we defend this in court?" was the ultimate test for forensic decision making.

The question remains whether the checks and balances in the courtroom are an effective means for holding medical examiners accountable. As Sheila Jasanoff has argued, legal views about science often diverge from scientists' own views.[116] Critics of the court system might point to how Coakley turned Dr. Baden's credibility into chopped liver or the way Scheck reduced Dr. DeGirolami to a remorseful underling and decry these strategies as excessively harsh, even abusive instruments for revealing the truth—practices in which legal preoccupations prevail over scientific concerns. Supporters of the legal checks on science argue that adversarial proceedings offer an opportunity to reveal methodological or theoretical flaws that might be glossed over by an insular scientific community (as happened with DNA typing).[117] Both views presume a clear demarcation between scientist and court expert. For medical examiners, however, the boundary between science and law is barely perceptible. Rather, forensic pathology constitutes a "law-medicine hybrid," in which medicine and law are so intertwined that separating them is difficult.[118] Indeed, the manners of death can be evaluated to deduce primary legal information. Designation of a death as natural, accidental, or suicidal confirms that a homicide did not take place and thus that further legal action is unnecessary. The far-reaching investigative powers of the institution of forensic pathology and the resources spent on it make sense only in light of its utility in gathering and interpreting bodily evidence for court applications, rather than merely for public health purposes. Other observers agree:

> For forensic science and pathology, the legal process itself has created their particular type of professional interaction and expert knowledge. The social integration of the law is such that forensic experts have learnt to reconcile themselves to the regular adversarial skepticism of legal processes, while maintaining the normal consensual discourses of scientific expertise. Whereas other disciplines may manage this by defining the courtroom interaction as "unscientific," this is not so easily available to forensic experts, because the courtroom is their ultimate professional arena.[119]

This feedback loop from courtroom to workplace is not unique to medical examiners but is also typical for other court experts, such as those engaged in DNA-typing and fingerprinting identification techniques.[120]

Rather than separating good science from junk science, the courtroom provides a powerful socialization experience in a legal and forensic paradigm, informing standards of practice for a widely diverse group of death investigators. Most trials in which medical examiners testify do not delve into the scientific principles underlying pathology but center instead on the chain of custody and pathologists' hands-on expertise.[121] Still, in the post-*Daubert* era, when judges have greater latitude in determining the admissibility of science, forensic pathology is vulnerable, in part because it developed not as an independent science but a legal utility. Some legal scholars have argued that judicial functioning requires the *Daubert* criteria to exempt forensic pathology, because a criminal court without pathological data is inconceivable.[122] If medical examiners' scientific authority were to be legally questioned, as happened with fingerprinting expertise, individual credibility would not matter any longer; all interpretations made by forensic pathologists could be disbelieved.

Court testimony offers a vehicle for expressing medical examiners' forensic authority. By successfully translating pathological findings into medical evidence at trial, medical examiners appropriate some of the authority vested in the legal system. A skeptic of forensic authority, therefore, would need to cast doubt not only on medical practice, but also on evidence that is routinely admitted in court. Such dual authority, however, raises issues of independence: how independent are medical examiners if their expertise is nourished by the legal system? In the next chapter, I will show that the integration of legal and medical authority already takes place in the autopsy room, when medical examiners investigate homicides, and that the law-medicine hybrid carries a price for society when medical examiners hesitate to classify certain deaths as homicides.

CHAPTER FOUR

THE PERFECT CRIME

And more than once I was able to uncover evidence of murder in so-called "perfect crimes."

THOMAS NOGUCHI, Los Angeles County chief medical examiner, *Coroner*

The thought of getting away with murder, with "the perfect crime," has intrigued mystery writers, the general public, and forensic pathologists alike. At the center of most crime fiction is a mysterious corpse to be explained by a detective. Similarly, with every suspicious death investigated in real life for "foul play," the possibility of a perfect crime hovers over the forensic work. By definition, however, perfect crimes are never discovered, because once identified, a crime cannot be perfect. If investigators fail to identify a corpse as a homicide victim, someone gets away with murder. Stories about near misses are abundant in the corridors of forensic conferences and in true-crime collections; but for "an unforeseeable grain of sand jamming a well-oiled mechanism,"[1] these perpetrators would have gotten away with homicide. Forensic specialists' most formidable weapon in the battle between good and evil is presumed to be their professional and technological prowess.

Medical examiners' professional blend of science and politics sets them apart from coroners. The expectation is that medical examiners' scientific approach leads to more accurate detection of suicide and homicide. As with suicide, however, homicide classifications run into the problem of human intent. Here, the larger problem is that medical examiners do not have to take an intent to kill into consideration. In a forensic context, a homicide is simply a "death caused by another." One textbook specifies forensic homicide as "violent death at the hand of another person. For practical purposes, we suggest that in most instances this can be refined to include deaths due to the hostile or illegal act of another person."[2] This definition, however, fails to stipulate how directly a person responsible for the death needs to be involved or whether that person needs to have intended to kill the deceased. This latter criterion is important to the criminological meaning of homicide. In jurisprudence, homicide is subdivided into manslaughter and murder, each with different degrees depending on intent to kill, premeditation, and whether malice or other felonies were involved. In forensic pathology, such factors should not play a role. Indeed, the authors of the forensic textbook add, "In contrast to the category of suicide, the demonstration of intent is not necessary for a determination of homicide. The certifier is not required to differentiate murder from manslaughter or justifiable homicide."[3]

The forensic definition of homicide, lacking all consideration of intent, is like a rudderless ship, drifting in all directions with changing winds and currents. The definition is too vague and broad to be useful. As medical examiners' cases reveal, every death includes some direct or indirect human involvement. Every death might therefore be considered a homicide, or very few might qualify, depending on the criteria applied. In forensic practice, however, suspicions arise only with telltale signs, and those signs depend on broader political and moral norms and on previously detected patterns. Instead of a vessel adrift in a spacious ocean, a death investigation becomes a carefully piloted ship, traveling through narrow channels, steering clear of danger spots, and navigating toward predictable ports. As with suicide, which deaths will be classified as homicides depends on their match with medical examiners' expertise, the evidence at hand, evolving categories of death, and organizational work practices.[4]

This chapter explores the professional practices that allow specific clusters of homicides to remain undetected. We know from the previous chapter that the legal system provides checks and balances on some of the determinations that medical examiners make. Yet the legal system does not check the claims that medical examiners *fail* to make. Thousands of deaths come to medical examiners' attention that are considered insufficiently suspicious to warrant an autopsy or even a case number. Some of those deaths may have been caused by others. Medical examiners' lack of action makes these deaths, by default, unsuspicious. Other deaths might involve undeniable evidence of homicide—such as gunshot wounds inflicted by others—but are not determined to constitute a homicide. In still other deaths, medical examiners' particular scientific expertise might not pick up on ways of killing others.

I will argue that getting away with murder does not depend on a mythical battle between evil personalities and an astute detective but, rather, follows from the "good" features of death investigation. The weakness of forensic death investigation that allows a specific set of perfect crimes to slip by is a necessary consequence of medical examiners' professional strengths: their dependence on allies—primarily law enforcement agencies and clinicians—and on scientific pathological methods makes classifying some deaths as homicides extremely difficult. These allies, unlike the lay public, have inside knowledge of the ways in which medical examiners function and the assumptions that guide their work. They know that medical examiners cannot investigate deaths without their cooperation, and they are cognizant of the limitations of forensic methodologies. Rather than risk confrontation with allies and a devastating assault on their credibility, medical examiners avoid potentially volatile death investigations by excluding them, giving their allies the benefit of the doubt, or classifying deaths as almost-but-not-quite homicides. By creating order in messy deaths, forensic pathologists and their tools also produce a specific new disorder: that which escapes classification, remains unclassified, or is unnecessarily vaguely classified.[5] In short, forensic procedures lead to the misclassification of perfect crimes involving law enforcement or clinical professionals.

At the core of these perfect crimes lies a professional quandary. For medical examiners, the immediate professional issue in their work is to secure collaboration with forensically knowledgeable parties. The broader problem is professional regulation. One characteristic of professional groups is that they monitor and regulate themselves.[6] Only if criminal transgressions occur will outsiders—that is, the justice system—be called upon after the fact, when lawsuits are brought against individual practitioners for negligence or malpractice; even then, an evaluation of evidence depends on the collaboration of professional insiders. When forensic pathologists direct their investigative powers toward deaths that may have been caused by clinicians or police officers, they are perceived as unqualified outsiders unable to evaluate the intricacies of these professionals' work. The perfect crime is thus a consequence of medical examiners' professional position spanning law and medicine. While they are generally trusted to make authoritative statements about causes and manners of death, when deaths involve their close professional allies, medical examiners lack forensic authority.

This chapter elaborates the analysis of earlier chapters. I have shown that pathologists, through their work, establish forensic authority that makes contesting their findings difficult for outsiders. The autopsy report and death certificate are constructed as a fortress, with every step calculated to defend the investigator against future incursions. Pathologists err on the side of caution, privileging hard pathological findings over alternative interpretations suggested by circumstantial data. When I argue that some deaths with all the characteristics of a homicide are classified otherwise, I claim no special knowledge that trumps forensic evidence. Instead, I show recurring inconsistencies in the application of homicide classifications—inconsistencies that medical examiners themselves discuss in professional journals. Unlike with suicide, where any chance for discovering intent dies with the decedent, homicidal intent lives on and can be confessed after the victim has been buried. Occasionally, a revelation prompts reevaluation of a death previously deemed natural or accidental, and the reassessment illuminates weaknesses in the death investigation system. Thus, this chapter discusses a secret hidden from the general public, a weakness in the fortress known only to insiders. Like earlier chapters, this one looks at the consequences of the work practices of medical examiners, and here we find that a specific set of perfect crimes follow from these practices. The investigations that miss those perfect crimes are almost identical to any other forensic investigation. The key difference in perfect crimes is that medical examiners cannot trust their close allies and, in turn, are not trusted by them. To show the far-reaching consequences of this distrust, I first review medical examiners' role in routine homicides.

THE ROUTINE HOMICIDE

Although forensic pathologists occasionally discover a homicide, their primary objective in routine cases with a strong suspicion of foul play is to turn the case into a forensic homicide, to establish homicide as an embodied fact. The following case offers an example of such critical embodiment.

Dr. Douglas examines the body of a young man on the stretcher in front of him. The man was shot after a minor altercation about a dirty sidewalk got out of hand. Witnesses to the shooting testified that up to five bullets had been fired, but the police recovered none of them. Dr. Douglas carefully checks every inch of skin, looking for signs of injury. The pathologist locates three wounds: two on the upper right arm and one on the chest. He presumes that the bullet went through the arm and then reentered the body at the chest, yet the X-rays show only a bullet in the groin. The doctor is puzzled that the deceased has a bullet in the "wrong" place. To complicate the matter, hospital personnel had opened the chest for open-heart massage and put in a chest tube; these actions may have obscured more bullet wounds. Turning to Dr. Brown, who is preparing for an autopsy on a young girl run over by a car, Dr. Douglas wonders aloud whether the bullet might have been embolized (entered an artery). Dr. Brown considers this an unlikely possibility. Instead, he wonders whether the victim was shot from above. Dr. Douglas admits that he knows of only one previous case of an embolized bullet.

Dr. Douglas begins the autopsy at the groin. He digs for the bullet and, to everyone's amazement, finds it exactly as he predicted, lodged neatly in an artery. The doctor's assistant takes pictures of the embolized bullet—jacketed, .22 caliber. Dr. Douglas explains that a .22 caliber bullet should not kill. His mentor used to tell him that if you shoot someone with a .22, the victim will be very pissed. The other pathologists, police officers, and assistants now group around Dr. Douglas to see whether the bullet had indeed pierced a major artery. Mindful of the audience, the doctor carefully opens the chest cavity and frees the heart and the aorta. Right again! Everyone can see a small hole in the aorta—one hole, not two. With a thin metal pointer, the doctor traces the bullet's deadly path: it went through the arm, entered the chest, ricocheted off a rib, penetrated one lobe of the lung, left the lung through a different lobe, then pierced the aorta, where it was pumped down into the leg. From the bullet's trajectory, the doctor confirms witnesses' reports that the victim was sitting on the sidewalk when shot, probably lifting his arm to shield himself. The doctor also deduces that the shooter stood more than four feet from the victim when firing the gun.

Dr. Douglas's solving of the case of the seemingly misplaced bullet is an instance of a deft forensic homicide investigation. During homicide investigations, the pathologist's main task is to check the corpse for lethal violence and reconstruct the sequence of events that preceded death. In shootings, this process means accounting for entrance and exit wounds, recovering bullets, estimating how close the shooter stood to the victim (from gunpowder patterns), and deciding whether a slug was lethal. These are not trivial issues. Claiming that a person has been shot is difficult without the bullet as evidence. Why all this effort to retrieve a deadly piece of metal? Dr. Cahill told me that to bury a body with bullets is bad forensic practice. Bullets have great criminological value: much as fingerprints may identify people, bullets may identify the gun that fired them.[7] The pathologist weighs the bullet to determine the caliber of gun that fired it and whether pieces of the bullet are missing. Investigating a different homicide, Dr. Douglas found a second bullet from a gun with a caliber different from that of the first bullet, a finding that surprised both the pathologist and the police officers. The police inquiry had focused on one suspect, but Dr. Douglas's unexpected find threw the investigation into doubt. Then the doctor noticed that the bullet was encapsulated in fat, and no second entrance wound could be found. The second bullet had apparently been lodged in the victim for several years (medical examiners refer to such bullets as "souvenir bullets"), and the case once again made sense.

Pathologists are also adept at interpreting wounds caused by blunt-force trauma and sharp objects, even if the murder weapon is unavailable. In the partly decomposed body of a young woman found in a hastily dug grave and allegedly killed by two men in the woods, the pathologist observed deep stab wounds in her left flank and extensive blunt-force trauma wounds on her head and back. The pathologist traced the wounds on transparent film and removed a large piece of skin surrounding them. Looking over the wounds with the state police, we figured out that the death was likely caused by a small folding army shovel locked in the 90-degree position. This particular type of army shovel also had a pointed axe to dig small holes. The axe had been used to make the deep stab wounds in the woman's chest, but she was likely killed by a blow to her head from the shovel, delivered while she was lying down. Before the fatal blow, she had received a blow to her back that had brought her to her knees. When asked about this scenario, one of the suspects admitted that such a shovel had indeed been used. The state police then retrieved the murder weapon from a pond. In a different case, the pathologist determined that a homicide victim was first strangled and subsequently stabbed in the throat, because the serrated edge of the knife made a small laceration over the strangulation mark. The knife would have left different traces if the events had occurred in reverse order.

Between 1996 and 2000, the medical examiners in my study classified 183 deaths as homicides. In 55 percent of those cases the deceased had been shot; in 17 percent the death was due to blunt-force trauma (e.g., the victim was beaten with a baseball bat); in 14 percent death was preceded by a stabbing with a knife or other sharp instrument; 4 percent of the deaths were due to strangulation; 8 percent were due to hit-and-run motor vehicle incidents; in 2 percent the mode of death was unknown or due to other factors (one case was a drowning, two others were suffocations).[8] Most deaths classified by medical examiners as homicides are thus obvious—impulsive acts recognizable as homicide by their violence and by witnesses' reports. Although opportunistic homicides between strangers do occur, homicides usually involve a gradual escalation of conflict, challenges and counterchallenges, loss of face, and use of weapons.[9]

I found only three instances in which the medical examiner's office was the first to identify a homicide. In one case, a neighbor found a woman dead in her bathtub after she failed to show up for an appointment. When the police were summoned, they found a plugged-in electric hair dryer arcing in the dirty bathwater and presumed that the woman had accidentally electrocuted herself. The scene investigator from the medical examiner's office, however, noticed blood streaks on the walls and multiple facial and chest bruises on the victim. He informed the police that they might have a homicide, and the officers quickly found more traces indicating foul play, a murder weapon, and eventually a suspect, who was identified through DNA evidence. Although it was a member of the medical examiner's staff who alerted the police to the possibility of a homicide, this information came not from the autopsy but from the investigator's taking a closer look at the scene than had the police, who mistakenly thought that the blood in the bathtub was from the electrocution. The second case looked like an accidental self-inflicted shooting, but the office determined that the gun had been fired by a person other than the deceased. The third case was a baby whose death was already clouded by suspicion. The father claimed to have tripped over an older child while holding the baby, but the investigation revealed extensive internal injuries inconsistent with a fall.[10]

In most deaths classified as forensic homicide, the pathologist is confirming the initial determination made by police. Before the body arrives in the medical examiner's office, police detectives have already launched an extensive investigation and concluded that the death was a homicide. The scene investigator might write, for example, that he was summoned for "a house fire with a homicide," or the description of the scene might make it obvious that the police and scene investigator assume the death to be a homicide. For example, "38 y o [year old] white male was stabbed inside the White Horse bar" leaves little doubt. In the latter case, the scene investigator's report contained details about the argument that preceded the stabbing, the resulting robbery attempt, the location of the knife before and after the stabbing, the people involved, the name and phone number of the homicide detective investigating the case, and his request to attend the autopsy. Even before the morning meeting, the case was discussed in the pathology assistants' office as a homicide. During morning meeting, Dr. Cahill noted that the case seemed clear. Although she would spend the next four hours carefully describing and documenting the stab wounds and torn clothes, she saw no ambiguity about the cause and manner of death.

Law enforcement personnel and medical examiners collaborate closely during homicide investigations. In most cases, police officers initially formulate the possibility of a homicide on the basis of their scene investigation. They notify the scene investigator from the medical examiner's office, who takes custody of the body after surveying the scene.[11] Several of the scene investigators at my research site were retired police officers. The next day, the medical examiner conducts the autopsy in the presence of the police. Detectives hand over a police report and any guns, clothing, drug pipes, or other evidence taken into custody at the crime scene. They often also help identify the victim, particularly if they have fingerprints on file or if the victim has a police record with mug shots. Medical examiners, in turn, interpret medical and psychiatric reports for police. If the pathologist takes pictures of wounds or identifying marks on the body with the special 1:1 camera, police officers receive copies. Before an autopsy begins, the pathologist asks the police whether they want to gather additional trace evidence—for example, from hands covered in brown paper bags to preserve evidence—or take pictures of the corpse (although this gesture is often unnecessary, because police have usually taken pictures at the crime scene). Police detectives wait in the back of the room, leaving the autopsy to the doctor. When the pathologists find something, they summon the police officers to take a closer look—to see, for example, the hemorrhaging or pierced lung for themselves. Police detectives may take additional pictures of the corpse, examine and photograph clothing, and then return to the back of the room, waiting for the pathologist to finish the case. Sometimes they answer questions about the scene that remain unclear to the pathologist, or they recall surprising or humorous exchanges with witnesses or suspects. When the autopsy is finished, the doctor explains the findings to the police officer, and they often plan a joint meeting with the district attorney's office to discuss the case.

The mutual exchange of evidence and information, the coordination of schedules, and the prerogative of police to attend autopsies as a matter of course underscore the routinized collaboration of a joint investigation. When one of the parties violates the understanding of a good working relationship, however, repair work will be required. In one situation, a police officer started fingerprinting the body while Dr. Douglas was dressing for the autopsy. When the pathologist found out what she had been doing, he yelled at her for destroying evidence and touching the body without his permission. In a different case, Dr. Brown had washed the body of a homicide victim while waiting for the detectives to arrive. When the police turned up, they were deeply disappointed that they could not take pictures of the body in its original condition and muttered disparagingly about Dr. Brown's forensic skills. Dr. Brown expressed surprise at their disappointment, because the victim had spent three days in intensive care, and most evidence must have been removed in the routine handling of a hospital patient. In a third situation, a police officer refused to provide the scene investigator with basic identifying information about the deceased. When the senior scene investigator found out, he immediately called the officer's chief, who apologized and explained that the offending officer was a rookie who had been told that he could not divulge anything about the case to anyone. The junior officer was unaware that "anyone" did not include the medical examiner's staff.[12]

Consistent with their cautious approach to forensic evidence, medical examiners are more likely to negate police suspicions of homicide with natural explanations than they are to discover a homicide. In one of several similar cases, the body of a young woman was found naked in a state park's garbage can. The same day, the town's mayor, flanked by the chief of police and other officers, gave a televised press conference denouncing the brutal murder of the young woman and promising that the police would not rest until they caught the offender. He urged anyone with information to come forward. When Dr. Douglas conducted an autopsy of the body, however, he found multiple needle marks on the woman's arms, and toxicology tests indicated lethal levels of a variety of illegal drugs. After the woman was identified, her boyfriend was tracked down. He admitted to having dumped her body in the park but claimed that the woman died of an overdose. The police declined further comment on the case.

In routine homicide investigations, medical examiners thus document the pathological and toxicological signs of murder in an ongoing dialogue with law enforcement agencies. In the same way that medical examiners depend on medical histories written by their clinical colleagues to make the case for natural death and suicide, they depend on law enforcement to initiate what will become a forensic homicide determination. As distinct yet interlinked professionals, police and forensic pathologists continuously and closely coordinate findings and evidence during the evolving investigation, further reflecting the privileged role of law enforcement in the organizational ecology of death investigation. Although forensic pathologists do occasionally discover a homicide, they are more likely to remove the suspicion of it in ambiguous cases. This caution is in line with their conservative approach to drawing inferences from forensic evidence.

THE MORALITY OF MURDER

Medical examiners readily admit that the mesh of the forensic net is not fine enough to distinguish deliberate human actions from some natural processes or self-inflicted injuries. In the same way that coronary arteriosclerosis is easier to observe during an autopsy than electrolyte imbalances, medical examiners easily recognize gunshot wounds, knife injuries, or strangulation marks but are less likely to notice signs of poisoning. Certain substances—some pathologists would specify to me which ones, while others would not—have a fairly high chance of remaining undetected. If swallowed or injected in fatal dosages, they easily kill, but in only a few hours they break down in the body and are undetectable. Widely available fine syringes would make even detection of the injection site difficult. Thus, if the pathologist were not alerted, such deaths could easily be classified as natural. Dr. Brown illustrated this point with a possible scenario.

You have a wife who has a diabetic husband with a bad heart who gave him a very high dose [of insulin] and then calls the police to say he complained of chest pain and when she checked on him he was dead. We get that kind of story once or twice a week. It would be ruled a bad heart, natural death with diabetes. We might not even bring him in. An insulin overdose is difficult to find out, because insulin level decreases to zero anyway after twenty-four hours. In addition, we now have artificial insulin [that is] very similar to natural insulin. Before it was porcine or bovine insulin and much easier to check, but now it is difficult.[13]

To lower the chance for infection, the office has a rule that a body needs to remain in storage for twenty-four hours before an autopsy. By then, some substances are undetectable. For some drugs, too, the difference between a therapeutic and a fatal dose is minimal, and even after identifying the drug, the pathologists might need to leave the manner of death undetermined. Dr. Douglas remembered a deceased factory worker with an unusually pink color. He checked for cyanide, and the man tested positive. Even then, the death was listed as undetermined because no suspect could be found in the poisoning, and the possibility that the man accidentally swallowed cyanide—which is still used extensively in woodworking and electronics—could not be excluded. The standard toxicological screen does not check for arsenic. Five years of medical examiners' records at the office I studied revealed no forensic homicides due to poisoning. Researchers note a possible explanation: "Many poison cases are undetected because many of the symptoms displayed by toxic substances mask themselves as symptoms of disease."[14]

The forensic pathologists in my study were not alarmed by the possibility that the investigative system was missing cases of homicide. Dr. Franken summarized their confidence.

Well, you know, it's a funny thing. I do think that with time—if there is a homicide and it is going to be undetected—with time it will come out. The only time someone is going to get away with a homicide is if nobody else ever knows about it. If I don't talk, I can get away with it. As long as somebody else knows it—I don't care who it is—the chances are that it is going to come out. We don't have that many cases coming out down the line: "Geesh, twenty years ago I saw this guy killing . . ." It's not coming up. So I don't think there are too many getting out of the system. Otherwise we would have a string of these.

According to this view, employing detection technologies is necessary only in cases of moral transgression. Social protection against homicide resides in a moral defense grounded in the Judeo-Christian commandment "Thou shalt not kill." The robustness of this defense is proven negatively: because we do not know of many undetected homicides, it must be that they do not happen. Such a defense rests on three assumptions about human nature, rather than on pathological evidence. These assumptions, which are embedded in forensic work practices, sketch a moral spectrum of the likelihood that death at the hands of another has taken place.

1. *People are good.* The first assumption is that lethal violence does not constitute a rational way to solve problems, that penalties for murder and general moral disapproval of homicide deter most people who might contemplate killing others. Dr. Brown shrugged, "My only hope is that most people are decent. Most people will not harm someone else without some reason." Although they are confronted daily with an endless pattern of maltreatment and despair—seemingly random violence, crippling depression, and devastating poverty—forensic pathologists expressed an upbeat view of humanity. Even Dr. Douglas, who tended to be cynical about people's motives, admitted that one needs to give people the benefit of the doubt and presume innocence. It would be impossible to do his job, he noted, if one assumed homicides everywhere. The result would be witch hunts that ruined lives and challenged the reputation of forensic pathology. Robert Dingwall, John Eekelaar, and Topsy Murray observed a similar "rule of optimism" in their study of child-protection agencies, adding that child-protection staff sought to justify seemingly abusive behavior. Outsiders were surprised that so few cases qualified as abuse. The researchers explained that staff actively tried to give parents the benefit of the doubt: "Child protection agencies may actually relieve parents of the burden of producing [explanations] by volunteering or imputing acceptable reasons for apparently untoward actions."[15] Social workers justified behavior that appeared abusive by appealing to a form of cultural relativism (we should not judge culturally different parenting styles), or they excused such behavior as an imperfect manifestation of "natural love" (e.g., when a mentally disabled mother hits her infant out of frustration but otherwise exhibits a loving relationship to the child). The result was that the staff rationalized much apparently abusive behavior.

2. *People fear making mistakes.* When Dr. Brown stated his hope that most people are decent, he added, "and most people are scared to botch it." The second assumption reflects the practical difficulties of killing someone without leaving identifiable traces. Even though an overdose of insulin can theoretically be used to kill without leaving signs in the body, administering the substance remains difficult. Injecting someone requires intimacy, and there are many opportunities for mistakes that could foil the crime. A cry for help might summon witnesses; a scrape could provide DNA evidence; the insulin needle might break; the dose might be insufficient; fingerprints

might be left behind; the perpetrator could be overpowered; a getaway car might draw attention. The list of possible errors is endless. The medical examiners noted that most homicides they saw occurred during the heat of an argument and did not involve the deliberate preparation and careful execution needed to commit what the perpetrator hoped would be a perfect crime. Murders were often sloppy, witnessed affairs with an abundance of evidence. Criminals either took something from the scene or left something behind. A suspect might not always be found, but a homicide was usually obvious. They pointed to the case of a closeted gay doctor who was bludgeoned to death in his bedroom. A year later, the police had few leads but no doubt that the doctor had been killed. While this assumption depended on the presence of forensic evidence, the medical examiners provided many examples of cases in which such evidence was initially lacking or could have been easily disguised.

3. *People talk out of guilt or pride.* The third assumption is that people who somehow get away with murder will boast about it or become overconfident, kill repeatedly, take more risks, and ultimately be detected. Even if a person succeeds in disguising the homicide, sooner or later the offender will talk about the crime, and then the story will reach the police. A perfect crime loses its perfection because of human weakness. The medical examiners at my research site gave me countless examples of people who had killed initially without being suspected but were later caught because they talked. The case mentioned earlier in which a young woman was found bludgeoned to death in the woods illustrates this situation. After allegedly killing the woman, the two men buried her body in a shallow grave, disposed of the army shovel by throwing it in a pond, and swore each other to secrecy. They believed their secret was safe because the chances of someone stumbling upon the body were small. Yet days after the victim disappeared, a "muscular and tattooed" (according to the investigating police detective) female roommate of the victim confronted the two men about her friend's whereabouts. Scared and intimidated, they sought protection from a police officer but subsequently implicated each other in the killing. The men had lured the woman into the woods with the promise of crack cocaine in exchange for sex. When she refused a sex act, at least one of them killed her with the shovel. Dr. Douglas was sure that because of the many people involved, the case was certain to have been solved eventually. Two of the woman's roommates had seen her leave with the men, and a third man, originally part of the plan, had changed his mind at the last minute. In a classic prisoner's dilemma, the men, separated in jail, accused each other and provided detailed descriptions of the crime.[16]

These three assumptions about humanity weave a *moral safety net* that prevents people from getting away with murder. They provide the terms for averting disorder and are apparent in every aspect of the death investigation. Yet these assumptions also indicate possible dangers, where the safety net may be frayed and law enforcement and medical examiners find transgressions. Their task is to detect the moral violation with forensic technologies. Routine homicides embody traces of moral breach: most are impulsive or opportunistic events involving guns or blunt-force trauma; even when the murder is planned, the perpetrator will make mistakes or boast about the killing. The overwhelming majority of routine homicides involve greed, lust, anger, or mental disorder and occur in a context of drug trafficking, corruption, organized crime, domestic violence, love triangles, or extreme psychopathology such as serial killing.

Such moral slippage becomes apparent in forensic practice. When discussing the case of a murdered young man with "THUG LIFE" roughly tattooed on his back (the "I" in "life" was a speeding bullet) and little blue envelopes with white powder spilling out of his pants pockets, the pathology assistant commented, "Live by the sword, die by the sword." The staff, particularly the scene investigators, mocked newspaper obituaries and testimonials that described homicide victims as people who had had some trouble in the past but were about to turn their lives around. Although the staff members never justified a killing—they regularly expressed outrage at loss of life, and homicide clearly ranked as worse than any criminal involvement by the murder victim—most routine homicides were seen as making moral sense. Sometimes the victim of an opportunistic murderer was simply in the wrong place at the wrong time. One such case was the sidewalk altercation in which a man uninvolved in the dispute was shot, apparently having been mistaken for someone else with a similar body type. Often the perpetrator had a long record of run-ins with the law, and if not, the homicide itself constituted proof of the perpetrator's moral deficiency. At the same time, the staff recognized that order and disorder rarely fell into a neat moral opposition. The medicolegal administrator noted, for example, that the disorder of homicide might actually be normatively ordered. He connected the increase in drug-related homicides with the incarceration of the dominant organized-crime family that once controlled the drug market in the region. In the era preceding my research, crime families had used homicides to regulate the drug market. Killing was part of doing business. The breakdown of this "order" was characterized by impulsive, violent outbursts by drug traffickers without central leadership. The administrator described it as a "free-for-all."

The moral safety net, reinforced with forensic detection technologies, protects against the possibility of getting away with murder and helps medical examiners and police officers distinguish homicides among the mass of deaths that come to their attention. These same work practices, however, allow a particular kind of perfect crime to slip by. We must add one more assumption to the moral safety net: *while some professionals might be involved in the deaths of others, we trust that they do not kill.* This assumption trumps the other three. Professionals on whom medical examiners depend in carrying out routine forensic investigations enjoy a generous benefit of the doubt. This fourth assumption affects, again, every aspect of medical examiners' death investigations. The justifications are institutionalized into office policies and procedures. They take effect before the office is notified of a death, and they affect the selection of cases, the ability to find evidence, the interpretation of findings, and the authority of medical examiners. The moral force in such cases is so convincing that medical examiners seem to neutralize their investigative technologies and see ambiguity rather than suspicion. Overlooking homicide in certain deaths is the flip side of investigating routine homicides; medical examiners knowingly, actively, routinely, and inevitably let some people get away with murder. Not surprisingly, the professionals getting away with murder are allies of medical examiners in the organizational ecology of death investigation: health care providers who kill their patients and law enforcement officers who kill suspects.[17] For deaths in health care institutions and deaths in police custody, the medical examiner often writes "undetermined," "natural death," "accidental death," or even "suicide" on the death certificate. These designations provide the perfect cover-up.

PRIMUM NON NOCERE: FIRST, DO NO HARM

When Dr. Harold Shipman was first arrested in 1998, one of his patients posted a note in his office window stating, "We don't believe it."[18] Soon, even the hard-core skeptics reluctantly accepted that the family physician in the town of Hyde, Britain, might be one of the world's most prolific killers. Shipman was convicted of murdering fifteen patients and suspected of killing between 220 and 240 others, mostly elderly women. Dr. Shipman would make unannounced visits to his patients during the afternoon, give them a lethal injection of diamorphine (heroin), and return later to sign the death certificate.

Avoiding detection was surprisingly easy for the doctor. A review of his records showed that Dr. Shipman issued 180 of 267 death certificates of elderly women who died under his care. Under British law, an autopsy was unnecessary if a doctor had seen the patient within seven days. Dr. Shipman always assured the coroner that he had met that requirement. When relatives requested an autopsy—for example, when the doctor found heart disease to be the cause of death even though the deceased had no known history of heart disease—he convinced them that a postmortem was unnecessary. When cremation certificates would have otherwise needed to be countersigned by another physician, Dr. Shipman provided false details and fabricated information on medical records in order to avoid that requirement. Two of the deaths were investigated by coroners (without public inquests), but both were attributed to "natural causes." Murder was so easy that Dr. Shipman killed in his office, sometimes three patients in one day. Even when he made obvious mistakes, he easily escaped suspicion. In 1997, he killed someone other than the person he had intended, afterward misidentifying the deceased. When the relatives complained, he pleaded confusion. He also killed someone while, unbeknownst to him, a relative was in the house. In a third instance, the dose was insufficient, and the patient remained in a persistent vegetative state for fourteen months; the autopsy discovered only "natural causes."

Eventually a funeral worker, having become suspicious after so many women died with their clothes on, alerted other physicians in the same town. The doctors, however, were unable to investigate, because Dr. Shipman's records were confidential. They contacted an insurance group and were told to drop the matter because they had no proof. Next, they notified the coroner and a police officer, who analyzed medical records. The detective found no pattern of suspicious death because the records were incomplete and fabricated; he wrote no report. Dr. Shipman made his final mistake when he clumsily forged a will for one of his patients, making him the beneficiary of her estate. Questions about the forged will led to an exhumation of the body and the detection of diamorphine. From there the investigation mushroomed, leading to his conviction. During the trial, the prosecution depended on immunoassay and gas-chromatography analyses of morphine and diamorphine in skeletal muscles. Dr. Shipman argued that one of his patients had been abusing medication (morphine is available in small dosages in over-the-counter medicine in Britain). The circumstantial evidence sealed his fate, however, and he received fifteen life sentences. He was found hanging by his bedsheets in his cell on January 14, 2004.

Dr. Shipman is not the only health care provider who has killed deliberately. In 2000, a U.S. physician, Dr. Michael Swango, pleaded guilty to four counts of murder, four counts of attempted murder, and five felonies.[19] He had poisoned co-workers and patients, writing in his diary how much he enjoyed the "internal homicide." From the time he entered medical school, Dr. Swango's career had been dogged by suspicions of incompetence, fabrication of records, and negligence. He was dismissed several times after internal investigations but easily found new jobs, because his supervisors wrote glowing recommendations. He is suspected in at least thirty-five deaths. In March 2001, a jury convicted Kristen

Gilbert, a nurse in a Veterans Administration (VA) hospital, for killing four patients with injections of a cardiac stimulant. In 2002, pharmacist Robert Courtney was sentenced for diluting the medication of more than four thousand terminally ill patients, thereby potentially shortening their lives. In December 2003, former nurse Charles Cullen claimed to have killed more than forty patients, and he pleaded guilty in April 2004 to killing at least fourteen patients. A team of investigative reporters wrote: "More than a decade ago, a medical examiner neglected to order a test on a dead patient that investigators now say might have stopped Mr. Cullen. Another coroner believed that a death was not accidental but did not alert prosecutors or the police. And several times when the police, prosecutors, medical examiners and licensing authorities investigated deaths that might have been linked to Mr. Cullen, they did not look deep enough to learn of previous investigations."[20] His ability to keep killing was particularly galling because wherever he went, people found his behavior "erratic, suspicious, even criminal."[21] In the past twenty-five years, at least twenty health care providers have been charged with killings in medical facilities.[22]

At regular intervals, a health care provider is put behind bars, but never for killing only a single patient. Perhaps detecting the hand of a health care provider in a single death is impossible, but medical examiners are unlikely to answer that question. The death investigation system is stacked against applying the concept of forensic homicide to iatrogenic (care-provider-induced) deaths. At least six obstacles prevent medical examiners from applying forensic homicide to a death under medical care.

First, the death investigation system has a built-in triaging obstacle. Legal guidelines for hospitals and physicians determine which deaths under medical care must be reported to the medical examiner's office.[23] The Shipman case shows, however, that many physicians in the United Kingdom lack familiarity with reporting procedures, a concern echoed by the Institute of Medicine in the United States.[24] Furthermore, reporting does not mean that there will be an investigation. When scene investigators answer calls reporting deaths under medical care, they assume that a death is natural if a combination of illness and age criteria are met. Documented heart disease in a man under forty years of age would be an insufficient explanation, and the investigators would have the man brought in for an autopsy. If this man's father had died with reported heart disease at age seventy, however, investigators would be unlikely to make the death a medical examiner's case. After consulting with the medical examiner, the scene investigator would not only communicate that an autopsy was unwarranted (after asking questions to rule out trauma) but also try to convince the attending physician to sign the death certificate. If the hospital or emergency-department physician felt uncomfortable signing a death certificate without prior knowledge of the patient, the scene investigator would ask the patient's primary physician for a signature. If no physician were available to sign and the patient had an extensive medical history, one of the forensic pathologists would cull a likely cause and manner of death from hospital records. And as I explained in chapter 1, if no medical history is available, the default cause of death without autopsy is coronary artery disease. Once the cause of death has been determined, the legal next of kin can request immediate cremation. If suspicion of foul play arises later, nothing can retrieve the body (several of Dr. Shipman's victims were cremated). Dr. Anthony in the medical examiner's office shivered at the thought of cremation certificates allowing evidence of foul play to be burned. A full investigation and autopsy ensue only if other health care providers report suspicions of neglect or intentional death.[25]

Whenever relatives brought to the medical examiner's attention a "medical" case that was not covered under the office's legal jurisdiction, the pathologists advised family members to hire a private pathologist and even volunteered to interpret the pathology findings. Only if relatives insisted would the office conduct a death investigation. The difference between medical and forensic investigation reflects an entrenched division of labor between hospital and forensic pathologists. Until the early 1980s, hospital pathologists often conducted autopsies to correlate clinical diagnosis and treatment with pathological findings for patients who had died in a hospital.[26] The autopsy served as quality control, checking pathology against diagnostic prediction; its primary goal was to increase medical knowledge. With fewer hospital autopsies, medical examiners have not filled the breach. The forensic investigation of a "medical" case is done primarily to help relatives understand what happened to their loved one.

A second obstacle to forensically investigating deaths that occur under physicians' care is that pathologists assume that medical records are complete and accurate. When the potential "perpetrator" is a medical expert, knowledge of the autopsy process and the limits of a forensic investigation may well inform the medical records to be scrutinized by the death investigators. In one crass instance of psychologizing, Dr. Swango wrote that one patient who had accused him of attempting to poison her "had apparent paranoid ideation as to the cause of her respiratory arrest."[27] Still, pathologists are aware that fear of adversarial death investigations might lead to inaccurate records. One pathologist writes, "The forensic expert may be seen by hospital personnel and the deceased's physicians as an adversary rather than a seeker of the truth. As a consequence, the forensic pathologist may be given only limited cooperation by medical colleagues."[28] Physicians are advised that the best defense against criminal suspicions is good record keeping,[29] but medical examiners have no way to determine whether medical records have been doctored, so to speak.

Third, even when the medical examiner's office investigates hospital and nursing home deaths (such investigations occur rarely), not only is the investigation complex and time-consuming, but the cause of death is likely to remain undetermined, or the verdict is a natural death. In a case I observed, a nurse reported in a written, signed statement that a nursing home patient was found facedown with her head stuck between the bed rails. The nurse's colleagues reported that the patient was found faceup. By the time the scene investigator entered the room, the scene had been disturbed, because the patient had been moved. No police or rescue personnel attended this scene, and the medical examiner was left with two conflicting stories. The autopsy provided no indication of smothering—which is very difficult to discern anyway—and the manner of death was noted as "natural." In suspicious deaths due to a surgical error, the body will likely have advanced disease, marks from surgery, and then the complication itself. To disentangle these factors and determine a straightforward cause and effect are challenging tasks. A determination of natural death is the likely outcome.

Occasionally, a relative of an elderly person who has died is convinced that the nursing home or hospital mistreated the deceased. In one case, an elderly woman who had been staying in a nursing home was transferred to a hospital after experiencing shortness of breath, and she subsequently expired. The daughter claimed abuse in the nursing home (none was ever documented), and the hospital offered to do an autopsy. The daughter declined, stating she was going to sue the hospital as well, and instead badgered the medical examiner's office into taking the case. The autopsy, however, was negative. It failed to find anything suspicious, and the death was classified as natural. Hospitalized and elderly people usually have extensive medical histories that readily provide counterexplanations for suspicious signs. Even if a body is badly bruised, concluding that blunt-force trauma caused the death is difficult, because the elderly bruise easily. As one pathologist explained to a police officer, simply putting a Band-Aid on the parchment-like skin of a frail, elderly person could create a two-inch bruise. During the autopsy, the pathologist looks for any signs of long-term neglect and abuse, such as extreme pressure wounds or signs of untreated infection. Building a forensic homicide case on these signs, however, is difficult. When I asked medical examiners what cases might be misclassified homicides, all mentioned nursing home patients.[30] Of the six hundred thousand people who die yearly in nursing homes, few receive autopsies—in part because Medicaid, a major payer, does not reimburse for autopsies.[31] Dr. Franken stated, "Some of our patients that die in our nursing homes, we sign them out as hypertensive ASCVD, but they might have been improperly treated. You don't always look for the drugs and abuse. I am sure that it is out there." A fifteen-year review of homicide among the elderly found no deaths due to abuse in an institutional context (the authors did, however, find two instances of spousal abuse and one of relative-caretaker abuse). Commenting on this unexpected finding, the authors postulated that

one explanation for our few cases is that abuse in our jurisdiction occurs more frequently, but it is not being detected by our office. Abuse might go undetected if a case were never referred to us, or if we declined to accept jurisdiction in an elderly individual for whom the circumstances surrounding death did not seem unusual. We routinely decline jurisdiction in cases where the elderly decedent has a medical history, such as hypertension, which accounts for death and which is in keeping with the circumstances surrounding death. If the police who investigate the death are concerned that foul play might be involved, we accept jurisdiction. Another possibility is that elder abuse sufficient to cause death is an unusual occurrence.[32]

A fourth obstacle is the expected high mortality rate of many serious illnesses and diseases. Even if a health care provider contributes to the death of a patient, proving malpractice is still difficult, because standard treatment results in death for a high percentage of patients. For example, sociologist Isabelle Baszanger reported that in cancer research, oncologists faced an ethical dilemma: "Are we going to kill the patient or let the cancer do the job?"[33] When death seemed inevitable, oncologists could either let the disease take its course or try to manipulate the dying process with innovative, experimental therapies, which often produced lethal side effects. Deaths due to experimental and innovative procedures become the collateral damage of advancing medical knowledge. Whether these deaths should be considered homicide is further complicated when people volunteer for experimental clinical trials and surgeries, signing waivers stating that they understand that death might be the result of their participation. Are such deaths forensic homicide? Suicide? Whether the result of the "normal" therapeutic course, a physician's inexperience, or malice, they remain outside the forensic realm.

In a classic study of mistakes during surgical residency training, Charles Bosk differentiates among technical, judgmental, normative, and quasi-normative errors.[34] Technical errors are due to shortfalls in skills in an imperfect surgical science. They are inevitable but presumably rare in surgical training and are usually reported promptly to supervisors. A judgmental error involves the wrong course of surgical treatment, usually over-

or undertreatment. A normative error involves bad professional behavior, such as trying to cover up a technical error rather than reporting it, or quarreling with nurses. It is behavior unbecoming a surgeon. A quasi-normative error occurs when a resident fails to adhere to the attending surgeon's idiosyncratic style. Any of these mistakes might result in serious complications or death. Bosk discusses how surgeons collectively manage these mistakes in informal conversations between superiors and subordinates during rounds. Mistakes are further discussed in weekly mortality and morbidity reviews, where even senior surgeons might "put on the hair shirt" and offer a public (i.e., in front of colleagues) mea culpa, although usually without specifying who was personally responsible for the complication or death. Mistakes are also reviewed in end-of-year meetings, when the senior staff decide who will be promoted. None of these deliberations extend beyond the surgical department. Bosk shows, instead, professional self-regulation in action. He remarks about the mortality and morbidity conference, "The major punishment of the practice is the embarrassment of a public confessional and the pain the outcome itself actually causes the surgeon's conscience. As a form of social control, this admission of error rests on the self-surveillance and self-reports of the individuals involved. . . . So this is hair shirt on the outside only; for the wearer it has the silken lining of unconditional professional support."[35] As suggested by the book's title, *Forgive and Remember,* surgeons confess technical breaches expecting redemption. Errors are viewed as opportunities to learn and to gauge the moral fiber of future surgeons. Close supervision during training is expected to weed out "bad" surgeons, those who make grievous or repeated normative errors.[36] After training is completed, a surgeon is professionally inviolate, and "you hope for the best."[37] Individual professional conscience prevails over external accountability.

A fifth obstacle to forensic investigation of deaths under medical care is medicine's engagement in a host of initiatives aimed at helping old and terminally ill people die. "Helping" implies injecting drugs to make patients physically comfortable, knowing that some drugs will hasten death. The "double effect" of morphine and other drugs is one example: "The idea is that the physician intends only to relieve the patient's pain; while morphine will also kill the patient, this second effect is not intended, and the physician's act is therefore not wrong."[38] Initially the hospice movement and now growing "right-to-die" organizations have argued that suffering from lengthy, painful terminal illnesses is worse than death. Palliative care aimed at symptom control and pain management, however, is a small step from helping a patient die and often depends on only a slight increase in the administered dose. Right-to-die and assisted-suicide advocates argue that physicians and other health care providers should be able to take that step and "allow" patients to die. Advocates consider this interference not homicide but fulfillment of a physician's duty to facilitate humane, dignified dying. The elderly and terminally ill are not the only patients vulnerable to such actions. The forensics and bioethics literatures contain several case histories of infanticide, purportedly committed because the infants were severely disabled.[39]

The result of these initiatives is a number of mixed categories designating actions that technically qualify as forensic homicide. These categories include active and passive euthanasia and physician-assisted suicide. The terms imply an explicit acknowledgment that death was directly or indirectly caused by others, but disease, the imminent death, and caring intentions are felt to "soften" the murder. In passive euthanasia, health care providers cease to slow down death. The focus on "hastening" death in active euthanasia underscores the inevitability of a passing. The neologism *physician-assisted suicide* emphasizes that a physician provides only the pharmaceutical means for a patient's wish to take his or her own life.[40]

How do medical examiners classify these "mercy killings"? Medical examiners spare themselves from wrangling with the ethical fine points, because policy in medical examiner's offices in general exempts these deaths from forensic investigation. At my research site, hospice deaths were treated as hospital deaths, even if the patient died at home under hospice care. Unless the death occurred within twenty-four hours of admission to a hospice program, the hospice physician filled out the death certificate and the office was not notified. When the Death with Dignity Act was enacted by the Oregon legislature in 1997, it explicitly stated that physician-assisted suicide deaths "do not constitute suicide, assisted suicide, mercy killing or homicide." Larry Lewman, Oregon's chief medical examiner at the time, exempted these deaths from investigation by his office.[41] A review of case law in Maryland showed that even when medical examiners are charged with investigating health care personnel who assist in another person's death, "there is really no reason that a palliative care provider should have any concern about criminal prosecution or administrative sanction. . . . to criminally convict a palliative care provider of a homicidal act essentially requires an admission of guilt."[42] Indeed, in one of the presented cases, an administrative judge overruled the medical examiner, who had noted lethal morphine levels as a primary cause of death for a woman who died with a history of breast cancer and Alzheimer's disease; the medical examiner had classified the death as undetermined. The judge gave greater weight to the opinion of the palliative pain specialists, who explained the morphine levels by the patient's acquired pain tolerance. The death was reclassified as having been caused by pneumonia and thus natural. This was one of only two medical examiner's cases that the Maryland study found to have appeared before an administrative judge in a ten-year period.

Sixth and finally, when medical examiners declare medical deaths to be homicide—despite the first five obstacles—the investigation will likely either fizzle out or backfire. Doctor Cahill remembered a case in her office in which a surgeon in a VA hospital administered an overdose of morphine and killed a patient. Nurses reported the case when they noticed that the morphine pump had been turned up. After a lengthy investigation, the medical examiner's staff felt that proof of a homicide was definitive. Staff members even suspected a motive: the surgeon had recently botched an operation on this patient. For "circumstances" on the death certificate, Dr. Cahill wrote, "giving morphine in excess of a medically recommended dosage." Because the death occurred in a VA hospital, she notified the FBI, and it became a federal case. The FBI, however, declined to prosecute. The surgeon claimed that he had acted out of pity for this terminal patient. Doctor Cahill admitted that if the nurses had not alerted her office, she would never have taken the case.

In 1998, Ronald Reeves, medical examiner of Volusia County, Florida, made headlines when he accused hospice doctors of giving nineteen terminally ill patients morphine overdoses to hasten their deaths. The medical examiner classified four of the deaths as forensic homicides. Within days of making these allegations, he was suspended (partly for an unrelated case of allegedly bungling a homicide investigation), and he resigned five months later. Morphine is often the pain reliever of choice for terminal patients because it relieves pain without putting patients to sleep. However, it can also cause respiratory arrest (the "double effect"), and as patients develop tolerance to it, they require progressively higher doses. A high level of morphine found in a hospice patient at autopsy might therefore be explained by the length of treatment and the patient's medical condition. A panel of national experts reviewed the Florida cases and exonerated the hospice. Although the morphine levels in some patients were indeed high, the experts felt that the hospice staff was not negligent. The medical community, the patients' relatives, and law enforcement officials rallied to the hospice's defense.

The reluctance of medical examiners to investigate their clinical colleagues is systemic. In 1995, the National Association of Medical Examiners (NAME) distributed a survey to its members consisting of various death scenarios. The death investigators were asked to classify the manner of death. Close to two hundred surveys were completed (a response rate of 23 percent). In one of the scenarios, a relatively healthy woman died of a surgical complication: the tip of a subclavian line (a catheter inserted in the subclavian vein that runs behind the clavicle) was protruding in the right chest. The cause of death was excess fluid in the right pleural cavity (right hydrothorax). Eighty-two percent of the respondents classified her death as accidental; 12 percent considered it natural; 1 percent classified the death as a forensic homicide; and the remaining respondents listed "undetermined" or left the question blank. The results of the survey were discussed during a plenary session of the annual NAME conference. One person suggested that the death could be considered a homicide because the patient died at the hands of another. Most of the audience, however, "appeared to feel that making such judgments places Medical Examiners in a difficult and precarious position, although a few audience members seemed to think that making such judgments was within the realm of responsibility." One expert "expressed his unwillingness to second guess clinical colleagues or to create a potentially inflammatory situation."[43] Another panel member noted that something must have gone wrong in the surgery and therefore put down "accident."

Charles Hirsch, a well-known expert in forensic pathology, has suggested "therapeutic complication" as a new manner of death when a death is due to a predictable complication from an appropriate therapy.[44] Although this new category would be reserved for cases in which death was not due to negligence or malpractice, most pathologists at the 1995 NAME meeting considered it "unduly inflammatory" to use such a designation.[45] Deaths due to therapeutic complications are generally classified as natural. A forensic textbook warns, "therapeutic complication *is prone to misinterpretation as implying negligence and should be avoided.*"[46]

The wide disparities in the results of the NAME survey stimulated the creation, in 2002, of a manner-of-death manual, approved by the NAME board of directors. The manual defines a process of classification for ambiguous deaths. It was written by three experts and incorporated suggestions given by the NAME membership during a six-week comment period. The manual substantiates the hands-off approach of forensic pathologists when reviewing possible iatrogenic deaths: "Deaths resulting from gross negligent medical care may be classified as accident unless there is clear indication of intent to do harm, in which [case] homicide might apply. The criminalization of medical malpractice is of great concern to both the medical and legal professions, and whether or not medical acts of commission or omission meet a legal definition of negligent or other homicide is better left to others more familiar with the legal issues involved."[47]

The notion that "inflaming" colleagues is sufficient reason for taking a hands-off approach in iatrogenic cases fits with a history of safeguarding internal professional regulation. The medical profession has a state-sponsored monopoly over a body of specialized knowledge. Peers determine whether negligence or malpractice has occurred. Physicians regulate entrance to the profession through certification and licensing, and, as Bosk reported, they handle professional mistakes internally. Every state has a board that licenses physicians in its territory, investigates complaints, and disciplines physicians found to be in violation of state law or the board's administrative rules. Only if a settlement cannot be reached is the case referred to legal authorities.

Although medical examiners are usually board-certified pathologists who spend long days investigating foul play and evaluating medical records, they do not investigate licensed physicians. Medical examiners are low in the medical hierarchy. In the eyes of their clinical colleagues, their daily experience has little resemblance to the work of clinicians. Following the work of cultural anthropologist Mary Douglas, sociologist Andrew Abbott explained that relative status within professions is related to the perceived purity of professional work. Professional groups working on clear, difficult yet definite professional problems (such as issues faced by thoracic surgeons) trump workers "tainted" by ambiguity, human complexity, and nonprofessional issues (such as the workload of emergency medicine). Forensic practitioners are, to use Abbott's word, "defiled" by their work in the eyes of their clinical peers.[48] For some investigative purposes, working on the border between law and medicine is a powerful position,[49] allowing insight into problems unintelligible to practitioners of either realm. Medical examiners know how to construct a tight legal case with medical evidence by examining a dead body. Within medicine, however, medical examiners are considered marginal, and their close collaboration with law enforcement is a sign of professional weakness. Their clinical colleagues do not trust that forensic pathologists have the in-depth knowledge to distinguish an easily preventable surgical oversight from deliberate neglect. Only true peers, physicians in the same subspecialty, are qualified to evaluate whether a physician followed the appropriate standards of care. Inquiries by the medical board, therefore, rarely rely on autopsies. Most depend instead on a review of records.

In addition, the ability of medical examiners to conduct any forensic investigation depends on the willingness of health care providers to share the patient's medical history. How can pathologists and clinicians create a collaborative relationship when the investigation might hold health care providers accountable? This is a recurring dilemma in death investigations. As we will see in the next chapter, medical examiners struggle with a similar problem when dealing with the parents of dead infants: how to persuade grieving parents to collaborate with the forensic investigation when they might be held legally accountable for their child's death. In that case, medical examiners hold out the possibility of formal exoneration; if this enticement fails, they try to legally coerce parents to collaborate. Neither the carrot nor the stick, however, works with health care providers. They are more likely to fight back by arguing over evidence and trying to discredit forensic professionals. In light of the strongly entrenched power of the medical professions and the dependence of medical examiners on their clinical colleagues, the investigative system resolves the collaboration-suspicion dilemma by exempting medical deaths from full forensic investigation. Clinicians and medical institutions share medical records with forensic pathologists with the understanding that the records will not be used against them. In this implicit agreement, physicians and other health care providers do not kill; rather, they make fatal errors. A widely publicized study carried out under the auspices of the National Academy of Sciences and the Institute of Medicine estimated that between 44,000 and 98,000 people die every year in the United States because of medical errors.[50] The title of the report—*To Err Is Human*—places the findings outside the criminal realm. The term "error" implies that the actions of the physician constitute unintentional deviance from a standard of practice. Iatrogenic deaths thus fall largely into a jurisdictional vacuum.

For criminal prosecution of a health care provider—such as in the cases of Drs. Shipman and Swango—the prosecutor needs to make the leap from malpractice and professional incompetence to criminal murder.[51] The jump to homicide requires a preponderance of evidence that is difficult to obtain. Dr. Shipman was discovered only after the forged will, exhumations, and toxicology tests. Suspicious co-workers set traps for Dr. Swango. The VA nurse Gilbert was discovered after a group of other nurses notified the hospital administration of unexplainable cardiac deaths. The diluting pharmacist was caught after a sting operation and independent laboratory tests. Nurse Cullen was finally arrested after the director of a toxicology lab threatened to reveal a list of suspicious deaths to state authorities when hospital officials had been dragging their feet for months in an internal investigation. If these care providers had stopped killing after one patient or only a few patients, they likely would have remained undetected. Forensic death investigations were little help in solving these criminal cases. Indeed, these homicides were detected in spite of the extra barrier of deaths having been certified as due to natural causes.

DEATHS IN POLICE CUSTODY

In modern democratic societies, police officers have the legal right to use violence to neutralize threats and maintain public order. Indeed, a classic treatise on police work states that "the police are nothing else than a mechanism for the distribution of situationally justified force in society."[52] Yet the line between justifiable force and police brutality is contentious. Sociologists have argued that the threat of violence protects the interests of the privileged, including the interests of the state.[53] In the United States, on average, one person is killed by law enforcement officers every day.[54] Social scientists have found that such lethal violence is not simply a reaction to interpersonal violence encountered by police; rather, it varies significantly by political factors, most notably the racial makeup of urban environments and economic inequities. Sociologists David Jacobs and Robert O'Brien found that police are more likely to use lethal violence in populous cities, particularly those characterized by greater racial inequalities. Greater economic differences between blacks and whites reduce both the black population's ability to curb police violence and the willingness of the dominant majority to intervene in law enforcement. Cities with black mayors have fewer police killings of blacks, presumably because black mayors are more dependent on black votes and appoint different law enforcement administrators.[55] In recent years, the general public has been sensitized to police brutality, with harrowing images of police beatings, officers restraining victims forcibly, the "accidental" shooting of an off-duty black officer by white officers, and a special "vice" squad riddling an unarmed suspect with nineteen bullets (out of forty-one fired). Two leading medical examiners acknowledge that "in our specialty, there is no more slippery slope than deaths in [police] custody. Justice must be served, and served fairly, first and foremost. Judgments made have legal ramifications and are often rendered without recourse to legitimate second opinions. Political fallout may result, regardless of the conclusions reached."[56] Another forensic expert explains, "Clearly, correct certification of cause-of-death while in police custody is essential to protect the public from undue harm and to protect the police from wrongful allegations."[57]

Lethal police action usually leads to an intense inquiry to determine whether the police used force justifiably, in self-defense or to protect civilians. Medical examiners participate in such investigations. The key issue in these inquiries is not whether a suspect died at the hands of police—in most instances, the police use weapons that leave little ambiguity—but whether lethal force was warranted by the circumstances. In contrast with cases of physician-induced mortality, the death investigation centers not on revealing a homicide but on determining the intent behind the chain of events preceding the fatality. Even if the police killed someone, was the death provoked by the deceased, or did the police overstep the bounds of their legal prerogative to use lethal force? As is clear with suicide, probing intent is a messy affair, involving consideration of split-second decision making, the difference between perceived and actual threats, changing public sentiment, jurisprudence, and professional policies about the use of force. According to the standard definition of forensic homicide, medical examiners should always classify deaths at the hands of another as homicides. Their determination is part of a fact-finding investigation, and while it is admissible at trial, it is not binding in a criminal investigation. A conclusion of forensic homicide for a death that receives intense public and legal scrutiny—with careers hanging in the balance and the potential of civil and criminal liability—will inevitably be a highly charged decision.

At my research site, deaths involving police on duty received the highest investigative priority. The chief medical examiner would conduct the autopsy herself after a careful review of all medical and law enforcement files and an extensive scene investigation. Forensic experts recommend a step-by-step reconstruction of the confrontation between law enforcement officials and the detained person (a freeze-frame approach).[58] The close collaboration that takes place between law enforcement officials and medical examiners in every aspect of routine homicides, however, will necessarily be constrained in these cases. If police officers are the "eyes and ears" of the medical examiners on the scene, this "sensory information" may be unreliable or incomplete in investigations of police actions. The routine exchange of information, the elaborate investigative etiquette, and the integration of interpretations during the autopsy will be restrained. As with iatrogenic deaths, medical examiners will depend largely on information written by the potential "perpetrators." In some police agencies, the officer involved in the use of force is expected to submit a report.[59] Even if other law enforcement agencies conduct the scene investigation and interrogation, they face exceptionally skilled "suspects" who are fully aware of the implications of every word they speak or write. While they cannot avoid these forensic investigations, medical examiners will retrench their efforts and stick to purely pathological fact-finding. Whereas an evidentiary standard of 51 percent is sufficient to declare a suicide, the standard for a death to be classified as a homicide in cases involving police seems closer to 99 percent. In such cases, forensic pathologists rely on ultraconservative standards of evidence. If any natural disease might allow for an alternative explanation, it will likely weigh heavily. Unless there are extraordinary circumstances, law enforcement officials will receive a generous benefit of the doubt. The medical literature offers two specific instances in which medical examiners provide alternative explanations when deaths caused by police have all the characteristics of a forensic homicide.[60]

"Suicide by Cop"

The lethal use of guns, even by police, seems to override any explanation other than forensic homicide. An accidental firing of a police gun constitutes a breach of professional responsibility. How can a death caused by a bullet not be a forensic homicide, justified or not? Researchers have recently developed a new category of almost-but-not-quite homicide: "suicide by cop," sometimes called "suicide by homicide." "Suicide by cop" refers to an incident in which an allegedly suicidal individual intentionally engages in life-threatening and criminal behavior toward law enforcement officers with what appears to be a lethal weapon. The victim is presumed to provoke, as a means of suicide, the police officer's right to use lethal force. Presumably, this is a more macho way of dying than taking one's own life.[61] My research site witnessed one such case, involving a man in his late forties who was drinking in the parking lot of a liquor store and waving a gun around. The store employees had notified police, as had the man's father, who told police that his son had threatened him. Three police cars pulled up at the same time. The officers told the man to put his hands in the air, but he drew a gun from his waistband, waved it at the officers, and, aiming the gun at them, dared them to shoot him. After police officers opened fire, they found the gun unloaded. This death was classified as a forensic homicide, but the pathologist wrote that the man had provoked the police.

Initial researchers relied on suicide notes left by the deceased to classify deaths as suicide by homicide.[62] Over time, however, a broader definition has taken hold: if a person expresses to police officers a verbal wish to die (e.g., shouting "Shoot me" or "You won't get me alive"), the situation qualifies as suicide by homicide. In one study, most cases of suicide by cop were determined in that way,[63] so that the interpretation of the person firing the gun justified the shooting. While in most suicide cases people have given verbal or behavioral clues that they intend to take their lives, suicide researchers agree that most people expressing verbal threats to commit suicide will not in fact attempt it.[64] Another complicating factor is the presence of cocaine or alcohol, which suggests that the shooting victim might have been delirious or under the influence and may not have intended to die. Interpretation of intent quickly becomes murky, and it inevitably seems self-serving. In one case study, a father angry about problems with the special schooling of his disabled son was shot after taking several school officials hostage at gunpoint and claiming to have explosive devices. According to psychiatrists presenting the case, "The meta-goal here was suicide."[65] Perhaps the meta-goal was a better education for his son. If a person in the midst of committing a robbery swears not to be taken alive by police, is that person truly suicidal? Is pointing a gun at a police officer a clear indication of suicidal behavior? In a standoff, are biblical references to the book of Revelations a sign of suicide? For some researchers and police officers, the answer is yes.[66]

Studies show that medical examiners variously classify such deaths as forensic homicide, suicide, or undetermined. In one unusual article, coauthors disagreed with one another about classifying such deaths. Focusing on the intent to die, one author argued for suicide, but the other contended that medical examiners should not second-guess the victim's state of mind and should apply homicide definitions uniformly.[67] In the 1995 NAME survey, for a scenario similar to a suicide by cop, 82 percent of respondents selected homicide as the manner of death, while 11 percent chose suicide and 5 percent classified the death as undetermined. Whether such a death is classified as homicide or suicide depends on how much weight the medical examiner gives to the mind-set of the victim in comparison to the source of the lethal bullet. The determination will put the onus of death on either the victim or the police. Even if a gun were fired deliberately to kill someone, some death investigators might certify the death as a suicide if the victim presumably wished to die. I could not, however, find a single case in which someone outside law enforcement shot another person and the death was interpreted as a provoked suicide.

Positional Asphyxia

In the medical examiner's office of my study, police were implicated in forensic homicide only when guns were fired. Virtually all "justifiable homicides" by law enforcement in the FBI's Uniform Crime Reports between 1999 and 2003 involved firearms.[68] Whether blunt-force trauma contributed to the death of a person in police custody is trickier to determine. Any signs of trauma can be explained by the victim's having resisted arrest, and if traces of illegal drugs are detected at autopsy, they offer a natural explanation for death. One recently contested area of police involvement in custody deaths, however, is a rash of delirious people dying after being placed in restraints.[69] In 1982, Seattle medical examiner Donald Reay successfully made the case that a popular restraining maneuver—the "neck hold," or "choke hold," in which the restrainer put an arm around the neck of the subject—could be lethal. The neck hold caused trauma observable during the autopsy, and its effects were experimentally supported with studies of reduced carotid blood flow.[70] The research and costly civil litigation led law enforcement agencies to abandon this method of restraint.

Three years later, forensic pathologist Charles Wetli and psychiatrist David Fishbain reported seven cases of death in cocaine users, four of whom had been placed in a "hog-tie like restraint." The deaths were attributed to cocaine intoxication complicated by other factors, including "restraint stress," a psychiatric term referring to sudden death associated with acute exhaustive mania. Wetli and Fishbain explicitly excluded mechanical asphyxia as a cause of death in these cases, because witnesses testified that none of the deceased had been restrained with the discredited neck-hold method. Instead, the authors drew attention to "excited delirium," which was becoming relevant to forensic pathologists because of increased drug use and a growing uninstitutionalized population with severe paranoid and manic disorders: "Delirium is an acute organic mental disorder characterized by a disturbance of attention and perception, impaired thinking, disorientation for individuals around the patient, visual hallucinations and illusions. The cases presented here are best characterized as an excited delirium secondary to cocaine intoxication. . . . the outcome may be fatal."[71] The notion of excited delirium could explain why some people under the influence of cocaine died with relatively low toxicological evidence (although there are no agreed-upon lethal levels for cocaine). While the article did not specify a manner of death, the authors clearly had in mind a classification of either natural or accidental death.

In 1992, Reay and associates presented three cases in which victims were restrained with the hog-tie method, put in the rear seat of police vehicles—apparently still alive—and then found dead upon arrival at their destination. In "hog-tie" restraining, the person is placed facedown with wrists tied behind the back and ankles tied together (hobbling); then the knees are bent and the bound wrists are tied to the hobbled ankles. Autopsies found no anatomical or toxicological findings that could explain sudden death, and Reay and his colleagues applied the term "positional asphyxia" as a specific cause of death: "Positional asphyxia occurs when the position of the body interferes with respiration, resulting in asphyxia. The deleterious positional effect may result either from interference with the muscular or mechanical component of respiration, from compromise of the airway, or from some combination of these. . . . In our view, the application of hog-tied-type restraints and subsequent positioning of the victim led to the respiratory compromise that caused these men's death." Here, the position of the deceased is apparently more significant than other findings: "There will be deaths, particularly those where cocaine, methamphetamine, and high levels of alcohol are present, in which it becomes tempting to assign the cause of death solely to these intoxicants, and to ignore or discount the final position in which the victim was found dead. . . . The same dilemma occurs in deaths where significant, but not necessarily fatal, natural disease exists."[72] Reay and associates reinterpreted the work of Wetli and Fishbain as evidence of the lethality of the hog-tie method. They supported their argument with earlier research in which healthy individuals were placed in the hog-tie restraint after exerting themselves on an exercise bike and showed prolonged recovery times for both the heart rate and oxygen saturation.[73] In an accompanying editorial, James Luke and Donald Reay further specified that "if the method or means used in the restraining process has been defined as representing deadly force, and death results during its application, the death is appropriately certified as homicide."[74] The criterion for determining the manner of death is thus whether the police officer putting on the restraints should have known that such restraining positions might be lethal.

Medical examiner and substance-abuse researcher Elizabeth Laposata disagreed with her colleagues, noting that the correlation of the deaths with a restraint method was insufficient to single out positional asphyxia as the cause of death and asserting that more research with control groups was needed. She further pointed out that exertion and struggle against restraints should be considered contributing causal factors.[75] The next year, Ronald O'Halloran and Larry Lewman published a report of eleven cases in which people died after being put in the hog-tie position. Although all the deceased had been in an excited delirious state (usually due to cocaine intoxication) and drug intoxication had been accepted as a sufficient cause of death, these pathologists argued that the cases fell into "the category of positional asphyxiation."[76] Several other case reports discussing hog-tie methods listed positional asphyxia as the sole or contributing cause of death.[77]

Independent of these developments, the San Diego Police Department and San Diego medical examiner's office issued a report in 1992 about the deaths of seven young men who had died suddenly while in custody after exhibiting agitated and delirious behavior. At least three of the men had been constrained by the hog-tie method. The police department conducted a national survey of law enforcement agencies, finding that 39 percent of them reported in-custody deaths and confirming at least ninety-four cases of restraint-associated in-custody deaths. The department then banned the restraining technique. In 1994, Los Angeles County officials also forbade hog-tie restraints after settling a lawsuit in a case in which an epileptic patient restrained by paramedics died.[78] A similar concept of mechanical asphyxia, referring to deaths caused by jackets and other restraints used in geriatric settings, circulated in the emergency and psychiatric literatures. The idea that a restraint could cause death thus gained a foothold in forensics. In 1995 the Wichita, Kansas, police department issued a training bulletin explaining that the hog-tie method could result in death if other risk factors were present, and in 1996 the *FBI Law Enforcement Bulletin* reprinted an adaptation of Reay and associates' 1992 article.[79] The same year, another study determined that the hog-tie restraint can depress breathing and cardiac function.[80] The conclusion for medical examiners is to "consistently classify as homicide this type of death."[81]

Referring back to the original interpretation by Wetli and Fishbain, opponents of the concept of positional asphyxia focused on the paranoid delirium of psychiatric illness or illegal drugs and the deleterious cardiac effects of chronic drug intoxication and stress as aggravating factors. Excited delirium results in an impairment of consciousness with abnormalities of mood, perception, and behavior, including violence, incoherent speech, and aggression toward shiny objects. Subjects often threaten or attack bystanders, destroy property, or run into traffic. When police arrive, the delirious person fights back with extreme strength, often expressing fear of the police, and many officers are required to subdue and restrain the subject.[82] The delirious person then suddenly lapses into tranquility and dies. The hog-tie restraint is considered an appropriate response to drug- or illness- induced aberrant behavior. Critics of the positional-asphyxia hypothesis noted that besides causing neurochemical changes, cocaine also depresses respiration and cardiac function, might lead to high circulation of catecholamines, and could be associated with myocardial hypertrophy and fibrosis.[83] Excited delirium can also occur in patients who combine cocaine with alcohol, in patients with mental disorders—particularly when receiving tranquilizers during manic periods—and in patients taking antipsychotic medication.[84] Noting that many victims of excited delirium die in police custody, critics also recommended that the hog-tie method be phased out but gave it little explanatory credence in death investigations.[85]

In 1998, emergency physician Theodore Chan and associates challenged the science behind positional asphyxia. They presented experimental data showing that although the hog-tie method reduced pulmonary function, the results were still in the normal range, and pulmonary function was reduced in other positions as well. While acknowledging that experimental conditions did not replicate the agitation and resistance of police interventions, these researchers concluded that "factors other than body positioning appear to be more important determinants for sudden, unexpected deaths in individuals in the hogtie custody restraint position."[86] In reaction, Donald Reay and John Howard acknowledged that "an association does not necessarily indicate causality" and that the hog-tie method should be seen as "an inherently neutral position . . . with no significant physiologic consequence in normal people."[87] The catch is "in normal people." According to Reay and Howard, the violence of a hog-tie restraint suggests that respiration might be stressed. They argued for a national database that would list all pertinent factors in custody deaths.

The divisive debate over positional asphyxia in the forensic literature has all the characteristics of a controversy about evolving scientific evidence, with at least four different positions in question: Is the delirium—whatever its cause—the most important aspect of the death scene? Is the hog-tie method the culprit? Should the explanation instead be sought among *all* procedures for restraining delirious people?[88] Or is positional asphyxia actually a long-recognized, broad mechanism of death in which the airway is obstructed due to the position of the body at the time of death?[89] For Reay and others, the repeatedly observed deaths in hog-tie restraints all over the country make the restraining method a strong contributing factor. These deaths should therefore be classified as homicides, especially now that the potential lethality of these restraints should be widely known. For Laposata, Chan, Wetli, and other skeptics, restraints are not necessarily more meaningful a factor than the clothes a restrained person wore or the fact that most victims are male. The key issue is the deceased's drug- or mental-illness-induced delirium. Police therefore have little responsibility in deaths that occur when they restrain combative victims. The skeptics provide alternative examples in which appearances have misled. Scalp wounds and a minor skull fracture sustained during the arrest of a person with cocaine-induced excited delirium were considered at autopsy insufficient to explain the death, although medical personnel and witnesses initially presumed that the head injury caused the death.[90] Both sides agree that "death during police restraint is generally viewed with extreme suspicion."[91] Yet they classify similar deaths differently, either exonerating police or implying their responsibility in the deaths.

As research continues, forensic pathologists have to determine the manner of death when confronted with these cases. The scientific determination of causality is inevitably influenced by medical examiners' presumption of justifiable homicide and the institutionalized relationship between police and forensic investigators. The interpretation of evidence determines in which cases the police will receive the benefit of the doubt. If a pathologist presumes that police officers generally use violence only to protect themselves or the public, then the evidence of a deceased suspect in restraints might be given less weight than the natural factors and the toxicology results. If, on the other hand, a medical examiner has concluded that some police violence is unwarranted and might be harmful, even if unintentionally, the medical examiner can imply police accountability on the death certificate. Institutionally, the former choice is the path of least resistance. Medical examiners depend on law enforcement for their scene investigations and can ill afford an antagonistic relationship with police. Even though the NAME manual with guidelines for manner-of-death determinations suggests that death investigators classify deaths in police custody as homicide to avoid the impression of a cover-up, two case-review studies indicate that most deaths involving excited delirium and positional asphyxia are classified as accidental.[92]

★ ★ ★

As with physician-induced deaths, medical examiners are faced with a stronghold of professionalism: the right of law enforcement to self-regulate. Only highly skilled officers familiar with the daily demands of policing are presumed qualified to evaluate police conduct.[93] Law enforcement agencies have their own internal-affairs divisions to check officer violations, and some cases go through an additional review by a civilian oversight board.[94] Civilian reviews, however, depend greatly on internal police investigations. Here, too, certain professional protections are systemic, with legal barriers and discretionary practices insulating police against civilian complainants. Reports and collected volumes do point to abuse. In the 1981 U.S. government report *Who Is Guarding the Guardians?* and its 2000 follow-up report, congressional commissions documented the correlation between a reduction in violent crime and an increase in civil rights violations by police and repeated the decades-old complaint about a lack of clear policies on the use of lethal force.[95] Medical examiners are, then, implicated in the self-regulation of police work: they might not investigate independently, but they still sign death certificates that say "natural," "accidental," "suicide"—or "homicide."

THE JANUS FACE OF ORDER AND DISORDER

The current death investigation system reflects a tension in American professionalism. Clinicians and police have the professional prerogative to use lethal means on people, and if potential transgressions occur, they are evaluated internally, within the profession. As medicolegal professionals, medical examiners depend heavily on the collaboration of their clinical and law enforcement allies in routine death investigations. Aggressively applying the category of forensic homicide to law enforcement and medical deaths not only risks that much-needed collaboration but also can lead to the heavy-handed contestation of forensic evidence that can devastate the credibility of medical examiners.

A forensic investigation of a law enforcement or medical death lacks the independence required of medical examiners in routine investigations. The investigation of routine homicides requires medical examiners to take information from police and clinicians at face value. Even more important than information is collaboration with clinical and law enforcement colleagues; it is fundamental to *any* forensic investigation, from the moment the office is alerted until the death certificate is signed. When confronted with the possibility of a death caused by their allies, medical examiners' gut reaction is to proclaim that determining the culpability of police and clinicians is the task of the criminal justice system. Yet in routine homicides, medical examiners have no problem writing "forensic homicide" on a death certificate. What death investigators actually mean when they disavow responsibility for investigating their allies is that because of the deeply symbiotic relationship, they are unable to make independent pronouncements.[96] The investigation cannot achieve its typical detached momentum: either medical examiners forgo investigating or they investigate too intensively, affecting their ability to resolve ambiguity. What are red flags in the investigation of routine homicides become uncertain findings in deaths at the hands of health care providers and law enforcement. The standard of evidentiary proof is always high in forensic determinations, but when medical examiners are investigating these professionals, the standard is all but impossible to meet. Not only do medical examiners need to show that the death was caused by others, but they also have to prove that it falls outside professional norms. Some "deaths caused by others" might thus slip by the investigative procedures.

For medical examiners' authority, the investigation of deaths involving police and iatrogenic deaths is a lose-lose situation: whatever pathologists decide, they open themselves up to heated criticism. In investigations of deaths under police custody, "some medical examiners have gone so far as to ask the family of the decedent to retain their own pathologist to witness the autopsy,"[97] and similar arrangements are regularly recommended in medical deaths. Medical examiners are thus willing in these cases to abandon their greatest professional asset—autonomy in the morgue. When evidence later reveals that health care providers or police officers killed their charges, death investigators can be swept up in the outrage. In Britain, for example, the Shipman case led to an extensive parliamentary inquiry into the reasons why the coronial investigation failed to detect the crimes during the twenty-four-year period over which they were committed.[98] On a national level, the inquiry documented the lack of training of coroners, variability in practice, the wide latitude coroners have in determining whether deaths fall under their jurisdiction, the great dependence of coroners on information from physicians, and the lack of leadership in the coroners' community. More specifically, the inquiry documented ad hoc decision making and lack of expertise on each level of death investigation and certification, which allowed Shipman to get away with murder. The inquiry recommended an overhaul of the coroner system aimed at strengthening its independence of any governmental branch, with broader judicial and medical powers and stricter guidelines for the inquiry in cases of hospital deaths.

The perfect crime and the routine homicide are two inseparable aspects of the same death investigation system. Whatever the outcome of a death investigation, it represents neither the consequence of criminal cunning nor a lucky break favoring the perpetrator. It does not involve an intentional conspiracy to cover up for allies. And it cannot be explained by flaws in forensic technologies. Perfect crimes committed by professionals and routine homicides are both investigated by following standard procedures involving similar processes to establish causality, reveal forensic evidence and transform it into causes and manners of death, write meticulous autopsy reports, anticipate contestations, and safeguard forensic authority. The only difference is that with perfect crimes, medical examiners are unable to connect with their usual allies, and consequently the investigation is unanchored. The ambiguity resolved in routine homicides is actively maintained in these perfect crimes. The moral safety net that allows routine homicides to be picked up by forensic detection becomes an impenetrable moral wall in the perfect crimes of professionals. In deaths involving their allies, medical examiners apply neutralized forensic techniques: they reveal but fail to notice. Even if forensic detection technologies do not achieve their promised accuracy, their use inevitably affects the final outcome of the investigation.[99] According to current forensic standards, potential homicides are classified as unsuspicious. The disorder of this perfect crime follows its own order; it does not occur randomly but is an anticipated product of the death investigation system.

At the same time, the order of declining homicide rates might hide its own disorder. Inevitably, when deaths that appear to be forensic homicides are not counted as such, one can question whether a reduction in crime has actually occurred. This is not an academic question, but one that affects policing in cities in the United States and the way we perceive others while walking down the street.[100] Homicide detection has recently gained attention, with research on U.S. crime statistics showing a drop in homicide rates beginning in the early 1990s after a steady ascent during the late 1980s.[101] In 1991 the homicide rate reached a peak of 9.8 deaths per 100,000 population, and by 1998 it had declined to less than 6.3 per 100,000—a rate not seen since the late 1960s.[102] By 2003 the figure had dropped to 5.7 per 100,000, and the preliminary figures for 2004 suggested a further decline.[103] The drop was most pronounced among teenagers and among young adult black males using handguns to murder other young black males, the group that had largely contributed to the earlier increase in homicides.[104] The homicide rates for intimate partners, people over twenty-five years of age, and those using weapons other than handguns have generally been declining or have remained flat since the 1980s.[105] The drop in homicide has been explained by demographic changes, the shifting economics of crack dealing, the economic expansion of the late 1990s, gun control, community policing, new computerized tracking systems that speed up police response to crime, and innovations in emergency care.[106]

Various public officials have taken credit for the decline and instituted policies based on their presumed success in reducing violent crime. The most controversial set of policies relates to no-tolerance or "quality-of-life" law enforcement based on the "broken-windows" theory.[107] This theory advances the notion that petty vandalism and neglect beget serious crime. Several police commissioners in Boston, New York City, Chicago, and Los Angeles instituted a no-tolerance policy for so-called quality-of-life crimes, such as graffiti, panhandling, public drunkenness, and vandalism—a policy singling out those deemed to be potential murderers. As the authors of the broken-windows theory put it, "A lot of serious crime is adventitious, not the result of inexorable social forces or personal failings. . . . If each [domestic-dispute] call is treated as a separate incident with neither a history nor a future, then each dispute will be handled by police officers anxious to pacify the complainants and get back on patrol as quickly as possible. All too often, however, the disputants move beyond shouting insults or throwing crockery at each other. A knife or a gun may be produced, and somebody may die."[108] Or, as former New York mayor Rudolph Giuliani—an advocate of the broken-windows approach—stated to the press, "Obviously, murder and graffiti are two vastly different crimes. But they are part of the same continuum, and a climate that tolerates one is more likely to tolerate the other."[109] It is no wonder that advocates of the broken-windows theory have used falling homicide rates to shore it up. The assumption here is that homicide statistics truly measure deaths caused by others. Researchers admit that they do not know much about forensic classification of homicides, but homicide rates—unlike suicide statistics, whose accuracy is debated at length—remain generally uncontested.

The drop in homicide rates has thus been a cornerstone of the justification of the broken-windows theory and the resulting no-tolerance and quality-of-life policing initiatives. This theory singles out rowdy teenagers, prostitutes, panhandlers, and derelicts who disturb public spaces as the cause of homicides in neighborhoods, justifying "stop-and-frisk" policing, antigang loitering ordinances, order-maintenance crackdowns, and a high rate of arrest for misdemeanors. While the correlation between such aggressive police surveillance and the drop in homicides remains controversial, even more doubt might be cast on the policies supported by the broken-windows theory if one realizes that only one of two homicide trends reaches the spotlight.[110] Mortality statistics perpetuate a worldview in which danger almost naturally lies with the panhandler, the young black man, and the "squeegee man"—but not with the physician or the police officer. These statistics help constitute the lens through which we judge homeless people, perceive safety, and call for changes in public policies. Overestimating the gradual nature of danger, public officials might overreact in places where disorder has been fabricated and overlook sites where it festers undetected. Complaints of police brutality in New York City, for example, have increased sharply since the institution of the no-tolerance policy. While the two phenomena might be unrelated, police misconduct has received little policy attention.[111] It is not part of official disorder.

CHAPTER FIVE

A BABY DIED. WHERE WERE THE PARENTS?

For centuries, infancy—like old age—was a time to die. While exact figures are difficult to find, historians estimate that about 15 to 30 percent of American infants born in the second half of the nineteenth century died before their first birthday.[1] In contrast, the current infant mortality rate in the United States—still higher than in many other developed countries and widely varying by race—is less than 1 percent.[2] In a remarkable reversal that began during the first decades of the twentieth century, infants are now expected to survive into old age. The reasons for this shift in mortality include better nutrition and housing, a higher standard of living, multiple advances in pediatric knowledge, public health campaigns, the spread of contraception, and a lower fertility rate.[3] Overall infant mortality covers a great variety of causes of death, only some of which demand a forensic investigation. Some infants succumb to congenital or well-known infectious illnesses, and their deaths raise little suspicion. Backed by a documented medical history, the attending pediatrician will sign the death certificate. And like all people, children, unfortunately, die from gunshot wounds, knife wounds, obvious blunt-force trauma, car accidents, and drownings. While these deaths require intense forensic attention, the investigation differs little from that for an adult death: medical examiners conduct an autopsy to document the damage of the trauma and to rule out alternative, natural explanations.

The challenge for death investigators lies with infants who enter the morgue with few or no signs of trauma: babies put down in a crib after a midnight feeding who are dead when the parents wake up or babies dead after seemingly inconsequential falls. Often the autopsy of such infants is nonspecific and nonconclusive, and the investigation depends on the actions of the child-care provider. The forensic pathologist will need to evaluate whether adult supervision was sufficient or, as in the Matthew Eappen case, whether the adult caretaker might be the source of the death. Even when the autopsy does not reveal trauma, an adult might have inadvertently or deliberately harmed the baby. One of the first questions posed during a forensic investigation of an infant death, therefore, is "Who was with the infant? Who was watching the baby? Where were the parents?" Because infants are not responsible for their own fate, the clue to solving the forensic puzzle of an infant death without obvious trauma lies in what the parents or other child supervisors were doing in the moments preceding death.

The forensic investigation of infant death constitutes a conflict of norms with two sets of rules grounded in deeply held values orienting medical examiners to different investigative stances.[4] The first set of norms reflects the call for justice when infants die. The death of an infant is by definition suspicious because such deaths, in light of the advances in health care and safety research, are deemed preventable. The default responsibility for infant care lies with the parents or legal guardians: their task is not only to offer basic shelter, food, and clothing, but also to vigilantly keep the infant out of lethal danger. Justice demands that the medical examiners go all out and fully investigate an infant's death, closely scrutinizing the quality of parenting. Medical examiners, such reasoning insists, should act as child advocates.

At the same time, a second set of norms, grounded in psychodynamic grieving theory and a general humanism, recognizes that because children should not die, the loss of a child constitutes one of the worst tragedies that can befall parents and child-care providers.[5] With an infant's death, the deep existential anguish and grief that any death invokes are magnified. Bereavement for a baby is indescribably painful and psychologically taxing.[6] As parents and care providers mourn, they wonder what they could have done to prevent the death. Forensic probing inevitably exacerbates guilt feelings. Inquiries about possible child abuse in the aftermath of a baby's death are intrinsically invasive and accusatory. Medical examiners recognize such grief. During the autopsy of a five-year-old who drowned in the ocean's undertow, Dr. Cahill sighed, "I can't even imagine what those parents are going through." Adding the ordeal of an aggressive death investigation to the experience of parental bereavement risks further victimizing those already deeply wounded. Normative grieving suggests compassion and restraint in a forensic investigation of an infant death.

The call for justice in light of possible infanticide thus clashes with the need to be sensitive to bereaved parents. What, then, are forensic pathologists to do? On the one hand, they are assailed by sensational investigative journalism for allowing adult caretakers to "get away with murder" if they do not investigate infant deaths fully.[7] On the other hand, they are berated by psychologists and members of interdisciplinary death-review teams for casting undue suspicion on parents when deaths are ultimately classified as natural. A forensic textbook advises, "The investigator should be neither excessively suspicious of the circumstances nor totally unaware of the possibility of child abuse. . . . It behooves the investigator to proceed professionally, with compassion and due caution."[8] The investigator's attitude should be "supportive and not accusatory throughout the investigation of the cause of death."[9] Of all suspicious deaths, infant death is the most extensively researched in the forensic and pediatric literatures, which detail aspects of a forensic investigation that for other deaths are lumped together, such as distinguishing injuries from CPR and the legal aspects of child abuse.[10] The investigation of infant deaths has also undergone considerable standardization, which is not the case for other areas of forensics. For example, in 1996 the U.S. Department of Health and Human Services convened a consensus conference to create a standard scene investigation protocol for sudden unexplained infant death, and an international autopsy protocol for sudden unexpected infant death exists as well.[11]

The investigation of infant deaths constitutes a prime site for observing forensic authority at work, because these unexpected deaths require careful balancing of the sources of legitimacy underlying medical examiners' authority. The conflict of norms with respect to the appropriate level of investigation results in a great cultural need to find the cause and manner of infant deaths. Few deaths invoke more existential questions about the meaning of life than the sudden loss of an apparently healthy baby. The forensic investigation of sudden infant deaths attempts to settle a violated moral universe. At stake in such seemingly random deaths is the foundation of parent-child love. Why love an infant if it might die for no apparent reason? Indeed, anthropologists have reported that in some impoverished areas of developing countries with high infant mortality rates, parents suspend love at the beginning of life.[12] The authority to make cultural sense of infant deaths will be reflected in the credibility and relevance of medical examiners' conclusions about the risks of parenting infants and the vulnerabilities of postneonatal lives.

It is not only the cultural need undergirding medical examiners' forensic authority that is highly charged; the other two sources of legitimacy for their authority—the legal mandate and scientific expertise—are also scrutinized in infant death investigations. While the legal power to autopsy infants is provided by statutory law, medical examiners need to convincingly show that their mandate is warranted for the benefits they bring to various stakeholders in infant deaths. The legal mandate solves the problem of receiving permission for the investigation, but it does not foster a collaborative investigative relationship. To generate a minimum level of parental cooperation, medical examiners have to persuade caregivers that an investigation is to their advantage, even though the investigation may legally implicate them in the death of their child.[13] Showing such benefits is further complicated by the limits to medical examiners' scientific acumen. Even after exhaustive investigations, medical examiners often have few definitive answers as to why a baby died. Whereas autopsies of old people often offer too many clues of potential causes of death, infants often provide too little pathological evidence for a conclusive determination. This problem is most striking during the intensive investigations of abandoned newborns: they simply show too few signs of social and biological life to answer forensic questions.[14] The limits of pathological evidence are partly compensated for by extensive interviews with relatives and others involved in the death. These people, however, have a clear stake in the outcome of the death investigation. Infant mortality thus requires a careful balancing of forensic powers to make sure that death investigators' procedures and findings are accepted as authoritative.

As with other suspicious deaths, medical examiners approach the investigation of infants with particular professional skills and institutional characteristics that may or may not easily fit the puzzle of unexpected postneonatal deaths. Throughout their work, they align professional skills and categories of death to reach conclusions they can legally defend. Even if medical examiners achieve a match and become authoritative experts to explain categories of death, their authority may still vary between different instances of suspicious death. Heart disease, with its strong, detectable pathological signs, becomes natural for medical examiners to reveal, while their authority in clinical homicides may be complicated by an inability to acquire an independent medical history. Infant mortality, with its high cultural expectations, norm conflict between parental grieving and justice, complicated pathological picture, standardized investigative protocols, and legal mandate that may thwart collaboration with caregivers, could be another instance in which medical examiners follow a cautious course, staying close to the pathological picture and steering away from a messy evaluation of parental responsibility in the baby's death. In fact, the opposite occurs. In comparison with potential suicide and homicide investigations, where the fit between medical examiners' skills and the deaths they aim to explain rests largely on a conservative interpretation of pathological evidence, unexpected infant death investigations showcase an expansive forensic authority. When filling out death certificates of infants, medical examiners feel comfortable making liberal interpretive claims.

In individual investigations, medical examiners' broad forensic authority becomes apparent in how they manage suspicion, strategically use the ambiguity of inconclusive findings to explain infant deaths, and comfortably interpret nonpathological evidence. Death investigators may offer unambiguously redeeming answers, even if their inquiry fails to find conclusive clarity. While the process of an extensive death investigation might be deeply unsettling for care providers, the final result might allow them to grieve knowing that they are officially cleared in the death. In situations where in spite of unanswered questions investigators conclude that maltreatment contributed to a baby's death, an extensive investigation will weave a web of culpability from which it is difficult to escape. Well-chosen words on the death certificate will taint the care provider, emotionally and often legally as well.

Forensic authority reaches further than a case-by-case evaluation of individual parental behavior. On an aggregate level, medical examiners indirectly help determine the cultural standards of good parenting. Death brokering for infant deaths feeds back into social life, singling out specific behaviors as risky and life-threatening. In this effort, medical examiners ally themselves with public health officials. Medical examiners alert public health officials to anomalous findings, incorporate a shifting research consensus into their investigations, consolidate evidence in court cases, and support both implementation and evaluation of public health initiatives by providing raw mortality data. Although separated by different views of causality and standards of evidence, public health officials and medical examiners join forces to preserve young human lives.

In the investigation of unexpected infant deaths, medical examiners largely succeed in expanding their interpretive powers. Not everyone will be satisfied with the answers they provide, but their findings, based on an exhaustive investigation, explain why a baby died and what can be done to avoid the death of other infants. One telling indicator of medical examiners' authority is that they succeed in explaining infant deaths with a strategic interpretation of ambiguity rather than with specific causes and manners of death. In perfect crimes, ambiguity stumped medical examiners, leading to an ultraconservative interpretation of evidence or even an exemption of a forensic investigation. Here, ambiguity becomes a means to impose a definitive moral order. The basis for such liberal interpretations is laid gradually throughout the entire investigation.

RAGING SUSPICIONS OF ABUSE

With dead babies, the ingredients of suspicion are present like pyres of dried-out timber in a scorching summer heat. Suspicion takes form in the questions asked, the answers given, the notes taken, and the procedures followed. Some case files, however, will contain repeated disclaimers in order to avoid an inferno. For example, one scene investigator, summarizing his impressions of a scene visit, noted, "No apparent signs of any kind of physical trauma, foul play or anything suspicious, and the parents have been described as very devoted and extremely distraught over this incident." The impression of a lack of foul play was repeated by the emergency physician in her notes and by the police officer interviewing the parents. The lack of signs of abuse, an assessment of parental devotion, and a display of appropriate grieving act like a cooling cloud of mist over the parched timber. And this cooling off is welcomed by pathologists: no one likes to presume that a baby was killed deliberately. In one autopsy, Dr. Gibran began to perspire and shake her head after she noted a small bruise on the penis of a dead baby. Under her face mask, she audibly pleaded and prayed that the bruise was a mere postmortem artifact.

The spark lighting the fire of suspicion in cases of infants without obvious trauma is usually a *discrepancy:* a disparity between the stories of different child-care providers, inconsistencies within the story of one provider, a child-care provider who presents different accounts of what happened, or an inconsistency—discovered at the scene, in the emergency department, or in the morgue—between the story and the trauma on the baby.

In the case of baby Manoel, a seven-month-old boy of Portuguese descent, the discrepancies between stories came to light in the morgue. The police officer who had briefed Dr. Douglas on the case explained that Manoel's ten-year-old sister Lucita was bathing him at home in the bathroom, made a phone call, and came back to find that the baby had lost consciousness in the bath. The baby died after spending three days in a hospital. Dr. Douglas expected a straightforward drowning and first conducted the postmortem of a young fisher who had been swept off the rocks by a wave. As the pathology assistant prepared the autopsy room for the baby, I noted a change in the pathologist's attitude:

Looking over the emergency-room records and the police file, Dr. Douglas notices that the sister altered her story a number of times. Lucita first stated that the baby was vomiting white milky stuff and she took him to another room, where he died. In another version, she was talking to her aunt on the phone and afterward found the baby dead in the bath. In a third variant, Lucita called the aunt because the baby was unconscious. In a fourth version, she reported that

Manoel turned blue while she was feeding him in a high chair. The pathologist is outraged. Because of the inconsistencies in the story, he might have a homicide instead of an accident. He announces that he will not release the baby to a funeral home until he receives answers. "She could as well have *made* him drown, in my book," he says.

One can see the onset of suspicion, an apprehension—even without clear evidence—that something is awry. The different stories imply that Lucita is hiding something, yet her motivation is unclear. She might be simply anxious and confused.

In the case of eleven-month-old baby Juan, coincidentally also of Portuguese descent, suspicion stemmed from conflicting stories given by the father and a daughter. The police officer who first responded to the emergency call wrote his report with an attentive ear for discrepancies. He noted the different stories sequentially with minimal interpretation and suggested that he was seeing lax parenting.

I attempted to question the father as to what happened. He was stating that while he was in the kitchen getting Alisa [his five-year-old daughter] blue lunch box ready, the child [Juan] fell off a chair. I asked him to show me where it happened. . . . Jorge [the father] then corrected me saying that the child fell off the top of the table. I examined the floor and the immediate area to where the father indicated the child had fallen. I could not identify any marks or indications of the incident. . . . Alisa stated that brother fell down the flight of stairs from the second floor to the first floor. Knowing that this story was different from Jorge's, I asked her again where Juan fell and she repeated that he fell down the stairs. I asked Alisa to go back to the house with me and show me where it happened. Jorge picked up Alisa and started talking to her in his native Portuguese language. I tried to keep the two separated, but Jorge was overly insistent that he needed to put shoes and a coat on Alisa. . . . After he placed the slippers on, he left her unattended [on the table] as he went over by the back door to grab a jacket for Alisa. Having just had one child reportedly fall off the table, I picked Alisa up and took her off the table and had her stand on the floor.

In his study of courtroom interactions, sociologist Robert Emerson distinguishes a pitch from a denunciation.[15] A pitch normalizes potentially suspicious behavior; for example, courtroom personnel present a suspect to a judge in a more favorable light than would seem appropriate. The opposite—presenting evidence that tends to discredit someone—is a denunciation. In light of a seriously injured child, the police officer's account reveals multiple denunciations: a lack of evidence where one would expect it, conflicting stories, a rapid exchange in a foreign language, and then a demonstration of "bad" behavior in front of the officer. The denunciations muffle the weak pitch of putting a coat on the daughter. The situation worsens for the father. The police officer radioed the different versions of the father's story to the emergency department. The emergency physician found it hard to believe that the baby had fallen either from a three- to four-foot table or from the stairs, because he showed no signs of bruising. The physician alerted the hospital's child-protection team. The hospital ophthalmologist noticed "extensive retinal hemorrhage of varying sizes, depth throughout both retinas and extensive serious detachments." A CT scan showed increasing cerebral edema (swelling) and perioptic nerve sheath hemorrhages. The social worker transferred custody of Alisa from her parents to her grandparents. Alisa was also brought in for a medical examination. Juan's death was thus already suspicious before the body reached the medical examiner's office.

Suspicion is further fueled by inappropriate *emotional reactions*. In baby Manoel's investigation, a hospital social worker and a police officer described the sister as emotionally "indifferent." "She rolled her eyes" when told that her brother would die. In the case of Juan, the police officer reported the body language with ethnographic detail: "Father's demeanor to this point was what appeared to be a tearless cry with loud incoherent screaming. However, when we would ask Alisa questions he would stop to listen to what was said"; and "Jorge continued to get more hysterical and began breathing in a hyperventilating manner. He was breathing short rapid breaths. He was speaking Portuguese and broken English while crying. 'Please God don't let my baby die. My parents are coming next week to see my baby, my baby.' "

What do these emotional displays mean? Are these the emotions of a sibling shocked by the possibility of her brother's dying and a father about to lose his only son? Or are these the emotions of perpetrators realizing what they have done? The attention to emotional responses suggests that expression might negate or confirm suspicion. The presumption of the investigators is that the overwhelming emotional impact of a fatality renders bodily composure difficult to maintain and reveals the true state of mind of the care provider. Emotional understatements are suspicious; grieving parents are expected to embody their distress. In the case of one father whose baby had extensive head trauma, the father claimed to have tripped over another child. The man called the medical examiner's office five times the day of the autopsy, asking only whether the doctors had discovered any trauma. Not only the staff but also his girlfriend and her mother found it strange that this was his only concern. In a different case, a mentally retarded father whom witnesses had observed slamming his baby against a wall appeared indifferent. The police officer taking him into custody observed, "He had a very blank expression on his face and showed little emotion. He would sit with his head down and would occasionally look up and make an utterance." The practice of checking the displayed emotions against a standard of appropriate grieving is a form of psychologizing behavior.[16] Psychologizing presumes a universal emotional language and a firm scientific basis for the appropriate emotional display. Both assumptions are questionable, but the effect of psychologizing is to credit or discredit people on the basis of their emotional expressions.[17]

Another accelerant for suspicion is *apparent lies*. Manoel's father initially told police that he was in the basement and his daughter was upstairs with the baby. Police investigators quickly found out that he actually had been at work, received a phone call, and then clocked out. His boss testified to the phone call, and the police had his time card. Confronted with this evidence, the father explained that he was afraid he would be in trouble for leaving his young daughter to care for his baby son. He lied because he knew that leaving children unsupervised would raise questions about his parenting. For investigators, the discovery of a lie sheds doubt on all other statements. This lie even reflected back on Manoel's sister. If the father lied, Lucita might also be lying. After all, she had several accounts of what had happened when the baby died.

In the autopsy room, smoldering suspicions flare up when discrepancies are confirmed or pathological evidence points overwhelmingly to abuse. Suspicions are checked against any signs of trauma, patterns of injury, or presence of natural disease. When a group of police cadets visited the medical examiner's office for a lecture on forensics, Dr. Douglas showed them a slide of an infant's face with a tiny bruise under the right ear. The boyfriend of the baby's mother claimed that the baby might have received the bruise from bumping into the slats of its crib. He had found the baby boy dead after the child's mother returned to work after taking maternity leave. The next slide showed the infant's severely bloodied skull after the doctor had folded back the scalp during the autopsy. The X-rays did not show much of the trauma. Such an injury required a great deal of force and could not have been caused by a simple fall in a crib—particularly when the infant could not even stand up.

In the case of Manoel, the police officer brought to the autopsy room the bath and a pile of clothing from the bathroom and the hospital. The tub was a molded plastic oval with a seat covered with purple padding.

Dr. Douglas orders water run into the tub to the same level as when the baby was found (about three inches). Then he puts Manoel in it. He is a big baby for a seven-month-old. The water barely covers part of his buttocks. The bath looks too small for such a baby; it seems more appropriate for a newborn or a two-month-old. The detective and the doctor agree that the baby would have almost needed to stand on his head to drown in so little water. The pathologist grimly takes pictures. An accidental drowning seems very unlikely.

Manoel has curly black hair and gold-colored skin and seems to have been well taken care of. Dr. Douglas finds no bruises on external examination, only some petechiae in the eyes. He asks me to lay out all the evidence on a sheet so that it can be photographed while he starts the incision. I ask him whether we will find anything in the trachea. He doubts it, because the infant spent three days in the intensive-care unit, where they probably put a tube in his lungs. When he cuts the tiny lungs and heart, he takes off his blue rubber gloves and protective sleeves and relies on simple latex gloves. He explains that the heart valves should be fully developed in a baby of this age, and the thinner gloves will allow him to inspect them properly. Many things could be wrong with a child this young, and they all need to be looked for. Dr. Douglas will freeze pieces of the liver and lungs to check for metabolic diseases. He puts pieces of all the organs in laboratory cassettes and preserves most of the remaining organ parts in a formaldehyde bucket, to recheck in case the histology results come up abnormal.

Dr. Douglas's suspicion seems warranted when he opens the bowel. To our surprise, we see big white globs of a wet, claylike material. The homicide detective concludes that the girl is now in trouble. The doctor pokes at the stuff, but he is unable to determine what it is and saves it in a cup.

Unless Manoel was bathed in a different bathtub, the autopsy made the possibility of an accidental drowning less likely. The pathologist had conducted the autopsy attempting to find a correspondence between at least one of the stories and the signs on the corpse. Instead, he found more anomalies.

In Juan's investigation, the autopsy confirms what the emergency physician already suspected.

The pathologist examines the eyes and notes extensive bilateral hemorrhages in the optic nerve sheaths. Juan also has extensive cerebral edema with separation of sagittal and frontal sutures, focal subarachnoid hemorrhage of the cerebrum and cerebellum, and hemorrhage beneath the dura, extending the length of the spinal cord. The medical examiner's staff sees little ambiguity in the meaning of these extensive brain and spine injuries. The findings are inconsistent with a fall from a table or down a flight of carpeted stairs; they are a textbook case of either shaken-baby or shaken baby/impact syndrome.

Police detectives, social workers, and the medical examiner's staff returned to the only witnesses—who were also the suspects—with pointed questions. They repeatedly zoomed in on what they considered the key autopsy findings, which magnified the likelihood of maltreatment. At this point, the private realm of parenting was closely scrutinized in order to look for a pattern of fatal abuse. Investigating Juan's death, police and social workers interviewed the mother, daughter, neighbor, uncle, and grandfather, asking them about domestic and child abuse. The neighbor, uncle, and grandfather denied that Juan's parents physically disciplined their children. The grandfather emphasized that the parents talked issues out with the children. The mother stated that her husband still brought her flowers. Sure, they had problems in their marriage, but no physical violence. Still, extinguishing suspicion is difficult. Five-year-old Alisa admitted that she was afraid her parents would put her in the cellar with tape over her mouth, although they had never done this, and she told investigators that her parents sometimes slapped her face, pinched her arms, pulled her ears, and spanked her. She added that she was also frightened by her grandparents, because they once hit her with a wooden spoon. Contradictions and suspicious behaviors created more ambiguity and accentuated discrepancies. A review of the medical history also showed that Juan hit his head on a toy box at seven months and required stitches. In light of the infant's death, any aspect of parenting that would otherwise have been considered innocuous might now indicate a pattern of abuse.

The police return with a Portuguese interpreter to interrogate Juan's father. The father is confronted with the inconsistencies in his accounts of the fall. He breaks down and states that he lied because he was afraid that he would be in bigger trouble if he reported that he had left the baby unattended upstairs. He confirms his daughter's version of events: his daughter had taken the baby out of the crib; the baby crawled out of the room and was climbing down the stairs. He had been in the kitchen preparing lunch for his daughter. He then saw his son at the top of the stairs, and when he looked up again, Juan was tumbling down. For the police interrogators, this account does not make sense. Does he realize that this is a different version from the one he provided earlier?

The father replies, "I was nervous and thought that I would be apprehended [go to jail]."

"So you thought that the story with the baby falling off the kitchen table wasn't that bad?"

"Yes, *because I'm always around him,* that is why."

The father believed that he usually kept an eye on his children and knew that it reflected badly on his parenting to leave children unsupervised, even for a few minutes. Reporting that the baby fell while under his supervision may have seemed like a small distortion to present himself as a good father. When uncovered, his lie undermined not only his image, but also his credibility.

The police officers prepare for a total denunciation. They confront the father with something they had learned from the mother. "Is it true," they ask, "that the baby was sick during the week and cried a lot?" The father nods. Indeed, the baby had had flulike symptoms, and the mother had given him some medication. He had been on the phone with her when the baby fell; she had called to check on how Juan was doing. The police officers then confront him with the abuse scenario, implying that the father lost it and shook his son out of frustration.

"What we are asking is—we are all parents, some of us work second shift—is it possible that this happened: you are tired, you work a lot of hours, you have to watch a five-year-old and a one-year-old, the baby has been sick, a lot of crying, you are tired and want the baby to stop, you can't take it anymore, and you pick the baby up, you get nervous and upset and you want the baby to stop crying so you shake the baby, did that happen?"

"No, never in my life," the father responds. The officers repeat this question in different ways, pointing out that the injuries do not correspond with a fall down the stairs, but the father refuses to back down. He adamantly repeats that he would never harm his children, and he begs the interpreter to write down that he loved his boy. To offer proof, he mentions that he tried to revive his son.

The interrogation is at a common impasse. The police treat the father as a suspect, and, like many suspects, he denies involvement in the death, even when confronted with a plausible yet incriminating scenario. Because of the many accounts of what may have happened in the death of Manoel, that investigation is also at an impasse.

Dr. Douglas arranges a meeting with Manoel's sister and father; an uncle comes along to serve as interpreter. The sister maintains that she was bathing the baby and had only filled the small tub. She sticks to the story that she received a phone call from her aunt (the aunt stated that she did not call but was called by her niece) and that when she returned to the bathroom, the baby was spitting up white, milky stuff. She took her brother into a different room to dress him, and he turned blue. Dr. Douglas, however, believes that the girl is hiding something.

During morning meeting the next day, a scene investigator suggests a cultural homicide motive.[18] Speaking from personal experience of what he refers to as "paternalistic Portuguese culture," he postulates that the oldest girl might have resented the attention her younger brother received and might have drowned or smothered him. This homicide motive is tossed around as one of many possibilities to make the pieces of the puzzle fit.

Much as the stigma of suicide affects the deceased, the relatives, and death investigators, the investigation of a dead baby collectively enacts the suspicion of abuse in an attempt to remove ambiguity. Both fathers anticipated that their son's death would be considered suspicious, and they actively changed their story to conform to the norm of constantly watching infants. Unfortunately, because their stories were later found to contain discrepancies and lies, their presentation of good parenthood backfired. Death investigators weighing the appropriateness of emotions, checking discrepancies between stories against the signs in the corpse, and asking confrontational questions about the intimacies of parenting isolate the potential for abuse and at the same time generate further suspicion. Once aroused, suspicion is difficult to contain or suppress. Doubt clouds everyone's vision, taking on a life of its own that is anchored in the materiality of the corpse, the scene pictures, and the interrogation transcripts. In the midst of a suspicious haze, child-care providers need to convince others that they truly loved their baby.

A FOOTPRINT AND A LOCK OF HAIR FOR GRIEF

While the medical examiner's staff aggressively generated suspicion in baby Manoel's investigation, some workers in the office promoted a more moderate approach. Staff members' views depended on whether the person expressing an opinion had children. Those who had raised children were more likely to believe that the baby had been chewing on something— probably a piece of soap left in the bathtub—noting that when babies are teething, they gnaw on almost anything and might be attracted by the texture of soap. Staff workers with children were more disturbed that the parents had left the baby alone with a ten-year-old, and they wanted social workers to send a strong message to the parents. Some also shook their heads wondering what their office was doing to the sister. Staff members without children were less clear on whether a properly supervised baby would die from chewing on soap. They thought that a baby would probably not like the taste. They tended to focus on the seemingly callous sister and noted that in a male-dominated culture, the only son had died. They occasionally suggested moderation in order to ease collaboration with the relatives. The office was divided because the child-care providers were not only the suspects, but also the bereaved family members. The staff worried that if the fatality was indeed accidental, the investigation could have deleterious effects on the grieving family.

Some aspects of the death investigation still confirmed the relatives as mourners. In infant deaths, regardless of abuse allegations, the staff of the medical examiner's office would create a memento for the parents. The pathologist would ink the left foot of the baby to make a print on a special card and would cut off a lock of hair. The hair was carefully tied with a soft blue ribbon for a boy or a rose ribbon for a girl. The card and lock of hair were given to the funeral director to offer to the parents as a remembrance.

The contrast between infant and adult deaths became clear when Dr. Hughes inked the small foot of a six-month-old baby girl next to a stretcher on which lay a twenty-three-year-old male covered by tattoos with violent themes. The man had been shot in his car and had crashed into a pole. Out of the man's left front shorts pocket, the assistant drew a big wad of cash, a plastic bag with three small white rocks, and ornamental golden upper front teeth.[19] The police officer had difficulty answering Dr. Cahill's questions about how he had found the deceased, because the young man's deeply distraught mother and grandmother had distracted him at the scene. No one would think, however, to ease the mother's grief by making a footprint from the suspected drug dealer. Instead, the homicide detective took fingerprints for identification purposes. The infant girl had been put on a futon by her mother and propped up with pillows. She must have fallen over, gotten tangled up in the sheets, and became trapped under the metal arm of the black futon, where she died from asphyxiation. Dr. Hughes shook her head angrily when looking over the pictures from the scene: the futon was next to a crib. If only the mom had put her daughter in the crib. Even for a mother who had inadvertently been involved in her baby's death, however, the memento recognized her as a grieving parent.

CONTINUING OR REVERSING THE MOMENTUM OF SUSPICION

The results of the death investigation provide the most important confirmation of parents' grieving. Medical examiners hold out the possibility that the final cause and manner of death will absolve the child-care provider of culpability. When suspicion has permeated a forensic investigation, however, reversing the momentum and treating parents as victims is difficult. Forensic pathologists can reflect their opinions about parents' involvement in the choice of words on the death certificate. The result is a well-supported indictment that holds the parents responsible for the infant's death. But when suspicions largely dissipate by the end of the investigation, the pathologist can tweak the words on the death certificate to imply the least culpability, *even if the medical examiner's findings suggest a less equivocal conclusion.* The medicolegal result might be an explicit exoneration of guilt. Manoel's case and Juan's case illustrate the different culpability trajectories.

Confirming the Denunciation

During his meeting with the sister, father, and uncle of Manoel, Dr. Douglas asked in passing whether the baby had been washed with a bar of soap. The father replied that they used liquid soap in the bathroom. Around 11:15 a.m. on the day of the meeting, the uncle who had served as interpreter called to say that the mother had found small chunks of soap on the surface of the bathtub when she was cleaning it. They did not know where it came from but thought the sister might have carried it in from a different room. Laboratory tests showed the white globs found in the bowel to be soap. At that point, Dr. Douglas decided to release the body to the funeral home (he was also leaving for a long weekend). Although he had now identified the white material, he still did not know how it had got there and whether it had killed Manoel. The pending cause of death was amended to asphyxia due to unknown etiology; the manner of death was recorded as undetermined.

The cause and manner of death constituted an uneasy draw. Asphyxia due to unknown etiology suggested that the medical examiner had not excluded either drowning in the bath or choking on the soap.[20] The presence of the soap in the colon after a three-day stay in the hospital was consistent with the possibility that Manoel died due to an obstruction caused by the soap, but it remained unclear how the material had entered his body. The medical examiners consulted with a pediatrician specializing in digestive problems and scoured the medical literature in vain for additional information. The undetermined manner of death implied that the pathologist, after considering all evidence, did not find any manner of death more compelling than competing ones. The deliberate ambiguity left the case hanging. It would be resolved only if further information became available. The staff, however, thought more information would likely never be available, because it would have to come from the sister—and she had been discredited as a reliable source. From a medicolegal perspective, the death remained suspect. About a month later, I asked the detective who had been present during the autopsy whether the family was ever charged with anything. He did not think so. The last he had heard about this case was that the sister had been admitted to a psychiatric hospital. When I mentioned this to Dr. Douglas, he raised his eyebrows and rolled his eyes upward.

When there is less uncertainty, medical examiners express suspicion on the death certificate, as in the case of the father who claimed to have tripped over an older child and kept calling the office asking whether the doctors had discovered any "trauma" during the autopsy. In this case, the medical examiner's staff distinguished markedly between the mother and the father. The autopsy indeed revealed extensive blunt-force trauma to the head. The mother reacted to the revelations of the postmortem investigation with active grieving. Rather than take the forensic findings as a consolation and remember her child, she became energized and wanted to hold the father responsible in court. At no point in the investigation was the father treated as a mourner. In the eyes of the investigators, he did not show any grief. His goal had been to remove suspicions, but, as with Juan's and Manoel's fathers, these attempts backfired.

Sociologists Barney Glaser and Anselm Strauss introduced the notion of mutual pretense to describe interactions between terminally ill patients and health care providers.[21] In the 1960s, when physicians did not routinely tell patients that they were dying, patients could often determine that they were terminally ill by comparing their symptoms to those of patients who had recently expired,[22] glancing at medical files, or overhearing relatives and care providers. Patients would often pretend, however, that they did not know they were dying, although they suspected that the care providers were aware that they were in on the secret. The result was a confusing and painfully isolating set of interactions, with both parties pretending not to know while knowing or suspecting that the other party knew. Phone conversations between the medical examiner's staff and the father who claimed to have tripped reflected a variation on an awareness context of mutual pretense.[23] When the father called, the case manager suspected that he was aware that he had fatally injured the baby, but both parties pretended not to know. Instead, the case manager replied generally to his questions, stating that the investigation was pending further study, that doctors were still performing microscopic examination and viral cultures to rule out a natural cause of death. Making a note of the phone conversations, the case manager observed, "I chose this route of death so as not to let him know the real cause of death, which was head trauma inflicted by another." The father, in turn, pretended not to know what had happened so that he might figure out what the office thought had occurred. The case manager thought the father had the impression that he had gotten away with murder. Mutual pretense, however, became open awareness when the homicide detective summoned the man for an interview. He immediately retained a lawyer and refused to answer any questions.

With the mother, the same case manager's interactions were conspicuously different. After the father was arrested, the mother also called the medical examiner's office asking for additional information. Without revealing too much about an ongoing investigation, the case manager gently suggested that the child's injuries resembled abuse. The mother initially considered this suggestion preposterous, because the father had run down three flights of stairs with the baby in his arms to find help and had called rescue, an indication of having the child's best interests in mind. Reflecting on her own observations, the mother thanked the case manager for being "frank" with her. In future interactions with the medical examiner's office, the mother seemed to have channeled her grief into a resolve for justice. She chided the office staff for "delaying" the autopsy report and expressed concern that the pathologist who performed the postmortem had left the office to work elsewhere. She was also frustrated with delays in the trial. The autopsy report and the death certificate for this baby were unambiguous: the baby died from blunt-force trauma to the head (subdural hematoma and brain injuries due to application of traumatic motion to the head). The manner of death was "homicidal, assaulted by another." Dr. Cahill, who finished the file after Dr. Brown left the office, and the case manager, who had kept notes of her phone conversations, testified to the grand jury and later at the trial. The father was indicted and convicted of second-degree murder. The forensic investigation was critical in building the criminal case.

Reversing the Momentum

Although the circumstances and the cultural background of the families were remarkably similar, Juan's death investigation ended differently from Manoel's. Juan's older sister was interviewed by a trained social worker. After the interview, the sister waited in the social worker's office and spontaneously described the scene at the time of Juan's death.

While Alisa was at headquarters waiting for her grandfather, she spent some time with me. She told me that her brother fell, and she showed me the look he had on his face after he fell. When she demonstrated that look for me, her eyes were fixed straight ahead, and her mouth was open. She then told me that her father picked up her brother and brought him to her grandparent's house. She said that Daddy and Granddad were holding her brother, and she started shaking her head forward and back, saying that this is what her brother's head was doing when they were holding him. She then blew air out of her mouth with puckered lips and said that her father and grandfather were doing that, and she said that they were pushing on her brother's chest.

Later that day, the detective and the Portuguese interpreter interrogating the father asked him to demonstrate how he had tried to revive the baby.

At this point, I asked Jorge if he could demonstrate how he shook his child with an anatomical doll. Jorge stated he could. I placed the anatomical doll on the floor and asked Jorge to show us what he did. Jorge told us that the baby fell down.

"I grabbed the baby, and went Juan, Juan, Juan. He cried and then stopped and was not breathing. I opened the door and went outside to the next door neighbor and banged on the door, there was no answer. I kept running with the baby and ran to my father-in-law's house. I opened the door to my father-in-law's house and told him the baby fell down, the baby fell down."

Jorge stated that his father-in-law told him to give the baby to him. Jorge stated he gave the baby to his father-in-law and he put him on the table.

"Michael [brother-in-law] was there and he shook the baby, my father-in-law kept on moving him, move, move, move. Michael then called 911 and put the phone down, I then grabbed a cup of water to put on the baby, he didn't wake up. My brother-in-law then went outside. We kept on shaking the baby. Juan wake up, wake up."

During this time, Jorge demonstrated with the doll how he shook his son.

Detective Jordan stated, "Do you see how hard you are shaking that doll, do you see how hard you are shaking that, that is a one-year old baby, how can you shake him that hard?" Jorge replied, "I was very nervous, I gave him mouth-to-mouth, what are you going to do when a baby stops crying, the baby stops breathing."

It should be noted that when Jorge demonstrated how the baby was shaken, he placed both hands around the anatomical doll's chest, leaving the neck and head unsupported. Jorge would shake the doll very hard causing the neck and head of the doll to shake violently.

Again, a case conference convened with child-abuse experts, pathologists, police investigators, and the district attorney's office to strategize about the case. In preparation for this meeting, Dr. Cahill retrieved an article on stairway injuries in children published in the journal *Pediatrics*. Among the highlighted sentences was the following statement: "Falls down stairways seldom result in severe injury."[24] During the meeting, the chief pathologist presented the opinion that the baby had died from severe shaking. The demonstration and the corresponding accounts from Juan's father and sister suggested that the shaking occurred after the fall. The fall backward down the stairs probably only knocked the baby out, likely causing a hematoma that could have been treated in the hospital. Juan's father did not know CPR and had only seen it on a TV show; his panicky, violent shaking probably caused the lethal shearing injuries. During the meeting, the participants decided not to pursue the case legally. Prosecution presented many barriers,[25] but the case manager explained to me that a majority of those present at the meeting believed that the parents had already suffered enough. The final death certificate reflected this opinion. The cause of death was "brain injuries due to application of traumatic motion to head," and the manner of death was left undetermined. In the narrative summarizing the findings, the pathologist concluded, "It appears that the force administered to Juan during the panic and attempt at revival was sufficient to induce the central nervous system injuries which caused his death."

In Juan's death, the appearance of any new information would not have changed the undetermined ruling. The pathologists were confident that they knew what caused his death. Medically, the case was a shaken baby, and legally it fit the category of involuntary manslaughter. A more precise forensic manner of death would have designated the death as "homicide" or at least "accident."[26] Leaving the manner of death undetermined constitutes a forensic exoneration of the parents. Taking the position that the parents had suffered enough from their son's death, the office amplified the remaining ambiguity. The father's intentions, the parents' deep grieving—witnessed by all who had talked to them—and the police transcripts all featured in the decision-making process. Whether the parents appreciated these redemptive intentions, however, was unclear. No one in the medical examiner's office maintained contact with them, and relatives did not request information.[27] One can only speculate that although they were relieved when suspicion was lifted, they probably found the extensive interrogations unsettling.

In the death of one two-month-old, a case mired in suspicion even before the baby died, the autopsy led to an explicit exoneration. The parents of this child had been closely monitored by the state's child-protection agency after a respected pediatric radiologist, treating the child for pneumonia, had diagnosed the infant a month before his death with broken ribs due to trauma. The parents were unable to explain the broken ribs, and an investigation by child-protection authorities required the parents to take a lie-detector test. When the infant died, the suspicion of child abuse was strong; both child-protection and law enforcement agencies met even before the results of the autopsy were known. During the autopsy, however, Dr. Douglas found no signs of broken ribs and no swelling, ecchymosis (bruise or contusion), or callus formation. He cut out the rib cage, carefully removed all tissue, X-rayed it, and held it up against a special light. He could not discern the slightest indication of a previous fracture. He checked the original hospital X-rays but was unable to detect broken ribs there either. Although the radiologist claimed that broken ribs could have healed in one month in a newborn without any pathological sign, the death was declared natural. The consensus in the office was that the radiologist and child-protection team had overreacted. The medical examiner's conclusion precluded any legal prosecution of the case.

★ ★ ★

The forensic authority achieved during the investigations of Manoel's and Juan's deaths depends on a strategic management of the ambiguity of forensic findings. In both cases, medical examiners encapsulated inferences in their final verdict that went beyond the pathological evidence they were working with. The scope of medical examiners' authority lies exactly in such inferences: they interpreted the ambiguity of the case to favor the version of events that ordered the diverse pieces of evidence. As in adult homicide investigations, these inferences are agreed upon with allies in law enforcement. But, unlike for some homicide inquiries, the investigation of infant deaths is not constrained by a conflict of interest between equal partners. Medical examiners still depend on parents to provide an account of what happened. But if families refuse to collaborate, their refusal will become part of the evidence, and the investigation will proceed nevertheless. Unlike with suicides, where medical examiners' pathological skills may not be able to retrieve an intent to die, the autopsy, coupled with extensive interviews with parents, allows death investigators to retrospectively reconstruct a deadly sequence to the best of their ability. In the cases of Manoel and Juan, the medical examiners felt that they had left no source of evidence unexamined, and this made them comfortable with their inferences. The closure of the cases implied a definitive moral verdict of the caregivers' responsibility in the sequence of events preceding the babies' deaths. Ambiguity was overstated in order to either suggest or remove culpability. Such liberal interpretive inferences are formalized in medical examiners' use of the category of sudden infant death syndrome (SIDS). In SIDS deaths, an extensive investigation without positive findings still leads to parental exoneration.

SIDS: THE NATURALIZATION OF THE UNKNOWN

In 2002, out of all infant deaths in the United States, 2,295 (8.2 percent) were classified as SIDS, making it the third leading cause of infant death.[28] SIDS cases usually involve deaths during sleep in a crib or bassinet, and the parents find the baby dead in the morning. Emergency personnel then try unsuccessfully to revive the infant in the bedroom. Scene investigators and police officers monitor the parents for inconsistencies and contradictions, watch for signs of appropriate grieving, and take the bedding, toys, bottles, and related items in and around the crib as evidence. But suspicions develop only if the autopsy reveals signs of trauma. In a SIDS case, such trauma is absent. The medical examiner, in an extensive investigation of the corpse, will conduct the autopsy with an eye for congenital malformations, order special genetic tests to check for common metabolic disorders, save the brain for a neuropathological examination, take tissue samples from all major organs and tissues for histology, swab the lungs for microbiology, run comprehensive toxicology and electrolyte laboratory tests, and send the corpse out for an extensive skeletal X-ray survey. Staff will review the birth records, growth charts, and records of wellness visits for any indication of natural disease, injuries, or "failure to thrive." If these findings fail to point to a specific cause of death, the unexpected death will be attributed to SIDS.

SIDS means forensically that the cause of death is undetermined. Instead of ambiguity, there is no positive finding: all pathological and scene evidence is unremarkable. The category of SIDS is medicine's cryptic acknowledgment that, although hypotheses abound, current knowledge is insufficient to account for these deaths.[29] SIDS constitutes a rare example of a forensic diagnosis by exclusion. While everything else the medical examiner puts on a death certificate needs to be positively proven, SIDS is the only cause of death established negatively, by the lack of any specific finding.[30] The "syndrome" refers to a presumed set of similar causes of unknown origin. Over the past fifty years, medical researchers have pursued a range of hypothetical factors, including race, socioeconomic status, seasonal variations, sleeping position, feeding preferences, bacteria, toxins, viruses, pollutants, pacifier use, maternal alcohol and caffeine consumption, maternal smoking, birth weight, apnea,[31] and a wide variety of physiological abnormalities.[32] "Despite extensive epidemiological, pathological and developmental biology research efforts, the immediate cause of death in cases of SIDS remains elusive."[33] The current theory is that SIDS babies are not completely normal in development and that some anomaly becomes obvious only when the infant is subjected to stress.

At the same time, SIDS has become a specific and substantial cause of death. On a death certificate, when a child has died from SIDS, the death is considered natural. Thus, when medical examiners in my study concluded that a death was due to SIDS, the manner of death was not "undetermined" but "natural." The National Association of Medical Examiners' guidebook for manner-of-death classification suggests that SIDS deaths "may be classified as either natural or undetermined, depending on the certifier's philosophy and approach."[34] An important fact with respect to public perception of such deaths is that the acronym is more specific than an "undetermined" ruling. It thus dispels suspicion: parents are not to blame for their child's death. The medical examiner's office in my study reinforced parental exoneration in a letter to parents of SIDS babies. All next of kin received a standard bereavement letter, but the SIDS letter was different. It began: "May I express our heartfelt sympathy for the loss of your child. At this time we are not sure of the exact cause of death. One common cause of death in infants is Sudden Infant Death Syndrome (SIDS), also known as 'Crib Death.' " The letter next summarized its exculpatory message: "SIDS is neither predictable nor preventable; it happens unexpectedly without warning." The letter provided the name and phone number of a nurse—herself a SIDS parent—who had started a support group.

SIDS has become a socially validated forensic death classification, even without medical substance. Its morally powerful forensic meaning follows a singular history: the medical concept gained currency through the lobbying of parent groups.[35] SIDS was initially championed by forensic pathologists doubting the prevalent theory that accidental suffocation always caused "crib deaths." Between 1945 and 1961, pathologists hypothesized that respiratory problems, rather than parental neglect, might be responsible for smothered infants. Without the validation of research, this hypothesis reinforced the conviction that the parents were not responsible for the child's death and provided hope that such deaths could be avoided. During the death-awareness period of the late 1960s, parent groups organized around SIDS and lobbied Congress to provide funding for research, which was eventually sponsored by the National Institute of Child Health and Human Development. The result is the hypothesis that SIDS babies suffer from a developmental abnormality that can lead to death if the child experiences stress. Although parents initiated the research, it has not completely excluded parental responsibility but now suggests that some factor in a pregnancy might cause a child's death. Still, research support and articles in popular and medical journals have generated awareness of SIDS as a specific cause of death and have prompted national public health campaigns recommending particular sleeping positions (e.g., the 1994 national "Back to Sleep" campaign).[36]

Forensic pathologists estimate that 10 percent of deaths attributed to SIDS and thus classified as natural might actually be infanticide.[37] A forensic textbook admits that "it is at times, most difficult to distinguish homicidal smothering from SIDS."[38] Another textbook is more blunt: "In addition to a natural etiology, some of the deaths that are certified as being due to SIDS are undoubtedly accidents due to overlay, while others are homicides usually due to smothering."[39] Indeed, an easy way to kill an infant is to smother it with a hand, pillow, towel, or blanket. This "gentle" homicide[40] might leave no sign of trauma, and autopsy findings are unremarkable.[41] An Ohio coroner observed wryly that "the only difference between SIDS and a suffocation is a confession."[42] Forensic pathologists Vincent and Dominick DiMaio offer the following guideline to determine whether SIDS covers up murder.

It is the general policy of the authors to ascribe the first death in a family presenting as SIDS to SIDS. The second death by the same mother is labeled as undetermined and a more intensive investigation of the circumstances surrounding the death are conducted. The police are usually asked to interview the family, though in a discreet fashion. A third such death in the family is felt by the authors to be homicide until proven otherwise. It is the authors' opinion that while a second SIDS death from a mother is improbable, it is possible and she should be given the benefit of the doubt. A third case, in our opinion, is not possible and is a case of homicide.[43]

Positive proof consists here not of any substantive finding but the frequency of deaths in one family! Other pathologists have looked for distinctive pathological findings, particularly petechiae, to distinguish SIDS from infanticide.[44]

Medical examiners' repeated application of SIDS exemplifies their broad cultural authority in postneonatal deaths. The deaths of infants during sleep for no apparent reason is unsettling and threatening for parents, because it presumes a mortal capriciousness that undermines the basis of child love. The disorder threatens even the altruistic dilemma of forensic investigation: how to convince parents to allow a postmortem investigation if no scientific answer is likely available? The forensic designation of SIDS removes the threat of disorder. The classification socially absolves parents from involvement in their infant's death by generously applying the rule of optimism, even if homicide may have occurred.[45] The designation is scientifically weak but exhaustively researched with all the tools and procedures available to forensic pathologists. Autopsy rates for sudden infant deaths approach 90 percent, and these deaths often receive a second review by interdisciplinary child-death teams. SIDS does not provide an answer as to the specific cause of death, but it officially validates the parents as guiltless and tragic victims of an unpredictable and unpreventable event. The interpretive leap from evidence to final designation characterizes forensic authority: forensic pathologists turn lack of findings into a specific manner of death. From a professional perspective, SIDS is an amazing accomplishment of expert death brokering, as medical examiners' legitimacy depends on medicolegal proof and on a cautious engagement with socially contentious categories such as suicide and homicide.

GUIDING PARENTS: BED SHARING

Medical examiners' authority in infant deaths extends from individual cases to population health when pathologists tinker with categories of death and suggest new risk categories in order to include anomalous findings. At one Monday morning meeting in the middle of July, one of the new cases involved the death of Anne, a four-month-old baby. Her mother had fed her at 11:00 p.m., and the mother and father then went to sleep with the baby between them in the same bed. The mother woke up around 4:00 a.m. and found the baby motionless. She called 911. Rescue came and found the baby difficult to intubate and already stiff. A resuscitation effort proceeded nevertheless, and the infant was transported to the hospital. The baby was pronounced dead shortly after arrival in the emergency department. Anne was the third white baby in two weeks to die in similar circumstances. The Monday before, the office had discussed the separate deaths of an eight-week-old girl and a three-month-old boy, both sleeping in the mother's bed. In the boy's death, his older sister had also shared the bed. Each baby had been rushed to the emergency department and expired after a futile resuscitation effort. During the morning meeting when Anne's death was discussed, the staff commented on the similarities among the three cases. Dr. Cahill wondered whether bed sharing could be considered a positive investigative finding and thus negate a SIDS diagnosis. The pathologists reasoned that in order for bed sharing to be involved in a deadly causal chain, other pieces of evidence would need to confirm it. Staff members were reluctant to consider bed sharing sufficient for a positive finding but agreed that they had to look at the bedding and check for soft pillows, "extra-soft" bedmates (i.e., obese parents), or bedmates who were intoxicated or on drugs—which would increase their threshold for arousal and thus make the possibility of accidental overlying more likely.

In this morning discussion, the pathologists tinkered with the boundaries of SIDS in an attempt to push the limits of forensic expertise. The question was whether bed sharing renders infant death more likely and thus lacking the unexplainable facets of a SIDS death. Extracting bed sharing deaths as a separate entity is a reaction against the popularity of SIDS and the frustration of unexplained sudden infant deaths. The discussion at that morning meeting suggests a possible new research track to explain SIDS deaths. Here, we observe the emergence of potentially anomalous findings that may remain assimilated in the category of SIDS or may follow their own discovery trajectory.[46]

Because knowledge in medicine accumulates by precedent, Dr. Cahill and her colleagues consulted the public health literature to review the current scientific consensus on bed sharing as a risk factor. As with suicide, medical examiners and public health officials rely upon different notions of causality and different standards of evidence. Unlike with suicide, however, infant death may render these professional differences complementary, allowing medical examiners and public health researchers to join forces to prevent untimely deaths. Epidemiologists work not with unfolding stories but with tabulated mortality statistics. They can access the medical examiner's data in two ways: by viewing the aggregated national mortality data maintained by the National Center for Health Statistics or by retrospectively reviewing the medical examiner's files. While national mortality data sets do not document the circumstances of death, reviewing the files could establish bed sharing as a risk factor on the basis of the frequency of its occurrence. In one such retrospective review of medical examiners' files, 29 out of 56 infants (52 percent) who were found dead in bed slept alone, and 27 infants (48 percent) slept with adults or twin siblings. The authors concluded that "the high incidence of cosleeping suggests that external factors may have contributed to some of these deaths. These findings support recent studies that suggest that cosleeping is a potentially dangerous practice."[47]

The key element for epidemiological risk profiles is their *calculability*.[48] Contemporary public health researchers single out variables to calculate odds ratios that quantify risk associated with particular factors. As a consequence, epidemiological variables include everything from host factors that determine individual susceptibility (e.g., age, gender, genetic makeup) to environmental factors that determine the host's exposure to individual agents (e.g., car size, weather, visibility). Epidemiological researchers assume that each independent variable can be isolated from others and correlated to demonstrate statistically the extent to which it affects outcomes.[49] If modifiable, these variables become targets for education campaigns, such as the supine position in the "Back to Sleep" campaign to reduce SIDS: "Mortality from the sudden infant death syndrome dropped dramatically in the late 1980s and early 1990s in most developed countries. This was attributed to the sleep position after the "Back to Sleep" campaign, which advised parents not to place their baby to sleep on their front."[50] Although the decline in SIDS is associated with a supine sleeping position, epidemiologists are unable to state that prone sleeping *caused* sudden infant deaths: "Prone sleeping is strongly associated with cot death but we are not certain the role this position plays in the chain of causality."[51]

In spite of fundamental differences about causality and evidence, epidemiological and forensic experts feed off each other's findings to create partially overlapping notions of good parenting. When conducting an autopsy and a scene investigation, the medical examiner's staff considered factors documented in the public health literature. Dr. Gibran, for example, had attended a conference on forensic pediatrics in which a speaker listed bed sharing under the heading of "risk factors for SIDS" and "risk factors for accidental overlying," and she had added "tired cosleeper" to the list of risk factors for accidental overlying.[52] Only weeks after the three cases, when the office's count had climbed to an unusual six dead babies, Dr. Cahill distributed copies of an article on sudden death in infancy attributed to bed sharing.[53] She explained that she did this to keep her staff up to date on the latest bed sharing research.

For epidemiologists calculating exposures, pathways, and outcomes, the crucial issue is to determine what is relevant and what is not. As sociologist Stephen Hilgartner has noted, no aspect of life is inherently risky, but some can become risky after being singled out.[54] One of the better studies on bed sharing, a British case-control study, interviewed bereaved parents and a control group with a survey containing six hundred items "including demographic and social data, the medical history of the infant and other family members, use of cigarettes, alcohol and drugs, the precise sleeping arrangements for the infant, and full details of the events preceding and the circumstances surrounding the death. Information was collected both with regard to the family's usual practices by day and by night and to the period when the baby died."[55] Even with six hundred items, researchers need to make sure that they have identified all possibly relevant variables. Here medical examiners and other death experts come in. In a reaction to the British study, two forensic pathologists confirmed that their experience corresponded to the research findings and suggested a potential marker of accidental asphyxia (intra-alveolar hemorrhage).[56] Death investigators thus alert epidemiologists to patterns or clusters they observe, fill in surveys for consumer-protection agencies, issue reports about child fatalities,[57] and alert authorities to patterns of mistake or neglect. In addition, they continue the search for specific physical signs that might indicate overlying: livor patterns (postmortem skin discoloration), intrathoracic petechiae (red or purplish dots on organs within the chest), and fabric imprints on the skin.[58]

The epidemiologically validated data derived from forensic cases are fed back into the debates about bed sharing. The pediatric community is still divided about the risks: on the one hand, evolutionary anthropologists note that parent-infant bed sharing is and has been the routine sleeping arrangement for most of the world's nonindustrialized cultures, suggesting that it might have some adaptive value for infants. They point out that research indicates that sleeping in the parental bed promotes breast-feeding and might be protective, because bed sharing babies are more likely to be placed in the supine position, indirectly lowering the risk for SIDS.[59] On the other hand, the number of deaths due to overlying increased two- to threefold between 1980 and 1995.[60] Overshadowed by the attention to SIDS, bed sharing has in the last five years reemerged as a modifiable risk factor in infant deaths.[61] One study reported a tenfold increase in the risk of SIDS among infants sleeping in parental beds and a fiftyfold increased risk among infants sleeping with parents on a couch.[62] Another major study found that bed sharing increased the risk of SIDS 2.7 times.[63] Debates continue on whether bed sharing per se or the particular circumstances in which bed sharing occurs (soft duvets, pillow use, sleeping on a couch, small spaces with wedges, intoxication, maternal smoking, etc.) might increase the risk for SIDS and on whether bed sharing with the mother might be protective while sharing the bed with others might not be. Most North American public health experts, however, err on the side of caution and have begun issuing warnings against bed sharing. Reviewing the available epidemiological literature, the American Academy of Pediatrics formulated a policy reflecting the cautionary approach. It warns that "bed sharing or cosleeping may be hazardous under certain conditions."[64] The U.S. Consumer Product Safety Commission also opposes bed sharing by an infant and an adult, particularly if there is more than one adult in the bed.[65]

As the "Back to Sleep" campaign demonstrates, these warnings shape broader norms of good parenting. Parents who love their children, it is implied, might need not only to place them on their backs, but also to keep them in separate cribs. Suspicious deaths thus generate moral momentum when they are tabulated by public health and consumer-protection advocates and translated into public health campaigns. Dr. Cahill predicted that bed sharing would be singled out as a major risk factor for sudden infant deaths in the near future. Her office could not only make this risk visible but also implement and safeguard norms of good parenting.

ALTRUISM

All death investigations reflect the fit between the death at hand, forensic pathologists' expertise, organizational characteristics, and evolving categories of death. In unexpected infant deaths, forensic pathologists use the fit to achieve a broad cultural reach. Medical examiners' authority in suicide and homicide depends on their ability to stay close to pathological findings, erring on the side of lethal natural processes rather than implying human intent. In spite of high cultural stakes, unexpected infant deaths form a stronghold of medical examiners' expertise. They are able to make uncontested interpretive leaps from evidence, and their liberal interpretations contribute to the understanding of infant mortality in epidemiological and public health circles. Medical examiners have even been able to defend their jurisdiction over infant mortality from interlopers. In February 2001, the American Academy of Pediatrics published a guideline to help pediatricians distinguish SIDS from child abuse.[66] The academy rescinded this guideline when the National Association of Medical Examiners pointed out that "medical examiners and coroners have the sole legal authority to investigate" such sudden infant deaths and that "examination or manipulation of the deceased body by child maltreatment experts without proper statutory authority or family permission may constitute a tort or be a violation of criminal law."[67]

Among all deaths, why do medical examiners have great authority in unexpected infant deaths? The answer is that during infant death investigations, medical examiners directly address the needs and interests of parents, even if taking those needs into consideration generates a conflict of norms. The touchstone of a forensic investigation of infants remains the pathological data triangulated with scene investigation and a medical history. Standardized protocols for infant deaths prescribe an exhaustive, interdisciplinary list of procedures. While these examinations do not necessarily provide positive clues, they still give medical examiners comfort that they can at least exclude most forms of trauma and known natural killers. Next, medical examiners and police officers repeatedly contact the child's caregivers during the investigation. The usually closed door of the office is opened somewhat for relatives who are interviewed to check evolving explanations. And unlike in potential medical or police homicides, there is no conflict of interest between medical examiners and relatives. Pathologists are in a strong position to extract information and draw conclusions, but the repeated interactions with parents have as an unintended consequence that the parents' viewpoint becomes part of the investigation. Such direct interactions may backfire when relatives fail to cooperate or are obviously implicated in the deaths. In more ambiguous cases, however, the recognizable pain and bewilderment of grieving suggest caution and compassion. These scientific and institutional factors add up to a unique opportunity to assess parenting in the forensic investigation.

Forensic pathologists further address the needs of parents by demonstrating direct benefits of the investigation. The guiding moral principle of any forensic investigation is a form of utilitarian altruism: although this life is lost, someone else might benefit from the acquired knowledge. Utilitarian altruism constitutes a kind of solidarity that sacrifices the private right to dispose of the dead for benefits for the living. The dead live on, indirectly, in the living. This altruism has been used for centuries to justify postmortem investigations in medical pathology and safety research. [68] Occasionally, death inquiries offer a direct illustration of such altruism: forensic pathologists confronted with a cluster of fatal respiratory cases have been credited with the discovery of the hantavirus pulmonary syndrome. [69] In other death investigations, preventive knowledge is advanced not by a discovery, but by the quantity of similar cases. For example, pathologists see hundreds of motorcycle deaths and rarely question why unrestrained people crashing against inanimate objects on a machine going forty to eighty miles per hour die. Still, medical examiners note whether the motorcyclist was intoxicated or wearing a helmet and provide raw data that can be used for the evaluation of policy. Seemingly useless deaths become useful when aggregated in mortality statistics to form the building blocks for a large public health and biomedical industry of research, risk prevention, lifestyle changes, surgical treatment, and drug regimens. [70] In most contemporary death investigations, utilitarian altruism remains an abstract notion; few relatives realize how they may directly benefit from a forensic inquiry. As we will see in the next chapter, tissue and organ procurement works from similar altruistic principles but offers concrete body parts for specific individuals rather than abstract knowledge for the general good, leading to clashing forms of hope.

In infant deaths, altruism does not remain an abstract notion; parents may directly benefit from the outcome of the investigation. The catch for relatives in the forensic postmortem investigation is that they will be judged as well. When the carrot of altruism is insufficient, the stick of legal coercion compels acquiescence. Parents and other relatives profit tangentially in forensic investigations: not only will they receive medical information about the cause of death, but their own responsibility will be established. Medical examiners have the power to preempt further legal steps and exonerate caregivers. The interpretive leaps that medical examiners make in infant investigations purposefully center on the caregivers' role in the baby's death. The difference between an unexpected infant death investigation and other forensic inquiries is that in the former, medical examiners explicitly take the interests and needs of parents into consideration. Justice still matters greatly, but it is not the only stakeholder in the inquiry.

Even such direct benefits for parents do not necessarily ease the existential sting of mortality. Only when the corpse can be objectified as an empty vessel for the soul are death investigations allowed to take place. The answers, however, fail to resolve the existential quandaries of premature dying. While explaining deaths, medical examiners also confirm in case after case the limits of preventive measures and medical acumen, the randomness of death in spite of precautions, the seeming inevitability of accidents,[71] and the ravages of natural disease. Death certificates highlight the futility of an obsession with death in every aspect of life.[72] For grieving relatives, an explanation might occasionally soften the blow of sudden death, but it does not bring their loved one back. At best, the death certificate specifies the answer to the existential "why" questions, but it never provides a meaning for the passing. Ultimately, the dead remain existentially mute, but even their muteness might be meaningful when it results from validated processes: "In our largely secular society, sometimes meaning can be reduced to the admission that we do not yet know the mechanism, that medicine cannot intervene in certain predetermined illness trajectories, that some disorders remain mortal. Anxiety and mystery can be ordered, if not precisely allayed."[73]

Viewed in light of the way that people in late modern North American societies cope with death, the forensic expert system thus offers a reformulation of the age-old question of why babies die. Infusing forensic authority with hope and justice leads to a social valuation of the deceased, relationships, and life itself. The forensic investigation validates the infant as a social being supervised by adult caretakers and judges the quality of parenting. Without defining "good" or even "acceptable" infant deaths, medical examiners use their powers as death brokers to confirm that each infant death is a great loss. While some deaths remain medically unexplainable, every death constitutes a moral lesson to be deciphered for the living. The truth that comes of the death investigation connects death with life, medicolegal science with morality, parents with children, families with the state, individual cases with general guidelines, and past behavior with future parenting. Consequently, death brokering frames social life: its values, its rules for living, its health care, its social relationships, even the tools and materials of living. In the next chapter, I will show that forensic institutions require strong structural and cultural resources to weather strains on their jurisdiction. At stake in conflicts with organ and tissue procurement organizations is the issue of who contributes most to the public good.

CHAPTER SIX

THE ORGAN AND TISSUE TRADE

Hit in the head with a baseball bat during a shoplifting spree, seventeen-year-old Jonathan Draper lies fatally wounded on the floor of an electronics store. An ambulance transports him from the store to the local hospital's emergency department. The ER physicians attempt to stabilize Jonathan but, noticing his rapidly deteriorating condition, transfer him to the university hospital's surgical unit. Surgeons insert a pressure catheter and perform a CT scan. The scan shows massive subarachnoid hemorrhage and a possible occipital fracture. Two neurologists conduct a full neurological exam and apnea challenge. Jonathan fails the test and at 8:00 p.m. is declared brain-dead. The attending surgeon alerts the organ bank and speaks to Jonathan's parents. They agree to organ donation and sign off on an almost full donation: every organ except bone marrow. Yet before organ transfer can proceed, the medical examiner needs to be notified.

Because it is a Saturday evening, scene investigator Tony Best takes the call from the surgical unit. He writes down the information about the circumstances of death and then talks to the organ procurer. The transplant coordinator notes that this is his lucky night. Tony cautions that his docs might not go for organ removal. He senses the disappointment and annoyance in the organ procurer's voice: "But it is a full procurement." Tony replies, "Sure, but it's also a homicide." He predicts that the procurers will receive permission only for removal of the corneas. He promises to talk to the doctor on call and get back to the organ procurer.

Tony calls Dr. Douglas and explains the situation. Dr. Douglas forbids organ procurement and restricts tissue removal to the corneas before the autopsy, the heart valves after the external inspection, and bones and skin after the autopsy. When Tony relates this to the procurement coordinator, the man protests angrily. Tony ends the conversation bluntly, stating that he is not in charge. Around 10:00 p.m. the phone rings again. This time Tony talks to Dr. Bircher, chief of organ and tissue transplantation for the region. He demands to talk to the chief medical examiner. Dr. Cahill sticks to the decision: she will not allow organ procurement in this homicide. Dr. Bircher is furious and considers this arrangement unacceptable. He threatens to contact his political connections. He darkly predicts that on Monday the medical examiner's budget will be discussed in the state senate.

At 3:30 a.m. Tony Best fields another call. He cannot believe his ears when he hears the state's governor inquiring about the homicide. Apparently, Dr. Bircher asked Jonathan's relatives to call their state representative and the press. Tony explains that policy forbids organ transfer in some cases of homicide. The governor decides not to interfere but will discuss the policy with the attorney general's office. These discussions and a budgetary review do not ensue. Jonathan tests positive for HTLV, excluding the possibility of any organ or tissue transfer. The next Monday, Dr. Douglas conducts a full autopsy. The cause of death is recorded as subarachnoid hemorrhage due to laceration of left vertebral artery associated with fracture of C-1 vertebra due to blunt-force trauma to head and neck. The manner of death is homicide.

This incident is an extreme example of conflict over professional turf. Early in the development of organ transplantation, a warning about a "moral and legal dilemma" between transplant and forensic science suggested that medical examiners might be required to accept brain death as the new definition of death.[1] Over time, the debate has shifted drastically, from clarifying brain death to access to bodies,[2] and the level of acrimony has increased. A 1994 article in the *Journal of the American Medical Association* (*JAMA*) described the relationship between medical examiners and organ procurement organizations as having been "laced with tension for years. But the stress might be mounting."[3] A survey of procurement organizations showed 36 percent of respondents reporting "bad" and "horrible" experiences with medical examiners,[4] while forensic practitioners cited "communication problems" and a blatant disregard for each other's work.[5] One forensic pathologist complained that the conflict was "detrimental to medical examiners and their offices."[6]

Organ and tissue procurement pits the living against the dead and transplant surgery against criminal justice. Jonathan Draper's body could have been a "gift of life" to several seriously ill people on long waiting lists; or it could have become, as it did, part of a complete death investigation that led to the conviction of his killer. Before conducting an autopsy, medical examiners wait twenty-four hours following death in order to lower the risk of infection and then proceed with their routine slicing of organs. Forensic investigations and procurement of tissues and organs are therefore often mutually exclusive. If medical examiners cut organs during autopsy, procurement organizations are left with only corneas and skin. If organ procurers recover body parts, medical examiners cannot conduct full investigations, and their findings are vulnerable to court challenges. Unfortunately, organ procurement organizations are interested in the cases that pose difficult medicolegal questions. Many bodies in the medical examiner's office are gold mines for tissue procurement, and some also qualify for organ donation. Those particularly prized for procurement are bodies of children and adolescents who have died as the result of a sudden trauma. In these cases, however, a full death investigation might make the difference in criminal court.

Virtually every article discussing organ transplantation offers a "ritualistic recitation" of similar stark statistics:[7] by the end of 2002, there were 82,749 patients waiting for organs in the United States; the number of transplanted organs in 2002 was 24,000, and more than 6,000 people died waiting for a transplant. Of the 12,800 donors in 2002, 48 percent were cadavers.[8] This recitation is followed by the moral claim that the shortage is unnecessary, because sufficient numbers of people die with reusable organs and tissues. Because coroners and medical examiners have forensic jurisdiction over about one-fifth of the deaths in the United States,[9] an organ recovery depends not only upon permission of the next of kin but also on the coroner's or medical examiner's approval. Noting that a person dies every four hours waiting for an organ, procurers offer veiled accusations of medical examiners' complicity in manslaughter when they "deny" organ or tissue procurement. For example: "Since an average of 3.37 organs were recovered per donor in 1992, it is *possible* that as many as 2979 people were denied transplants in the United States from 1990 to 1992 because of medical examiner denials."[10] Or: "The paradox that exists when the investigator denies release for just one potential donor is that up to seven waiting recipients are also denied the chance for a lifesaving transplant."[11] Recent attempts at public education to expand voluntary donation and a number of high-profile legislative initiatives to encourage donation have not significantly increased the number of donors.[12] The organ procurement organizations have therefore made organ and tissue release from medical examiners and coroners a priority.

The fundamental issue at stake is the cultural ethic of postmortem manipulation. The transplantation and forensic communities share a public relations problem: they need to overcome a widespread and long-

entrenched sense of distrust, repugnance, and outrage at physicians' violating the integrity of the corpse. In spite of decades of education, relatives
have difficulty accepting that a warm, breathing body with a heartbeat is
brain-dead and should be readied for organ removal, and although most
people favor organ donation, they remain reluctant to sign donor cards.[13]
For most North Americans, a corpse is never just a thing.[14] The forensic
and transplantation communities counter this cultural barrier with a call
for altruism grounded in utilitarianism.[15] In the conflict over access, the
struggle is about whose altruism rules. Both forms of altruism rely on a
loosely defined Judeo-Christian ethic of the Good Samaritan: one gives
selflessly to help another in time of need and should expect nothing in return. In organ and tissue transplantation, altruism benefits from a clearly
identifiable gift with direct life-prolonging effects. The ethical justification
for forensic work—to provide answers about a death and hope that it did
not occur in vain—confronts the utility of saving terminally ill people.
Expanding the knowledge base about causes of death is no match for the
tangible gift of a transplant.

The two parties also bring different resources to the conflict. Medical
examiners have tradition and the law on their side, but organ procurers
have more resources, political power, and vocal public support.[16] The procurement and transplantation interests constitute one of the most adapt-
able, technologically savvy, and powerful professional groups in contemporary biomedicine. Transplant interests are at the forefront of developing
and incorporating innovative medical technologies, including genetics and
cloning, and have flexibly expanded their market and jurisdiction with
Medicare funding and private insurance reimbursement for a growing array of conditions.[17]

Anthropologist Nancy Scheper-Hughes observed that "wherever transplant surgery moves it challenges customary laws and traditional local
practices bearing on the body, death, and social relations. Commonsense
notions of embodiment, relations of body parts to the whole, and the
treatment and disposal of the dying are consequently being reinvented
throughout the world."[18] Longtime organ transplant observers Renée Fox
and Judith Swazey add, "The determination to procure organs has become
so powerful that we believe there is an almost predatory obliviousness
to where the organs come from and how the donors died."[19] Regardless
of where a death investigation office draws the line on organ and tissue
procurement, the encounter with transplant organizations challenges the
legal, moral, financial, and technical equilibrium that has allowed death
investigators to conduct their inquiries. For the traditional field of forensics, the encounter with procurement organizations has become a crash

course in the high-stakes commodified body market. Although the professional struggle involves relatively few corpses, it has, over the last decade, become the largest organized threat to the medical examiner's position as death broker. The results have been far-reaching for the sources of legitimacy underlying medical examiners' forensic authority. Procurement organizations have challenged the legal mandate that forms the foundation of the forensic market shelter, they have questioned the scientific basis of forensic pathology, and they have created conflicts of interests. They justify these profound challenges by claiming a superior ethical position. Procurers argue that they speak for life rather than for death and so offer true altruism.

QUESTIONING THE LEGAL MANDATE OF DEATH INVESTIGATORS

When analyzing the events that led to the explosion of the *Challenger* space shuttle during takeoff in 1986, sociologist Diane Vaughan explained the "normalization of deviance." NASA engineers had standard risk-assessment procedures to determine whether the risk of a launch was acceptable. Over time, despite deviation from standards, the risk of launching the shuttle became acceptable as launches occurred without accident. Vaughan locates this gradual normalization process in the development of an engineering culture at NASA.[20] To offset the perennial shortage, organ and tissue transplantation has undergone a similar process that has, to some degree, normalized deviance in cases of suspicious death. Organ and tissue transplantation initially involved ethical and legal policies that restricted the sources of organs to be transplanted, the consent procedures to be followed, the incentives for organ donation, the risks involved in transplantation, and the appropriate recipients. Over time, these restrictions have been greatly relaxed, and risks once deemed unacceptable have become acceptable. For example, organs of HIV patients, intravenous-drug users, and alcoholics—all once considered marginal—are now welcomed for donation. Age criteria for donation have been relaxed: elderly people used to be excluded from donation but are now encouraged to consider it. The biggest taboo in organ donation has been providing a financial incentive enticing vulnerable people to donate. As anthropologist Donald Joralemon explained, most transplantation advocates in the 1980s agreed that selling organs was "morally repugnant and reprehensible," although some advocates argued that financial incentives should complement altruist gift-giving.[21] Yet even this moral center has shifted. Several organizations, transplant surgeons, and advocates have proposed financial incentives to entice more people to donate organs. In January 2004, Wisconsin became the first state to offer a tax break to organ donors, and New York and Indiana have introduced similar laws.

The interaction of procurement interests with the forensic community exemplifies a similar shifting of well-entrenched boundaries. Since the deceased's property rights to the body terminate at the moment of death, jurisdiction over a body for the past century has remained with surviving relatives or death investigators, depending on the circumstances of the death. The next of kin or other designated person has a "quasi property right to possession of the cadaver for the purposes of proper disposition. Interference with this right can give rise to a claim against anyone not releasing the body or in any other way altering it prior to release, without permission of the next of kin. This prerogative was not absolute and yielded to the public good where the demands of justice required such subordination. Until the latter part of the 1960s, the interests of the public and justice were represented by the medical examiner/coroner."[22] For example, Minnesota's Hennepin County medical examiner is required to issue a death certificate for every sudden or unexpected death. The state statute authorizes the medical examiner to take charge of the body, claim any property of the deceased needed in the investigation, summon all health-related records, and conduct an autopsy when "advisable and in the public interest." The autopsy includes the "removal, retention, testing and use of organs and parts of organs and tissues."[23]

In certain states, the legal next of kin can raise religious objections against the mutilation that occurs during autopsy. The medical examiners in my study honored such requests (except when they suspected a homicide or a public health hazard). They either avoided an autopsy and had the family sign a waiver, or they modified procedures to take the religious beliefs of the deceased into consideration. If no autopsy was performed, the manner of death was left "undetermined due to family objections to autopsy." The waiver explained that a refusal could affect insurance payments and litigation. During autopsies of Jewish people, the staff would make sure that all blood and tissues stayed with the body. They would keep the body in the body bag instead of laying it directly on the autopsy table, and they would wipe off all instruments instead of washing them and enclose the wipes with the body. They would also perform the autopsy soon after death, so that the body could be buried the same day. Although religious objections have been used by legal next of kin to hide drug abuse,[24] the medical examiner can get a court order to perform an autopsy. Thus, even if religious objections are offered, the medical examiner's jurisdiction over the body usually prevails in the public interest.[25]

Over the past decades, funeral directors have also occasionally tried to contest the jurisdiction of medical examiners over dead bodies. Funeral directors want to embalm and bury the body as quickly as possible and balk at waiting twenty-four hours for the medical examiner to perform an autopsy. In essence, funeral directors have tried to eliminate the intermediaries in order to deal unencumbered with relatives. Dr. Douglas characterized the office's relations with funeral directors as a partnership between two parties who have been forced to work together. At worst, the relationship is marred with distrust and bickering. A funeral worker complained to me, for example, that he could not understand why the office conducted an autopsy on a five-year-old boy who drowned, the cause and manner of death being obvious to everyone. Usually, however, this medical examiner's office tried to accommodate funeral directors, giving priority to autopsies of decedents who had designated a funeral home and making sure not to cut through arteries in the neck needed to circulate embalming fluid. These medical examiners also took advantage of the funeral director's privileged relationship with relatives to distribute information about support groups. Yet because of their often opposing interests, pathologists have been suspicious of electing funeral directors to the position of coroner.

In one county in the mountains of eastern Kentucky—I am sure it is not an isolated case—every four years the residents elect a coroner to investigate their deaths. Every election year, the same two people run for office. They are not experienced medicolegal investigators, pathologists, or even doctors. They are the directors of the two local funeral homes. The one that gets elected automatically gets a hand up on the competition because he gets to steer the family of the deceased toward his funeral home. This is completely unacceptable. Who knows how many murders disguised as suicides or accidental deaths occur and these people would not have a clue as to the difference. All they are concerned about is making money.[26]

Relatives and funeral directors have thus been unable to sever the link between forensic medicine and the public good. This leaves the challenge from tissue and organ transplant interests. Forensic pathologist Donald Jason has argued that transplantation interests have intruded on the legal quasi rights of the next of kin to dispose of the body and, in some instances, on the legal mandate of the medical examiner.[27] Here we observe the gradual shifting of norms and a reinterpretation of relationships in the wake of the growth of transplantation. The 1968 Uniform Anatomical Gift Act, adopted by all states with minor variations and updated in 1987, authorized any person eighteen years or older and of sound mind to designate organs for transplantation even if the next of kin objects. The "donee" of a part must remove the part "without unnecessary mutilation" and then relinquish custody of the body to the next of kin or other person to dispose of.[28] However, to avoid negative publicity or possible litigation, current transplantation services seek the permission of the next of kin as a practical matter and will not procure organs over their objections. Yet Jason warns, "Since there is no legal requirement for this [custom], . . . the practice may not be universal and need not be retained indefinitely."[29] Indeed, the organ procurement organization of New York, Pennsylvania, and West Virginia recently adopted a controversial policy of acting on the documented wishes of individuals to donate, independent of family consent.[30] Instead of asking permission, organ procurers will simply *inform* relatives that the deceased signed an organ donor card.

In addition, some states allow tissue procurers to remove eye tissue (corneas) and pituitary glands for research and manufacture of drugs without asking permission from the next of kin when the body is under the jurisdiction of a coroner or medical examiner.[31] These laws also shield the medical examiner from liability if, after removal, the family sues because of the lack of consent.[32] In 1997, investigative journalist Ralph Frammolino of the *Los Angeles Times* discovered that the Los Angeles County coroner's office was abusing a state law known as the "medical examiner's law" to obtain corneas at autopsy if the next of kin had offered no known objections.[33] The law had been passed after lobbying by California's eye banks, because corneas disintegrate within twenty-four hours after death, and asking for permission was considered too time-consuming when relatives could not be located. Tissue procurers, however, interpreted the law as a license to take corneas without asking permission. Only if the next of kin had the insight to mention that they did not want organ or tissue procurement would the corneas not be removed. Disregarding the protests of scene investigators and other staff, the Los Angeles office made cornea removal routine by discouraging staff from asking relatives whether they had any objections. The de facto and de jure presumed consent led to absurd situations. In some cases, the coroner decided that an autopsy was not necessary, but because the corneas had already been removed, the pathologists were required to do an autopsy. The journalist also discovered that corneas were removed from people with lengthy jail terms for "multiple drug violations," a high-risk group for contagious diseases.

The day after the *Los Angeles Times* published the report, the coroner's office changed its procedures and required staff to ask permission from relatives. Shortly after the policy went into effect, the number of procured corneas dropped sharply, by nearly 70 percent. Ronald Smith, director of the Doheny Eye and Tissue Transplant Bank, wrote a letter defending the procurement of corneas on humanitarian grounds and highlighting the many people who had regained their eyesight.[34] In October of 1998,

California governor Pete Wilson signed a new law requiring coroners' offices to secure permission from relatives before removing the eye tissue for transplants. Twenty other states, however, including Florida and Texas, have laws similar to the original California statute. In Washington, D.C., the law goes even further and allows procurers to remove heart valves without asking permission from relatives.[35] According to some legal scholars, such laws violate due process and constitute a taking without just compensation.[36] At a minimum, they constitute an erosion of the long-held common-law rights vested in the next of kin to possess the undisturbed corpse for the purposes of burial or other disposition.

To date, in the event of a suspicious death, the right to possession of the body has remained with the medical examiner or coroner, even if the corpse might be used for organ or tissue donation. This jurisdictional prerogative was confirmed in section 4 (a) of the 1987 update of the Uniform Anatomical Gift Act (UAGA): "The [medical examiner] may release and permit the removal of a part from a body within that official's custody, for transplantation or therapy, if: (1) the official has received a request for the part from a hospital, physician, surgeon, or procurement organization, (2) the official has made a reasonable effort . . . to locate and examine the decedent's medical records and inform persons listed in Section 3 (a) of their option to make, or object to making, an anatomical gift, . . . and (5) the removal will not interfere with any autopsy or investigation." In Minnesota, for example, the Hennepin County medical examiner statute specifies that "the medical examiner may facilitate donation of organs and tissues in compliance with the Uniform Anatomical Gift Act."[37] There, as in many other jurisdictions, organ procurement in suspicious deaths depends on the judgment of the medical examiner.[38]

Recently, local organ procurement organizations have been successful in changing medical examiner statutes to make the death investigation secondary to organ removal, subordinating medical examiners' legal mandates. Since the early 1990s, New York, Tennessee, New Jersey, and Texas have had laws dictating that the needs of transplantation take precedence.[39] The New York and Tennessee laws go farthest, requiring the release of organs in medical examiners' cases, while the laws of New Jersey and Texas make it more difficult for medical examiners to deny organ recovery. For example, the New York law states that the medical examiner "who has notice of such donation shall only perform an autopsy and/or analysis of tissue or organs in a manner and within a time period compatible with the preservation for the purposes of transplantation of said donation."[40] The New Jersey and Texas statutes require a medical examiner who wants to withhold one or more organs to be present at organ recovery. A medical examiner who denies organ donation must then provide written objections to block the procedure and explain why the organ might be involved in the cause of death. In New Jersey, "a case occurred in which, despite the warning to the organ procurement team that more time was needed prior to release to allow further investigation, the medical examiner was forced to go to the operating room where the recovery team had already been assembled, and deny recovery."[41] In spite of a joint policy statement issued by the National Association of Medical Examiners (NAME) and major organ procurement organizations in 1995 that appealed for collaboration and case-by-case evaluation and argued against legislative changes,[42] legislation similar to the Texas law was introduced in Colorado during the 2000 legislative year.[43] It failed, but such legislation passed both houses of the legislature in California in 2003. Organ and tissue transplantation interests have also interfered on the federal level. A 2002 advisory committee on organ transplantation appointed by the secretary of the Department of Health and Human Services directs the secretary to add a new subsection to the UAGA that mirrors the Texas and New Jersey laws.[44]

When disputes arise, therefore, organ transplantation organizations already have the law on their side in four states. In addition, transplantation organizations threaten to undermine the legal protections of the medical examiner, as happened in the death of Jonathan Draper. In West Virginia, where the organ transplant bank lobbied to change the law,[45] the state's chief medical examiner called state legislators and learned that the measure was likely to pass. If the issue were debated, advocates would parade children who had received a "second chance at life" with transferred organs, and few legislators would resist the political clout of the organ procurers, the medical groups, and patient organizations. The organ procurement group and the chief medical examiner therefore compromised in order to make additional resources available to forensic investigators.

The legal attacks on medical examiners' jurisdiction over corpses may suggest that death investigators actively boycott organ and tissue procurement. The few available studies, however, indicate that medical examiners and coroners routinely and overwhelmingly accede to the requests of organ procurers. In 1994, *JAMA* published a retrospective study conducted by several organ procurement organizations to find out how many bodies are actually denied by medical examiners and coroners for organ and tissue transfer.[46] The same authors published a follow-up study in 2003. The studies showed that in more than 90 percent of requests, the medical examiner had provided the organ procurement organization with permission to remove organs. During 2000–2001, there were 354 denials, mostly for homicide and child-abuse cases. In addition, the rate of organ recovery from medical examiners' cases was ten times that of non–medical examiners' cases. Medical examiners provided an astonishing 62 percent of all donors. The studies revealed that in several major areas of the country, no donors were denied for recovery during the years studied. The authors did not provide information on how many relatives refused organ transfer after medical examiners gave permission, but other studies show that about 30–40 percent of the families who are approached refuse donation.[47] Relatives are three times as likely to deny donation as medical examiners.[48]

Although these results could indicate a growing collaboration between medical examiners and organ procurement organizations, the articles instead advocated for organ recipients, emphasizing that in the last decade the rate of denials has decreased only slightly, from 7.2 percent to 6.9 percent. The authors complained about the lack of accountability for medical examiners' denials—suggesting that decisions for organ release were arbitrary—and dismissed the argument that forensic or criminal evidence could be compromised. No defendant, they noted, had been successfully acquitted with that argument.[49] Rather than consider the ten areas of the country without denials, the authors faulted medical examiners and coroners for refusing any dead body for organ procurement. In a reply to the first article, medical examiner Randy Hanzlick bristled at the negative interpretation of the findings and noted that even if medical examiners complied in 100 percent of cases, the donor pool would be only marginally larger.[50] Instead of the "ignorance and contrariness" attributed to medical examiners, he argued, sound forensic and legal considerations lay behind most denials. He urged the organ transplant stakeholders to improve the donor pool from non–medical examiner cases and to educate relatives of donors to accede to donation.

The transplant interests have dismissed death investigators' public health and criminal justice mandates and instead have countered that the benefits of organ transfer overshadow any goal medical examiners might accomplish. The most vocal proponent of this position is Teresa J. Shafer, affiliated with the LifeGift Organ Donation Center of Fort Worth, Texas, and the lead author on the two studies mentioned above. Because organ donation literally makes the difference between life and death for terminally ill people, she argues, organ procurement organizations act from an ethically superior position. Ultimately, she insists, ethics, not old laws, should guide people's actions. Using a principles-based ethics, Shafer, with the help of philosopher Timothy Mahoney, claims that "the harm to society caused by not releasing the organ results in a preventable death, the ultimate harm."[51] When releasing organs, Shafer elaborates, medical examiners need not worry about violating the ethical principle of autonomy, because the UAGA resolved that issue legally when it granted primary authority over the dead body to the deceased.[52]

The trickiest dilemma permeating this conflict is whether a medical examiner's denial defies the principle of justice. Medical examiners have argued that allowing organ transfer endangers criminal justice. Again, advocates such as Shafer dismiss such concerns: "Available data do not support the belief that there are substantive concerns in this case nor that the fear of miscarriage of justice warrants being given such weight that lives be lost due to [medical examiners/coroners'] denials of organ recovery." And "even if such a 'miscarriage of justice' did exist, it would, initially, still be only a *single* case, and, given the severity of the organ shortage and the near certainty that when suitable organs are not recovered someone will die, would the sacrifice of hundreds and even thousands of lives be justified by one case?" One miscarriage of justice might not count for much, such reasoning says, but one denied organ constitutes unethical practice bordering on the criminal: "Finally, one should not minimize the importance of just one donor denied by a medical examiner. To do so is unethical and trivializes the life of the next potential heart, liver, or lung recipient who will die. To cause such a death through denial of organ recovery in a [medical examiner/coroner] case is to cause the ultimate harm to a person."[53]

The claim that medical examiners are morally obligated to release organs under all circumstances because organ transplantation holds the ethical higher ground is an amazing intellectual feat. Ethicists and social scientists have long considered organ procurement and transplantation a hotbed of ethical conundrums.[54] Ultimately, however, Shafer's goal is not to stake out the ground of higher ethics, but to employ ethical rhetoric to undermine the legal authority of death investigators over dead bodies.

It is time that the issue of loss of life due to [medical examiners/coroners'] denials of organ recovery be given the same amount of attention from the government that other impediments to organ donation have been given. The facts in this case, as well as the stakes involved, justify such attention. The public should be part of this discussion. Federal regulations or legislation could assist in gaining the release of more organs for transplantation. Further, states should begin earlier rather than later to move legislation through state governments similar to that passed in Texas and New Jersey.[55]

The procurement groups thus frame the conflict over the jurisdiction of dead bodies largely as an ethical issue with legal implications. Because people can be directly helped with organs and because such help is lifesaving, organ procurers act more ethically and should have priority over the body. The death investigator's legal mandate is an obstacle that needs to be cleared, with the help of lawmakers, regardless of the large number of organs that death investigators already release. This legal displacement involves an ethical shift from public to private interests. What matters when a person dies is not the potential criminological or public health information gathered during a death investigation but the condition of the organs for transplantation into individuals. The transplant community presents itself as indispensable lifesavers, speaking on behalf of dying patients. The framing of the conflict exaggerates the role of medical examiners as sole decision makers, holds them directly accountable for any organs that are not transplanted, and glosses over the difficult ethical choices common even in "ordinary" transplants. [56]

Organ procurers have also tried to portray medical examiners as physicians with mixed loyalty serving both the medical and the criminal justice systems. The recent history of forensic medicine shows that instead of emphasizing medical examiners' dual role, reformers sought to tie forensic pathology closely to the medical model of other subspecialties, to shore up the scientific objectivity of death investigation. [57] Forensic pathologists' certification has downplayed their legal knowledge while emphasizing their primary role as physicians. Organ procurement advocates exploit this unresolved tension between law and medicine when they call upon medical examiners as fellow physicians to save lives, thus offering forensic pathologists a way to redeem themselves as professional healers. [58] The catch is that death investigators have to abandon their niche of professional jurisdiction and dedicate their jobs to securing organs and tissues.

During the legislative changes in the early 1990s, medical examiners assumed that they were easy targets for the transplant interests. Organ and tissue procurers determined that less effort and fewer resources were required to force several thousand death investigators to release transplant materials than to launch educational campaigns to convince millions of people to donate. The organ procurement community generally admits that national campaigns, federally mandated communication between hospitals and organ procurement organizations, extensive studies and surgeon general workshops about the organ shortage, various legislative and policy initiatives, increased use of "marginal" organs, and tinkering with donor-suitability criteria have not led to a substantive expansion of organ transfer. [59]

Legally, only one party can have first access to a corpse, and statutes in four states (New York, Tennessee, New Jersey, and Texas) explicitly render the interests of medical examiners secondary to organ procurement. Such policy may seem appealing in light of the perennial organ and tissue shortage, but changing legal mandates is a risky strategy for both professional groups. Medical examiners clearly lose the most when they are forced to relinquish legally guaranteed first access to dead bodies. Procurement organizations, however, also face a difficult situation if they do not assume *all* the responsibilities of medical examiners. Forensic pathologist Michael

Baden pointed out the doomsday scenario: "If there is a 'not guilty' verdict, [the procurement organizations] want to make sure it's not blamed on them. If there is just one case in which a murderer gets off because an organ wasn't there, they know people will stop giving permission" for donation.[60] Indeed, legally subordinating the medical examiner's interests to organ procurement might render the procurement profession vulnerable in cases that present a clear need for a forensic death investigation. An argument that the standard procedure in homicide investigations is to conduct a full forensic autopsy unless the victim has organs that can be recovered for transplantation would be untenable in court. In light of the great variation in death investigation systems in the United States, however, the organ and tissue procurement interests have concluded that changing legislation, preferably at the federal level, is the easiest means to obtain organs and tissues. Shafer and coauthors noted that between 1990–93 and 2000–2001, medical examiners' "denials" dropped 83 percent in New Jersey and Texas, while there were no "denials" in New York and only two in Tennessee.[61]

QUESTIONING THE SCIENTIFIC BASIS OF FORENSIC PATHOLOGY

Nowhere are the conflicts between procurers and death investigators more intense than in the cases of child abuse, adult homicide, and SIDS. In the two surveys of medical examiners' and coroners' denial of organ procurement, Shafer and her associates noted that roughly 27 percent of refused cases were probably child abuse, while an additional 4 percent of denials likely involved SIDS (half of SIDS cases are denied).[62] Other studies report similarly that the most likely categories of denial are child abuse, SIDS, and adult homicide.[63] In order to obtain tissue materials from those corpses, transplant organizations question the scientific basis of the death investigation and implement changes under the guise of increasing collaboration.

For procurers, the problem with denying organs after death from child abuse or SIDS is a critically short supply and too large a demand. Relatively few children die with organs ready for transplantation, and those who do are likely to have been involved in trauma, qualifying the death as a medical examiner case. Relatives of children often agree to organ transfer with greater willingness than the families of adult patients,[64] although relatives of pediatric patients are still more likely to refuse organ donation than are medical examiners (29 percent versus 16 percent in one study).[65] Discussing the lack of organ transfer in cases of SIDS and child abuse due to medical examiners' prerogatives, Shafer and coauthors remark,

This is especially unfortunate for two reasons. First, pediatric organs are in critically short supply and are essential for needed transplantations in young recipients for whom size is crucial. Second, nonfatal probable child abuse cases are routinely prosecuted with evidence that can be gathered through external physical examination, laboratory results, roentgenograms, computed tomographic scans and the like. In the case of organ donation, all of these medical data can still be provided, and, in addition, direct examination and photography of internal organs and tissues can be offered as further evidence.[66]

Medical examiners are most likely to deny organ procurement in child-abuse and SIDS cases because death investigation requires a careful medicolegal inquiry to exclude natural causes of death and to document the forensic evidence. To compromise such an investigation might result in the death of another child at the hands of an abuser. Even if the cause and manner of death are apparent, circumstantial evidence might be destroyed. Organ procurers question why the medical examiner needs to do a full autopsy on a decedent with a gunshot wound to the head. Pathologists point out that the entire body might provide trace evidence, such as gunpowder patterns or blood spatters. An analysis of the organs might reveal factors contributing to the cause of death (e.g., the presence of cocaine). Such circumstantial evidence is rarely revealed later, and no one, including prosecutors or defense attorneys, will know what has been destroyed or missed. A medical examiner told me about her initial confusion after an apparent SIDS case came back with bruised lungs after organ transfer. The organ procurers explained that the kind of retractors they used had caused the bruising. Documenting such artifacts not only creates extra work for the medical examiner but also potentially challenges the pathologist's expertise. When organ procurers point out that in no case has the state been unable to prosecute a criminal defendant because organ donation had removed necessary evidence,[67] medical examiners counter that compromised investigations with questionable evidence fail to come to trial and that defense counsels routinely allege evidence manipulation in order to generate reasonable doubt.[68]

Compromised cases rarely appear in professional journals but are instead the stuff of hallway conversations. Occasionally, conflicts spill over into the media. A medical examiner reported the case of a five-month-old boy brought to the hospital by the mother's boyfriend, who claimed that the infant had suddenly collapsed in his arms. The organ procurement organization requested tissue transfer, but the medical examiner refused after noting superficial injuries to the child's penis. The pathologist alerted the police, who interviewed the boyfriend. He confessed to having squeezed the infant by holding him tight against his chest and was convicted of second-degree murder in a jury trial.[69]

In another case, the Washington, D.C., medical examiner's office asked for a federal inquiry into the Washington Regional Transplant Consortium after the agency removed the organs of a gunshot victim before an autopsy could be performed. The organ transplant agency had removed the organs after receiving permission from the deceased's relatives but without contacting the medical examiner's office, thereby compromising the forensic investigation. The transplant surgeon did not map the trajectory of the bullets in the victim—who had been shot in the head, chest, buttocks, and extremities—and even incorrectly counted the number of bullets. In another case, the organ transplant agency tried by legal means to block the transfer to the medical examiner's office of the body of a man who had died under suspicious circumstances and whose relatives had given permission for organ donation. The judge ruled in favor of the medical examiner's office, but the delay generated confusion and created difficulty in explaining the cause and manner of death. The death remained undetermined.[70] The most egregious and conflict-ridden clash occurred in Harris County, Texas, in 1999. Officials of the LifeGift Organ Donation Center kept a homicide victim on life support after the medical examiner twice denied permission for organ donation. The decedent had apparently died after having been hit in the head by two men wielding two-by-fours. The transplant organization subsequently obtained a restraining order that also forced the medical examiner to be present at the organ retrieval and to put all objections in writing. According to the medical examiner's office, the procedures to keep the body viable for the purpose of organ donation created artifacts for the study of the brain, jeopardizing the determination of the cause of death. The district and county attorneys argued that the actions of the transplant agency were illegal and jeopardized the prosecution of a murder case. The director of LifeGift, on the other hand, took pride in his office's aggressive stance and emphasized that four people had received organs.[71]

Particularly vexing for the organ transplant interests is that death investigators lack uniformity in their denials. In some states and counties, they seem to release all child-abuse victims for organ procurement, while in other jurisdictions no such cases are released. The transplant community has therefore concluded that with more education and incentives, medical examiners can be coaxed into releasing some of the bodies and that a national policy can be implemented. Such initiatives might make sense from a medical perspective, but not from the perspective of criminal justice. Criminal investigation and litigation are not uniform across jurisdictions. The depth of the investigation depends on the local legal climate, including admissibility standards used in evidentiary hearings, a history of adverse court outcomes based on handling of evidence, and the scope of expert testimony used at trials.[72] When organ transplant officials surveyed medical examiners and coroners in Colorado to find out how to increase organ release, they found that death investigators first had to consult with district attorneys before releasing organs. District attorneys were hesitant to have doctors other than medical examiners touch bodies in cases of suspicious death, because trials were delayed when busy organ transplant surgeons canceled their court testimonies.[73]

Throughout the country, various procurement organizations and medical examiners have developed protocols to facilitate organ recovery, particularly in the contested domains of child abuse and SIDS. These protocols aim to explicate the different jurisdictions of medical examiners and procurement coordinators in fine detail. The various protocols include:

1. Decision guidelines for medical examiners delineating the kinds of cases that can be released and those that should not be released.[74]
2. Communication protocols that delineate when a medical examiner should be notified, what kind of information should be provided, and the possible decisions a medical examiner can make with regard to organ release.[75] Some protocols also specify that objections should be put in writing.[76]
3. Attendance of the medical examiner at organ removal.[77]
4. Providing extra imaging tests in the hospital (full-body roentgenograms, abdominal CT scans, other CT scans, MRI) to compensate for the lack of access to the corpse,[78] and/or providing blood and urine samples in special evidence kits.[79]
5. Check-off protocols and information sheets filled in by transplant surgeons, aimed at fulfilling the basic medicolegal needs of the medical examiner.[80]
6. Making transplant surgeons available to testify in court.[81]
7. Videotaping the transplant procedure for medical examiners. (This has only been suggested and may not have been implemented.)[82]

The decision guidelines remain the terrain closest to the medical examiner's traditional forensic jurisdiction. The author of the guidelines, medical examiner William Sturner, distinguishes six kinds of child death and evaluates whether they qualify for organ release. In an accidental drowning, for example, the medical examiner could allow organ release; but if a child is the victim of a hit-and-run accident, then organ donation should be denied because of the criminological value of the investigation. Yet specifying decision criteria in formal guidelines carries professional risks.

As sociologist Andrew Abbott has noted, professions thrive when they can bring abstract knowledge to bear on the tasks they perform. Abstract knowledge provides professionals with legitimation and opportunities for research and instruction. Although the knowledge base of a profession can be so abstract that it loses all relevance to the tasks at hand, too much clarity also limits professional judgment.[83] Spelling out tasks in fine detail, as in standardized protocols and guidelines, thus invites outside interference. The worldwide turn to evidence-based medicine in the contemporary health care field exemplifies this risk. Physician researchers have attempted to develop clinical protocols based on epidemiological principles to decrease variation in practice and to educate their colleagues. Third parties (insurance companies and government payers) have attempted to seize these guidelines in order to hold the profession accountable, institute reforms, and determine financial reimbursement.[84]

The danger for professional power lies not only with standardization but also with the content of the protocol. None of the proposed protocols grants medical examiners jurisdiction over any of the procurement tasks. Instead, the protocols allow transplant surgeons to provide forensic evidence and testimony for medicolegal purposes, provide alternative procedures and techniques for forensic investigations, and set timetables for communication and attendance at a transplant procedure that are out of the medical examiner's control. Such developments, although less confrontational than legislative changes, might still weaken the authority of medical examiners. Training others to complete forensic documentation of the external and internal examination of the corpse and sign off on it could lead to a gradual decentralization of the medical examiner's office. The range of alternatives in the protocols implies a critique of the forensic autopsy. Pathologists have long claimed that imaging technologies are at best complementary to autopsies,[85] but in hospitals such technologies have already supplanted autopsies, altering the tasks and position of hospital pathologists. Many of the quality-control tasks traditionally performed by pathologists have disappeared or have shifted to other medical subspecialties. In their quest for more transplants, therefore, procurement advocates question the need for, and usefulness of, autopsies in the medicolegal investigation. As we saw in chapter 4, criticism from fellow physicians can be particularly damning for death investigators. Clinicians might question the basic causal assumptions embedded in forensic work and reveal them as out of step with contemporary medicine.

Protocols for decision making may thus be used to specify, subdivide, and partly appropriate the jurisdiction of medical examiners, sometimes with their active collaboration. While medical examiners retain the forensic jurisdiction over death investigation, such protocols redistribute the actual work of conducting a medicolegal investigation. They define conditions that need to be met and processes that need to be followed before the medical examiner can deny organ and tissue recovery, and they offer substitutions for tasks central to forensic pathology.

QUESTIONING FORENSIC AUTONOMY

"Although organs are frequently described as 'gifts of life' (an expression that originates in the blood industry and that likewise is used to describe surrogacy), it is, in fact, a multi-million-dollar medical industry where clients in need pay steep fees for the procurement, preparation, transportation, and surgical replacement of body parts."[86] Indeed, the procurement and transplantation organizations frame their work in terms of offering the "gift of life" to people who would otherwise die—yet most of the "donation," "sharing," or "recovery" in the office of the medical examiner relates not to potentially lifesaving organs but to nonvital tissue. The removal of skin, bones, heart valves, and corneas is less regulated and restrictive than organ recovery. When the Clinton administration adopted rules in 1998 that required hospitals to notify procurement agencies of all deaths, organ donations increased by less than 1 percent, but donations to tissue banks and companies increased by about 40 percent.[87] Unless the eyes were involved in the cause of death, the medical examiners in my study almost always permitted the harvesting of corneas. Such routine tissue recovery, however, threatens another pillar of forensic jurisdiction: independence. When tissue recovery is accompanied by financial payments, conflicts ensue.

While social scientists have written extensively about the commodification of body parts,[88] no scholar has tracked the money that changes hands when tissues are recovered. In 2000, however, investigative journalists Mark Katches, William Heisel, and Ronald Campbell from the *Orange County Register* revealed that the profit margin for tissue processing is lucrative. Although the National Organ Transplantation Act, approved by Congress in 1984, made it a federal crime to engage in interstate selling of organs, the law does allow a harvesting company to charge a "handling and processing fee." No court has ever decided where a reasonable fee ends and a profitable markup begins. Reviewing company records, these journalists found that the entire tissue trade has sales of about $500 million per year, while the chief executives in this for-profit tissue industry were paid six- to seven-figure salaries. Every dead body becomes a potential gold mine: "A typical donor produces $14,000 to $34,000 in sales for the nonprofits. But yields can be far greater. Skin, tendons, heart valves, veins, and corneas are listed at about $110,000. Add bone from the same body, and one cadaver can be worth about $220,000."[89] Nonprofit tissue banks spin off private and publicly traded firms and the other way around; the nonprofit tissue banks send bone and other tissues to the for-profit bank, which pays processing fees to the nonprofits and then sells final products to surgeons, dentists, hospitals, and transplant centers. Dentists have been using powdered cadaver bone to treat severe gum disease for nearly thirty years, making processed bone as valuable as diamonds. Often the same people run both profit and nonprofit organizations.[90]

Organ transplantation is tightly regulated to make sure that organs reach patients with the greatest needs. Skin, bone, and corneas are sold to the highest bidder, and hospitals often cannot compete with the burgeoning plastic surgery industry. Skin, according to the *Register* article, is purchased by two major companies: Collagenesis Inc. of Massachusetts and LifeCell Corporation of New Jersey. Both companies process skin collagen for plastic surgery and reconstructive urinary surgery. "Collagenesis Inc. in Massachusetts can make $36,000 on skin from one body by turning it into a gel that is injected to smooth wrinkles and inflate lips."[91] Although skin procurers originally intended that skin be used for burn victims, the potential profits in cosmetic and reconstructive surgeries are ten times larger. The result is that burn units are regularly faced with shortages for skin grafting, while cosmetic-surgery patients do not wait. In a 2000 survey of the American Burn Association, 32 percent of burn centers reported delaying or altering treatment in the preceding year because of inadequate supplies of skin.[92] For-profit skin procurers prefer to supply companies like Collagenesis, because the demand for skin in cosmetic surgery is steady, while burn-victim units require skin sporadically; furthermore, the cosmetic-surgery industry pays a "processing fee" four times higher than a hospital's payment. Stung by the controversy and bad publicity caused by these reports,[93] Collagenesis developed a program awkwardly called Burn First to double the amount of available skin—with a new device that removes the first skin layer for use as a burn graft and the second layer for use in cosmetic surgery and other applications—and to establish a formal network among tissue banks to facilitate coordination of skin supply and demand.[94]

With potentially $220,000 worth of commodities in each body, the altruistic notion of the "gift of life" has become closely intertwined with the prospect of more profits. Tissue procurement organizations have strong financial incentives to pressure for the release of as many cadaver tissues as possible from the medical examiner's office. Procurement organizations dismiss medical examiners' financial concerns over the costs incurred (in time, personnel, and resources) in tissue recovery: "It is not acceptable public policy for a medical examiner's/coroner's office to deny cases, citing loss of forensic evidence, because the office does not have the resources to send someone to the hospital. If the issue is resources, and not the scientific loss of evidence, then the resource issue must be addressed."[95] Yet lack of resources and compromised scientific evidence can coincide when medical examiners lack personnel to attend procurement and forensic evidence is therefore lost. To address the lack of resources, procurement organizations have begun to pay medical examiners' offices a processing fee. Although some observers consider the cash flow from organ and tissue procurement organizations a boon for medical examiners,[96] the NAME takes a more prudent stance. Its policy on organ and tissue procurement states that payment for expenses incurred by medical examiners in the administration of an organ or tissue recovery program should be made to the government agency of which the forensic office is a subdivision and not directly to the medical examiner's or coroner's office.

When Ralph Frammolino of the *Los Angeles Times* investigated the Los Angeles County coroner's office as a "cornea mill," he discovered disturbingly tight connections between the coroner's office and the eye and tissue bank. Eye-bank employees had keys and twenty-four-hour access to the morgue and could thus enter and possibly disturb evidence. In contrast, during my research, I observed Dr. Cahill interviewing building contractors about the personnel that would have access to her building. She told them that she needed to know at all times who was in the building, in case she needed to testify about who might have had access to evidence. In Los Angeles, the tissue bank hired employees and their relatives from the coroner's office, paid to renovate an autopsy suite, and bought two vans for the coroner's office. The coroner's office was paid between $215 and $335 for each pair of recovered corneas. Over a five-year period, the total amount of money received from the Doheny Eye and Tissue Transplant Bank was $1.4 million. The company charged transplant surgeons a "processing fee" of $3,400 for a pair of corneas.[97]

For cash-strapped county and state medical examiner's or coroner's offices, the abundant flow of organ and tissue procurement money is seductive. Between 1991 and 1997, the budget of the Los Angeles County coroner's office was slashed by 8–10 percent, falling by six million dollars. An extra $275,000 a year for corneas likely provided some financial relief.[98] Other medical examiners have reported that organ and tissue procurers contributed to new facilities or that they leased space in the medical examiner's office. In Louisiana, a tissue procurement agency paid staff in the coroner's office to notify the agency when bodies arrived and also paid for bone and cornea transfers.[99] A lawsuit filed by a mother whose son's brain was removed without permission revealed that the agency had taken bones out of 117 unidentified bodies. In one New England state, the local organ procurement organization even paid for administrative personnel to answer phone calls coming in to the medical examiner's office. The organ procurement staff thus executed the important task of triaging and had direct access to information about all dead bodies. Some of the pathologists I talked to in various locations took similar initiatives to deal with financial duress, while others charged that the procurement organizations bought their way into the medical examiner's office. The medicolegal administrator of the office in my study had also been approached by the local tissue procurement organization with offers of administrative support, equipment, and "grants." The Texas health and safety statutes allow medical examiners to charge a fee of up to a thousand dollars (on top of any processing fees) to organ procurement organizations to "facilitate the timely procurement of organs."[100] Such payments are reminiscent of the debate on paying funeral costs to relatives in exchange for organ procurement, or on creating a futures market for organs—which is illegal under the National Organ Transplant Act of 1984.[101] Payments might lead to the sale of organs and tissues in financially unstable forensic offices.

When medical examiners depend on the monetary resources of procurement agencies to conduct everyday activities, these financial incentives for tissue procurement invoke the image of the corrupt coroner of the beginning of the twentieth century. The familiar question is *cui bono:* who benefits? Is the access of medical examiners to corpses primarily for forensic purposes, or do medical examiners first respond to their new paymasters, the procurement organizations?[102] Organization sociologist Michael Reed summarizes the dilemma: "Professional practice has traditionally distinguished itself from 'business' practice through the authoritative claim to 'disinterested universalism' in which the liberal professions portray their activities as fulfilling natural and social needs. Once they become 'tainted' through a much closer incorporation into business practice, this disinterested claim to moral and cultural authority is increasingly difficult to sustain."[103]

A CULTURAL DEFICIT

In their quest for organs and tissues, procurement organizations have steamrolled over the medicolegal death investigation system. Nothing that medical examiners have held sacred has been left untouched if change might generate more tissues and organs for transplant. Altering the legal mandates, doubting medical examiners' methods, questioning their selection criteria, and flashing hard cash have been justified by increasing the organ supply and feeding the tissue market. The transplant community has remained mostly unscathed in its encounter with death investigators.

In some communities, procurement staff need to fill out additional forms if they retrieve organs from a medical examiner's office or may be summoned to court to discuss the condition of the body before retrieval, but none of the procurement values, principles, or aims have required adaptation. In recent years, most medical examiners' offices have come to accommodate the demands from organ procurers. At the 1999 NAME conference, Edmund R. Donoghue, the president of the organization and medical examiner of Cook County, Illinois, urged his colleagues to aim for zero refusals.[104] The NAME's 2002 strategic plan recognizes that medical examiners "are dedicated to assisting in the utilization of scarce organs and tissues for transplantation. Medical examiners assist families and organ procurement agencies in assessing the suitability of the decedent for organ/tissue donation. Medical examiners are at the frontline in recognizing the importance of rapid organ retrieval, family notification and consulting."[105] As with iatrogenic deaths, when confronted with possible collusion among clinical colleagues, forensic pathologists have retreated.

The organ transplant interests have questioned the legitimacy of death investigators both in the public, legal-political arena and in the workplace. These advocates have reframed medical examiners' access to dead bodies as secondary to the public good of saving lives. The preferred strategy has been to exploit medical examiners' dual loyalty as physicians and as investigators in the criminal justice system and to claim the higher ethical ground. The organ procurement organizations have downplayed the significance of medical examiners' forensic observations for the criminal justice system; instead, the transplant surgeons have called upon medical examiners—invoking their shared background as physicians—to choose life. Still, the transplant community has not rendered forensic pathology obsolete nor completely usurped its jurisdiction. By working in alliance with the criminal justice system, medical examiners still hold a trump card. When procurement organizations take on medical examiners, they inevitably affect the conduct of criminal investigations. To meddle with evidence in a criminal case carries high risk for procurers.

Anesthesiologists and surgeons, midwives and obstetricians, nurse practitioners and primary care physicians, nursing aides and registered nurses, allergists and pulmonologists—the list of groups embroiled in similar turf fights to gain or protect professional power is long.[106] If we add hospitals, research-funding agencies, government regulators and payers, and patients to the mix, struggles over jurisdiction become the rule rather than the exception in the field of medicine.[107] Because medical examiners work as government officials, out of the public purview, protected by legal statutes, with a fixed workload and well-defined audiences, they have been insulated from most conflict and lack an incentive to change their mode of operation. Rather than consolidating their power over death investigation, they have allowed a variety of systems to flourish. And instead of positioning themselves as the team leaders in forensic investigations (similar to the vision of forensic pathology promoted by Dr. Michael Baden in the Woodward trial), they have retreated to a narrower expert role centered on autopsies (as defined by Drs. Gerald Feigin and Jan Leestma at that trial). The struggle with procurement organizations over access to cadavers reveals the weakness of protected forensic jurisdiction: to remain unchallenged for too long can make a professional group outdated.

These weaknesses are not simply structural ones (such as the lack of resources and funding, which is the usual explanation for chronic problems in medical examiners' offices) but also cultural. Organ transplant advocates have the upper hand in this conflict because they frame their work with the rhetoric of giving life. When transplant organizations publicize the growing list of children waiting for organs, death investigators are at a disadvantage, lacking appealing counterexamples. Medical examiners' call to altruism is not as convincing as that of procurement advocates, who deploy the public relations model of successful charitable organizations. They broadcast celebrity profiles and organize "transplant games," where people with transplanted organs engage in sports competitions sponsored by pharmaceutical companies and where organ donors are honored as well. They also allow restricted contact between recipient and donor families (usually letter-writing) to maximize the ethic of gift-giving, further consolidating the sense of reciprocity.[108]

Forensic pathologists assume that a full investigation of a death is necessary in order to meet their professional standards. Such an argument, however, pales in comparison to a media-friendly campaign with children smiling after their organ transplant. This conflict between organ transplant organizations and death investigators is therefore permeated with a narrative inequity. As Renée Fox and Judith Swazey explain, organ transfer is a tyrannical gift, because it creates an unequal relationship between donor and recipient[109]—yet organ procurers tell sunny stories of altruism, hope, life, healing, second chances, and redemption. They position themselves at the summit of medical practice, using technology to create deeply valued new chances for life. Medical examiners' narratives, in contrast, are relegated to the back pages of newspapers. The best they can accomplish is an accurate description of child abuse or infanticide, leading only to an indirect form of justice that—as victim-impact statements during court sentencing emphasize—never replaces the loss of a loved one. Compared to the altruism of forensics, the altruism of organ procurement is aimed at extending, restoring, and beautifying life and is never explicitly about death. If medical examiners are death brokers, procurement organizations claim to broker a new lease on life. As in the forensic investigation of children's deaths, medical examiners can simply rely on their legal mandate to conduct a full postmortem when the argument of their altruism is unconvincing. But when procurement altruism trumps forensic altruism, such legal mandates become vulnerable to change as well. When forced to make a choice, politicians and, increasingly, elected district attorneys favor organ and tissue transplantation. The question is whether accommodating procurement has affected the medical examiner's record of detecting and documenting homicides, child abuse, SIDS, and suicide.

THE HOPE OF FORENSIC AUTHORITY

In the morgue, medical examiners bring society and body together to make sense of suspicious death. Writing about British coroners' determination of suicide, sociologist Maxwell Atkinson observed, "The role of coroners in maintaining and sometimes changing shared definitions of suicidal situations attains a crucial importance, for they can be seen as defining for their society what kind of behaviour constitutes suicide at a particular point in time."[1] Medical examiners are our society's main death brokers: expert intermediaries who establish the varying meanings of violent or suspicious death. Death brokers situate lethal bodily trauma in a network of responsibility, risk, and intentionality. They code bodies to determine which deaths qualify as suicide, homicide, accident, or natural death and so inform us when suspicions are warranted. In their work, they sort out how pathology and social life may have come together to constitute a lethal chain of events. Their knowledge claims turn the individuality of a death into generalizable findings that feed the work of others, such as health researchers and homicide detectives. In short, medical examiners are the authorities on suspicious death.

In his seminal writing on power in modern society, sociologist Max Weber proposed that the basis of authority is a belief that lends prestige.[2] Authority, Weber argued, can be enforced or can be established through processes of legitimation. When power is legitimate, affected parties consider the exercise of authority valid. In Weber's typology, medical examiners apply a modified rational-legal authority typical of state bureaucracies.[3] Their authority rests on the legality of rules and presumes an organization where position is based on certified expertise and where social actors follow a chain of command and apply rules impartially. The crux of legitimate authority is voluntary compliance with decisions that run counter to personal, legal, or political interests. Medical examiners have authority if their determinations are accepted by others, even though these parties may disagree with their forensic conclusions. Even when parties mobilize to contest death determinations, medical examiners maintain authority if their decisions prevail. Their conclusions then seem natural, objective, and inevitable.

A legal mandate, scientific methods, and a cultural need legitimate medical examiners' authority. Weber emphasized that bureaucratic authority rests on "a belief in the legality of enacted rules and the right of those elevated to authority under such rules to issue commands."[4] Bureaucratic authority invokes formal rules specifying what must, may, or may not be done, by whom, and under what conditions. Medical examiners indeed draw legitimacy from the statutory mandate to conduct postmortem investigations as they see fit, when the death satisfies legally defined conditions. Their mandate, codified in law, silences those parties reluctant to allow a death investigation and protects medical examiners' jurisdiction from those offering alternative explanations. Requiring a death certificate before burial or cremation reinforces the legal mandate and positions the medical examiner as gatekeeper.

Weber saw such legal rules as the self-legitimating hallmark of modern rationalization, but other scholars have expanded on the role of science in legitimization, elevating the infusion of science into professional life as another marker of a rational modernity.[5] Scientific methods legitimate death investigation by supplying the aura of neutrality and objectivity, thereby reducing the potential for conflicts of interests. Finally, medical examiners' legitimacy is bolstered by their fulfillment of the cultural need to explain suspicious deaths for the public good. Embedded in medical examiners' cultural covenant is the hope that suspicious deaths have not occurred in vain. Without authoritative explanation, such deaths raise the threat of an omnipresent disorder ready to strike its next victim. In responding to a cultural need, medical examiners acquire some political capital when pleading with legislators for financial support.

None of these sources of legitimacy, however, guarantees authority. Rather, each carries weaknesses that may delegitimize medical examiners as brokers for suspicious death. A legal mandate may generate compliance but stifle innovation. Scientific methods may promise objectivity but require continual proof of their superiority. And response to a cultural need may not seem tangible enough when legislators confront more pressing requests on which elections may hinge. Medical examiners thus need to make the basic sources of their legitimacy work for them. Authority is never static. Exercising authority both risks delegitimization and carries the potential for further legitimization.

Forensic authority is achieved in practice: "Professions both create their work and are created by it."[6] Medical examiners claim the authority to explain forensic deaths for the public good. As the list of credentialed medical examiners relieved of their duties indicates, the authority of forensic pathologists to make sense of suspicious death is not an a priori professional characteristic but a locally situated accomplishment. Medical examiners work hard to make their statements authoritative. With every forensic inquiry, they put their reputations on the line. Through postmortem examinations, meetings, and documentation, they establish themselves as the authorities on suspicious death.

The core argument of this book is that *the kind of specialists who have the mandate to inquire into deaths and the character of the work they conduct influence what will be written on the death certificate and, consequently, how we understand and give meaning to suspicious deaths.* Forensic authority is profession-specific. The fact that medical examiners, whose scientific strength lies with observing the morphology of organs and tissues, are the preferred death investigators affects the detection, classification, and explanation of suspicious deaths. Similarly, the relationships that pathologists develop during an investigation explain why they are willing to make interpretive leaps in some deaths but stick close to pathology in others. Ultimately, medical examiners' work affects the ways in which people in Western societies memorialize those who die under suspicious circumstances.

I have approached forensic authority from the standpoint of a medical sociology of practice. This sociology privileges what pathologists do rather than what they say they did: it reconstitutes the network of their work.[7] The primary analytical principle is to follow the connections medical examiners make as they process suspicious deaths and link pieces of tissues, ripped clothing, or a psychiatric history to the events preceding death, thereby transforming these elements into causes. From practice, the relevance of policies, relationships, and other structural elements becomes apparent. This approach gives medical sociologists a way to talk about the substantive content of medicine. Specific kinds of suicide or natural death follow from medical examiners' expertise and relationships with third parties. Moreover, a medical sociology of practice focuses on how death investigators fulfill the broader normative purpose of forensics.

Norms are situated in practice: forensic pathologists may claim to offer hope for the living, but it is in their daily work that many different public goods are prioritized.

In this concluding chapter, I will draw several analytical strands together to offer a comprehensive view of the ways in which medical examiners achieve different kinds of forensic authority, depending on their ability to investigate deaths according to professional standards and on the cultural resonance of their findings. Different kinds of forensic authority affect medical examiners' vulnerability as individual practitioners, as investigative offices, or as a profession. My analysis also indicates points at which medical examiners might strengthen their authority by developing strong relationships with stakeholders and expanding their methodology. I locate this discussion in a simmering debate in the sociological literature about the loss of professional power. I then return to the cultural value that organizes forensic work: hope.

AN ANSWER TO A RIDDLE OF PROFESSIONAL THEORIZING

The last decades of the twentieth century saw medical professionals taking salaried positions in bureaucratic or corporate settings rather than moving into independent practice. To account for this shift in professionalism, sociological writing about medical professions has been preoccupied with whether health care professionals have lost or gained power. Pointing to growing managerial oversight, information technologies, and knowledgeable clients, some social scientists have concluded that health professionals have lost autonomy.[8] Others, notably Eliot Freidson, have maintained that because medical professionals retain control over the content of their work, they have lost little of their professional luster. This debate has reached a stalemate because of selective data and lack of common standards to assess professional power. As Freidson puts it: "Some are saying, 'the cup is half empty,' and others, 'the cup is half full.'"[9] Conceptualizing professional power on different levels, both sides of the debate may be partly right.[10] The study of forensic professionals safeguarding their authority, however, offers an opportunity to reconcile the different perspectives.

Sociologist Donald Light proposed the theory of countervailing powers to explain the overall decline of the medical profession at the end of the twentieth century.[11] According to Light's theory, when one player in the health care field dominates, others will react and redress the "excessive" power of the dominator. Health care thus takes place in a market of "interdependent yet distinct" parties vying for resources, favorable public opinion, territory, and control.[12] The so-called golden age of professional dominance during the 1950s and 1960s was a period of excess, when the medical profession dominated the health care market. Other parties then attempted to chip away at medicine's control. The rise of managed care, cost-containment, and the broader buyer's revolt thus constitutes one of the "ironies of success."[13] Because the profession was so powerful in protecting markets for health care providers, it created captive markets for pharmaceutical and other health-related, for-profit corporations. The weakening of professional power is thus an unintended consequence of its political dominance. The theory of countervailing powers suggests that challenges to the legitimacy of forensic work may instigate a counterreaction in which outside parties will contest the manner-of-death determination and attempt to limit death investigators' authority through structural means. Among the factors leading to change, ignoring the concerns of clients and institutional partners seems most likely to limit authority.[14]

Freidson, in contrast to Light, maintains that while some professional decline might indeed be occurring, the core of medicine's dominance remains resilient, because professionals still maintain autonomy over the everyday content of their work.[15] Professionals distinguish themselves from other occupations because they routinely exercise discretion and judgment. Professional credentialing systems institutionalized through lobbying provide a firm but not completely secure framework for professional livelihood. The professional market shelter is thus a state-sanctioned means of independent professional control.[16] Consolidated professional status bolstered by esoteric technical knowledge, therefore, offers professionals both control and discretion in work, so that "their modes of formulating and interpreting events permeate both popular consciousness and official policy."[17] Freidson dismisses the importance of organizational changes and third-party encroachment on professional power because outsiders have been unable to dictate how professionals perform their work. Employment status, Freidson asserts, has little bearing on autonomy. Moreover, health care professionals innovate, creating an insatiable demand for their services. The main effect of greater bureaucratic involvement is to stratify health care providers, with elite physicians formally controlling other professionals.[18] Forensic authority, this perspective suggests, depends on the profession's consolidated monopoly over the content of daily work.

While Freidson privileges autonomy in the workplace, Light situates professional work in a larger organizational context, and consequently they reach different conclusions. For Light, the proliferation of computer-aided decision-making tools in health care indicates the subordination of professional expertise to managerial control aimed at rendering health care more cost-efficient.[19] For Freidson, the same information technologies may actually bolster professional power if health professionals themselves input data and can adapt their resources to new directives.[20] Hence, they frustrate third-party implementation of health care reform.

The challenge of maintaining forensic authority indicates that a division between the workplace and the broader organizational arena is untenable: medical examiners need to consider the interests and needs of various parties while investigating deaths, although their work itself determines the extent of third-party involvement. At the heart of forensic claims making is the staff's work: the triaging, scene survey, and collection of police and medical reports from the scene investigator; the autopsy performed by the forensic pathologist and assistant; the laboratory orders; the meetings with various parties; and the gradual filling out of forms. The aim of medical examiners' work is to gather a wide variety of data and then reduce those data to essentials that point to the cause differentiating life from death. Rather than being passive observers of the finality of life, medical examiners actively create causes of death by transforming bits of life, first into evidence and then into causes. One connection at a time, they create knowledge about death—not by extinguishing these last bits of life, but by revealing certain causes while eliminating other factors. With photographs, histology slides, and sketched drawings, the evidence is triangulated until one explanation becomes more plausible than the others. Medical examiners' creative process is highly disciplined by the available evidence. If the corpse offers excessive or insufficient clues, ambiguity ensues.

Medical examiners' strength may lie with pathological evidence, but their findings are never pure pathology. Instead, they inevitably depend on a mix of biology, history, and social behavior. Because ultimately the pathology of all death reflects the cessation of respiratory and cardiac functions, this finding is not insightful. It simply attests to death. Pathological findings become interesting when their causal role can be situated within a temporal chain of events inside and outside the body.[21] At the very least, pathological evidence needs to be consistent with the scene investigation, but more often it also needs to match police reports and medical files. The deceased's social life is relevant only in light of an evolving pathological understanding of the death, but the circumstances of the death also suggest lethal pathological pathways. Moreover, autopsy findings may reveal undocumented medical conditions or may mediate between conflicting versions of the end of life and so change our understanding of the deceased's life. Similarly, the question of what occurred in the person's life may remain unresolved because of contradictory pathological findings. While dissecting organs and removing tissues, medical examiners render certain forms of social life more plausible than others.

This work of medical examiners is embedded in an organizational ecology of exchange relationships. Medical examiners depend on health and law enforcement professionals to alert them to a suspicious death and provide information about a case. They consult with law enforcement agencies before finalizing the cause and manner of death. And they communicate their findings to relatives, health care providers, a broad variety of regulatory state and professional agencies, law enforcement bodies, public health institutions, insurance companies, and media. The state and professional organizations are thereby alerted about potential institutional problems against which they might take action. Funeral directors and organ and tissue procurement organizations have interests that compete with those of medical examiners; other agencies, such as the Occupational Safety and Health Administration (OSHA), child-protection agencies, and law enforcement may conduct parallel investigations but depend on forensic pathologists for postmortem interpretations. Finally, medical examiners closely collaborate with laboratory experts in toxicology, histology, genetics, and other related sciences.

Each of these parties exerts some degree of leverage on the work of medical examiners, depending on that party's ability to make its needs and priorities relevant for death investigations. Professional interdependence varies with the kind of relationship, the source of influence, and the effects of relationships on everyday work.[22] In spite of presumably close collaboration with medical examiners based on common interests, public health officials have had little effect on the process of investigating deaths. They may suspect that forensic pathologists underestimate certain kinds of suicide, but they can do little besides offer guidelines on identifying suicide, which are among the weakest tools for changing professional behavior.[23] In contrast, organ and tissue procurement organizations have maneuvered themselves into the thick of death investigation by cutting off medical examiners' access to bodies valued for procurement, thereby attempting to alter medical examiners' legal mandate and challenging both their scientific basis and their service to the public. Forensic pathologists must consider the position of tissue and organ procurers and either resist or adapt to the resulting intrusions. Within the same group, some people may have more influence than others. For example, relatives of suicide victims have little leverage, because administrators deflect their attempts to shape the death investigation. In contrast, relatives of deceased infants may have considerable influence over the interpretation of evidence, because forensic pathologists extensively engage them during the investigation. From Freidson's perspective, the professional subordination of allied laboratory workers renders forensic pathologists dominant in much the same way that physicians may subordinate nurses in clinical settings.[24] This dominance in a division of labor, however, may fail to carry weight with stakeholders in forensic investigations.

The touchstone for explaining changes in professional power is not the presence of third parties vying to usurp professional turf, but professional work itself. Rather than looking at the threat that managed care, computerization, or knowledgeable patients pose to the powers of health professionals, an empirical investigation analyzes the effect of such third parties on care providers' ability to work as they see fit.[25] The picture that emerges in clinics and hospitals reflects the resilience of medical professionals in their ability to absorb, appropriate, or subvert reform measures. Computerized decision-making tools, for example, have not automated the difficult task of reaching a diagnosis;[26] evidence-based medicine has not led to cookbook doctoring;[27] greater knowledge about birthing procedures has not reversed a medicalization trend;[28] alternative medicine has generally not usurped biomedical treatments but has instead complemented them;[29] once-progressive women's health centers have been incorporated into for-profit hospital structures;[30] and managed-care reforms have not led to cheaper health care.[31] All these developments have affected medical care, but without dramatic shifts in power. Oncologists, for example, talk to knowledgeable patients differently than they did before patients' health movements, but they retain control.[32]

Resilience, however, does not imply continued dominance. While Light may overestimate the effects of third parties, analyzing their presence rather than their actual involvement in medical work, he conceptualizes change in professional power. One major problem with Freidson's perspective on professional power is his inability to account for changes over time: Freidson suggests that once a profession gains dominance in a division of labor, it remains dominant.[33] Such views fail to square with the tremendous changes in medicine since the 1960s. Over time, professional groups may achieve a monopoly over an area of work, but the work may gradually become marginalized or irrelevant. Or groups may remain dominant for reasons different from the conditions that led to their ascendance. As Andrew Abbott explains, the history of professions is littered with once-dominant professions that have now vanished. The solution is to examine the components of professional power and the shifts that occur under pressure. Rather than asking whether the proverbial glass is half-empty or half-full, we should examine its contents.

DIFFERENT KINDS OF FORENSIC AUTHORITY

In forensic work, authority is multidimensional. A first broad differentiation is the relationship between professional and cultural authority. Medical examiners achieve professional authority if they can investigate deaths according to their standards. A loss of professional authority implies that medical examiners work under the direction of others. Professional authority matters in individual death investigations and may be challenged either case by case or through a review of similar cases investigated. With challenges to the basic sources of medical examiners' legitimacy, the entire profession may lose the authority to investigate or interpret certain deaths. Medical examiners may also achieve cultural authority if they define suspicious death. Cultural authority is apparent in individual death investigations when medical examiners tinker with inclusion criteria, or it may appear in the cumulation of similar cases. For example, medical examiners might consistently come to classify deaths during games of Russian roulette as accidental, whereas outsiders might argue that such deaths are closer to suicide. By officially defining accidents, medical examiners exercise cultural authority. A lack of cultural authority renders forensic pathologists merely technicians who process pathological evidence but lack influence over the broader discourse on suspicious death. Cultural and professional authority do not necessarily overlap: medical examiners have greater professional than cultural authority in natural deaths, because these deaths have few stakeholders. They may have disproportionately less professional than cultural authority in homicides, where they map the injuries for consideration in criminal proceedings.

★   ★   ★

Professional authority varies between subcategories of death. In some deaths, medical examiners stay close to the pathological evidence, describing what their scalpel shows them; in others, they feel comfortable evaluating human intent and assessing culpability. *The scope of medical examiners' inferences depends on creating a tight fit with the death at hand, their expertise, the evolving category of death, and the leverage of parties in the organizational ecology.* Medical examiners will document only what they can prove, and they privilege proof in the area of their expertise: pathology. Their forte is deaths caused by visible trauma—manifested in the shape or constitution of organs (visible either with a trained eye or with the microscope)—or death that meets toxicology thresholds. Suicides by hanging thus constitute a good fit, but suicides by esoteric poison may not. The organizational ecology affects the leverage of the parties involved during the investigation. Medical examiners typically depend on information from law enforcement and health care professionals to evaluate the actions of a third party. In the absence of any conflicts of interest, medical examiners may presume that the information they receive is accurate and reliable. Finally, the scope of pathologists' inferences varies with the need to base interpretations on intent rather than on measurable medical evidence, witnessed accounts, or historical evidence recorded by other authorities. Some categories of death require a greater evaluation of intent than others. Natural deaths are presumed to be nonintentional. Homicide depends on the intent of others, but intent need not be evaluated in the forensic inquiry (although it inevitably is). Suicides are most difficult, because intent dies with the deceased.

Medical examiners render conservative, ultraconservative, or more liberal interpretations depending on the professional fit. The most common inference is a *conservative* determination. Medical examiners are the best death investigators for natural deaths caused by a visible lethal factor, where they can depend on a medical history from health care providers and a clean scene investigation from police officials. These deaths are so routine that medical examiners hesitate to even bring in the body—especially when it is an older person, in whom they are bound to find lethal heart disease. Determinations of suicide and homicide are routine when signs of trauma, scene evidence, and medical history triangulate to suggest a logical manner of death. A depressed person found hanging without signs of foul play in an apartment locked from the inside or a witnessed homicide with multiple stab wounds are examples of the cases that qualify.

Most motor vehicle accidents have a similarly routine feel. Multiorgan trauma leaves little ambiguity when medical examiners view pictures of an overturned SUV or a motorcycle wrapped around a tree. The dilemma may be whether it was the pierced lung or the torn aorta that caused death, but forensic pathologists can answer such questions authoritatively. Accidents often involve collaboration with other agencies, such as OSHA for deaths in the workplace, the National Transportation Safety Board (NTSB) for airplane and railroad deaths, or police from the department of recreation for deaths that occur in parks. Medical examiners have few conflicts of interest with these parties, and the exchange of information is generally congenial. In airplane disasters, the investigation is largely standardized, with tissue and fluid kits and checklists that specify the steps to be followed during the investigation. Accidents lie between natural deaths and suicides in the need to evaluate intent. In accidents, medical examiners need to exclude human intent. Their propensity for pathological trauma and their limited willingness and ability to evaluate intent tend to neutralize human responsibility in accidents. As with natural death, the category of accidental death may be used residually for deaths with ill-defined intent.[34] In cases of relative youth and lack of clear pathology, the death is unlikely to be natural, but it may lack the clear positive indication needed for a determination of suicide or homicide. Rather than probing more deeply and considering whether the death was preventable, due to neglect, or reasonably likely if the deceased had common sense, the designation of accident glosses over these nuances. Accident thus means that something went awry; life did not just take its course. The extent of disorder, however, may vary widely—from a random, freak event to a more or less predictable lethal course requiring the active participation of the deceased or others (e.g., teenagers "surfing" in the bed of a moving pickup truck).

Generally, medical examiners tend to make conservative inferences in routine homicides, accidents, suicides, and natural deaths. The seamless fit that links their skills, the organizational ecology, the evidence of trauma, and the category of death renders further inferences unnecessary. The naturalness of these explanations, however, depends on having medical examiners with specific resources to establish legitimacy in conducting death investigations. The social autopsy conducted by a sociologist, for example, may come up with an alternative explanation that sounds natural from a perspective invested in social determinants of mortality, but it would not make sense for medical examiners nor carry much legal or medical weight. The conservative nature of pathologists' inferences is calibrated in court, where homicides are subjected to an extensive public re-analysis centered on the plausibility of inferences and reflecting the medicolegal character of forensic determinations. Fortunately for medical examiners, most death investigations are routine: they show the obvious lethal trauma that satisfies pathological expertise.

When one or more of the components of the investigation do not fit the case at hand, however, medical examiners tend to limit their professional authority and opt for *ultraconservative* inferences. Several reasons might lead to a misfit. Most commonly, medical examiners work on cases in which a scene investigation suggests a homicide, a natural death, an accident, or a suicide but the postmortem investigation fails to produce conclusive evidence to settle the manner of death. Alternatively, forensic pathologists may be confronted with a scene investigation that suggests a manner of death involving human intent, but the autopsy shows a lethal natural cause. In those ambiguous situations, medical examiners become captives of their expertise: their usual pathological touchstone fails them. Because making claims about human intent in death is professionally risky without pathological backing, medical examiners tend not to make interpretive leaps but instead explain potential suicides and homicides as accidents or as natural or undetermined deaths.[35] When the parties providing medical examiners with information are involved in the death, the usual working relationship is even more disturbed. When police or health care professionals are suspected of involvement in a death, for example, medical examiners retreat further into pathology, preferring courts to make determinations about intent. Here, the misfit is located between the organizational ecology and the forensic procedures. Information provided to medical examiners that they might otherwise take for granted becomes suspect or subject to unresolved contradictions. Medical examiners try to avoid investigating these deaths by exempting them from a postmortem inquiry. Generally, forensic pathologists protectively resort to ultraconservative inferences when questions are bound to be raised about their ability to arbitrate evidence.

With infant deaths, medical examiners involve parents and caregivers in the investigation through repeated interviews. Medical examiners maintain the upper hand in these interactions, triangulating accounts of the hours and moments preceding death with evolving pathological evidence. The involvement of the third party gives them a much more extensive picture of the scene investigation and thus makes them comfortable about addressing parents' intent. In these deaths, medical examiners make more *liberal* inferences. They give themselves more leeway to interpret pathological evidence. Their liberal attitude, however, is skewed toward giving parents the benefit of the doubt by presuming that they had no role in the death. The final determinations in these cases and others are unlikely to be tested in court, because medical examiners' power includes disposing of otherwise court-bound cases.

The variety in medical examiners' professional authority becomes manifest in their management of ambiguous evidence. Routine cases lack ambiguity because of a tight professional fit linking the medical examiner's skills, relationships with third parties, manner of death, and available evidence. The same ambiguity in forensic evidence that may lead medical examiners to back down from determining intent in suicides and homicides may be an insurmountable obstacle to investigating deaths involving their close allies; or it may be an opportunity to make interpretive leaps in infant deaths.

★ ★ ★

Medical examiners have less control over their *cultural authority,* which depends on the number of parties affected by a classification of death, the extent to which they are affected, their leverage on forensic work, and the relative weight of forensic authority in comparison to the authority of others. Cultural authority reflects the relevance of forensic determinations, including the ability to define specific deaths. Still, medical examiners can foster relevance by nurturing relationships and explaining the relevance of a postmortem inquiry. As each new determination confirms the conceptual boundaries of a death category, medical examiners' cultural authority is expressed in their classifying of deaths. They may thus have cultural authority even over the deaths they do not investigate: lack of investigation, whether because of statute or triage, means a death is not suspicious. Consequently, information about these deaths is limited, and the knowledge they generate is constrained as well.

In most natural deaths, accidents, and suicides, medical examiners' cultural authority is restricted to what they write on the death certificate and how other parties use the findings. Thus, a suicide determination may void insurance policies and become a heavy burden for relatives, whereas a natural death may have less impact. Although medical examiners rarely detect homicides, their cultural authority in homicide investigations is greater than in suicides or natural deaths, because the final determinations and the investigative process are crucial for law enforcement and criminal courts. Medical examiners have the power to shape the understanding of homicide by determining which deaths qualify, the mechanism of homicide, and the time frame of death. While closely interpreting wounds and tissue damage, they may also confirm the likely interactional sequence between victim and perpetrator.

Medical examiners may increase their cultural authority—with moral and legal consequences—when they tinker with inclusion criteria and thus assert a new classification that may affect new categories of victims or redefine intent. Thus, medical examiners may revisit the relationship between SIDS and bed sharing, debate the deadly mechanism of positional asphyxia, or query a spate of potentially self-inflicted teenage deaths. These deaths may become their own subcategory, or they may remain on the periphery of forensic knowledge. In some cases, the redefinition may stimulate epidemiological or physiological research and affect the practice of clinicians or law enforcement. Often, the NAME will issue position papers about these topics or incorporate changing sentiment in new guidelines for death investigators. As medical examiners' reluctance to support shaken-baby syndrome has shown, forensic pathologists must not only redefine categories but also have their position prevail in situations where these deaths matter. In the aftermath of the Louise Woodward trial, the media coverage seemed to have supported the orientation of clinicians rather than pathologists. Consequently, medical examiners may relinquish cultural authority when they stop investigating some deaths or fold a separate category of death—such as "therapeutic complication"—back into natural death. Moreover, as Abbott discussed, they may also be forced to cede cultural authority when third parties assume part of their jurisdiction or successfully attack the sources of their legitimacy.[36]

★   ★   ★

Rather than assessing professional power as declining or dominant, a fine-grained analysis of the connections fostered by death investigators emphasizes the qualitative spectrum of forensic authority. Deaths cluster together because they pose similar problems for death investigators certified as forensic pathologists working in certain organizational settings. The classification of cases is not predictable. Classifying deaths may imply tinkering in order to match the details of a case to an evolving death category or may involve a shift in relationships within the organizational ecology. In the workplace, forensic authority becomes apparent in the ways medical examiners resolve or maintain ambiguity, feel comfortable assessing intent, and make interpretive leaps when evaluating evidence. The reception of their findings by various parties further confirms their cultural authority, as does their ability to define suspicious death. Analyzing the multiple dimensions of forensic authority can help in tracing shifts in authority under the pressure of third parties.

THREATS TO FORENSIC AUTHORITY

The order of forensic work rests on professional discretion, which creates some variation across difficult-to-classify cases. Decisions in ambiguous cases, therefore, may remain exceptional or may set precedents for future classifications. Such continuous change still implies a position of authority; indeed, the ability to conduct such boundary work is itself a marker of professional power and exemplifies forensic judgment.[37] For each cluster of deaths, medical examiners take a calculated risk in interpreting evidence, but they lower the risks by opting for a wide margin of error. Medical examiners need to feel very confident before they write "homicide" on a death certificate and even more confident before they classify a death in police custody as homicide. Their generally conservative approach to interpreting evidence thus buffers their authority against challenges.

Yet every classification, as a claim to forensic authority, inevitably entails some residual risk, especially if a medical examiner's evaluation of intent implies accountability in a death. Ideally, this risk falls within the margins of professional discretion, but outsiders may still challenge findings and so alter the calculation of risk. Whether these challenges lead to a loss of authority depends on the challenger's ability to untie the connections medical examiners have made. Death investigators expect relatives to disagree with suicide determinations, so that even if relatives mobilize an array of politicians and media, the staff is likely to prevail. Sustained challenges may cause medical examiners to fight back by mobilizing allies and initiating lobbying campaigns to maintain the status quo. Or they may adapt their jurisdiction by shifting tasks, methodologies, caseloads, and alliances. A challenge to their authority may become an opportunity to reassert or even expand forensic authority. As Bruno Latour has demonstrated for science, challenges—what he calls trials of strength—are useful to bolster alliances and convince new groups of one's merits.[38]

Radical change—the rapid decline of authority and autonomy alleged by Light and others—would involve a situation in which medical examiners lose control over their claims making and are discredited. Such a situation implies a breakdown in the routine legitimation that typifies forensic work. The connections between evidence and interpretation, which medical examiners foster, would no longer hold. Pressures by organ and tissue procurers have already cost medical examiners forensic authority and may cost them even more in the future. An analysis of the diversity of forensic authority indicates which deaths are most likely to bring medical examiners trouble and why. For example, procurement organizations target all bodies with valuable tissue and organs but particularly seek homicide and child-abuse victims. How widespread and complete the loss of authority will be depends on medical examiners' ability to contain the crisis of legitimacy. As the chapter on infant deaths explained, suspicion is difficult to contain once the fires of doubt are sparked. Loss of trust in authority may bring down (1) a career in forensics, (2) the workings of an office, or (3) the entire profession.

For most medical examiners, challenges to a single case of death classification should not be problematic as long as the inference in question followed from the evidence and the work fell within broad professional standards. Challenges that end careers in forensics typically involve proof of mishandled evidence, sloppy autopsy reports, changes of mind without new evidence, corruption, or unfounded speculation. These actions are evident to outsiders without confirmation by other forensic pathologists. Thus, when medical examiners make mistakes in autopsy reports that are easily verifiable with medical records, or when they change the manner of death in the middle of court proceedings without new evidence, any doctor or lawyer can point out the discrepancy and question their credibility. When forensic pathologists contradict each other, as occurs often in court testimony, the dispute can be written off as a professional disagreement. Worse for personal credibility is professional isolation, which is most problematic in deaths with high cultural stakes such as homicides, deaths in police or medical custody, infant deaths, and mass disasters. Because medical examiners try to anticipate challenges, the cases in which problems tend to occur are those that they considered long ago resolved or failed to flag as difficult. Once the allegation of incompetence takes hold, similar cases in which they have successfully testified may be reopened to critical scrutiny, and even the smallest oversights can have far-reaching consequences. In one homicide investigation I observed, an assistant brought four tubes of blood to the laboratory on the third floor. The form accompanying the tubes, however, noted five tubes. The laboratory worker signed the form and thus acknowledged receipt of five tubes. This error went unnoticed until preparations for the trial. The defense lawyer then seized on the "disappearance" of the tube of blood as an indication of a shoddy investigation and stated that the missing tube would have exonerated his client. The chief medical examiner, the assistant, and the laboratory worker testified that it was an innocent mistake.

If serious problems or a wide range of problems cannot be attributed to one wayward individual or an exceptional lapse in procedures, the chief medical examiner or department supervisor usually takes the fall, and the entire office may be reorganized. In the eyes of forensic practitioners, the quality of forensic work in their office may have eroded because of years of underfunding, and the public perception of problems may be exacerbated because medical examiners rarely make the news for having conducted an excellent postmortem investigation. The medicolegal administrator in the office where I conducted my research articulated and confirmed the ambivalence of communicating forensic findings: "No one wants to know what we're doing until they need us. Then they all want the best investigation possible. So, we're a silent office." Such "silence" compounds the problem of asserting a contribution. To counter such impressions, some medical examiners' offices have resorted to working with public relations consultants.

To bring down an entire profession requires undermining one or more of the sources of its legitimacy. Such a challenge to forensic pathology has not yet occurred. Medical examiners benefit from a legal market shelter, yet this shelter has also shielded them from the need for adaptation and may cause problems in the long run. The greatest weakness of forensic pathology may be the complacency of the field—its reluctance to innovate and to address the increasing gap between forensic pathology and the methodology and procedures of clinical medicine that support the growth of knowledge. The staying power of other groups of health professionals depends in large part on their ability to innovate their way through new diseases, areas of jurisdiction, and technologies. Over the past decades, health care professionals have responded to challenges from managed care, government cost-control measures, health care reform initiatives, and knowledgeable patients. In response, they have continued to constitute a strong political entity ready to respond to new threats in broad realms of health policy. Medical examiners, in contrast, do not constitute a formidable political force ready to expand jurisdictions, and changes in other fields may greatly affect their ability to conduct death investigations. The *Daubert* criteria, for example, may shift the rules of evidence and expertise that forensic pathologists have perfected. The emergence of new imaging technologies threatens the scientific primacy of the autopsy. Indeed, some researchers working with these technologies have proposed virtual autopsies, or "virtopsies," with multislice computed tomography to reveal cranial, skeletal, or tissue trauma and lessen the need for autopsies.[39]

The incomplete professionalization of death investigation further weakens the ability to innovate. Here, the gap between local and national practice may pose serious problems in the future. One problem inherent in professionalism is the balance between individual discretion and practitioners' uniformity. The ability to individualize cases, to adapt decisions to the idiosyncracies of a client, constitutes the heart of professional autonomy. At the same time, clients and other third parties expect uniformity in decision making. A death by Russian roulette should be classified the same way in Wisconsin, Oregon, and Pennsylvania. As Freidson explained, outside parties have difficulty imposing such uniformity because professionals retain control over their work and easily find ways to circumvent such pressures. In health policy, the lack of uniformity across geographic regions has become a major issue; researchers have shown variation among medical interventions that cannot be explained by factors other than physician preference.[40] If in one county a diagnosis of breast cancer requires a lumpectomy but in the neighboring county the preferred treatment is a radical mastectomy, patients have reason to be worried about the scientific basis of medical decision making. In addition, health insurers and other payers may question payment for a variety of expensive treatments prescribed without clinical rationale. Consequently, medical academies and colleges are exploring ways to promote greater uniformity without undermining clinical autonomy.[41]

In forensic medicine, the issue with variation in practice is not so much cost control as professional authority. Medical examiners with similar backgrounds classify comparable cases differently, and the variation suggests reliance on personal rather than scientific criteria. Unfortunately, such variability affects every aspect of death investigation in the United States. Differences are evident in personnel, training, accreditation, and governmental oversight. Some medical examiners have independent offices; others are part of law enforcement; still others work under public safety or public health. Funding levels vary from sixty-two cents to $5.54 per capita. Autopsy rates vary across locales by a factor of forty. Quality assurance, laboratory services, recording procedures, and facilities vary as well.[42] The variation is so thoroughgoing that even the data showing variability are incompatible or lacking. Such staggering differences point to the existence of only a few well-staffed and adequately supported medical examiner's offices and many neglected sites. This systemic organizational variability may result in variability in the screening, triaging, investigation, and determination of death. Except for the limited information gathered on the death certificate, aggregate data about suspicious deaths are inaccessible. The available data, including the death certificate, are thus open to challenges over reliability.

This situation greatly hampers the public health surveillance that death investigation purports to provide. Medical examiners might spark a new research hypothesis when they describe an unusual case or notice a pattern of accidents, but following such a clue requires tapping a different data source. Thus, researchers alerted by medical examiners about deaths of children locked in car trunks were stymied by the incompatibility of forensic data:

Over a 2-month period in 1998, 11 child deaths were identified through death investigations in three states: New Mexico, Utah, and Pennsylvania. The cluster of cases triggered a broader investigation, which uncovered a total of 21 deaths nationwide from 1987 to 1999. That investigation led to identification of the major risk factor: children's inability to get out of a car trunk. An expert panel was convened by the National Highway Traffic Safety Administration (NHTSA), and it recommended an interior trunk release. NHTSA responded by setting a new safety standard for automobile manufacturers in September 2001.[43]

Whereas a new safety measure may be a forensic success story, the research on child entrapment was hampered by incompatibility of forensic databases and variability in data quality. The public health researchers had to resort to media reports to calculate the prevalence of trunk entrapment.

Because medical examiners can satisfy local law enforcement agencies in most criminal investigations, geographical variability has so far failed to undermine forensic authority. A disaster crossing geographic boundaries, however, might reveal gaps in the current death investigation system that could, in turn, exacerbate the fatality rate with missed or misclassified suspicious deaths. One medical examiner predicts "the likelihood that sentinel bioterrorism deaths would probably be declined by the medical examiner system because the event would not necessarily have been identified as resulting from bioterrorism, leaving the private physicians with a responsibility for signing the certificate."[44] Britain reformed its coroner system after death investigators failed to unmask Dr. Shipman's years of killing. The attention to terrorism and potential mass disasters in the wake of the September 11 attacks, however, have not spurred an overhaul of death investigation in the United States. At the federal level, only the armed forces have a medical examiner's office; it specializes in airplane disasters and has not taken a leadership role in forensic pathology. After reviewing the lack of federal support for death investigation, one observer concluded that "the message seems to be that the federal government has no interest in forensic pathologists or medical examiners."[45] Incomplete professionalization further affects medical examiners' ability to recruit more members into the profession, replace coroners, monitor themselves, assure quality control, and conduct scientific research.

★　★　★

The sociological debate about loss of professional power requires careful empirical analysis of the processes through which third parties affect autonomy in the workplace *and* how professionals respond to such threats. Medical examiners may be strengthened by challenges; they may lose authority over some kinds of cases and compensate with other work; or they may be forced to shrink their jurisdiction. The key question is not whether medical examiners have lost professional power but rather, What does forensic authority look like? How has it evolved over time, and how does it compare to authority in related professions? In comparison to the rapid changes for clinicians, the past decades show a stagnant, increasingly anachronistic forensic profession. Medical examiners have held onto basic death investigations and even expanded their claims making in some small areas, but they have given up territory in others. Most worrisome is that they have provided little resistance to the most serious challenges, such as the raids by organ and tissue procurement organizations. Paradoxically, medical examiners' major professional weakness may be that they have been insufficiently tested and have not been able to showcase their contributions to the public good. Their survival strategy has depended more on an increasingly conservative interpretation of forensic evidence than on politically asserting their contributions.

STRENGTHENING FORENSIC AUTHORITY

Medical examiners strike a cautious balance in order to maintain authority: they generally opt for conservative interpretations to lower the chance of criticism, and when threatened by knowledgeable parties, they tend to retreat rather than confront. Compared to the coroners of the past, medical examiners bring greater professional authority to death investigation but have relinquished a certain amount of cultural authority. Their greater scientific expertise comes at the expense of political savvy: medical examiners rarely rally against the injustices they encounter, preferring that other agencies take the lead in improving safety and reducing risk. This balance affects both the message that medical examiners are willing to send about suspicious deaths and the usefulness of their investigation for third parties. In light of the history of political corruption and a weak scientific basis in former coroner offices, medical examiners' cautious stance is understandable. Yet they might now have reached a point where any further reduction so marginalizes them that they become, as the NAME's strategic-vision report put it, mere "body handlers."[46] Forensic pathologists are acutely aware of their vulnerable state; they plead in workshops and professional documents for more resources, in the areas of both funding and staffing.[47] More resources would, of course, allow medical examiners to continue doing their job but would not replenish the field or shore up its scientific base.

Although few social scientists have used their research as an opportunity to strengthen medicine, such an effort is indeed possible.[48] A sociology of medical practice reveals that medical examiners foster some connections but might need to strengthen others. Rather than asking, as Annemarie Mol does,[49] whether medical practices contribute to many diverse goods, we can look for ways to connect forensic practice to specific public goods and to broaden the base of forensic investigations, realizing that such connections will transform current investigative procedures. To be effective, such connections will need to become embedded in forensic work. Death classifications matter only if they gain social texture and facilitate or legitimate the actions of others.

For example, by cutting up parts of the body, medical examiners produce authoritative knowledge about suspicious death that was earlier unavailable. This added value relates to several public goods, though not all equally well. One way of strengthening forensic pathology is to involve the constituencies that are now secondary. With federal initiatives lacking, public health constitutes a natural ally. Aside from the causes and manners of death, medical examiners collect data on injuries, abuse, and violence in a variety of settings and geographical areas of interest to many health researchers. In addition, since the anthrax attacks of 2001, public health researchers and law enforcement officials have joined forces in "forensic epidemiology" to investigate health problems that suggest criminal behavior.[50] "Forensic pathology has a treasure trove of research assets, including population-based epidemiologic data, a window on unnatural deaths, and the only remaining significant source of autopsy tissues."[51]

Using this "treasure trove" of data is difficult because of variations in procedures and reporting forms and the lack of standards for data interchange. Rather than overhauling the current death investigation system, public health researchers are implementing a violent-death surveillance system that reports data from medical examiners and coroners, police crime reports, crime labs, and death certificates. This system has been pilot-tested in ten states and is transferred to the CDC, which intends to make violence surveillance part of the public health information network.[52] The NAME issued a statement in support of this surveillance system.[53] Other collaborative initiatives involve forensic participation in interdisciplinary teams for review of children's deaths.

Medical examiners might also foster stronger ties with the general public. Medical examiners aim both to educate relatives regarding health issues, such as inherited diseases and risks of infection, and to clarify legal issues surrounding the sudden demise of a loved one. Yet they might do more to implement those goals. Suggestions for attending to relatives were central in the report by Dame Janet Smith on the Shipman inquiry. Smith argues that some of the murders might have been prevented if death investigators had informed relatives that a forensic investigation was occurring, heard them out, and given them an opportunity to react to the results of the inquiry. In the medical examiner's office where I conducted my study, relatives were informed of an investigation and were mailed the results, but their stories and concerns were evaluated warily. A more consistent flow of information might instead lead to discussions with relatives before a death certificate is finalized. The precedent here is relatives' involvement in the forensic inquiry into infant deaths. The medical examiner's office I studied considered hiring a social worker who specialized in grief counseling as a liaison between pathologists and relatives. In the Smith inquiry, relatives called for a centralized death investigation service that would provide counseling. Although such a development would run counter to the history of decreased public involvement in death investigation, medical examiners might act as advocates for the decedent's family. Especially in potential suicides, greater family involvement could provide a less ambiguous picture.

These examples show possible directions for strengthening forensic death investigation by expanding both its methodological base and its community of stakeholders. The purpose is threefold: to take greater advantage of the expertise already present in the medical examiner's office, to expand the expertise produced by forensic investigations, and to embolden medical examiners by strengthening their political support. The principle is to connect forensic practice with new constituencies, realizing that each link to a new audience, new allies, a new set of technologies, or new concerns will affect medical examiners' tasks (and also runs the risk of rendering current tasks less salient). During autopsies, medical examiners are good scientists and savvy politicians. They link the corpse and its tissues with intentions, social identities, and motives while remaining cognizant of the ways in which their findings will be used by a wide variety of audiences. Once the autopsy report is signed, however, medical examiners remain scientists and become politicians only reluctantly, expecting others to determine the implications of their findings. Like the slices of coronary artery that indicate the difference between life and death, the autopsy report and the death certificate need to become factual pieces of knowledge, which in turn aid and transform the work of many third parties.

FINALLY: HOPE

The emblem of a medical examiner's office consists of an ornamental shield flanked by a single word: "Hope." The choice of "Hope" as a motto might seem strange and even inappropriate in a place that deals daily with grim and painful situations. Hope implies that we are not absolutely determined by either our biology or our circumstances but that we can exercise other options. "Hope can flourish only when you believe that what you do can make a difference, that your actions can bring a future different from the present. To have hope, then, is to acquire a belief in your ability to have some control over your circumstances."[54] A political economy of hope informs much palliative care and medical disciplines that have high mortality rates, such as oncology.[55] In an era of greater patient disclosure, medical specialists have to convey hope while suggesting invasive therapies that may only prolong life or alleviate symptoms. In forensic pathology, the deceased has no hope for cure or care. Death has occurred—often too suddenly, violently, and unexpectedly.

Hope, however, is intended not for the deceased but for the people left behind. The forensic investigators I met hoped that the expert knowledge they produced would provide closure for grieving relatives. A death investigator articulated this mission: "I can't give people back their loved ones. I can't restore their happiness or innocence, can't give back their lives the way they were. But I can give them the truth. Then they will be free to grieve for the dead, and then free to start living again. Truth like that can be a humbling and sacred gift for a scientist to give."[56] In this sense, hope has a benign, informational quality, dovetailing with psychodynamic notions of accepting death. Knowing what happened medically allows relatives to accept the inevitability of their loved one's death. Hope can also imply a call to action, to avoid similar fates for others, an incentive to channel energy toward prevention and safety. In yet another sense, hope has a sharper edge: it carries the aspiration for justice. On an aggregate level, hope refers to the knowledge that may accumulate from forensic inquiries. Here, hope comes mostly with incremental advances, because patterns emerge only after several cases pique an investigator's curiosity. Yet this hope also holds the greatest promise to affect many lives.

The current death investigation system reflects ambivalence toward hope: with laws mandating death investigations, people in North America are willing to learn about suspicious death—but not too much. Only the most reliable scientific knowledge is accepted, and even then, death investigators are rarely funded adequately. The inability to explore the implications of forensic findings or expand forensic methodologies reflects broader cultural discomfort about suspicious, violent, or unexpected deaths. Even when the benefits of an investigation are tangible, they are inevitably indirect and never bring the deceased back. Forensic investigation demands an acceptance that an individual corpse can tell us something important about the communal risks of living. This altruistic sacrifice for the public good is a tough sell when it clashes with religious and secular notions about the integrity of a body and personhood, when it involves deeply uncomfortable physical manipulation of the corpse, or when an investigation potentially assigns personal or institutional responsibility. Still, if the invasive steps of an autopsy are taken *only* for legal-criminal purposes, we have missed an opportunity.

Hope in forensics is about having the courage to probe death, realizing that some people should not have died and that we have an opportunity and a responsibility to learn from their deaths. To speak for the dead, as forensic specialists do, means to speak up, gently but insistently, with compassion and without obfuscation. If Cook County's medical examiner had not classified deaths as heat-related during the summer of 1995, a heat wave would never have received epidemiological, sociological, and political attention. Equally important, many other suspicious deaths that medical examiners have found to be natural deaths would have been rumored to be homicides, suicides, or accidents if no forensic investigation had been done. Without forensic workers officially bearing witness for the dead, these and other deaths might as well not have occurred. Forensic investigations are not only a treasure trove for research, but also a vantage point from which to examine health care, housing, welfare, and other policies. As indisputable signifiers of disorder, unexpected and violent deaths offer a window onto human suffering, abject marginality, social isolation, safety, and security. Forensic investigations constitute the last line of defense in a system of broad-based societal quality control. This is not to say that if we reform and strengthen forensic practice, we will finally know an unqualified truth about mortality. Even with forensic psychologists and others playing a key role in death investigations, suicide will always remain an enigma, because determining suicide hinges on an irretrievable intent to commit self-harm. Forensic knowledge will always depend on disciplines, professions, institutions, and bureaucracies. Some deaths will remain ambiguous in spite of the most extensive investigative efforts. Strengthening forensic investigations by tailoring methods to death categories and involving more constituencies, however, provides an opportunity to produce comprehensive knowledge and subject that knowledge to extensive review. Forensic hope is about applying hard-earned, precious authority for the broadest public good.

"HOW CAN YOU WATCH AUTOPSIES?"

How can someone look at corpses on a daily basis? This was inevitably one of the first questions I was asked when I told people about this study: How could I stand watching autopsies? Did I ever faint? Did I have night-mares? And how could the staff stand doing autopsies? Although outsiders wanted to know how medical examiners endure their jobs, Dr. Douglas made clear at the beginning of my research that this was an inappropriate research question. I was not to analyze the staff's coping mechanisms. He did not elaborate. Perhaps he was afraid of what I would find or afraid that I might inadvertently confirm the stereotype of death-obsessed medical examiners. Rather than obsession, however, I noted a potential for stress when working with fatal trauma. Stress resides in some aspects of the work, but stress comes also from incomprehension of outsiders' stereotyping of forensic work. Although I was not allowed to analyze others, I may talk of how I dealt with facing death. Of course, I did not experience full exposure to forensic trauma, because I was free to come and go and was not subjected to all the pressure from endless autopsies, budget problems, backlogs, and courtrooms. This is thus a partial, outsider's reflection on working with death.

★   ★   ★

My first autopsy. After a lengthy negotiation process to gain access to the medical examiner's office, I was determined to make a good impression when pathology assistant David Dings took me into the dressing room and asked me to put on the full-body Tyvek protection suit. Dr. Douglas told me to keep breathing through my mouth and sit on a chair if I felt queasy. The case was of a man who had left a note.

Hi Sarah,

If you are reading this then the both of us know where I'm going so would you say a few good words for me just in case. And explain it to Mickey and Steve. I'll be with them all the time. This much with my hands and arms behind my back. They'll know.

What struck me initially was the smell. When the pathologist put the scalpel in the body and made the Y incision, the air filled with a heavy stench. I asked Dr. Douglas whether this was the smell of death. "No," he replied soberly, "this is the smell of decomposition." I was too overwhelmed by the naked corpse with the chest cavity spread open, the sight of the wooden block under the shoulders pushing the dead man's mouth open in a wide O, and the small puddle of dark blood seeping from the man's shoulder to pay much attention to his level-headed reply. The assistant put it differently. David told me that the body on the stretcher is just an empty shell. The soul is elsewhere. He also punned that on Friday it had been dead in the morgue, dead as in quiet. When I asked Dr. Douglas how he remembers the condition of all the organs he cut during an autopsy, he answered that he writes it down after the autopsy and then forgets about it as soon as he gets out of the room.

Guided by the pathologist's clues and directions on what to look for, I felt a sense of fascination and anticipation. The small scalpel incisions on the heart showed that the man had coronary occlusions, adding another possible cause of death. Did he take his own life or die from natural causes? Dr. Douglas "pended" the case: the final cause of death would depend on toxicology results. Later, when debriefing this case with the medicolegal administrator, he laughed away both my anticipated anxiety and fascination with the possible cause of death. For him, the case constituted one of the most routine autopsies. When I mentioned that I was struck by the similarity between human and animal organs, he again shook his head and remarked that he had had a meatball sandwich for lunch.

After that first postmortem, I observed the autopsy of a nursing home patient who had broken both femurs and that of a patient who went in for a checkup and died in the hospital. The third day was occupied with a young woman who had overdosed on pills in the woods. Day in, day out, the white dry-erase board in the assistant's office filled with shootings, stabbings, falls, overdoses, abuse, trauma, accidents, bad luck, and reckless behavior. Not long after one stretcher was emptied, the phone would ring with another suspicious death. Forensic deaths are "bad" for reasons opposite to those that made good deaths good. Instead of capping a life with heightened self-awareness at the time of final transition, death has come suddenly, in an accident or from a drug overdose that suppressed awareness. Instead of spiritual guidance and prayer, it was curses and damnation that accompanied the death of the abused wife thrown down the stairs. Instead of the consolation of a ripe old age, the autopsy showed unfulfilled potential in the organs and arteries of the teenager extracted from the rolled-over pickup with the Jaws of Life. Instead of a traditional farewell with an open casket, the funeral of the elderly paranoid schizophrenic man whose body was shredded by the train's cowcatcher would be a service with a closed casket.

In those first weeks of observing, I was struck by the lurid aspects of the deaths. A month after I began observing autopsies, I went to London for a workshop on medical sociology. I remember telling colleagues about the mystery of a young man found with a bashed-in head at the bottom of a parking garage and the unanswered questions in the case of a boy who died in convulsions after playing a violent video game. I would play up the "gross factor" and describe how the spinal column had entered the skull of the man at the parking garage. Some police officers also experienced death voyeurism. Officers attending autopsies for the first time were intrigued by the sensational aspects of forensics or simply by the sights of the autopsy. They would bombard the doctors with questions about the contents of the body and the traces of lethality. I remember one police officer who wondered what piece of a body one should eat if stranded with a corpse on a desert island. Dr. Douglas was quite annoyed by his question. Such fascination with the macabre subsides. Months into the research, I would come home and, were it not for my notes, barely remember which cases I had observed that day. The deaths had blurred into autopsies.

The sights, the odors, and even the animal life devouring severely decomposed bodies did not faze me much. I, along with the staff, braced myself for the worst deaths, the "decomps," as a test of mettle. Decomposed bodies usually presented precious little conclusive evidence and were often autopsied quickly. The gripping aspects of those autopsies resided in sweeping up all the maggots that wiggled off the stretcher, or in observing the police officers who resented being there. During one homicide investigation, an officer kept sniffing a nasal spray to counter the stench of a body that had been partially buried. Of course, such nasal misting also kept his respiratory passages wide open.

Even though I had observed resuscitative efforts in emergency departments and terminal care on oncology wards, the variations and incon-sistencies of mortal disorder remained disturbing, and I began to notice patterns and exceptions. With heart disease running in my family, I was impressed by the people who lived into old age with greatly occluded arteries. How did they beat the major killer? I was also puzzled by the athletes, some young and others middle-aged, who died from heart dis-ease. Neither those who died young nor those who lived into old age were reassuring. Rather, they represented the uncertainties and perhaps the futility of preventing death. Also upsetting were the cases of people who lived unaware of severe disease processes festering until it was too late, the easily preventable accidents that went unprevented, and the moments of carelessness that cost someone's life. At every morning meeting in the medical examiner's office, I listened to the variations. A forty-one-year-old woman drives home from her aunt's funeral, deeply distraught. Her husband urges her to put on her seat belt, to let him drive. She slips off the road, overcorrects, and yanks the steering wheel. The car bounces against some trees, and she hits her head against the car frame. The car is fine except for some chipped paint and a flat tire. She is dead, with fatal brain injuries. What lessons do you take from such a situation? Even the more predictable deaths, such as weekend car accidents, drug overdoses, and gang violence, remained unsettling. Dr. Brown quipped that the office "selected for the underbelly of society," suggesting a logic in the violent deaths. I did not find such thoughts comforting. Landing on the dissection table seemed rather easy. A student robbed and killed while begging for his life, an abandoned newborn, a lonely elderly man—actually, many lonely elderly men and women—all these lives could have ended differently. The distance between life and death, as Dr. Cahill pointed out when autopsying the heart of a stabbing victim, can be measured in millimeters.

I also worried about my family. And I was not the only one. Zachary confided that his greatest nightmare was picking up the scene investiga-tor's phone to hear a police officer spell out D-a-r-l-e-n-e S-h-a-r-p-e, the name of his wife. He explained, "You never know who the call will be about. I have been living my entire life in this area, and sooner or later we might bring in someone I know." One of the last autopsies I observed was in fact that of one of his relatives. After the case of a two-year-old who ran into traffic, Zachary told me that he was going to give his kids a big hug that night. Dr. Brown was less bothered by autopsying kids: he instead identified with overweight fifty-year-old men with heart disease. Dr. Hughes remarked that she likely would die of cancer, because it ran in her family. A scene investigator took a leave of absence when his sons were teenagers and had learned to drive. Occasionally, the office autopsied a staff member's acquaintance or relative, and the staff member was under strict orders not to be involved in the death investigation. The medical examiner's consulting radiologist still looked from the doorway at his father lying on a stretcher.

★   ★   ★

Death investigations are structured not for contemplation but for detachment. Several pathologists told me that they were personally attracted to solving scientific puzzles. Dr. Brown reflected, "The first thing that intrigues me about the position is that I rarely know what case I am going to be doing in the morning. Even if I do know what the case is, there is always something unique about it. I learn something new about the case. I just increase my knowledge base on how a particular disease can present itself." Death investigators are rarely shocked by lurid details, noting that they had "seen it all before." A staff member might comment on the irony of a man who died from a drug overdose in a room that had a teddy bear wearing an anti-drug message knifed against a wall. Someone whispered "Poor child" during morning meeting when we heard that a woman was found dead on a water bed with her four-year-old daughter next to her watching TV. The discussion of the case, however, centered on a history of diabetes and high blood pressure that could explain the sudden demise. With so many cases coming in, all tragedies in their own way, deep empathy with the bereaved was scarce. Detachment resides in the ritual of processing cases. Every pathologist did the autopsy in more or less the same way, ordered tests on standardized forms, and then filled out the paperwork. Eventually, every dead body became a pathological and anatomical exhibit, with slight variations.

That's the way it should be, I was told. Routinization necessarily occurs in forensic medicine, but it is an imperfect coping mechanism.[1] Some days, routinization worked smoothly. Staff members did not seem bothered by dealing with deaths; they might as well have been cataloguing pieces of art. Particularly after a sunny spring weekend, one could just sense the positive attitude in the office. Everyone seemed to be in a jocular mood and willing to get the bodies out. A scene investigator chatted with a railway police officer who predicted that a new and faster train connection would bring the office more work. And that's how it felt: a job to be done.

On bad days, when the office had been short-staffed and overwhelmed with cases for two weeks straight, when people experienced personal problems and illnesses, when a disaster struck the state, or when staff members did not get along, the task of conducting scene investigations and autopsies became a heavy chore. People dug into themselves, avoided one another, and sniped at each other. During those days, the endless stream of bad deaths dragged the collective mood down. Repetition aggravated the grim atmosphere. Cases that I had easily observed in the past became more difficult. One abused child was bad enough, but three in a row became intolerable. Dissatisfaction grew; the workers eyed their colleagues with resentment, grumbling to me, "Why was I stuck with two babies when she comes in late every day and escapes the tough assignment?" Those days, working in the medical examiner's office felt like being trapped in a grinding war zone. Bodies became the enemy to get rid off. In spite of procedures aimed at maintaining detachment, death seeped through and stuck to the staff. One such day, when I was already feeling nauseated from a cold, I left early.

★ ★ ★

Outside the medical examiner's office, the idea of routinizing autopsies or violent deaths encounters incomprehension. The challenge is enormous: how do you convey to outsiders that you are a caring, considerate, trustworthy person when you spend your time cutting up dead bodies? Medical examiners are glorified in contemporary TV shows and mystery books as super-detectives who bring scientific rationality to crime fighting. At the same time, forensics, with its connotation of dirty death, retains an undertone of deviance. The image of solving crimes with the power of science is appealing until you find out that it involves taking fluids out of dead eyes with needles. As with sausage making, we might value the final product, but we do not necessarily want to explore the production process. Sociologist Erving Goffman noted how stigma contaminates people close to the stigmatized.[2] Medical examiners are, of necessity, professionally close to suspicious death, but conveying professionalism to the outside world is difficult. All too quickly, the association with dirty work isolates medical examiners: outsiders express disbelief if the staff normalizes violent death, and they do not understand why staff members continue working in the morgue if the continuous exposure to death becomes too much for them. The same stigma of contamination applied to me: during one holiday party, a Harvard scholar who had interviewed violent terrorists speculated at length about the alleged neuroses that must have led me to study forensics. I quickly learned to be careful when I mentioned this research to others. The mixture of fascination and repulsion that suspicious death evokes sticks to the researcher and the death worker. Medical examiners may want to do a good job, but they are not supposed to enjoy their job nor complain about it. The outside pressure is to either keep quiet or quit.

And some quit. The medicolegal administrator told me that most staff members take a year to decide whether to stick around. After one year, they would have experienced some bad days at work. During the three years I was observing, several pathologists and other staff members left or were asked to leave for a variety of reasons, including the daily insult of working with trauma. While staff members whispered that forensic work has high rates of burnout, depression, and suicide—even higher than in law enforcement—little of this is reported in the medical literature.[3]

As Goffman poignantly observed, the burden of coping and sheltering others from the stigma falls on the stigmatized: "The general formula is apparent. The stigmatized individual is asked to act so as to imply neither that his burden is heavy nor that bearing it has made him different from us; at the same time he must keep himself at that remove from us which ensures our painlessly being able to confirm this belief about him."[4] Staff members who confront the gruesome qualities of suspicious deaths must manage this contradiction. A worker in another morgue "commented that the thing he found most uncomfortable about the job was not the work entailed by autopsies and body transportation but the loneliness of that work."[5] In the medical examiner's office, some of the administrative staff working in the room adjacent to the morgue blocked out any mention of forensic work. Medical examiners are thus expected to hold back and not confront others with death. That first question—"How can you watch autopsies?"—serves also as a conversation closer.

NOTES

PREFACE

1. One year after the death, on May 20, 2004, a judge ruled that the death was accidental. "Death of Aide's Son Accidental," *Milwaukee Journal Sentinel,* May 20, 2004. It is very unusual for a judge to overturn a medical examiner's determination.

INTRODUCTION

1. Talcott Parsons, "The Sick Role and the Role of the Physician Reconsidered," *Milbank Memorial Quarterly Fund* 53, no. 3 (1975): 257–78.

2. Parsons does not make this leap. In a discussion of the sick role, he notes that "the case of clearly terminal illness, where death is regarded as not merely inevitable but likely to occur relatively soon, raises a few special problems, which, however, probably need not be entered here." Ibid., 269.

3. Renée Anspach, *Deciding Who Lives: Fateful Choices in the Intensive Care Nursery* (Berkeley and Los Angeles: University of California Press, 1993); Daniel F. Chambliss, *Beyond Caring: Hospitals, Nurses, and the Social Organization of Ethics* (Chicago: University of Chicago Press, 1996); Stefan Timmermans, *Sudden Death and the Myth of CPR* (Philadelphia: Temple University Press, 1999); Robert Zussman, *Intensive Care: Medical Ethics and the Medical Profession* (Chicago: University of Chicago Press, 1992).

4. See the National Mortality Followback Survey from the Centers for Disease Control and Prevention (CDC) at http://www.cdc.gov/nchs/about/major/nmfs/nmfs.htm (accessed September 19, 2005).

5. See Elisabeth Kübler-Ross, *On Death and Dying* (New York: Macmillan, 1969).

6. Karen E. Steinhauser et al., "In Search of a Good Death: Observations of Patients, Families and Providers," *Annals of Internal Medicine* 132, no. 10 (2000): 825–32. See also

Karen E. Steinhauser et al., "Factors Considered Important at the End of Life by Patients, Family, Physicians, and Other Care Givers," *Journal of the American Medical Association* 284, no. 19 (2000): 2476–82.

7. Margaret Lock, *Twice Dead: Organ Transplants and the Reinvention of Death* (Berkeley and Los Angeles: University of California Press, 2002).

8. While access to medical care is not a right in the United States, it is definitely an expectation.

9. The 20 percent figure is an estimate. I found it in Richard Bonnie, "Opening Remarks," in Institute of Medicine, *Medicolegal Death Investigation System: Workshop Summary,* 3–6 (Washington, DC: National Academies Press, 2003). I have never been able to find out the exact number of deaths that fall under the jurisdiction of death investigators. Dominick J. DiMaio and Vincent J. M. DiMaio, *Forensic Pathology* (New York: Elsevier, 1989), offers a lower number of 8 percent. Organ transplant organizations suggest that death investigators have jurisdiction in about a third of deaths (Teresa J. Shafer et al., "Ethical Analysis of Organ Recovery Denials by Medical Examiners, Coroners, and Justices of the Peace," *Journal of Transplant Coordination* 5, no. 4 [1999]: 232–49), but their numbers should be taken with a grain of salt (see chapter 6). The exact figure is difficult to determine because in most cases, death investigators do not conduct an investigation but simply write down that they have been contacted by physicians, hospitals, or the police. These short contacts are included in the 20 percent figure. Regional variations in how frequently death investigators are contacted render it even more difficult to determine an accurate number. Suicide and homicide, major topics in this book, make up less than 1 percent of death investigators' cases.

10. Historians and anthropologists have paid more attention to burial customs and rites. And although the work of coroners has been examined in Britain (Maxwell J. Atkinson, *Discovering Suicide: Studies in the Social Organization of Sudden Death* [London: Macmillan, 1978]; Ian Burney, *Bodies of Evidence* [Baltimore: Johns Hopkins University Press, 2000]; Lindsay Prior, *The Social Organisation of Death: Medical Discourses and Social Practices in Belfast* [London: Macmillan, 1989]), the work of medical examiners has not been looked at from a sociological perspective.

11. R. F. Hunnisett, *The Medieval Coroner* (Cambridge: Cambridge University Press, 1961), chap. 1. Chapter 7 shows that the medieval coroners also had corruption problems.

12. In England and Wales, the Coroners Act of 1860 changed the fee-for-service system to a salary. Burney, *Bodies of Evidence,* 3.

13. For examples, see William G. Eckert, "Medicolegal Investigation in New York City," *American Journal of Forensic Medicine and Pathology* 4, no. 1 (1983): 33–54.

14. George P. LeBrun, *It's Time to Tell; as Told to Edward D. Radin* (New York: William Morrow & Company, 1962), 145. That chapter is titled "Coroners for Sale"; another chapter, "Little Napoleon," is about a coroner who loved to see his name in print and used his powers to stretch out death investigations. A chapter titled "Business as Usual" talks about the attempts of businesses to influence the verdicts.

15. See the information at the Web site of the coroner of McLean County, Illinois: http://www.mcleancountyil.gov/Coroner/ (accessed September 7, 2005).

16. LeBrun, *It's Time to Tell;* Shabbir Ahmed Wadee, "Forensic Pathology—a Different Perspective: Investigative Medicolegal Systems in the United States," *Medicine and Law* 13 (1994): 519–30; Cyril H. Wecht, Mark Curriden, and Benjamin Wecht, *Cause of Death* (New York: Penguin Books, 1993).

17. The prerequisites for this certification vary from being self-taught in legal medicine to having four hundred hours of experience in a coroner's office. See the American Board

of Medicolegal Death Investigators Registry Certification site at http://www.slu.edu/organiza
tions/abmdi/certification.shtml (accessed November 26, 2003).

18. Julie Johnson-McGrath, "Speaking for the Dead: Forensic Pathologists and Criminal
Justice in the United States," *Science, Technology, and Human Values* 20, no. 4 (1995): 438–59.

19. Information on types of death investigation systems is gathered and updated by
the CDC; see http://www.cdc.gov/epo/dphsi/mecisp/summaries.htm (accessed November 26,
2003). The mixed systems include states with a combination of coroner and medical examiner
systems and states with a referral system, in which coroners refer cases for autopsy to medical
examiners. Randy Hanzlick, "Overview of the Medicolegal Death Investigation System in the
United States," in Institute of Medicine, *Medicolegal Death Investigation System,* 7–11.

20. U.S. Department of Health and Human Services, *Medical Examiners' and Coroners'
Handbook on Death Registration and Fetal Death Reporting* (Hyattsville, MD: Public Health
Service, 1987), 5.

21. See Burney, *Bodies of Evidence,* chap. 1, for historical precedents.

22. LeBrun, *It's Time to Tell,* chap. 6. The flamboyant Los Angeles County chief medical examiner Dr. Thomas Noguchi was involved in passing safety laws during the 1970s.
Thomas T. Noguchi, *Coroner,* with Joseph DiMona (New York: Simon & Schuster, 1983),
248–49. Although Dr. Noguchi worked in a coroner's office, the office was actually structured
as a medical examiner's office.

23. Eric Klinenberg, *Heat Wave: A Social Autopsy of Disaster in Chicago* (Chicago: University
of Chicago Press, 2002).

24. Paul Starr, *The Social Transformation of Medicine* (New York: Basic Books, 1982), 13.
Starr also added social authority to professional authority, but this does not apply to medical
examiners.

25. World Health Organization, *Prevention of Suicide,* Public Health Paper No. 35 (Geneva:
World Health Organization, 1968).

26. Edwin S. Shneidman, *Definition of Suicide* (New York: John Wiley & Sons, 1985), 203.

27. Simon A. Cole, "Jackson Pollock, Judge Pollak, and the Dilemma of Fingerprint
Expertise," in *Expertise in Regulation and Law,* ed. Gary Edmond, 98–120 (Burlington, VT:
Ashgate Publishing Company, 2004).

28. Among philosophers, see Martin Heidegger, *Being and Time,* trans. Joan Stambaugh
(Albany, NY: SUNY Press, 1996; first published 1927); M. J. Inwood, ed., *Hegel Selections,*
The Great Philosophers (New York: Macmillan, 1989); and Jean-Paul Sartre, *Being and Nothingness: A Phenomenological Essay on Ontology* (New York: Pocket Books, 1966; first published
1943); among psychoanalysts, see Herman Feifel, ed., *The Meaning of Death* (New York:
McGraw-Hill, 1959); Sigmund Freud, *Reflections on War and Death* (New York: Moffat, Yard,
1918); and Carl Jung, "The Soul and Death," in Feifel, *The Meaning of Death,* 3–16; among
historians, see Philippe Ariès, *The Hour of Our Death* (London: Allen Lane, 1977); and Michel
Vovelle, *La mort et l'occident: De 1300 à nos jours* (Paris: Gallimard, 1983); among social sci-
entists, see Zygmunt Bauman, *Mortality, Immortality and Other Life Strategies* (Palo Alto, CA:
Stanford University Press, 1992); Norbert Elias, *The Loneliness of the Dying* (Oxford: Basil
Blackwell, 1985); Ivan Illich, "The Political Uses of Natural Death," in *Death Inside Out,* ed.
Peter Steinfels and Robert M. Veatch, 25–43 (New York: Harper & Row, 1974); and Herbert
Marcuse, "The Ideology of Death," in Feifel, *The Meaning of Death,* 64–78.

29. Elias, *Loneliness of the Dying,* 5.

30. Freud, *Reflections on War and Death;* Illich, "Political Uses of Natural Death"; Marcuse,
"The Ideology of Death."

31. Aries, *The Hour of Our Death,* 36.

32. Illich, "Political Uses of Natural Death."

33. See, for example, Peter Glover Forster, "Religion, Magic, Witchcraft, and AIDS in Malawi," *Anthropos* 93 (1998): 537–45.

34. Nicolas Rose, *Governing the Soul* (London: Free Association Books, 1989); Irving Kenneth Zola, "Medicine as an Institution of Social Control," *Sociological Review* 20 (1972): 487–504.

35. Aries, *The Hour of Our Death;* David Armstrong, "The Invention of Infant Mortality," *Sociology of Health and Illness* 8, no. 3 (1986): 211–32; Jan Bondeson, *Buried Alive: The Terrifying History of Our Most Primal Fear* (New York: W. W. Norton & Company, 2001).

36. Freud, *Reflections on War and Death.*

37. Elias, *Loneliness of the Dying;* Barney Glaser and Anselm Strauss, *Awareness of Dying* (Chicago: Aldine, 1965).

38. Bauman, *Mortality,* 137–40.

39. Geoffrey Gorer, *Death, Grief, and Mourning* (Garden City, NY: Doubleday, 1965), 114.

40. Ulrich Beck, *Risk Society: Towards a New Modernity* (London: SAGE Publications, 1992).

41. Bauman, *Mortality,* 17.

42. Sheila M. Rothman and David J. Rothman, *The Pursuit of Perfection: The Promise and Perils of Medical Enhancement* (New York: Pantheon Books, 2003).

43. Hanzlick, "Medicolegal Death Investigation System."

44. For a review, see Timmermans, *Sudden Death,* chap. 1.

45. For example, do not push off from a sandbank in a powerboat with roaring engines; do not light a cigarette while wearing an oxygen mask. The term for such cases in the medical examiner's office where I observed was "terminal stupidity." For more examples, see Wendy Northcutt, *The Darwin Awards II: Unnatural Selection* (New York: Penguin Group, 2001).

46. Bill Bass and Jon Jefferson, *Death's Acre: Inside the Legendary Forensic Lab the Body Farm, Where the Dead Do Tell Tales* (New York: Putnam, 2003), 222.

47. Bauman, *Mortality,* 192 (my emphasis). Bauman argues that center stage is now held by the late modern strategy of "deconstructing immortality." "It is now immortality, not mortality, which is deconstructed; but deconstructed in such a way as to show that permanence is nothing but the sequence of evanescences, time is nothing but a succession of episodes without consequence, immortality is nothing but an ongoing sequence of mortal beings. Deconstructed, immortality reveals mortality as its only secret. Mortality need not be deconstructed: it ought to be lived." Ibid., 190–91. Bauman argues that in a time when everyone can hope for fifteen minutes of fame, when histories are written about mundane lives and not just reserved for kings and queens of yore, the notion of immortality has lost its special character, to be shattered and turned into a mundane mass commodity. The death brokers of late modernity are the advertisers and television entertainers promising eternal yet evanescent youth to restless, infinitely mobile consumers. Things and people disappear before they can die, and death is infinitely rehearsed in the same way that widowhood is rehearsed in serial divorce or separations. While the deconstruction of mortality led to the omnipresence of death in life (e.g., in the fight against risk factors), Bauman suggests that the deconstruction of immortality once again leads to a reappearance of mortality. Death constitutes a stark reality check in the fleeting global consumer culture.

48. On the importance of legal authority, see Max Weber, *Economy and Society,* ed. Guenther Roth and Claus Wittich (Berkeley and Los Angeles: University of California Press, 1978; first published 1914).

49. Donald Jason, "The Role of the Medical Examiner/Coroner in Organ and Tissue Procurement for Transplantation," *American Journal of Forensic Medicine and Pathology* 15, no. 3 (1994): 193.

50. For a complete list of cases that fall under the medical examiner's jurisdiction in Utah, see http://www.health.state.ut.us/ome/act.html (accessed April 23, 2003).

51. Some jurisdictions in the United States allow religious exceptions for pediatric cases. The National Association of Medical Examiners has issued a position paper to repeal such exemptions on religious grounds. See the position paper at http://www.thename.org/index.php?option=com_docman&task=cat_view&gid=38&Itemid=26 (accessed September 7, 2005).

52. Andrew Abbott, *The System of Professions: An Essay on the Division of Expert Labor* (Chicago: University of Chicago Press, 1988), 63.

53. Eliot Freidson, *Professional Dominance: The Social Structure of Medical Care* (New York: Atherton Press, 1970). Abbott refers to this condition as "full jurisdiction."

54. Barbara Barzansky and Sylvia I. Etzel, "Educational Programs in US Medical Schools, 2002–2003," *Journal of the American Medical Association* 209, no. 9 (2003): 1190–96.

55. Hanzlick, "Medicolegal Death Investigation System," 10.

56. At her retirement in June 2000, chief medical examiner Joan Wood of Pinellas-Pasco County in Florida earned $145,000. A beginning medical examiner in the state where I conducted my research earned around $110,000 in 2000, and the deputy chief earned about $20,000 more.

57. National Association of Medical Examiners, *Strategic Plan 2002*, http://www.thename.org/library/NAME_strategic_plan2002.pdf (accessed October 5, 2004).

58. http://www.thename.org/medical_detective.htm#what%20is%20a%20coroner (accessed February 7, 2004); my italics.

59. Michel Foucault, *The Birth of the Clinic* (New York: Vintage Books, 1973), 145.

60. Charles E. Rosenberg, "The Tyranny of Diagnosis: Specific Entities and Individual Experience," *Milbank Quarterly* 80, no. 2 (2002): 237–60; Russell C. Maulitz, *Morbid Appearances: The Anatomy of Pathology in the Early Nineteenth Century* (Cambridge: Cambridge University Press, 1987).

61. Rolla B. Hill and Robert E. Anderson, *The Autopsy: Medical Practice and Public Policy* (Boston: Butterworths, 1988), 48.

62. Frederic Hafferty, *Into the Valley: Death and the Socialization of Medical Students* (New Haven, CT: Yale University Press, 1991).

63. Branko Emerc, "Minimizing Mistakes in Clinical Diagnosis," *American Journal of Forensic Medicine and Pathology* 44, no. 4 (1999): 810–13; Linda T. Kohn, Janet M. Corrigan, and Molla S. Donaldson, eds., *To Err Is Human: Building a Safer Health System* (Washington, DC: National Academy Press, 2000).

64. Jack Hasson and Herbert Schneiderman, "Autopsy Training Programs to Right a Wrong," *Archives of Pathology and Laboratory Medicine* 119 (1995): 289–91.

65. Randy Hanzlick and Jesse K. McKenney, "Education of a Pathologist," *Annals of Internal Medicine* 159, no. 9 (1999): 907–8; George D. Lundberg, "College of American Pathologists Conference: Restructuring Autopsy Practice for Health Care Reform," *Archives of Pathology and Laboratory Medicine* 120 (1996): 736–39.

66. Hafferty, *Into the Valley;* Frederic Hafferty, "Reconfiguring the Sociology of Medical Education: Emerging Topics and Pressing Issues," in *Handbook of Medical Sociology,* ed. Chloe E. Bird, Peter E. Conrad, and Allen M. Fremont, 238–57 (Upper Saddle River, NJ: Prentice-Hall, 2000).

67. Edward A. Gall, "The Necropsy as a Tool in Medical Progress," *Bulletin of the New York*

Academy of Medicine 44 (1968): 829. Medicare pays for autopsies, but most hospitals use the money for other services. Pathologists have lobbied the Department of Health and Human Services to require certain autopsy-performance rates but have not succeeded. George D. Lundberg, "The Role of the Medicolegal Autopsy in Health Care," in Institute of Medicine, *Medicolegal Death Investigation System,* 44.

68. Kurt Nolte, "Research Issues," in Institute of Medicine, *Medicolegal Death Investigation System,* 15–18.

69. The recent turn to evidence-based medicine in the health care field is predicated on a replacement of pathological by epidemiological principles of knowledge production. See Evidence-Based Medicine Working Group, "Evidence-Based Medicine: A New Approach to Teaching the Practice of Medicine," *Journal of the American Medical Association* 268, no. 17 (1992): 2420–25.

70. I reviewed the three volumes of the *American Journal of Forensic Medicine and Pathology* between 2000 and 2002 and coded the articles based on their methodology used. Of a total of 241 articles, 38% were based on a single death investigation, 15% were based on multiple cases (usually two or three), 19% were methodological articles, 18% offered a retrospective case review, and 10% were other types of articles. The "other" category included, for example, a meta-analysis, a position paper, a professional survey, a survey of families, and several experimental studies. The single and multiple case reports regularly contained the word "unusual" or "rare" in the abstract and were aimed at alerting death investigators to equivocal deaths. An example is Russell Deidiker, "Return of the Killer Fish: Accidental Choking Death on a Bluegill (*Lepomis Macrochirus*)," *American Journal of Forensic Medicine and Pathology* 23, no. 2 (2002): 197–98. The abstract says it all: "An unusual case of choking is presented. In this case, a 45-year-old man, while fishing and drinking with friends, attempted to swallow a whole fish. He subsequently asphyxiated as a result of upper airway obstruction." Such a death would probably qualify as another example of "terminal stupidity" (see note 45 above). This was not the only article about animals; the three volumes of the journal contained a similar fish story and articles about wild dogs, a hunting dog shooting its owner, and attack by big cats. Sexual asphyxiation and unusually inventive blends of suicide and homicide are also often published as single case studies. The methodological articles generally aimed to introduce death investigators to new techniques or their applications and involved DNA technologies or tissue harvesting. Only one methodological article in the three-year period offered a new technique to be used in autopsy procedures: Kevin D. Horn and William A. Devine, "An Approach to Dissecting the Congenitally Malformed Heart in the Forensic Autopsy," *American Journal of Forensic Medicine and Pathology* 22, no. 4 (2001): 405–11. The September 2003 issue (not included in my review) contained the first article to use an evidence-based medicine approach: Mark Donohoe, "Evidence-Based Medicine and Shaken Baby Syndrome, Part 1: Literature Review, 1966–1998," *American Journal of Forensic Medicine and Pathology* 24, no. 3 (2003): 239–42. Finally, the December 2003 issue reorganized the journal into three categories: original articles, reviews, and case studies. See Nolte, "Research Issues," for a similar analysis.

71. According to the February 2003 newsletter of the National Association of Medical Examiners, the winners that year were Laura Knight, MD, who offered a platform presentation titled "Co-sleeping and Sudden Unexpected Infant Deaths in Kentucky: A 10-Year Retrospective Case Review"; and Michael Leman, MD, who made a poster presentation titled "Suicide in Cancer Patients: A Retrospective Review, 1996–2001."

72. According to several forensic pathologists I spoke with, the standard textbook is Werner U. Spitz, *Spitz and Fisher's Medicolegal Investigation of Death,* 3rd ed. (Springfield, IL: Charles C. Thomas, 1993), followed by DiMaio and DiMaio, *Forensic Pathology.*

73. Edmond, *Expertise in Regulation and Law;* David L. Faigman et al., *Modern Scientific Evidence: The Law and Science of Expert Testimony* (St. Paul, MN: West, 1997); Sheila Jasanoff, "Judicial Fictions: The Supreme Court's Quest for Good Science," *Society* 38, no. 4 (2001): 27–36; Shana M. Solomon and Edward J. Hackett, "Setting Boundaries between Science and Law: Lessons from *Daubert v. Merrell Dow Pharmaceuticals, Inc.,*" *Science, Technology, and Human Values* 21, no. 2 (1996): 131–56. See also chapter 3.

74. I work this out in chapter 3.

75. Richard C. Froede, ed., *Handbook of Forensic Pathology* (Northfield, IL: College of American Pathologists, 1990), 2.

76. Paul Draus, *Consumed in the City: Observing Tuberculosis at Century's End* (Philadelphia: Temple University Press, 2004), 68.

77. Burney, *Bodies of Evidence,* 70.

78. Ibid., 136.

79. Although science studies is, of course, a diverse and interdisciplinary field and includes several people with dual loyalties, it is fair to say that science scholars have articulated their field largely in opposition to what they understand as traditional sociology.

80. Samuel Bloom, "The Institutionalization of Medical Sociology in the United States, 1920–1980," in Bird, Conrad, and Fremont, *Handbook of Medical Sociology,* 11–33.

81. Robert Straus, "The Nature and Status of Medical Sociology," *American Sociological Review* 22, no. 2 (1957): 200–204.

82. Howard S. Becker et al., *Boys in White: Student Culture in Medical School* (Chicago: University of Chicago Press, 1961); Everett Hughes, *The Sociological Eye: Selected Papers* (Chicago: Aldine-Atherton, 1971; first published 1945), pt. 3.

83. Hughes, *The Sociological Eye,* 426.

84. See in particular Abbott, *The System of Professions;* and Eliot Freidson, *Profession of Medicine: A Study of the Sociology of Applied Knowledge* (New York: Harper & Row, 1970).

85. See, for example, Adele Clarke, *Disciplining Reproduction: Modernity, American Life Sciences, and "the Problems of Sex"* (Berkeley and Los Angeles: University of California Press, 1998); Joan Fujimura, *Crafting Science: A Sociohistory of the Quest for the Genetics of Cancer* (Cambridge, MA: Harvard University Press, 1996); S. Leigh Star, *Regions of the Mind: Brain Research and the Quest for Scientific Certainty* (Stanford, CA: Stanford University Press, 1989); Anselm Strauss, *Continual Permutations of Action* (New York: Aldine de Gruyter, 1993); and Anselm Strauss et al., "Sentimental Work in the Technologized Hospital," *Sociology of Health and Illness* 4, no. 3 (1982): 254–78.

86. Anselm Strauss et al., *The Social Organization of Medical Work* (Chicago: University of Chicago Press, 1985).

87. Marc Berg and Monica Casper, "Constructivist Perspectives on Medical Work: Medical Practices and Science and Technology Studies," *Science, Technology, and Human Values* 20, no. 4 (1995): 397.

88. For useful reviews, see Karin Knorr-Cetina, *Epistemic Cultures: How the Sciences Make Knowledge* (Cambridge, MA: Harvard University Press, 1999); Bruno Latour, *Science in Action: How to Follow Scientists and Engineers through Society* (Cambridge, MA: Harvard University Press, 1987); and Michael Lynch, *Scientific Practice and Ordinary Action: Ethnomethodology and Social Studies of Science* (Cambridge: Cambridge University Press, 1993).

89. Robert K. Merton, *On the Shoulders of Giants: A Shandean Postscript* (Chicago: University of Chicago Press, 1993; first published 1965); Merton, *Social Theory and Social Structure* (Glencoe, IL: Free Press, 1957).

90. Thomas Kuhn, *The Structure of Scientific Revolutions,* 2nd ed. (Chicago: University

of Chicago Press, 1962). For various histories, see Stephen Cole, "Merton's Contribution to the Sociology of Science," *Social Studies of Science* 34, no. 6 (2004): 829–44; and Harry M. Collins, "The Sociology of Scientific Knowledge: Studies of Contemporary Science," *Annual Review of Sociology* 9 (1983): 265–85. When I was in graduate school in the early 1990s, it was as if the Mertonian sociology of science had never existed. We started a survey course with Imre Lakatos and Karl Popper and then moved into the works of David Bloor, Harry Collins, and Bruno Latour.

91. The extension of agency is a counterintuitive idea for sociologists, but explaining this in detail would sidetrack my argument. For a lengthier account, see the discussion between Harry Collins and Steven Yearley on the one hand and Michel Callon and Bruno Latour on the other in Andrew Pickering, ed., *Science as Practice and Culture* (Chicago: University of Chicago Press, 1992); and Pickering, *The Mangle of Practice: Time, Agency, and Science* (Chicago: University of Chicago Press, 1995).

92. For a provocative explanation of this position, see Latour, *Science in Action.*

93. Ibid. Some sociologists also argued that such variables need to earn their analytical value. See Barney Glaser and Anselm Strauss, *The Discovery of Grounded Theory* (New York: Aldine, 1967).

94. Troy Duster, "Medicine: Race and Reification in Science," *Science* 307, no. 5712 (2005): 1050–51; Jonathan Kahn, "How a Drug Becomes "Ethnic": Law, Commerce, and the Production of Racial Categories in Medicine," *Yale Journal of Health Policy and Law Ethics* 4, no. 1 (2004): 1–46.

95. Annemarie Mol, *The Body Multiple: Ontology in Medical Practice* (Durham, NC: Duke University Press, 2002).

96. Ibid., 151.

97. Mol also takes Foucault's critique of normativity seriously; see the subtext to her chapter 2.

98. Mol notes that when she shared her chapter drafts with the physicians she studied, they felt "alienated" by her analysis. *The Body Multiple*, 160. She explains the feeling of alienation by the fact that she explores the practices care providers routinely bracket. I wonder, however, whether the alienation is not a consequence of the erasure of normativity. During an author-meets-critics session at the 2004 annual meeting of the Society for Social Studies of Science in Paris, Mol explained that what she found fascinating about physicians was that they made important decisions about every three minutes. These kinds of decisions, and their fascination, is what I hope to retrieve with my study.

99. See Charis Cussins, "Ontological Choreography: Agency for Women in an Infertility Clinic," in *Differences in Medicine: Unraveling Practices, Techniques and Bodies,* ed. Marc Berg and Annemarie Mol, 166–201 (Durham, NC: Duke University Press, 1998).

100. Howard S. Becker, *Outsiders: Studies in the Sociology of Deviance* (New York: Free Press, 1963).

101. See, for example, Randy Hanzlick and Julia Goodin, "Mind Your Manners, Part III: Individual Scenario Results and Discussion of the National Association of Medical Examiners Manner of Death Questionnaire," *American Journal of Forensic Medicine and Pathology* 18, no. 3 (1997): 228–45.

102. When taking lung cultures, pathologists would cauterize the lung tissue.

103. This was tricky, because the assistants were unionized and had definite rules about who could perform what tasks in the morgue.

104. Glaser and Strauss, *The Discovery of Grounded Theory.*

105. I do not want to imply that acceptance of one's findings by research subjects should be the standard by which to evaluate ethnographic work. I was more concerned with my accuracy

in interpreting forensic details. In my book *Sudden Death and the Myth of CPR,* one reviewer used a typo in a medical term as an opportunity to dismiss the entire study. The pathologists who read this book disagreed with some of my analysis and conclusions (particularly in chapter 4) but hoped that the book would stimulate discussion within their field.

106. Bonnie, "Opening Remarks"; Randy Hanzlick, John C. Hunsaker III, and Gregory J. Davis, *A Guide for Manner of Death Classification* (National Association of Medical Examiners, 2002).

107. Richard Bonnie, "Closing Remarks," in Institute of Medicine, *Medicolegal Death Investigation System,* 63.

CHAPTER ONE

1. *The Duchess of Malfi* (1612), act 4, scene 2:

> I know death hath ten thousand several doors
> For men to take their exits; and 'tis found
> They go on such strange geometrical hinges,
> You may open them both ways: any way, for heaven sake.

Opening doors both ways refers to taking one's own life or waiting for death.

2. Robert L. Anderson and Betty N. Smith, "Deaths: Leading Causes for 2001," *National Vital Statistics Report* 52, no. 9 (2003): 1–86.

3. I checked a random sample of two hundred cause-of-death certificates issued in 1999 after a postmortem investigation and found that coronary artery disease was the immediate or an underlying cause of death in about 65 percent of natural deaths.

4. DiMaio and DiMaio, *Forensic Pathology,* 44.

5. Prior, *Social Organisation of Death.*

6. Burney, *Bodies of Evidence,* chap. 3.

7. Ibid., 93.

8. Ibid., epilogue.

9. Ibid., 167.

10. Massachusetts established the first medical examiner system in 1877, but the medical examiner had no authority to conduct autopsies. New York City introduced the first centralized, medically controlled medical examiner system in 1918 requiring the chief medical examiner to be a physician. Randy Hanzlick and Debra Combs, "Medical Examiner and Coroner Systems: History and Trends," *Journal of the American Medical Association* 279, no. 11 (1998): 870–74.

11. Forensic workers have commented on their banishment to less desirable spaces: "Why are crime labs and morgues always in the basements? Why not on the top floor, with big corner windows looking out across the city or countryside? Just because some of us like to look at bodies and bones, that doesn't mean we wouldn't appreciate a nice view out a window now and then." Bass and Jefferson, *Death's Acre,* 176. Dr. Randy Hanzlick has pointed out that some medical examiners now work in new, very nice facilities. Personal communication, January 13, 2005.

12. Prior, *Social Organisation of Death,* 27.

13. Ibid., pt. 1.

14. Clive Seale, *Constructing Death: The Sociology of Dying and Bereavement* (Cambridge: Cambridge University Press, 1998), 81. The comparison with the Marshall Islands community is on page 207.

15. For historical studies of how the link between cholesterol and cardiac mortality was fostered and on general cardiac mortality, see Robert A. Aronowitz, *Making Sense of Illness*

(Cambridge: Cambridge University Press, 1998); Anne Fagot-Largeault, *Les causes de la mort: Histoire naturelle et facteurs de risque* (Paris: L'Institut Interdisciplinaire d'Études Épistémologiques, 1989); Christopher Lawrence, " 'Definite and Material': Coronary Thrombosis and Cardiologists in the 1920s," in *Framing Disease: Studies in Cultural History,* ed. Charles E. Rosenberg and Janet Golden, 50–84 (New Brunswick, NJ: Rutgers University Press, 1992); and Reidar K. Lie, "The Angina Pectoris Controversy during the 1920s," *Acta Physiologica Scandinavia* 599, suppl. (1991), 135–47.

16. See Charles E. Rosenberg, "Pathologies of Progress: The Idea of Civilization as Risk," *Bulletin of the History of Medicine* 72, no. 4 (1998): 714–30.

17. In addition, the medical examiner's office is notified when body parts are found. During one Fourth of July weekend, the office received a finger that turned out to belong to a fourteen-year-old who had been playing with fireworks. More often, the office is alerted when bones thought to be human are found. Most bones turn out to be bovine, ovine, or canine; if human, they often seem to have come from a historic cemetery. In some situations, the office will need to notify the local tribal council to find out whether the bones are likely those of a Native American.

18. I did not attend any scene investigations as part of my research. The next part of this chapter is therefore based on extensive interviews with scene investigators.

19. Prior, *Social Organisation of Death,* 20.

20. I thank Stefan Hirschauer for alerting me to the notion of thanatography.

21. Bruno Latour, *Pandora's Hope: Essays on the Reality of Science Studies* (Cambridge, MA: Harvard University Press, 1999), chap. 1.

22. Ibid., 38.

23. Abbott, *The System of Professions,* 41. Abbott refers to this process as *colligation,* the process of bringing together isolated facts by a hypothesis or explanation, and he considers it a key component of the diagnostic quality of a professional.

24. The case number means that 2,405 deaths have been reported for 2001 so far in the state. Only a tiny minority of those deaths fall under the jurisdiction of the medical examiner's office. The case number is thus much higher than the number of autopsies done up to that time.

25. Harold Garfinkel, "Practical Sociological Reasoning: Some Features in the Work of the Los Angeles Suicide Prevention Center," in *Essays in Self-Destruction,* ed. Edwin S. Shneidman (New York: Science House, 1967), 174.

26. On the objectivity of DNA technologies, see Michael Lynch, " 'Science above All Else': The Inversion of Credibility between Forensic DNA Profiling and Fingerprint Evidence," in Edmond, *Expertise in Regulation and Law,* 121–35.

27. For more on difficult identifications, see Jehuda Hiss and Tzipi Kahana, "Trauma and Identification of Victims of Suicidal Terrorism in Israel," *Military Medicine* 165, no. 11 (2000): 889–93.

28. Identification becomes more complicated for skeletal remains. See Froede, *Handbook of Forensic Pathology,* 54–58.

29. Charles S. Hirsch and Vernard I. Adams, "Sudden and Unexpected Death from Natural Causes in Adults," in Spitz, *Medicolegal Investigation of Death,* 137–74.

30. Ibid., 140.

31. Geoffrey Bowker and S. Leigh Star, *Sorting Things Out* (Cambridge, MA: MIT Press, 1999), 24; Stuart A. Kirk and Herb Kutchins, *The Selling of the DSM: The Rhetoric of Science in Psychiatry* (Hawthorne, NY: Aldine de Gruyter, 1992).

32. "De ene zijn dood is de andere zijn brood."

33. Forensic entomology is a recent specialty; these scientists study insects to help death investigations. They are usually called to consult with medical examiners' offices or law enforcement authorities. See M. Lee Goff, *A Fly for the Prosecution: How Insect Evidence Helps Solve Crimes* (Cambridge, MA: Harvard University Press, 2000).

34. Timmermans, *Sudden Death*.

35. Dorothy Nelkin and Lori Andrews, "Do the Dead Have Interests? Policy Issues for Research after Life," *American Journal of Law and Medicine* 24 (1998): 261–91; Ruth Richardson, *Death, Dissection, and the Destitute* (London: Routledge & Kegan Paul, 1987).

36. Chambliss, *Beyond Caring*.

37. See, for example, Roland Bal, "How to Kill with a Ballpoint: Credibility in Dutch Forensic Science," *Science, Technology, and Human Values* 30, no. 1 (2005): 52–75; or most issues of forensic journals.

38. See Jack Katz, *How Emotions Work* (Chicago: University of Chicago Press, 1999).

39. Dr. Douglas is here using the Rokitansky procedure, named after Karl von Rokitansky, the obsessive nineteenth-century Viennese anatomist.

40. Kay Redfield Jamison, *Night Falls Fast: Understanding Suicide* (New York: Vintage Books, 1999), 126.

41. Latour, *Pandora's Hope*.

42. On the philosophical assumptions behind causes of death, see Lennart Nordenfelt, *Causes of Death: A Philosophical Essay* (Göteborg: Forskningradsnamnden, 1983).

43. Coronary artery disease's only competition for most frequent cause of death as recorded on the death certificate is acute intoxication from medications, alcohol, or narcotics. A toxicological overdose is a univocal cause of death. An alcohol level of .527 in a man who was in the habit of drinking a gallon of vodka a day constitutes a positive proof of death. Lethal toxicology levels have been put into tables; see Randall C. Baselt, *Disposition of Toxic Drugs and Chemicals in Man*, 6th ed. (Davis, CA: Chemical Toxicology Institute, 2002). As the Steve Albom case shows, however, the problem with toxicology is that results are available only after the body has been transferred from the morgue. Often the pathologist would find obstructed arteries but leave the case open "pending toxicology." This meant that if toxicology was negative and heart disease was present, the cause of death would become coronary artery disease. If toxicology was significant, the acute intoxication would become the cause of death, because acute events are presumed to more immediately cause death.

44. DiMaio and DiMaio, *Forensic Pathology*, 44.

45. Hirsch and Adams, "Sudden and Unexpected Death," 149.

46. All states employ a death certificate that is based on the U.S. Standard Certificate of Death. Variations occur, but all death certificates need to include a manner of death. Hanzlick, Hunsaker, and Davis, *Manner of Death Classification*.

47. Randy Hanzlick, *The Medical Cause of Death Manual* (Chicago, IL: College of American Pathologists, 1994), 19, 18.

48. A simple etiological causal chain is often problematic in chronic diseases with multiple coexisting conditions. Robert A. Israel, Harry M. Rosenberg, and Lester R. Curtin, "Analytical Potential for Multiple Cause-of-Death Data," *American Journal of Epidemiology* 124, no. 2 (1986): 161–79. See also chapter 4 of Fagot-Largeault, *Les causes de la mort*, on problems with the notion of causality.

49. Prior, *Social Organisation of Death*, 95–96.

50. Of the two hundred death certificates I checked, only one listed a cancer-related cause—carcinoma of the lungs.

51. Mita Giacomini, "A Change of Heart and a Change of Mind? Technology and the

Redefinition of Death in 1968," *Social Science and Medicine* 44, no. 10 (1997): 1465–82; Lock, *Twice Dead.*

52. Dale M. Atrens, "The Questionable Wisdom of a Low-Fat Diet and Cholesterol Reduction," *Social Science and Medicine* 39, no. 3 (1994): 433–47.

53. Hirsch and Adams, "Sudden and Unexpected Death," 144.

54. U.S. Department of Health and Human Services, *Medical Examiners' and Coroners' Handbook.*

55. Hirsch and Adams note that a generation ago, the deaths now attributed to coronary artery disease would have been classified differently. They suggest that the prevalence of coronary artery disease as cause of death is related to the discovery of CPR: "Two and three decades ago, pathologists and cardiologists aspired to attribute all sudden deaths from arteriosclerotic heart disease to coronary thrombosis with acute myocardial infarction. It was assumed that the infarcts occurred but were undetectable at autopsy in their early hours of evolution. Since the advent of cardiopulmonary resuscitation and cardioversion, numerous resuscitated survivors of cardiac arrest have been studied by serial electrocardiograms and cardiac enzymes. Only a small minority develop signs of an infarct. The majority simply evince profound electrical instability." "Sudden and Unexpected Death," 147. Hirsch and Adams also mention their suspicion that hypertension is often overlooked as a cause of death and is mistaken for coronary artery disease.

56. If the brain had been less decomposed, Dr. Douglas could have suspended it in a fixative for a week to let it harden.

57. Jessica Mitford, *The American Way of Death Revisited* (New York: Vintage Books, 2000).

58. But see Marc Berg, "Practices of Reading and Writing: The Constitutive Role of the Patient Record in Medical Work," *Sociology of Health and Illness* 18, no. 4 (1996): 499–562; Marc Berg and Geoffrey Bowker, "The Multiple Bodies of the Medical Record: Toward a Sociology of an Artifact," *Sociological Quarterly* 38, no. 3 (1997): 513–37; Timothy Diamond, *Making Gray Gold: Narratives of Nursing Home Care* (Chicago: University of Chicago Press, 1992); and Sally Macintyre, "Some Notes on Record Taking and Making in an Antenatal Clinic," *Sociological Review* 26 (1978): 595–611.

59. Although pathologists use a template form to facilitate writing down the sequence of findings, the autopsy report is adapted to each case. Because of the importance of this final report, several parties in the office double-check it for internal consistency. Pathologists first dictate their findings on tape; while transcribing the dictation, case managers flag any inconsistencies or incomplete parts. The doctor then reads over the draft, makes changes, and incorporates new laboratory findings when they become available. Finally, the penultimate draft goes to Dr. Cahill, the chief medical examiner, who checks the entire file and adds her changes. She then signs off on the final version of the autopsy report. Because of all this cross-checking and waiting for laboratory results, the office's major problem is a long delay in getting autopsy reports finished. Due to staffing problems and some transportation disasters involving many deaths, the office was about a year behind in finishing autopsy reports. Although everyone was frustrated with this delay, nobody suggested taking shortcuts. The office strove for the highest quality of autopsy reports because these documents would represent the medical investigators in courts and needed to satisfy the questions of relatives. Once the forms are mailed out to relatives and officials, they cannot be changed, only amended, so the medical examiner's office has to live with any mistakes it may have made.

60. For this reason, a study of death investigators that relies only on the final products misses the gradual construction of a cause of death.

61. The pathologists confirmed that alcohol might also cause a cardiac arrhythmia. Par-

ticularly during the holidays, people die after having drunk alcohol even when their alcohol level should not be lethal. This is called the *alcohol holiday syndrome*. See, for example, Abdel J. Fuenmayor and Abdel M. Fuenmayor, "Cardiac Arrest following Holiday Heart Syndrome," *International Journal of Cardiology* 59, no. 1 (1997): 101–3.

62. The death certificate is legally binding for administrative purposes. It is not legally binding in criminal investigations or for insurance purposes.

63. Prior, *Social Organisation of Death*, 43. Although on pages 78–79 Prior moves closer to the perspective that I favor, he does not resolve the contradictions with his earlier writing.

64. Rosenberg, "The Tyranny of Diagnosis," 250.

65. On the historical link between heart disease and risk factors, see Aronowitz, *Making Sense of Illness;* and Lawrence, "Definite and Material."

66. Michel Callon, "Some Elements of a Sociology of Translation: Domestication of the Scallops and the Fishermen of St Brieuc Bay," in *Power, Action, and Belief: A New Sociology of Knowledge?* ed. John Law, 196–229 (London: Routledge, 1986).

CHAPTER TWO

1. Albert G. Reitan, *Specialist's Factual Report of Investigation DCA00MA006* (Washington, DC: National Transportation Safety Board, 1999), 34–38.

2. National Transportation Safety Board, *EgyptAir Flight 990: The Final Report* (Washington, DC: National Transportation Safety Board, 2002).

3. William Langewiesche, "The Crash of EgyptAir 990," *Atlantic Monthly,* November 2001.

4. For example, compare the August 16, 2000, editorial in the *Cleveland Plain Dealer* with the August 18, 2000, article in the *Guardian.*

5. Atkinson, *Discovering Suicide;* Jack Douglas, *The Social Meanings of Suicide* (Princeton, NJ: Princeton University Press, 1967); Anthony Giddens, "The Suicide Problem in French Sociology," *British Journal of Sociology* 16 (1965): 276–95.

6. Hanzlick, Hunsaker, and Davis, *Manner of Death Classification,* 3.

7. Gregory M. Davis, "Mind Your Manners, Part 1: History of Death Certification and Manner of Death Classification," *American Journal of Forensic Medicine and Pathology* 18, no. 3 (1997): 222.

8. Prior reports that the coroner of Belfast, Ireland, refuses to use terms such as *homicide, suicide, accident,* or *misadventure.* "For him, the cause of death is always a medical cause; the coroner's court does not exist to assign or remove liability." *Social Organisation of Death,* 44.

9. Commission Internationale, Nomenclature International des Maladies (1910), quoted in Bowker and Star, *Sorting Things Out,* 144.

10. This view has not completely disappeared; see Jamison, *Night Falls Fast.*

11. An egoistic suicide is the result of insufficient integration. If an individual insufficiently participates in community life though the major institutions of politics, family, and religion, excessive individualism results: "Suicide varies inversely with the degree of integration of the social groups of which the individual forms a part." Emile Durkheim, *Suicide: A Study in Sociology,* trans. John A. Spaulding and George Simpson (New York: Free Press, 1979; first published 1897), 209. Altruistic suicide, on the other hand, is correlated with an overidentification of the individual with the society. Particularly in kinship-based societies, people sacrifice their own lives for the sake of the group. Anomic suicide results from insufficient social regulation and is marked by a sudden displacement of a person's status. Divorce, for example, produces anomie for individuals because it uproots the individual from established family roles. Finally, excessive social regulation generates fatalistic suicide. Individuals feel that they lose control over their lives and that efforts to make changes are hampered by pow-

erful institutions. According to Durkheim, suicide is not an individual issue but reflects the relationship between a person and society.

12. See, for example, Jack P. Gibbs and Walter T. Martin, *Status Integration and Suicide* (Eugene, OR: University of Oregon Books, 1964); and A. F. Henry and J. F. Short, *Suicide and Homicide* (New York: Free Press, 1954).

13. Durkheim, *Suicide*, 148–51.

14. Gregory Zilboorg, "Suicide among Civilized and Primitive Races," *American Journal of Psychiatry* 92 (1936): 1347–69.

15. Coming from an interpretive framework, these authors argued for studying "deviance" from the perspective of the people labeled as such and not by "causally" explaining their actions on the basis of statistical variables; see, for example, Becker, *Outsiders;* and David Matza, *Becoming Deviant* (Englewood Cliffs, NJ: Prentice-Hall, 1969). They believed that researchers should focus on the meaning of, for example, criminal behavior for the criminal and his or her career in the correctional system. Deviance was not an intrinsic characteristic of an individual; rather, behavior became deviant when it was defined as such by others. Influenced by critical theory, this school of research saw social statistics as an instrument in the armamentarium of the political power establishment to maintain the status quo and oppress the powerless.

16. Douglas, *Social Meanings of Suicide.*

17. For a more elaborate but similar critique of statistics, see John I. Kitsuse and Aaron V. Cicourel, "A Note on the Uses of Official Statistics," *Social Problems* 11 (1963): 131–39.

18. Douglas, *Social Meanings of Suicide*, chap. 12.

19. Douglas's project of investigating the social meanings of suicide is methodologically and existentially impossible: how can a researcher reconstruct the meaning of suicide in the suicidal person's own words and from their embodied perspective when all potential respondents are dead and have left, at best, cryptic, self-serving messages? Douglas relied on psychiatric records to grasp the meaning of suicide. His social meanings of suicide amounted to three notions: the wish to transform oneself in an afterlife, getting revenge, and receiving sympathy. Ibid., chap. 17. While his book was hailed for its programmatic quality, his actual results have largely been dismissed because of empirical flaws. See, for example, Christopher Bagley, "Authoritarianism, Status Integration and Suicide," *Sociology* 6 (1972): 395–404.

20. Atkinson, *Discovering Suicide;* Maxwell J. Atkinson, "Societal Reactions to Suicide: The Role of Coroners' Definitions," in *Images of Deviance,* ed. Stanley Cohen, 165–91 (New York: Penguin Books, 1971).

21. Atkinson, *Discovering Suicide*, 144.

22. On "moral entrepreneurs," see Becker, *Outsiders.*

23. Brian M. Barraclough, "Poisoning Cases: Suicide or Accident," *British Journal of Psychiatry* 124 (1974): 526–30; J. H. Brown, "Reporting of Suicide: Canadian Statistics," *Suicide* 5, no. 1 (1975): 21–28; Richard Gist and Q. B. Welch, "Certification Change versus Actual Behavior Change in Teenage Suicide Rates, 1955–1979," *Suicide and Life-Threatening Behavior* 19, no. 3 (1989): 277–88; Trevor A. Holding and Brian M. Barraclough, "Undetermined Deaths—Suicide or Accident?" *British Journal of Psychiatry* 133 (1978): 542–49; Solomon Jacobson, Christopher Bagley, and Ann Rehin, "Clinical and Social Variables Which Differentiate Suicide, Open and Accident Verdicts," *Psychological Medicine* 6 (1976): 417–21; Michael J. Kelleher et al., "Improving Procedures for Recording Suicide Statistics," *Irish Medical Journal* 89, no. 1 (1996): 14–15; Ashok Malla and John Hoenig, "Differences in Suicide Rates: An Examination of Under-Reporting," *Canadian Journal of Psychiatry* 28, no. 4 (1983): 291–93; Guido F. Moens, "The Reliability of Reported Suicide Mortality Statistics: An Experience

from Belgium," *International Journal of Epidemiology* 14, no. 2 (1985): 272–75; Jan Neeleman and Simon Wessely, "Changes in Classification of Suicide in England and Wales: Time Trends and Associations with Coroners' Professional Backgrounds," *Psychology and Medicine* 27, no. 2 (1997): 467–72; Annakatri Ohberg and Jouko Lonnqvist, "Suicides Hidden among Undetermined Deaths," *Acta Psychiatrica Scandinavia* 98, no. 3 (1998): 214–18; Dennis L. Peck and Kenneth Warner, "Accident or Suicide? Single-Vehicle Car Accidents and the Intent Hypothesis," *Adolescence* 30 (Summer 1995): 463–72; Bernice A. Pescosolido and Robert Mendelsohn, "Social Causation or Social Construction of Suicide? An Investigation into the Social Organization of Official Rates," *American Sociological Review* 51 (1986): 80–101; David P. Phillips and Todd E. Ruth, "Adequacy of Official Suicide Statistics for Scientific Research and Public Policy," *Suicide and Life-Threatening Behavior* 23, no. 4 (1993): 307–19; Judy Schaechter et al., "Are 'Accidental' Gun Deaths as Rare as They Seem? A Comparison of Medical Examiner Manner of Death Coding with an Intent-Based Classification Approach," *Pediatrics* 111, no. 4 (2003): 741–44; Chester W. Schmidt et al., "Suicide by Vehicular Crash," *American Journal of Psychiatry* 134, no. 2 (1977): 175–78; Arnold R. Soslow and Alan D. Woolf, "Reliability of Data Sources for Poisoning Deaths in Massachusetts," *American Journal of Emergency Services* 10, no. 2 (1992): 124–27; Mark Speechley and Kathleen M. Stavraky, "The Adequacy of Suicide Statistics for Use in Epidemiology and Public Health," *Canadian Journal of Public Health* 82, no. 1 (1991): 38–42; Debbi Stanistreet et al., "Accident or Suicide? Predictors of Coroners' Decisions in Suicide and Accident Verdicts," *Medicine, Science, and Law* 41, no. 2 (2001): 111–15.

24. Dennis L. Peck, " 'Official Documentation' of the Black Suicide Experience," *Omega* 14, no. 1 (1983–84): 21–31; M. Ellen Warshauer and Mary Monk, "Problems in Suicide Statistics for Whites and Blacks," *American Journal of Public Health* 68, no. 4 (1978): 383–88; P. N. Cooper and C. M. Milroy, "The Coroner's System and Under-Reporting of Suicide," *Medicine, Science, and Law* 35, no. 4 (1995): 319–26; Speechley and Stavraky, "Adequacy of Suicide Statistics"; Daniel J. Fisher, "Equivocal Cases of Teenage Suicide," *Forensic Examiner* 9, nos. 9–10 (2000): 24–27; Gist and Welch, "Certification Change"; Emad Salib, "Coroner's Verdicts in the Elderly: A Suicide or an Open Verdict?" *International Journal of Geriatric Psychiatry* 12, no. 4 (1997): 481–83; Brendan Walsh, Dermot Walsh, and Brendan Whelan, "Suicide in Dublin," *British Journal of Psychiatry* 126 (1975): 309–12.

25. Patrick W. O'Carroll, "A Consideration of the Validity and Reliability of Suicide Mortality Data," *Suicide and Life-Threatening Behavior* 19, no. 1 (1989): 1–16; Phillips and Ruth, "Adequacy of Official Suicide Statistics."

26. Birgitta Jonasson, Ulf Jonasson, and Tom Saldeen, "Suicides May Be Overreported and Accidents Underreported among Facilities Due to Dextropropoxyphene," *Journal of Forensic Sciences* 44, no. 2 (1999): 335–56; Gary Kleck, "Miscounting Suicides," *Suicide and Life-Threatening Behavior* 18, no. 3 (1988): 219–36.

27. Pescosolido and Mendelsohn, "Social Causation or Social Construction of Suicide?"

28. Michael MacDonald and Terence R. Murphy, *Sleepless Souls: Suicide in Early Modern England* (Oxford: Clarendon Press, 1990); Phillips and Ruth, "Adequacy of Official Suicide Statistics"; Peter Sainsbury, "Validity and Reliability of Trends in Suicide Statistics," *World Health Statistical Quarterly* 36, nos. 3–4 (1983): 339–48.

29. Erwin Stengel and Norman L. Farberow, "Certification of Suicide around the World," in *Proceedings of the Fourth International Conference of Suicide Prevention*, ed. Norman L. Farberow, 8–15 (Los Angeles: Delmar Publishing Company, 1967).

30. Christopher Henry Cantor, Antoon A. Leenaars, and David Lester, "Under-Reporting of Suicide in Ireland, 1960–1989," *Archives of Suicide Research* 3, no. 1 (1997): 5–12.

31. Michael J. Kelleher, Paul Corcoran, and Helen S. Keeley, "Suicide in Ireland: Statistical, Social and Clinical Considerations," *Archives of Suicide Research* 3, no. 1 (1997): 17.

32. Peck, "Official Documentation"; Phillips and Ruth, "Adequacy of Official Suicide Statistics."

33. See http://www.mentalhealth.org/suicideprevention/calltoaction.asp (accessed May 3, 2004).

34. Sara K. Goldsmith et al., *Reducing Suicide: A National Imperative* (Washington, DC: National Academies Press, 2002), 55. See also chapter 10.

35. Breon G. Allen et al., "The Effect of Cause of Death on Responses to the Bereaved: Suicide Compared to Accident and Natural Causes," *Omega* 28, no. 1 (1993): 39–48; Michael Bloor, "A Minor Office: The Variable and Socially Constructed Character of Death Certification in a Scottish City," *Journal of Health and Social Behavior* 32 (September 1991): 273–87; Hanzlick and Goodin, "Mind Your Manners, Part III."

36. Brian M. Barraclough, Trevor Holding, and Peter Fayers, "Influence of Coroners' Officers and Pathologists on Suicide Verdicts," *British Journal of Psychiatry* 128 (1976): 471–74; John L. deJong and Randy Hanzlick, "Level of Agreement between Opinions of Medical Examiner Investigators and Forensic Pathologist Medical Examiners regarding the Manner of Death," *American Journal of Forensic Medicine and Pathology* 21, no. 1 (2000): 11–20; C. Jennings and Brian Barraclough, "Legal and Administrative Influences on the English Suicide Rate since 1900," *Psychology and Medicine* 10, no. 3 (1980): 407–18; Neeleman and Wessely, "Changes in Classification of Suicide."

37. M. W. Atkinson, Neil Kessel, and J. B. Dalgaard, "The Comparability of Suicide Rates," *British Journal of Psychiatry* 127 (1975): 247–56; Jan C. Giertsen and Inge Morild, "Reliability of Norwegian Suicide Statistics," *Nordisk Medicin* 108, no. 2 (1993): 58–59; David A. Jobes, Alan L. Berman, and Arnold R. Josselson, "Improving the Validity and Reliability of Medical-Legal Certifications of Suicide," *Suicide and Life-Threatening Behavior* 17, no. 4 (1987): 310–25; Franklyn L. Nelson, Norman L. Farberow, and Douglas R. MacKinnon, "The Certification of Suicide in Eleven Western States: An Inquiry into the Validity of Reported Suicide Rates," *Suicide and Life-Threatening Behavior* 8, no. 2 (1978): 75–88.

38. O'Carroll, "Validity and Reliability of Suicide Mortality Data."

39. William Massello III, "The Proof in Law of Suicide," *Journal of Forensic Sciences* 31, no. 3 (1985): 1000–1008.

40. DiMaio and DiMaio, *Forensic Pathology;* S. Russell Fisher, "History of Forensic Pathology and Related Sciences," in Spitz, *Medicolegal Investigation of Death,* 3–13; Froede, *Handbook of Forensic Pathology.*

41. Bass and Jefferson, *Death's Acre,* 203.

42. The decomp room was a separate, small autopsy room with one sink used exclusively for decomposed bodies. It also contained a hood for drying clothes and other materials.

43. Paul R. Vanatta and Charles S. Petty, "Limitations of the Forensic External Examination in Determining the Cause and Manner of Death," *Human Pathology* 18, no. 2 (1987): 170–74.

44. Mark L. Rosenberg et al., "Operational Criteria for the Determination of Suicide," *Journal of Forensic Sciences* 33, no. 6 (1988): 1445–55.

45. DiMaio notes that in most cases where the deceased was said to be cleaning a gun that went off, the gunshot injury shows a contact wound, and the death is therefore more likely to be a suicide than an accident. Vincent J. M. DiMaio, "Characteristics of Wounds Produced by Handguns and Rifles," in Froede, *Handbook of Forensic Pathology,* 217–25.

46. Julia Goodin and Randy Hanzlick, "Mind Your Manners, Part II: General Results

from the National Association of Medical Examiners Manner of Death Questionnaire, 1995," *American Journal of Forensic Medicine and Pathology* 18, no. 3 (1997): 224–27.

47. Edwin S. Shneidman, *The Suicidal Mind* (Oxford: Oxford University Press, 1996).

48. See, for example, Amy L. Bradfield and Gary L. Wells, "The Perceived Validity of Eyewitness Identification Testimony: A Test of the Five Biggers Criteria," *Law and Human Behavior* 24, no. 5 (2000): 581–94; Gary L. Wells, "The Psychology of Line-up Identifications," *Journal of Applied Psychology* 14 (1984): 89–104.

49. DiMaio, "Characteristics of Wounds," 223; Edwin S. Shneidman and Norman L. Farberow, eds., *Clues to Suicide* (New York: McGraw-Hill, 1957).

50. Derek Humphry, *Final Exit: The Practicalities of Self-Deliverance and Assisted Suicide for the Dying*, 3rd ed. (New York: Dell Paperbacks, 2003).

51. Peter M. Marzuk et al., "Increase in Suicide by Asphyxiation in New York City after the Publication of *Final Exit*," *Publishing Research Quarterly* 10, no. 4 (1994–95): 62–68.

52. LeBrun, *It's Time to Tell*.

53. Elizabeth Hallam, Jenny Hockey, and Glennys Howarth, *Beyond the Body: Death and Social Identity* (London: Routledge, 1999), 95.

54. H. R. M. Johnson, "The Incidence of Unnatural Deaths Which Have Been Presumed to Be Natural in Coroners' Autopsies," *Medicine, Science, and the Law* 9 (1969): 103.

55. One therapist I know explained that at the end of every therapy session, she checks off "si/hi" (suicidal ideation/homicidal ideation) as "absent" or "present," depending on the client's answers during the session. If she asks her client explicitly whether he or she intends suicide and the client denies it, she writes "client denies suicidal ideation" in her narrative. Other therapists write "client denies suicidal ideation" as a routine statement at the end of every session, regardless of whether they asked it or not. A client might report feeling suicidal but has no plan or weapon to carry out this intent; in such a case, the "suicidal ideation present" box might be checked and the therapist might still decide not to hospitalize the patient. Such a decision should be justified in the narrative part of the session report. Alana Levy, personal communication, May 10, 2001.

56. When depression is corroborated in a psychiatric file, it will be included on the death certificate as "clinical history of depression." If depression is described by relatives and friends, it might be mentioned in the autopsy report as "reported history of depression."

57. Virginia Woolf apparently killed herself by walking into the river Ouse with large stones in her coat to weigh herself down. See also Darren B. Wirthwein, Jeffrey J. Barnard, and Joseph A. Prahlow, "Suicide by Drowning: A 20 Year Review," *Journal of Forensic Sciences* 47, no. 1 (2002): 131–36.

58. See Dorothy E. Smith, "'K Is Mentally Ill': The Anatomy of a Factual Account," *Sociology* 12, no. 1 (1978): 23–53.

59. Douglas, *Social Meanings of Suicide*.

60. This is incorrect. He cursed the girlfriend, for whom he had moved to a new town. The person whom he asked to pray for him had a different female name; I suspect it was his former wife.

61. See, for example, Antoon A. Leenaars, *Suicide Notes: Predictive Clues and Patterns* (New York: Human Sciences Press, 1988); and Shneidman and Farberow, *Clues to Suicide*.

62. Edwin S. Shneidman, *Voices of Death* (New York: Harper & Row, 1980), 58.

63. Leenaars, *Suicide Notes*, 46–47.

64. A. Darbonne, "Suicide and Age: A Suicide Note Analysis," *Journal of Consulting and Clinical Psychology* 33 (1969): 46–50.

65. Shneidman, *Voices of Death*.

66. Jamison, *Night Falls Fast*, 181.

67. A. Alvarez, *The Savage God: A Study of Suicide* (New York: Random House, 1970), 237–38. But see also Peter Kramer, *Against Depression* (New York: Viking, 2005), for a book aiming to sever the link between depression and creativity.

68. Pescosolido and Mendelsohn, "Social Causation or Social Construction of Suicide?" 97.

69. Paul Atkinson, "Training for Certainty," *Social Science and Medicine* 19, no. 9 (1984): 949–56; Renée C. Fox, "Training for Uncertainty," in *The Student Physician*, ed. Robert K. Merton, G. Reader, and P. L. Kendall, 207–41 (Cambridge, MA: Harvard University Press, 1957); Fox, "Medical Uncertainty Revisited," in *The Handbook of Social Studies in Health and Medicine*, ed. Gary L. Albrecht, Ray Fitzpatrick, and Susan C. Scrimshaw, 409–22 (London: SAGE, 2000); Donald W. Light, "Uncertainty and Control in Professional Training," *Journal of Health and Social Behavior* 20, no. 4 (1979): 310–22; Stefan Timmermans and Alison Angell, "Evidence-Based Medicine, Clinical Uncertainty, and Learning to Doctor," *Journal of Health and Social Behavior* 42, no. 4 (2001): 342–59.

70. Massello, "Proof in Law," 1002–3.

71. Anspach, *Deciding Who Lives*.

72. Hallam, Hockey, and Howarth, *Beyond the Body*, 101.

73. Atkinson, Kessel, and Dalgaard, "Comparability of Suicide Rates," 248; Massello, "Proof in Law."

74. Becker, *Outsiders*.

75. Randy Hanzlick, "Lawsuits against Medical Examiners or Coroners Arising from Death Certificates," *American Journal of Forensic Medicine and Pathology* 18, no. 2 (1997): 119–23; Massello, "Proof in Law."

76. Michael MacDonald, "The Medicalization of Suicide in England: Laymen, Physicians, and Cultural Change, 1500–1870," *Milbank Quarterly* 67, suppl. 1 (1989): 69–91.

77. This is not totally correct. Rulings by medical examiners are not binding for insurance companies, but they do carry a heavy weight.

78. S. Bromberg and Christine K. Cassel, "Suicide in the Elderly: The Limits of Paternalism," *Journal of the American Geriatrics Society* 31, no. 11 (1983): 698–703; Alexander C. Leighton and Charles C. Hughes, "Notes on Eskimo Patterns of Suicide," *Southwestern Journal of Anthropology* 11 (1955): 327–38.

79. Fisher, "Equivocal Cases of Teenage Suicide," 26.

80. Elliot G. Mishler, *Discourse of Medicine* (Norwood, NJ: Ablex, 1984).

81. Erving Goffman, *Stigma: Notes on the Management of Spoiled Identity* (New York: Touchstone, 1963); Bruce Link and Jo C. Phelan, "Conceptualizing Stigma," *Annual Review of Sociology* 27 (2001): 63–85.

82. Schmidt et al., "Suicide by Vehicular Crash."

83. DiMaio and DiMaio, *Forensic Pathology*, 272.

84. Jonasson, Jonasson, and Saldeen, "Suicides May Be Overreported."

85. Even when researchers retrospectively conduct extensive psychological autopsies, the number of suicides discovered remains relatively small (three cases out of 278 deaths were reclassified in one study; Schmidt et al., "Suicide by Vehicular Crash").

86. Anspach, *Deciding Who Lives*, chap. 5. Needless to say, my use of "organizational ecology" has little to do with the formal theory proposed by Hannan and Freeman to account for the diversity, selection, adaptation, and survival of organizations. Michael T. Hannan and John Freeman, "The Population Ecology of Organizations," *American Journal of Sociology* 83 (1977): 929–84. My use is closer to the interactionist conceptualization proposed by Robert Park and grounded in human-ecology theory.

87. Donald MacKenzie refers to this phenomenon as the "certainty trough": those at intermediate social distances from the production of technical knowledge appear to evince greater certainty than those who take part directly in its production. Donald MacKenzie, *Mechanizing Proof: Computing, Risk, and Trust* (Cambridge, MA: MIT Press, 2001), 333–34. See also Ludwik Fleck, *Genesis and Development of a Scientific Fact* (Chicago: University of Chicago Press, 1979; first published 1935).

88. Ian Hacking, *Rewriting the Soul* (Princeton, NJ: Princeton University Press, 1995), 61.

89. T. Kircher, J. Nelson, and H. Burdo, "The Autopsy as a Measure of Accuracy of the Death Certificate," *New England Journal of Medicine* 313, no. 20 (1985): 1267–73.

90. Monroe G. Sirken et al., "The Quality of Cause-of-Death Statistics," *Journal of Public Health* 77, no. 2 (1987): 137–39.

91. See Jonasson, Jonasson, and Saldeen, "Suicides May Be Overreported."

92. See Pescosolido and Mendelsohn, "Social Causation or Social Construction of Suicide?"; Robert Dingwall, John Eekelaar, and Topsy Murray, *The Protection of Children* (Oxford: Basil Blackwell, 1983), 52.

93. Donald MacKenzie, *Inventing Accuracy: A Historical Sociology of Nuclear Missile Guidance* (Cambridge, MA: MIT Press, 1993).

94. Randy Hanzlick, "On the Need for More Expertise in Death Investigation," *Archives of Pathology and Laboratory Medicine* 120 (1996): 329–32; Hanzlick and Goodin, "Mind Your Manners, Part III."

95. Teresa L. Crume et al., "Underascertainment of Child Maltreatment Fatalities by Death Certificates, 1990–1998," *Pediatrics* 110, no. 2 (2002): 18–23; Marie Lundstrom and Rochelle Sharpe, "Getting Away with Murder," *Public Welfare* 49, no. 3 (1991): 18–29.

96. American Academy of Pediatrics, "Investigation and Review of Unexpected Infant and Child Deaths," *Pediatrics* 104, no. 5 (1999): 1158–60; Michael Durfee, Deanne T. Durfee, and M. Patricia West, "Child Fatality Review: An International Movement," *Child Abuse and Neglect* 26, nos. 6–7 (2002): 619–36.

97. Ibid.; George A. Gellert et al., "Fatalities Assessed by the Orange County Child Death Review Team," *Child Abuse and Neglect* 19, no. 7 (1995): 875–83; Joseph D. Hatina, "Shaken Baby Syndrome: Who Are the True Experts?" *Cleveland State Law Review* 46 (1998): 557–83.

98. Hanzlick, "Medicolegal Death Investigation System."

99. Stefan Timmermans and Marc Berg, *The Gold Standard: The Challenge of Evidence-Based Medicine and Standardization in Health Care* (Philadelphia: Temple University Press, 2003).

100. Schmidt et al., "Suicide by Vehicular Crash."

101. Shneidman, *Voices of Death.*

102. Stephen Turner, "What Is the Problem with Experts?" *Social Studies of Science* 31, no. 1 (2001): 133.

CHAPTER THREE

1. Turner, "What Is the Problem with Experts?" 145.

2. Personal e-mail communication, August 22, 2001.

3. I measured the distance at eleven steps.

4. Steven Shapin, "Cordelia's Love: Credibility and the Social Studies of Science," *Perspectives on Science* 3, no. 3 (1995): 255–75.

5. See Bal, "How to Kill with a Ballpoint," for an analysis of how expertise is achieved in a Dutch inquisitorial system rather than a U.S. adversarial justice system.

6. Sheila Jasanoff, "The Eye of Everyman: Witnessing DNA in the Simpson Trial," *Social Studies of Science* 28, nos. 5–6 (1998): 731.

7. Augustine Brannigan and Michael Lynch, "On Bearing False Witness: Credibility as an Interactional Accomplishment," *Journal of Contemporary Ethnography* 16, no. 2 (1987): 115–46.

8. William R. Levesque, "Medical Examiner Retires," *St. Petersburg Times,* June 29, 2000. The case involved the death of Scientologist Lisa McPherson. Wood traced the death to a blood clot in McPherson's left lung. When prosecutors charged the church with neglecting a disabled adult and practicing medicine without a license, she changed her mind and called the death accidental. Her resignation led to a review of more than 150 cases in her office.

9. Barry Siegel, "Judging Parents as Murderers on Four Specks of Blood," *Los Angeles Times,* July 11, 1999.

10. Donohoe, "Evidence-Based Medicine and Shaken Baby Syndrome," 241.

11. The full transcripts are available from the Middlesex County Superior Court in Cambridge, Massachusetts. The trial excerpts given in this chapter were taken from http://www.sbs-resource.org/map.htm in July 2003 (this site has now been discontinued). A great limitation of my analysis is that I was unable to get access to the visual displays used at the trial and did not observe tapes of the actual demeanor of expert witnesses. On the importance of visualization, see Tal Golan, "The Emergence of the Silent Witness: The Legal and Medical Reception of X-Rays in the USA," *Social Studies of Science* 34, no. 4 (2004): 469–99; and Jasanoff, "The Eye of Everyman."

I will reference the speakers at the trial on the basis of whether they were on direct, cross, re-direct, or re-cross-examination, using the page numbers of a printout of the Web site given above. All references are from the *Commonwealth v. Woodward* trial, unless otherwise noted. If the examination of a witness was spread over two days, I will indicate with "1" or "2" from which day the testimony came. Counsel Barry Scheck carried all direct and cross-examination for the defense, while Gerald Leone Jr. led direct examination for the prosecution and Martha Coakley conducted cross-examination for the prosecution.

12. In his opening statement, the judge put the task before the jury in the following terms: "The Government has to prove beyond a reasonable doubt that Louise Woodward intentionally performed an act which, in the circumstances known to her, created what a reasonably prudent person in her position would have known, according to common experience, created, that is, a plain and strong likelihood that the act would cause death. That's one of the things that the Government has to prove. The second thing that the Government has to prove is that the act was committed with extreme cruelty or atrocity. The Government does not have to prove motive, the Government does not have to prove that Ms. Woodward acted with deliberate premeditation, the Government does not have to prove that she knew or believed that her act was extremely atrocious or extremely cruel, so long as the Government proves that a reasonable person would have regarded it as such." *Woodward,* Zobel opening statement, 18–20.

13. *Woodward,* prosecution opening statement, 1.

14. *Woodward,* defense opening statement, 3.

15. *Woodward,* prosecution opening statement, 1.

16. *Woodward,* defense opening statement, 1.

17. Ibid., 3.

18. Ibid., 2.

19. Starr, *Social Transformation of Medicine.*

20. Jasanoff, "The Eye of Everyman," 723.

21. This claim of originality was disputed by Dr. Baden later in the trial.

22. *Woodward,* Leestma 1, cross-examination, 9.

23. Ibid.

24. *Woodward,* Leestma 2, cross-examination, 9.

25. Ibid., 15.

26. *Woodward,* Gean, cross-examination, 7.

27. Arthur Daemmrich, "The Evidence Does Not Speak for Itself: Expert Witnesses and the Organization of DNA-Typing Companies," *Social Studies of Science* 28, nos. 5–6 (1998): 746.

28. He had written a popular trade book aimed at a general audience but was not examined on its content. Michael M. Baden, *Unnatural Death: Confessions of a Medical Examiner* (New York: Random House, 1989).

29. According to a CV posted at http://www.selets.com (accessed September 21, 2004), Dr. Baden became a resident in pathology at New York's Bellevue Hospital in 1961. At the time of the trial, his career had spanned thirty-six years. Twenty thousand autopsies averages about 555 per year. The National Association of Medical Examiners bars certification of a medical examiner's office if pathologists conduct more than 350 autopsies yearly.

30. Harry M. Collins and Robert Evans, "The Third Wave of Science Studies: Studies of Expertise and Experience," *Social Studies of Science* 32, no. 2 (2002): 235–96. I disagree with Collins and Evans's focus on experience only at the expense of institutionalized credentialing. See Sheila Jasanoff, "Breaking the Waves in Science Studies: Comment on H. M. Collins and Robert Evans, 'The Third Wave of Science Studies,'" *Social Studies of Science* 33, no. 3 (2003): 389–400.

31. *Woodward,* Baden 1, cross-examination, 5–6.

32. Ibid., 6.

33. That case was *Massachusetts v. Azar* (Middlesex County, 1989).

34. *Woodward,* Baden 1, cross-examination, 8.

35. Joseph S. Oteri, Marty S. Weinberg, and Marty S. Pinales, "Cross Examination of Chemists," in *Science in Context: Readings in the History and Philosophy of Science,* ed. Barry Barnes and David Edge, 250–59 (Milton Keynes, UK: Open University Press, 1982).

36. Daemmrich, "Evidence."

37. *Woodward,* Feigin, cross-examination, 1.

38. *Woodward,* DeGirolami, cross-examination, 43.

39. *Woodward,* Feigin, cross-examination, 2.

40. The two additional rulings were *General Electric Co. v. Joiner* in 1997 and *Kumho Tire Co. v. Carmichael* in 1999. See National Research Council, *The Age of Expert Testimony: Science in the Courtroom* (Washington, DC: National Research Council, 2000).

41. Michael Saks, "Banishing Ipse Dixit: The Impact of Kumho Tire on Forensic Identification Sciences," *Washington and Lee University Law Review* 57 (2000): 879–900.

42. Gary Edmond and David Mercer, "Trashing 'Junk Science,'" *Stanford Technology Law Review* 3 (1998): 1–31; Edward J. Imwinkelried, "The Meaning of 'Appropriate Validation' in Daubert v. Merrell Dow Pharmaceuticals, Inc., Interpreted in Light of the Broader Rationalist Tradition, Not the Narrow Scientific Tradition," *Florida State University Law Review* 30 (2003): 735; Michael D. Risinger, "Preliminary Thoughts on a Functional Taxonomy of Expertise for the Post-Kumho World," *Seton Hall Law Review* 31 (2000): 508–37.

43. Saks, "Banishing Ipse Dixit."

44. *Woodward,* prosecution closing argument, 3.

45. *Woodward,* defense closing argument, 3–4.

46. *Woodward,* Leestma 1, cross-examination, 10.

47. *Woodward,* Baden 1, direct examination, 2. I am not the only observer to characterize

Baden in this way; see also Jessica Snyder Sachs, *Corpse: Nature, Forensics, and the Struggle to Pinpoint the Time of Death* (Cambridge, MA: Perseus Publishing, 2001).

48. Shapin, "Cordelia's Love," 265.

49. *Woodward,* Baden 2, cross-examination, 3.

50. Saul Halfon, "Collecting, Testing and Convincing: Forensic DNA Experts in the Courts," *Social Studies of Science* 28, nos. 5–6 (1998): 801–28.

51. Dr. Ommaya added, however, that in his opinion, Dr. Feigin's autopsy report was incomplete because it did not include histology. *Woodward,* Ommaya, cross-examination, 2.

52. *Woodward,* the charge, 4.

53. Harry M. Collins, *Changing Order: Replication and Induction in Scientific Practice* (London: SAGE, 1985); Bruno Latour, *The Pasteurization of France* (Cambridge, MA: Harvard University Press, 1988).

54. *Woodward,* Feigin, direct examination, 2.

55. Steven Shapin and Simon Schaffer, *Leviathan and the Air-Pump* (Princeton, NJ: Princeton University Press, 1985), 65.

56. *Woodward,* DeGirolami 2, direct examination, 2.

57. *Woodward,* DeGirolami, cross-examination, 36–37.

58. Harold Garfinkel, *Studies in Ethnomethodology* (Englewood Cliffs, NJ: Prentice-Hall, 1967); Lynch, *Scientific Practice and Ordinary Action.* A prime example of the inability of rules to capture work is the six-page manual of the British Standards Institution on how to make a cup of tea (BS-6008).

59. The gross autopsy revealed "massive right hemispheric disruption associated with epidural, intradural, subdural, and subarachnoid hemorrhage," "subfalcine herniation from right to left," and "bilateral inferior frontal lobe disruption." The microscopic analysis of the dura showed "acute subdural hematoma and intradural hemorrhage" and no signs of old bleeds. The right frontal cortex of the brain was destroyed, the right thalamus area was injured, the pons showed necrosis, the cerebellum exhibited reactive changes, the left frontal cortex showed acute hypoxic ischemic injury, and the midbrain contained widespread evolving infarction. *Woodward,* DeGirolami, cross-examination, 39–40.

60. Ibid., 41.

61. *Woodward,* Leestma, direct examination, 37.

62. Ibid., 11.

63. Dr. Leestma did not go over the major brain and skull injuries covered by Dr. DeGirolami; rather, he offered new evidence. He had created three to four magnifications of each of four additional dura sections and discussed these enlargements at length. Comparing the magnifications to a chart for dating subdural hematomas, he pointed out the existence of a membrane that he labeled a "neomembrane" and described it as "something that is probably related to a resolving subdural." He showed the jury traces of calcium deposits and identified them as signs of an older injury. On different magnifications, he pointed to red blood cells as signs of a weeks-old injury. He also found capillary formation and about thirteen layers of fibroblasts; and on a piece of the dura closer to the skull fracture, he located osteoblasts, all signs of healing.

64. *Woodward,* Leestma, direct examination, 21–22.

65. Michael Lynch, "The Discursive Production of Uncertainty: The OJ Simpson 'Dream Team' and the Sociology of Knowledge Machine," *Social Studies of Science* 28, nos. 5–6 (1998): 829–68.

66. The preservation of evidence came up even before the autopsy was discussed. The neurosurgeon who had performed Matthew's emergency surgery, Dr. Joseph Madsen, de-

scribed how when he opened the skull, a blood clot with the consistency of "currant jelly" squirted out at him and his assistant. When Scheck confronted the surgeon with his hospital's rules about the preservation of specimens removed at surgery, the physician admitted that the blood clot had not been preserved. He explained that it was too runny to preserve and that his first priority was to save the life of Matthew Eappen. Scheck asked Dr. Madsen and other witnesses whether the clot could have been preserved and could have been dated based on the growth of capillaries. He insinuated that the missing clot was the crucial piece of evidence that could have scientifically settled how old the subdural hematoma in Matthew's brain was. In addition, the prosecution did not send the skull fracture to a lab for aging—because, they argued, skull fractures heal very slowly, and the test would not have provided any information. The skull was instead buried with the rest of Matthew's remains. Several defense witnesses argued that the skull fracture could have been sectioned and dated, similarly to the wrist fracture, which was sent to the lab and came back as three weeks old.

67. *Woodward,* DeGirolami, cross-examination, 27.

68. Ibid., 32.

69. *Woodward,* DeGirolami, re-cross-examination, 3.

70. *Woodward,* DeGirolami, cross-examination, 46–47.

71. Lynch, "Discursive Production of Uncertainty." Scheck had used the same tactic in the Simpson trial. See Jasanoff, "The Eye of Everyman," 729–30.

72. *Woodward,* Leestma, direct examination, 35.

73. *Woodward,* Leestma 1, cross-examination, 11.

74. Ibid., 34.

75. Ibid.

76. Ibid., 30.

77. *Woodward,* Leestma 2, cross-examination, 34.

78. The judge wondered why the medical examiner's office would have an anthropologist on staff. Her main role was to help identify skeletal remains.

79. *Woodward,* DeGirolami 1, direct examination, 10.

80. Steven Shapin, *A Social History of Truth: Civility and Science in Seventeenth-Century England* (Chicago: University of Chicago Press, 1994).

81. *Woodward,* Baden 2, direct examination, 2.

82. *Woodward,* Leestma, direct examination, 34.

83. Judge Zobel allowed defense counsel to indicate what tests they would have conducted and the importance of those tests. He did not allow speculation about the likely test results.

84. On the Duhem-Quine thesis, see Imre Lakatos, "Falsification and the Methodology of Research Programmes," in *Criticism and the Growth of Knowledge,* ed. Imre Lakatos and A. Musgrave, 91–195 (Cambridge: Cambridge University Press, 1970). On interpretative flexibility, see Collins, *Changing Order.*

85. MacKenzie, *Inventing Accuracy;* Steven Shapin, "The Politics of Observation: Cerebral Anatomy and Social Interests in the Edinburgh Phrenology Disputes," in *On the Margins of Science: The Social Construction of Rejected Knowledge,* ed. Roy Wallis, 139–78 (Keele, UK: Keele University Press, 1979).

86. Collins, *Changing Order.*

87. John Abraham, "Distributing the Benefit of the Doubt: Scientists, Regulators, and Drug Safety," *Science, Technology, and Human Values* 19, no. 4 (1994): 493–522; Karin Garrety, "Social Worlds, Actor-Networks and Controversy: The Case of Cholesterol, Dietary Fat and Heart Disease," *Social Studies of Science* 27, no. 5 (1997): 727–73; Sheila Jasanoff, *Science at the Bar: Law, Science, and Technology in America* (Cambridge, MA: Harvard University Press,

1995); Evelleen Richards, *Vitamin C and Cancer: Medicine or Politics?* (London: Macmillan, 1991); Brian Wynne, "Establishing the Rules of Laws: Constructing Expert Authority," in *Expert Evidence: Interpreting Science in the Law*, ed. Roger Smith and Brian Wynne, 23–55 (London: Routledge, 1989).

88. Michael Lynch, "Discipline and the Material Form of Images: An Analysis of Scientific Visibility," *Social Studies of Science* 15, no. 1 (1985): 37–66.

89. *Woodward*, Feigin, re–direct examination, 2.

90. See Andrew Pickering, "Constraints on Controversy: The Case of the Magnetic Monopole," *Social Studies of Science* 11, no. 1 (1981): 63–93.

91. On the history of the use of visual technologies in expert testimony, see Golan, "Emergence of the Silent Witness."

92. *Woodward*, Leestma, direct examination, 54.

93. *Woodward*, Baden 1, direct examination, 6.

94. Brannigan and Lynch, "On Bearing False Witness," 127–35; Michael Lynch and David Boden, *The Spectacle of History: Speech, Text, and Memory at the Iran-Contra Hearings* (Durham, NC: Duke University Press, 1996), 141.

95. Lynch and Boden, *The Spectacle of History*, 122.

96. In their final exchange about absorption of impacts by fatty tissue in children's skulls, Dr. Baden's opinion contradicted earlier testimony by another expert defense witness, Dr. Lawrence Thibault. When Dr. Baden agreed with Coakley, she scored a bonus point for credibility bashing.

97. *Woodward*, Baden 1, cross-examination, 18–20.

98. Ibid., 21.

99. But even lawyers less familiar with the scientific techniques and underlying principles relevant to child-abuse cases might raise credibility questions. Daemmrich, "Evidence," 746.

100. Siegel, "Judging Parents as Murderers."

101. *Woodward*, Feigin, direct examination, 12.

102. *Woodward*, Leestma, direct examination, 51.

103. *Woodward*, Leestma 2, cross-examination, 46.

104. *Woodward*, prosecution closing argument, 1.

105. Fox, "Training for Uncertainty"; Fox, "Medical Uncertainty Revisited"; Timmermans and Angell, "Evidence-Based Medicine."

106. Hiller B. Zobel, *Memorandum and Order in Commonwealth of Massachusetts v. Louise Woodward*, Commonwealth of Massachusetts, Superior Court of Middlesex, ss. 97–0433, November 10, 1997.

107. Scheck admitted after the trial that the jury research had been flawed. More people from working classes believed Louise Woodward to be innocent. Both the defense and the prosecution had stacked the jury with highly educated people, because they wanted the jury to grasp the scientific evidence. On questioning jury trials, see P. Anand Rao, "Keeping the Science Court Out of the Jurybox: Helping the Jury Manage Scientific Evidence," *Social Epistemology* 13, no. 2 (1999): 129–45. Judge Zobel, a former academic, had also written about the effectiveness of jury trials. Hiller B. Zobel, "The Jury on Trial," *American Heritage* 46, no. 4 (1995): 42–52.

108. Harvey Silverglate, "Science and the Au Pair Trial," *Wall Street Journal*, November 11, 1997.

109. David L. Chadwick et al., "Shaken Baby Syndrome—a Forensic Pediatric Response," *Pediatrics* 101, no. 2 (1998): 321–23.

110. John Plunkett, "Shaken Baby Syndrome and the Death of Matthew Eappen," *Amer-*

ican Journal of Forensic Medicine and Pathology 20, no. 1 (1999): 17–21. See also Stephen D. Cohle, Anthony Foster, and Sandra L. Cottingham, "Shaken Baby Syndrome," *American Journal of Forensic Medicine and Pathology* 21, no. 2 (2000): 198–99; and Cyril H. Wecht, "Shaken Baby Syndrome," *American Journal of Forensic Medicine and Pathology* 20, no. 3 (1999): 301–2.

111. Mark Hansen, "Why Are Iowa's Babies Dying?" *ABA Journal* 84 (1998): 47–78.

112. Mary E. Case et al., "Position Paper on Fatal Abusive Head Injuries in Infants and Young Children," *American Journal of Forensic Medicine and Pathology* 22, no. 2 (2001): 112–22.

113. I work this out in chapter 5.

114. Turner, "What Is the Problem with Experts?"

115. Roger Smith goes even further; he considers forensic pathologists subservient to the law. "Forensic Pathology, Scientific Expertise, and the Criminal Law," in Smith and Wynne, *Expert Evidence.*

116. Jasanoff, "Judicial Fictions."

117. Daemmrich, "Evidence."

118. Edmond and Mercer, "Trashing 'Junk Science.' " This article uses the term "law-science hybrid."

119. Roger Smith and Brian Wynne, "Introduction," in *Expert Evidence,* 15.

120. Historian Arthur Daemmrich documented the case of DNA typing. During the 1980s, private DNA laboratories spun off from larger companies as subsidiaries or became entrepreneurial start-ups to offer their DNA-typing identification services. Paternity and forensic testing involved extracting DNA segments, testing them with probes, and calculating a match based on statistical population probabilities. These companies initially relied on competitive-marketing principles to distinguish themselves from their competitors (e.g., quoting endorsements by district attorneys) and asserted their credibility in courtroom testimonies by describing their procedures. In 1989, defense counsel in *N. Y. v. Castro* questioned the credibility of one of these firms. The company's scientific expert had claimed a match between the blood of two victims and blood found on the watch of the defendant and reported the odds of a random match as one in 100 million. Defense experts heavily criticized the laboratory's protocols, production of DNA profiles, and use of population statistics (one expert arrived at odds of one in 24), and the court ruled that the test's reliability had not been adequately established. This courtroom event initiated a defining moment of introspection for the industry. Moves to tighten the credibility of the DNA technologies led not only to more standardized and regulated laboratory practices, but also to a reorganization of the entire industry. While many factors and agencies contributed to the vertical integration of the companies (Daemmrich, "Evidence"; Jasanoff, "The Eye of Everyman"), it was clear that without reorganization, the credibility of DNA typing would remain vulnerable in courts. Interestingly, the firms aimed to circumvent courtroom-credibility questions with external validation through voluntary credentialing, standardization, and peer review. Still, as we saw in the Woodward case, such strategies can cut two ways in the legal-credibility struggles: a deviation from standards and peer review offers a clear opportunity to damage an expert's credibility.

Another group whose livelihood depends on courtroom testimony, fingerprinting experts, seemed to have achieved immunity against the courtroom-credibility struggles, but the uniqueness of these experts reveals a professional weakness that confirms the importance of the courtroom as the reference point for their work practices. As historian Simon Cole indicates, even for fingerprinting, the peculiar organization of experts, the standardization of their practices, and a system of independent validation were defensively instituted to ward off credibility challenges in court. Simon A. Cole, *Suspect Identities: A History of Fingerprinting and Criminal Identification* (Cambridge, MA: Harvard University Press, 2001); Cole, "Witnessing Identification:

Latent Fingerprinting Evidence and Expert Knowledge," *Social Studies of Science* 28, nos. 5–6 (1998): 687–712. The credibility of fingerprinting experts had been maintained because in the early twentieth century, when the technique entered the courtroom, latent-fingerprint examiners closed professional ranks and refused to testify against each other. Fingerprinting examiners adopted the injunction that "the testimony of a finger print expert is not subject to contradiction by another finger print expert" (Frederick Kuhne, quoted in Cole, "Witnessing Identification," 703), and they claimed absolute certainty and professional interchangeability for their interpretations. Fingerprinting experts were thus able to black-box their entire practice in court, obtaining the enviable status of unchallengeable expert authorities. When a fingerprint expert made an apparent error, his certification was swiftly revoked, sacrificing the individual for the credibility of the technique. Still, the risks in this high-standard strategy became apparent when a judge recently questioned whether fingerprinting was based on a scientific discipline and threatened to render the entire practice inadmissible because it did not meet the general-acceptance test of *Daubert.* Because fingerprinting had never been scientifically validated, the practice seemed an anachronism in contemporary courts.

121. Impression management also counts in maintaining professional credibility: Dr. Cahill was adamant that no kitchen tools enter the autopsy room, but that more expensive—and occasionally less versatile—surgical tools be used.

122. Edmond and Mercer, "Trashing 'Junk Science.'"

CHAPTER FOUR

1. Laurent Fanton et al., "The Perfect Crime: Myth or Reality?" *American Journal of Forensic Medicine and Pathology* 19, no. 3 (1998): 290. For some near misses, see Arthur E. Westveer, John J. Trestrail, and Anthony J. Pinizotti, "Homicidal Poisonings in the United States: An Analysis of the Uniform Crime Reports from 1980 through 1989," *American Journal of Forensic Medicine and Pathology* 17, no. 4 (1996): 282–88. The true-crime collections by forensic pathologists also play on this theme: Baden, *Unnatural Death;* Noguchi, *Coroner;* Thomas T. Noguchi, *Coroner at Large,* with Joseph DiMona (New York: Simon & Schuster, 1985); Morton Shulman, *Coroner* (Toronto: Fitzhenry & Whiteside, 1975); Tom Tullett, *Clues to Murder* (London: The Bodley Head, 1986); Cyril H. Wecht, *Grave Secrets: A Leading Forensic Expert Reveals the Startling Truth about O.J. Simpson, David Koresh, Vincent Foster, and Other Sensational Cases* (New York: Penguin Books, 1996); Wecht, Curriden, and Wecht, *Cause of Death.*

2. Spitz, *Medicolegal Investigation of Death,* 175.

3. Ibid., 176.

4. Classifying a death as a forensic homicide does not necessarily mean that it will be prosecuted as a crime. Medical examiners are part of the fact-finding of criminal investigations, and their conclusions are not considered legally binding for criminal justice purposes. Still, as the Louise Woodward trial shows, prosecutors need medical examiners as witnesses. In practice, therefore, district attorneys and medical examiners consult closely before a pathologist writes "homicide" on a death certificate.

5. S. Leigh Star, "Power, Technologies, and the Phenomenology of Conventions: On Being Allergic to Onions," in *A Sociology of Monsters: Essays on Power, Technology and Domination,* ed. John Law, 26–56 (London: Routledge, 1991); Stefan Timmermans and Marc Berg, "Standardization in Action: Achieving Local Universality through Medical Protocols," *Social Studies of Science* 26, no. 4 (1997): 769–99.

6. Eliot Freidson, *Professionalism Reborn: Theory, Prophecy, and Policy* (Chicago: University of Chicago Press, 1994).

7. "Rifles and guns have rifled barrels. A series of parallel spiral grooves have been cut the length of the interior of the barrel. . . . When a bullet is fired down a rifled barrel, the rifling imparts to the bullet a number of markings that are called 'class characteristics.' . . . In addition, imperfections in the metal forming the surfaces of the lands and grooves mark the bullet, producing 'individual characteristics.' These are specific for each barrel just as fingerprints are for each person." DiMaio, "Characteristics of Wounds," 218.

8. The following table shows a breakdown of the 183 homicides from 1996 to 2000 by several characteristics. Some deaths combined several modes of death; I classified them according to what the medical examiner considered the most lethal mode of death. Thus, if a death included a fatal gunshot wound with blunt-force trauma, I classified it as a gunshot wound.

	1996	1997	1998	1999	2000	Total
Age						
<1	1	1	2	0	1	5 (3%)
1–10	2	2	1	4	0	9 (5%)
11–20	7	6	6	9	9	37 (20%)
21–30	7	9	11	7	21	55 (30%)
31–40	9	5	9	9	11	43 (23%)
41–60	4	7	2	4	5	22 (12%)
61+	5	3	0	3	1	12 (7%)
Average age	32	32	24	36	27	30
Sex						
Male	22	24	24	26	40	136 (74%)
Female	13	9	7	10	8	47 (26%)
Race						
White	19	19	13	14	19	84 (46%)
Black	10	8	11	6	14	49 (27%)
Hispanic	5	4	6	14	12	41 (22%)
Other/unknown	1	2	1	2	3	9 (5%)
Mode						
Gunshot wound	16	15	16	22	31	100 (55%)
Blunt-force trauma	7	7	4	9	5	32 (17%)
Stabbing	4	5	5	4	8	26 (14%)
Strangulation	2	2	2	0	1	7 (4%)
Hit-and-run	6	3	2	1	2	14 (8%)
Other/unknown	0	1	2	0	1	4 (2%)
TOTAL	35	33	31	36	48	183 (100%)

9. David F. Luckenbill, "Criminal Homicide as a Situated Transaction," *Social Problems* 25, no. 2 (1977): 176–86.

10. I will discuss this case in more detail in the next chapter.

11. This division of labor, with the police responsible for the scene and the medical examiner responsible for the body, is legally defined. See, for example, the lawsuit by coroner William T. Anderson against the City of Bloomington in the McLean County, Illinois, Eleventh Circuit Court. In that case, the coroner was denied access to a possible crime scene and a corpse after the police secured it. The court confirmed that no law

enforcement officer can obstruct a coroner from performing the duties of his office. See http://www.ilcoroners.org/anderson%20lawsuit.htm (accessed December 31, 2003).

12. Such relationships go beyond cooperation on specific investigations. Concerned with understaffing and a heavy caseload in one crucial homicide unit—inexperienced or over-worked law enforcement units might hinder a homicide investigation, particularly in low-profile, difficult-to-prosecute cases—Dr. Cahill contacted the police chief, offering to provide political support for more hires. These favors are returned. When Dr. Bill Bass, a forensic anthropologist who has conducted pioneering research on the decomposition rate of corpses, became the subject of a highly critical TV show, he turned to his many friends among district attorneys and police. The legislation that would have rendered the donation of bodies for forensic research more difficult was tabled. Bass and Jefferson, *Death's Acre,* 200–209.

13. See Noguchi, *Coroner,* 205–8, for a murder case based on insulin injections. This case also fits in with the analysis that follows about iatrogenic deaths. The perpetrator was a medical professional, and his actions would have remained undetected if he had not benefited financially from the death. He was not caught until his seventh murder.

14. Westveer, Trestrail, and Pinizotti, "Homicidal Poisonings," 287.

15. Dingwall, Eekelaar, and Murray, *The Protection of Children,* 82.

16. The assumption that people talk thus presumes a rationality entailing the need to unburden oneself of guilt feelings. Such a rationality seems to be contradicted by the extensive psychiatric literature on the criminal mind, particularly its ability to rationalize "deviant" behavior. Serial killer Jeffrey Dahmer, for example, was diagnosed by a psychiatrist as "having a mixed personality disorder with sadistic, obsessive, fetishistic, anti-social, necrophilic features, typical of what has been called the organized, nonsocial, lust murderer." Jeffrey Jentzen et al., "Destructive Hostility: The Jeffrey Dahmer Case; A Psychiatric and Forensic Study of a Serial Killer," *American Journal of Forensic Medicine and Pathology* 15, no. 4 (1994): 283–94. Law enforcement agents rely on the FBI's profiling of serial killers: the organized, nonsocial killers, for example, are intelligent and socially and sexually "competent"; they are skilled workers, live with a partner, drive late-model cars, and follow their crimes in the media. They tend to use restraints on the victim, hide or transport the body, remove the weapon from the scene, and molest the victim prior to death, and they are methodological in their style of killing. Robert A. Ressler, Ann W. Burgess, and John E. Douglas, *Sexual Homicide: Patterns and Motives* (Lexington, MA: Lexington Books, 1988). The psychiatric literature thus suggests that criminals have a deviant morality different from the common morality.

17. Dead infants, another category of suspicious death that has been presumed for centuries to contain hidden homicides, will be discussed in the next chapter.

18. The summary of Dr. Shipman's case is based on Kurt Eichenwald, "Deadly House Calls," *New York Times,* May 13, 2001; Derrick J. Pounder, "The Case of Dr. Shipman," *American Journal of Forensic Medicine and Pathology* 24, no. 3 (2003): 219–26; and Janet Smith, "Third Report: Death Certification and the Investigation of Deaths by Coroners," in *The Shipman Inquiry,* 530 (Norwich, UK, 2003).

19. James B. Stewart, *Blind Eye: How the Medical Establishment Let a Doctor Get Away with Murder* (New York: Simon & Schuster, 1999).

20. Richard Perez-Pena, David Kocieniewski, and Jason George, "Death on the Night Shift," *New York Times,* February 29, 2004.

21. Ibid.

22. James M. Thunder, "Quiet Killings in Medical Facilities: Detection and Prevention," *Issues in Law and Medicine* 18 (2003): 211. I have added the two cases I have discovered since 2003 to the eighteen described in this article.

23. In the United States, these include all deaths due to trauma, deaths that occur under anesthesia or in the post-anesthetic period without the patient's having regained consciousness, all deaths thought to be instances of "therapeutic or diagnostic misadventure," all deaths occurring withing twenty-four hours of admission to a health care facility, all cases in which the patient is dead on arrival at the hospital, and all deaths for whose cause the attending physician has no adequate or reasonable explanation.

24. Hanzlick, "Medicolegal Death Investigation System."

25. Even then, inconsistencies persist. Nurses accused Dr. Swango of injecting a patient when it was not indicated; the patient almost died, but an internal hospital investigation dismissed the nurses' accusations as rumormongering. Stewart, *Blind Eye*. Similar interventions and suspicions marked the career of nurse Charles Cullen. Perez-Pena, Kocieniewski, and George, "Death on the Night Shift."

26. Hill and Anderson, *The Autopsy.*

27. Stewart, *Blind Eye*, 87.

28. Hill and Anderson, *The Autopsy,* 110.

29. Joseph P. Pestaner, "End-of-Life Care: Forensic Medicine v. Palliative Medicine," *Journal of Law, Medicine, and Ethics* 31 (Fall 2003): 371.

30. See also Hanzlick, "Medicolegal Death Investigation System," 10.

31. Lundberg, "Role of the Medicolegal Autopsy," 45. Medicare pays for autopsies but does not require that autopsies actually be conducted.

32. Andrew L. Falzon and Gregory G. Davis, "A 15-Year Retrospective Review of Homicide in the Elderly," *Journal of Forensic Sciences* 43, no. 2 (1998): 373.

33. Isabelle Baszanger, "Entre traitement de la dernière chance et palliatif pur: Les frontières invisibles des innovations thérapeutiques," *Sciences Sociales et Santé* 18, no. 2 (2000): 67–94.

34. Charles L. Bosk, *Forgive and Remember: Managing Medical Failure,* 2nd ed. (Chicago: University of Chicago Press, 2003; first edition published 1979).

35. Ibid., 145.

36. Bosk argues that because a consensus about acceptable technical-error rates is lacking and such mistakes are unavoidable, normative errors are more devastating to a surgeon's career than technical ones. Surgeons might not be able to avoid technical or judgment errors, but they need to comply with the norms of clinical responsibility. *Forgive and Remember,* conclusion.

37. Ibid., 185.

38. Mark A. Hall, Ira Mark Ellman, and Danile S. Strouse, *Health Care Law and Ethics in a Nutshell,* 2nd ed. (St. Paul, MN: West Group Press, 1998), 316.

39. Lawrence S. Harris, "A Killing of Baby Doe," *Journal of Forensic Sciences* 42, no. 6 (1997): 1180–82. This article reports on two nurses who killed an anencephalic child by pressing on its chest with their fingers. They got caught because one of them talked about it during a coffee break. See also Anspach, *Deciding Who Lives.* In Israel, fetuses with disabilities are routinely aborted and newborns abandoned; see Meira Weiss, *The Chosen Body: The Politics of the Body in Israeli Society* (Stanford, CA: Stanford University Press, 2002).

40. Advocates justify these actions because of the abundant reliance on life-extending medical technologies such as ventilators, heart pumps, intravenous lines, and mechanical feeding devices during the last days and hours of life. Such technologies are accused of "dehumanizing" and "corrupting" dying by unnecessarily extending the death and shutting out relatives while keeping patients captive. David Wendell Moller, *Life's End: Technocratic Dying in an Age of Spiritual Yearning* (Amityville, NY: Baywood Publishing Company, 2000). Here, perceived technological determinism justifies the moral equivalent of forensic homicide. In

response, some of the presumed beneficiaries of physician-assisted suicide, organized in the activist movement Not Dead Yet (see http://www.notdeadyet.org, accessed June 19, 2003), have fought against this lethal mercy. I have argued that the "humanistic" rally against technology actually depends on the extensive use of medical technologies and drugs to keep people comfortable. Stefan Timmermans, "Resuscitation Technology in the Emergency Department: Towards a Dignified Death," *Sociology of Health and Illness* 20, no. 2 (1998): 144–67.

41. Patrick O'Neill, "Rules Questioned for Assisted Suicide Reports," *Oregonian*, March 21, 1998.

42. Pestaner, "End-of-Life Care," 366.

43. Hanzlick and Goodin, "Mind Your Manners, Part III," 234–35.

44. Charles S. Hirsch and Mark A. Flomenbaum, *Forensic Pathology Check Sample FP 95-1: Problem Solving in Death Certification* (Chicago: American Society of Clinical Pathologists, 1995).

45. Hanzlick and Goodin, "Mind Your Manners, Part III," 236.

46. Froede, *Handbook of Forensic Pathology*, 257; italics in original.

47. Hanzlick, Hunsaker, and Davis, *Manner of Death Classification*, 12.

48. Andrew Abbott, "Status and Status Strain in the Professions," *American Journal of Sociology* 86, no. 4 (1981): 825. As with many functionalist arguments, Abbott rationalizes an existing status hierarchy based on perceived superiority—in this case, superior purity. Such a ranking is open to counterarguments. Forensic pathologists, for example, also work on issues in which human complexity, in the form of patient subjectivity, is minimal. For Abbott, this is an indication of high status and may account for pathologists' high position in the past, but it does not explain their current situation.

49. See Donna J. Haraway, *Simians, Cyborgs, and Women: The Reinvention of Nature* (New York: Routledge, 1991); and Star, "Power, Technologies, and the Phenomenology of Conventions."

50. Kohn, Corrigan, and Donaldson, *To Err Is Human*.

51. Malpractice includes acts of extreme carelessness, such as removing the wrong kidney. Incompetence refers to actions that a physician is not trained to do or does not do safely and effectively, such as continuing to perform a surgical procedure that others in the field stopped doing years ago because it was deemed unnecessarily dangerous.

52. Egon Bittner, *The Functions of the Police in Modern Society, Crime and Delinquency Issues* (Washington, DC: U.S. Government Printing Office, 1970), 39.

53. Peter K. Manning, *Policing Contingencies* (Chicago: University of Chicago Press, 2003).

54. According to the FBI's *Crime in the United States—2003,* based on Uniform Crime Reports, there were 366 justifiable homicides by law enforcement authorities in 1997, 369 in 1998, 308 in 1999, 309 in 2000, 370 in 2001, 341 in 2002, and 370 in 2003. See http://www.fbi.gov/ucr/cius_03/pdf (accessed April 4, 2005). Law enforcement killings are defined as "the killing of a felon by a law enforcement officer in the line of duty." According to the FBI's *Uniform Crime Reports Handbook* (2004 revision), the determination of justifiable homicide is made by law enforcement and not by a court, prosecutor, or coroner. See http://www.fbi.gov/ucr/handbook/ucrhandbook04.pdf. These figures might thus underreport the actual number of people killed by law enforcement personnel. See also Alexander Alvarez, "Trends and Patterns of Justifiable Homicide: A Comparative Analysis," *Violence and Victims* 7, no. 4 (1992): 347–56.

55. David Jacobs and Robert M. O'Brien, "The Determinants of Deadly Force: A Structural Analysis of Police Violence," *American Journal of Sociology* 103, no. 4 (1998): 837–62; see also David Jacobs and David W. Britt, "Inequality and the Police Use of Deadly Force," *Social Problems* 26 (1979): 403–12.

56. James L. Luke and Donald T. Reay, "The Perils of Investigating and Certifying Deaths in Police Custody," *American Journal of Forensic Medicine and Pathology* 13, no. 2 (1992): 98–100.

57. Elizabeth A. Laposata, "Positional Asphyxia during Law Enforcement Transport," *American Journal of Forensic Medicine and Pathology* 14, no. 1 (1993): 86–87.

58. Luke and Reay, "Perils of Investigating," 99.

59. Carl B. Klockars, "A Theory of Excessive Force and Its Control," in *Police Violence*, ed. William A. Geller and Hans Toch, 1–23 (New Haven, CT: Yale University Press, 1996), 15.

60. There may be more accounts of deaths involving law enforcement officials, such as deaths in prisons or during police pursuits. The problem is that little has been published recently about these deaths from a medical examiner's perspective, and the available information does not explain how the manner of death is classified. I found one review article of deaths under police custody, but it describes a coroner jurisdiction with juried inquests: Steven A. Koehler et al., "Deaths among Criminal Suspects, Law Enforcement Officers, Civilians, and Prison Inmates: A Coroner-Based Study," *American Journal of Forensic Medicine and Pathology* 24, no. 4 (2003): 334–38.

61. Katherine S. Newman, *Rampage: The Social Roots of School Shootings* (New York: Basic Books, 2004), 150.

62. Vernon J. Geberth, "Suicide by Cop: Inviting Death from the Hands of a Police Officer," *Law and Order*, July 1993, 105–9.

63. H. Range Hutson et al., "Suicide by Cop," *Annals of Emergency Medicine* 32, no. 6 (1998): 665–69.

64. Shneidman, *The Suicidal Mind*.

65. Kris Mohandie and Reid J. Meloy, "Clinical and Forensic Indicators of 'Suicide by Cop,'" *Journal of Forensic Sciences* 45, no. 2 (1999): 385.

66. Ibid.

67. Edward F. Wilson et al., "Homicide or Suicide: The Killing of Suicidal Persons by Law Enforcement Officers," *Journal of Forensic Sciences* 43, no. 1 (1997): 51.

68. Only ten out of 1,706 justifiable homicides (0.6%) by law enforcement between 1999 and 2003 involved "other dangerous weapons." There were no deaths due to knives or cutting instruments. See http://www.fbi.gov/ucr/cius_03/pdf (accessed April 4, 2005).

69. I am here mainly following the debate in the forensic community. A similar set of issues has been discussed among paramedics. See http://www.charlydmiller.com/RA/RAlibrary.html#fpasphyx (accessed January 7, 2004) for a library of articles on this topic.

70. Donald T. Reay and J. W. Eisele, "Deaths from Law Enforcement Neck Holds," *American Journal of Forensic Medicine and Pathology* 3, no. 3 (1982): 253–58; Donald T. Reay and G. A. Holloway, "Changes in Carotid Blood Flow Produced by Neck Compression," *American Journal of Forensic Medicine and Pathology* 3, no. 3 (1982): 199–202.

71. Charles V. Wetli and David A. Fishbain, "Cocaine-Induced Psychosis and Sudden Death in Recreational Cocaine Users," *Journal of Forensic Sciences* 30, no. 3 (1985): 878.

72. Donald T. Reay et al., "Positional Asphyxia during Law Enforcement Transport," *American Journal of Forensic Medicine and Pathology* 13, no. 2 (1992): 94, 96.

73. Donald T. Reay et al., "Effects of Positional Restraint on Oxygen Saturation and Heart Rate following Exercise," *American Journal of Forensic Medicine and Pathology* 9, no. 1 (1988): 16.

74. Luke and Reay, "Perils of Investigating," 99.

75. Laposata, "Positional Asphyxia."

76. Ronald L. O'Halloran and Larry V. Lewman, "Restraint Asphyxiation in Excited Delirium," *American Journal of Forensic Medicine and Pathology* 14, no. 4 (1993): 295.

77. Samuel J. Stratton, Christopher Rogers, and Karen Green, "Sudden Death in Individuals in Hobble Restraints during Paramedic Transport," *Annals of Emergency Medicine* 25, no. 5 (1995): 710–14.

78. Alan R. Cowen, "In a Bind," *Emergency Medical Services* 24, no. 6 (1995): 54–58.

79. Wichita Police Department, *In-Custody Sudden Deaths,* Wichita Police Department Training Bulletin (1995); Donald T. Reay, "Suspect Restraint and Sudden Death," *FBI Law Enforcement Bulletin,* May 1996, 22–25.

80. Martin Roeggla et al., "Cardiorespiratory Consequences to Hobble Restraint," *Wien Klinische Wochenschrift* 109, no. 10 (1996): 359–61.

81. Charles S. Hirsch, "Restraint Asphyxiation," *American Journal of Forensic Medicine and Pathology* 14, no. 1 (1994): 86.

82. Darrell L. Ross, "Factors Associated with Excited Delirium Deaths in Police Custody," *Modern Pathology* 11, no. 11 (1998): 1127–37.

83. Catecholamines are chemical compounds that act as neurotransmitters or hormones; they include epinephrine, norepinephrine, and dopamine. They are associated with stress and may increase blood pressure, heart rate, and blood-glucose levels. "Myocardial hypertrophy" refers to enlargement of the heart, while fibrosis is the formation of scarlike tissue.

84. See the literature review provided in Ross, "Excited Delirium Deaths"; and Haresh G. Mirchandani et al., "Cocaine-Induced Agitated Delirium, Forceful Struggle, and Minor Head Injury," *American Journal of Forensic Medicine and Pathology* 15, no. 2 (1994): 95–99.

85. Mirchandani et al., "Cocaine-Induced Agitated Delirium"; Ross, "Excited Delirium Deaths"; James Ruttenber et al., "Fatal Excited Delirium following Cocaine Use: Epidemiologic Findings Provide New Evidence for Mechanisms of Cocaine Toxicity," *Journal of Forensic Sciences* 42, no. 1 (1997): 25–31.

86. Theodore C. Chan et al., "Reexamination of Custody Restraint Position and Positional Asphyxia," *American Journal of Forensic Medicine and Pathology* 19, no. 3 (1998): 205.

87. Donald T. Reay and John D. Howard, "Restraint Position and Positional Asphyxia," *American Journal of Forensic Medicine and Pathology* 20, no. 3 (1999): 300–301.

88. Michael S. Pollanen et al., "Unexpected Death Related to Restraint for Excited Delirium: A Retrospective Study of Deaths in Police Custody and in the Community," *Canadian Medical Association Journal* 158, no. 12 (1998): 1603–7.

89. Maura Belviso et al., "Positional Asphyxia," *American Journal of Forensic Medicine and Pathology* 24, no. 3 (2003): 292–97; Stephan A. Padosch et al., "Death due to Positional Asphyxia under Severe Alcoholisation: Pathophysiologic and Forensic Considerations," *Forensic Science International* 149, no. 1 (2005): 67–73.

90. Mirchandani et al., "Cocaine-Induced Agitated Delirium."

91. Ibid., 99.

92. Ronald L. O'Halloran and Janice G. Frank, "Asphyxial Death during Prone Restraint Revisited," *American Journal of Forensic Medicine and Pathology* 21, no. 1 (2000): 39–52; Ross, "Excited Delirium Deaths," 1134.

93. Klockars, "Excessive Force."

94. Douglas W. Perez and William Ker Muir, "Administrative Review of Alleged Police Brutality," in Geller and Toch, *Police Violence,* 213–33.

95. U.S. Commission on Civil Rights, *Who Is Guarding the Guardians?* (Washington, DC: U.S. Commission on Civil Rights, 1981); U.S. Commission on Civil Rights, *Revisiting "Who Is Guarding the Guardians?" A Report on Police Practices and Civil Rights in America* (Washington,

DC: U.S. Commission on Civil Rights, 2000). See Bittner, *Functions of the Police,* for an early version of the argument about crime and civil rights violations.

96. Occasionally, forensic pathologists attempt to create distance and independence—for example, by keeping police officers out of the autopsy room when their departments are involved—but such ad hoc rules cannot make up for the advantage that police have in being knowledgeable about forensic procedures (in contrast to grieving relatives).

97. Steven B. Karch and Charles V. Wetli, "Agitated Delirium versus Positional Asphyxia," *Annals of Emergency Medicine* 26, no. 6 (1995): 760.

98. See Smith, "Third Report."

99. For example, Annemarie Mol discusses how the use of a simple technology—a blood-glucose monitor—requires financial resources, cleanliness, quietness, a predictable daily rhythm, and the ability to keep a log, not to mention a tolerance for pain and blood and the fear of a diabetic coma or blindness as a motivator. Annemarie Mol, "Wat diagnostische Technieken doen: Het Voorbeeld van de Bloedsuikermeter," in *Ingebouwde Normen: Medische Technieken Doorgelicht,* ed. Marc Berg and Annemarie Mol, 143–57 (Utrecht: Van der Wees, 2001). Failure to assess the blood-glucose level does not depend simply on the mere presence of a technology but on the monitor's shape, size, and weight, plus all the contingencies and elements of everyday living. Use of mini blood-glucose monitors should keep glucose around normal values, but what counts as "normal" has itself changed because of the device. The glucose levels of nondiabetic people vary between 80 and 120 mg per 100 ml, but diabetics monitoring their glucose levels about five times a day with the device strive for *lower values,* with less fluctuation. Achieving those low values requires proper diet, self-discipline, and support and reminders from friends, family, and doctors, but it also depends on the activities of the glucose monitor. And while glucose monitoring ultimately promises freedom from blindness, it requires a remarkable discipline of the self to make the technology work for the diabetic. If only one element of the heterogeneous network is out of place, the result is non-usage. Even non-utilization has the effect of personal and technical failure.

100. This point is based on Bernard E. Harcourt, *Illusion of Order: The False Promise of Broken Windows Policing* (Cambridge, MA: Harvard University Press, 2001).

101. Homicide data come from two sources: the FBI's Uniform Crime Reports, based on police agencies' data reporting; and the National Center for Health Statistics, whose figures are based on coroners' and medical examiners' records. Marc Riedel, "Sources of Homicide Data: A Review and Comparison," in *Homicide: A Sourcebook of Social Research,* ed. M. Dwayne Smith and Margaret A. Zahn, 75–95 (Thousand Oaks, CA: SAGE Publications, 1999). While differences exist between the two sources, this has rarely led to controversies (for an exception, see Gary Kleck, "Crime Control through the Private Use of Armed Force," *Social Problems* 35, no. 1 [1988]: 163–84), and the data sources are considered valid: "The high level of agreement between Return A estimates [FBI's Uniform Crime Reports] and NCHS homicide rates nationally is rather strong evidence that supports their validity." Riedel, "Sources of Homicide Data," 92. About how little is known on forensic certification of homicide, see Riedel, "Sources of Homicide Data," 85.

102. These figures are based on the FBI's Uniform Crime Reports. Alfred Blumstein, P. Frederick Rivara, and Richard Rosenfeld, "The Rise and Decline of Homicide—and Why," *Annual Review of Public Health* 21 (2000): 506; Anthony Harris et al., "Murder and Medicine: The Lethality of Criminal Assault, 1960–1999," *Homicide Studies* 6, no. 2 (2002): 128–66.

103. U.S. Department of Justice, *Crime in the United States, 2003* (Washington, DC: Federal Bureau of Investigation, 2004).

104. Blumstein, Rivara, and Rosenfeld, "Rise and Decline of Homicide."

105. There are some interesting race and gender differences in these declines; see Blumstein, Rivara, and Rosenfeld, "Rise and Decline of Homicide."

106. Ibid.; Benjamin Bowling, "The Rise and Fall of New York Murder: Zero Tolerance or Crack's Decline?" *British Journal of Criminology* 39, no. 4 (1999): 531–54; Harris et al., "Murder and Medicine."

107. See Bowling, "New York Murder"; Mitchell Duneier, *Sidewalk* (New York: Farrar, Straus & Giroux, 1999); and Harcourt, *Illusion of Order,* for ways in which the broken-windows theory has been implemented. For the theory itself, see James Q. Wilson and George L. Kelling, "Broken Windows," *Atlantic Monthly* 249, no. 3 (1982): 29–38.

108. James Q. Wilson and George L. Kelling, "Making Neighborhoods Safe," *Atlantic Monthly* 263, no. 2 (1989): 47.

109. Rudolph Giuliani, press conference, February 24, 1998.

110. Robert J. Sampson and Stephen W. Raudenbusch, "Systematic Social Observation of Public Spaces: A New Look at Disorder in Neighborhoods," *American Journal of Sociology* 105, no. 3 (1999): 603–51.

111. Harcourt, *Illusion of Order,* 168–71.

CHAPTER FIVE

1. Richard A. Meckel, *Save the Babies: American Public Health Reform and the Prevention of Infant Mortality, 1850–1929* (Baltimore: Johns Hopkins University Press, 1990), 1. See also Samuel H. Preston and Michael R. Haines, *Fatal Years: Child Mortality in Late Nineteenth-Century America* (Princeton, NJ: Princeton University Press, 1991).

2. Kenneth D. Kochanek et al., "Deaths: Final Data for 2002," *National Vital Statistics Report* 53, no. 5 (2004): 1–116.

3. R. I. Woods, P. A. Watterson, and J. H. Woodward, "The Causes of Rapid Infant Mortality Decline in England and Wales, 1861–1921," pts. 1 and 2, *Population Studies* 42, no. 3 (1988): 343–66; 43, no. 1 (1989): 113–32.

4. For a similar dilemma from a police perspective, see Innes Martin, "Organizational Communication and the Symbolic Construction of Police Murder Investigations," *British Journal of Sociology* 53, no. 1 (2002): 74.

5. Paul H. Wise, "The Anatomy of a Disparity in Infant Mortality," *Annual Review of Public Health* 24 (2003): 341–62.

6. See, for example, Ronald C. Oliver et al., "Beneficial Effects of a Hospital Bereavement Intervention Program after Traumatic Childhood Death," *Journal of Trauma* 50, no. 4 (2001): 440–48.

7. Lundstrom and Sharpe, "Getting Away with Murder."

8. Froede, *Handbook of Forensic Pathology,* 93.

9. Charles V. Wetli, *Laboratory Practice Management LPM-13* (New York: American Society of Clinical Pathologists, 1997), 231.

10. Charles V. Wetli, Roger E. Mittleman, and Valerie J. Rao, *Practical Forensic Pathology* (New York: Igaku-Shoin, 1988).

11. Henry F. Krous, "The International Standardized Autopsy Protocol for Sudden Unexpected Infant Death," in *Sudden Infant Death Syndrome: New Trends in the Nineties,* ed. T. O. Rognum, 81–95 (Oslo: Scandinavian University Press, 1995); U.S. Department of Health and Human Services, *Guidelines for Death Scene Investigation of Sudden, Unexplained Infant Deaths: Recommendations of the Interagency Panel on Sudden Infant Death Syndrome* (Washington, DC: National Institutes of Health, 1996).

12. Nancy Scheper-Hughes, *Death without Weeping* (Berkeley and Los Angeles: University

of California Press, 1992). Another example comes from Israel, where babies with slight visible deformities are often abandoned in hospitals and, if taken home, are neglected, isolated, and hidden. Weiss, *The Chosen Body,* chap. 2.

13. See also Freidson, *Professional Dominance,* chap. 4.

14. Early one spring morning, a slightly decomposed newborn boy of unknown race with the umbilical cord still attached was found in a plastic garbage bag, floating down a river. A boater alerted by the smell had opened the bag. The detective noted that the crime scene was basically twenty miles long, since the perpetrator had probably thrown the newborn into the water during the past two days and the bag could have floated about ten miles a day. Even if the detective had had a stroke of good luck and had been able to locate the mother, she would likely have argued that the infant had been stillborn and that she panicked and disposed of the body. The pathologist's difficult task was to determine that the newborn had been alive at birth. The presence of milk or food in the stomach is a decisive clue, but most such newborns are already dead before the first feeding. Another test is floating the lungs in water to find out whether they were aerated from the baby's breathing. But after decomposition, most lungs will float in water, and some first breaths do not fully aerate the lungs. In this particular case, putrefaction was too advanced to even check the lungs. Because the pathologist could thus not even determine with certainty whether the infant had been alive at birth, the question of what killed the boy was moot. The case ended up undetermined. This outcome is common for the dead newborns found in sewers, trash dumps, and public restrooms.

The presumption in those cases is that the mother—young, unmarried, and with insufficient access to contraception or abortion services—tried to hide the pregnancy or wished to dispose of an unwanted child. Although police and medical examiners will have a strong suspicion that the baby was at one point alive and that its death was caused by the mother and/or her helpers, forensically most of those cases do not go anywhere, because two crucial assumptions that allow a death investigation to take place remain unmet. First, its short presence on earth leaves the baby with little or no identifying information. Although pathologists have someone's physical remains, without social ties they have nobody. The newborn has fingerprints and a genetic DNA profile, but such information is useless without a means to link it to the parents. None of the additional clues that could identify the infant are usually present. The newborn looks like a neonate; he or she does not have any tattoos, surgical marks, or dental records that could help with identification. Usually there are also no towels, sheets, or clothing accompanying the baby. The only clues are the baby's sex and the time and location at which it was found. Identification is a matter of developing ties between the self and other people and things. For babies, the first tie—and the linkage that counts in the investigation—is the tie to the mother. If the mother cannot be located, the baby remains anonymous, to be buried by social services. In this particular case, a local funeral home volunteered to arrange the funeral and bear the costs.

The second assumption that remains unproven in such cases is that the birth was a live birth. Life at its beginning is usually certified by a midwife or physician attending the birth. In the first minutes after birth, the baby's vital parameters and Apgar scores are recorded. If the baby does not take its first breath after birth, the physician or midwife usually helps it with a gentle pat on the buttocks or by freeing the nasal passages; occasionally, more intrusive measures are needed. And when the birth is a true stillbirth, the non-beginning of life is measured and recorded as well. As Rayna Rapp puts it, "All newborns are conscripts to modern bureaucratic record keeping and discipline." *Testing Women, Testing the Fetus: The Social Impact of Amniocentesis in America* (New York: Routledge, 2000), 272. Birth, like death, is thus a socially witnessed event. Because newborns are at the beginning of life, they are the only kind of people for whom forensic staff need to establish whether they were alive. If there was no life, a death investigation does not make any sense. Then the medical examiner and police are dealing with unlawful disposal of human remains, and that is far from a possible homicide investigation. Interestingly, "human beings in every society studied to date are more likely to be murdered on the day they are born than on any other day of their lives." Randolph Roth, "Child Murder in New England," *Social Science History* 25, no. 1 (2001): 107.

15. Robert Emerson, *Judging Delinquents* (Chicago: Aldine, 1969).

16. Anspach, *Deciding Who Lives,* chap. 5.

17. Michael Eid and Ed Diener, "Norms for Experiencing Emotions in Different Cultures: Inter- and International Differences," *Journal of Personality and Social Psychology* 81, no. 5 (2001): 869–85.

18. Sita Reddy, "Temporarily Insane: Pathologizing Cultural Difference in American Criminal Courts," *Sociology of Health and Illness* 24, no. 5 (2002): 667–87.

19. No one in the office had seen such teeth before.

20. A straightforward drowning would have been written up as "asphyxia due to drowning," while choking might in this case have been formulated as "asphyxia due to a foreign substance."

21. Glaser and Strauss, *Awareness of Dying.*

22. Julius Roth, *Timetables: Structuring the Passage of Time in Hospital Treatment and Other Careers* (Indianapolis, IN: Bobbs-Merrill, 1963).

23. It is a variation because in this instance, the purpose was to find out whether the other party did *not* know, rather than whether he or she knew.

24. Mark Joffe and Stephen Ludwig, "Stairway Injuries in Children," *Pediatrics* 83, no. 3 (1988): 459.

25. Prosecutors would have had to argue that the fall down the stairs was not life-threatening and that the father had killed the baby while trying to revive it, an action that might be excused under Good Samaritan laws (although these laws have not been legally tested).

26. When I mentioned this case to Dr. Cahill a couple of years later, she actually thought that she had designated the death as accidental. Note here also that medical examiners only mete out justice negatively (i.e., by absolving people). If they were to try to indict people, the case would enter the justice system and be subject to the contestation discussed in chapter 3.

27. I was not allowed to contact the parents in these cases.

28. Joyce A. Martin et al., "Annual Summary of Vital Statistics—2003," *Pediatrics* 115, no. 3 (2005): 619–34. Most of the other leading causes of infant death are natural causes or are related to complications during delivery. The leading cause of death is "congenital malformations, deformations and chromosomal abnormalities" (5,523 deaths, or 20.1%), followed by "disorders related to short gestation and low birthweight, not elsewhere classified" (4,637 deaths, or 16.5%). The other forensic category in the top-ten list is the sixth leading cause of death: "accidents (unintentional injuries)," with 946 deaths, or 3.4%.

29. In Abbott's terms, SIDS functions as a professional "stopgap"; it is a well-recognized problem for which the profession lacks an effective answer. One could argue that in medicine, every "syndrome" represents such a stopgap, because a syndrome implies an unknown etiology. Abbott considers such stopgaps a professional vulnerability, because they open up the profession to poaching by other professional groups. Abbott, *The System of Professions,* 50–51.

30. When I discussed this issue with Dr. Cahill, she noted that in some cases, attributing death in a young adult to heart arrhythmia might also constitute a diagnosis by exclusion. Even in those cases, however, there is often a clinical history of heart problems, or the scene

suggests exertion or stress. In one case, a nineteen-year-old male collapsed while playing basketball, and another after a night of partying. No such positive clues from history or scene investigation are needed to make a diagnosis by exclusion in SIDS.

31. Sleep apnea initially became the main paradigm for SIDS. See J. Geoff Gregory, "Citation Study of a Scientific Revolution: Sudden Infant Death Syndrome," *Scientometrics* 5 (1983): 313–27. That article also shows the danger of talking about scientific revolutions soon after the establishment of a research agenda.

32. For a review, see Frank M. Sullivan and Susan M. Barlow, "Review of Risk Factors for Sudden Infant Death Syndrome," *Pediatric and Perinatal Epidemiology* 15 (2001): 144–200.

33. Ibid., 187.

34. The guidebook adds that "undetermined is probably the most objective case since the cause is, by definition, undetermined." Certifiers who classify SIDS deaths as undetermined are advised to explain their determination to the parents. Hanzlick, Hunsaker, and Davis, *Manner of Death Classification*, 16–17.

35. Gregory, "Scientific Revolution"; Michael P. Johnson and Karl Hufbauer, "Sudden Infant Death Syndrome as a Medical Research Problem since 1945," *Social Problems* 30, no. 1 (1982): 65–81.

36. Ulf Hogberg and Eric Bergstrom, "Suffocated Prone: The Iatrogenic Tragedy of SIDS," *American Journal of Public Health* 90, no. 4 (2000): 527–31; Marian Willinger, "SIDS Prevention," *Annals of Pediatrics* 24, no. 7 (1995): 358–64.

37. DiMaio and DiMaio, *Forensic Pathology*.

38. Spitz, *Medicolegal Investigation of Death*, 725.

39. DiMaio and DiMaio, *Forensic Pathology*, 289.

40. Ibid., 315. Smothering an infant with a pillow does not leave any pathological traces in the soft tissue.

41. For two highly suspicious cases, see Elizabeth Mitchell et al., "An Analysis of the Usefulness of Specific Stages in the Pathologic Investigation of Sudden Infant Death," *American Journal of Forensic Medicine and Pathology* 21, no. 4 (2000): 397. For a confirmed case, see Harris, "A Killing of Baby Doe." The perpetrators in this case were not the parents but health care providers.

42. Lundstrom and Sharpe, "Getting Away with Murder," 27. Another instance of deliberately killing a baby occurs if the child is a victim of Munchausen syndrome by proxy. In that situation, a parent—in the medical literature, it is usually the mother—repeatedly induces signs of illnesses in the child and rushes it to a hospital. The child is usually subjected to multiple admissions and extensive medical evaluations, most of which come up negative. If a child dies after repeated episodes of apnea and cyanosis, the possibility of infanticide following child abuse might be raised. Most smothering deaths will likely be classified as SIDS.

43. DiMaio and DiMaio, *Forensic Pathology*, 291.

44. Manfred Oehmichen, Ivana Gerling, and Christoph Meissner, "Petechiae of the Baby's Skin as Differentiation Symptom of Infanticide versus SIDS," *Journal of Forensic Sciences* 45, no. 3 (2000): 602–7.

45. Dingwall, Eekelaar, and Murray, *The Protection of Children*.

46. Stefan Timmermans, "Closed-Chest Cardiac Massage: The Emergence of a Discovery Trajectory," *Science, Technology, and Human Values* 24, no. 2 (1999): 213–40.

47. Tiffany L. A. Person, Wendy A. Lavezzi, and Barbara C. Wolf, "Cosleeping and Sudden Unexpected Death in Infancy," *Archives of Pathology and Laboratory Medicine* 126 (2002): 345.

48. Judith Green, "From Accidents to Risk: Public Health and Preventable Injury," *Health,*

Risk and Society 1, no. 1 (1999): 25–39; Ian Hacking, *The Taming of Chance* (Cambridge: Cambridge University Press, 1990).

49. John Last, *Public Health and Human Ecology* (East Norwalk, CT: Appleton & Lange, 1987).

50. Ed Mitchell, "Cot Death—the Story So Far," *BMJ* 319 (1999): 1457.

51. Peter Blair, "Re: Why the Danger in Sharing a Sofa?" electronic letter, *BMJ*, December 20, 1999, http://bmj.bmjjournals.com/cgi/eletters/319/7223/1457 (accessed September 13, 2005). See also Sullivan and Barlow, "Review of Risk Factors," 150.

52. Kim A. Collins, "SIDS, Overlaying, and Suffocation" (lecture presented at the Third Annual Pediatric Forensic Issues Conference, Orlando, FL, December 2, 1999). In my personal experience, most parents of infants qualify as "tired" cosleepers.

53. This article was Person, Lavezzi, and Wolf, "Cosleeping."

54. Stephen Hilgartner, "The Social Construction of Risk Objects; or, How to Pry Open Networks of Risk," in *Organizations, Uncertainties and Risk,* ed. James F. Short and Lee Clarke, 39–58 (Boulder, CO: Westview Press, 1992).

55. Peter J. Fleming et al., "Environment of Infants during Sleep and Risk of the Sudden Infant Death Syndrome: Results of 1993–5 Case-Control Study for Confidential Inquiry into Stillbirths and Deaths in Infancy," *BMJ* 313 (1996): 191.

56. N. Carter and G. N. Rutty, "Invoking Sudden Infant Death Syndrome in Cosleeping May Be Misleading (Letter to Editor)," *BMJ* 321 (2000): 1019.

57. These reports contain some of the most comprehensive recommendations drawn from forensic investigations. For New Hampshire, for example, see the reports at http://doj.nh.gov/victim/childfatality.html. For other states, see http://www.childdeathreview.org/state.htm (both accessed October 20, 2004).

58. Kim A. Collins, "Death by Overlaying and Wedging: A 15-Year Retrospective Study," *American Journal of Forensic Medicine and Pathology* 22, no. 2 (2001): 155–59.

59. See, for example, Christopher Richard et al., "Sleeping Position, Orientation, and Proximity in Bedsharing Infants and Mothers," *Sleep* 19, no. 9 (1996): 685–90.

60. Dorothy A. Drago and Andrew L. Dannenberg, "Infant Mechanical Suffocation Deaths in the United States, 1980–1997," *Pediatrics* 103, no. 5 (1999): e59.

61. Fiona L. R. Williams, Gillian A. Lang, and David T. Mage, "Sudden Unexpected Infant Deaths in Dundee, 1882–1891: Overlying or SIDS?" *Scottish Medical Journal* 46 (2001): 43–47.

62. Peter S. Blair et al., "Babies Sleeping with Parents: Case-Control Study of Factors Influencing the Risk of Sudden Infant Death Syndrome," *BMJ* 319 (1999): 1457–62.

63. Fern R. Hauck et al., "Sleep Environment and the Risk of Sudden Infant Death Syndrome in an Urban Population: The Chicago Infant Mortality Study," *Pediatrics* 111, no. 5 (2003): 1209.

64. Task Force on Infant Sleep Position and SIDS, "Changing Concepts of Sudden Infant Death Syndrome: Implications for Infant Sleeping Environment and Sleep Position," *Pediatrics* 105, no. 3 (2000): 653.

65. Suad Nakamura, Marilyn Wind, and Mary Ann Danello, "Review of Hazards Associated with Children Placed in Adult Beds," *Archives of Pediatrics and Adolescent Medicine* 153, no. 10 (1999): 1019–23.

66. American Academy of Pediatrics, "Distinguishing Sudden Infant Death Syndrome from Child Abuse Fatalities," *Pediatrics* 107, no. 2 (2001): 437–41.

67. American Academy of Pediatrics, "Addendum: Distinguishing Sudden Infant Death Syndrome from Child Abuse Fatalities," *Pediatrics* 108, no. 3 (2001): 812.

68. Richardson, *Death, Dissection, and the Destitute;* Mary Roach, *Stiff: The Curious Lives of Human Cadavers* (New York: W. W. Norton & Company, 2003).

69. Kurt Nolte, "The Potential Role of Medical Examiners and Coroners in Responding to and Planning for Bioterrorism and Emergency Infectious Diseases," in Institute of Medicine, *Medicolegal Death Investigation System,* 49–52.

70. Adele E. Clarke et al., "Biomedicalization: Technoscientific Transformations of Health, Illness, and U.S. Biomedicine," *American Sociological Review* 68 (April 2003): 161–94; Deborah Lupton, *Risk* (London: Routledge, 1999). These efforts, however, have been limited by incompatibilities in data gathering between jurisdictions.

71. Charles Perrow, *Normal Accidents: Living with High Risk Technologies* (New York: Basic Books, 1984).

72. Bauman, *Mortality.*

73. Rosenberg, "The Tyranny of Diagnosis," 256.

CHAPTER SIX

1. John E. Hauser, "The Use of Medical Examiner–Coroner's Cases as Transplant Donors," *Journal of Forensic Sciences* 14, no. 2 (1969): 501–6. The organ transplant interests forced death investigators to adopt a definition of death that was for their purposes unusable. Renée C. Fox, "An Ignoble Form of Cannibalism: Reflections on the Pittsburgh Protocol for Procuring Organs from Non-Heart-Beating Cadavers," *Kennedy Institute of Ethics Journal* 3, no. 2 (1993): 231–39; Margaret Lock, "Contesting the Natural in Japan: Moral Dilemmas and Technologies of Dying," *Culture, Medicine, and Psychiatry* 19, no. 1 (1995): 1–38. In an archival study of the correspondence of the Harvard Ad Hoc Committee on Death in 1968, Mita Giacomini confirmed the general suspicion that a leading factor in the tailoring of the redefinition of death was the interests of the transplant organizations. Giacomini, "A Change of Heart and a Change of Mind?" In 1967, after the first heart transplant in South Africa, the general public became sensitized to the potential conflict of interest of transplant surgeons declaring patients dead before their heart had stopped beating. Up until that time, physicians and laypeople had been unable to come up with criteria for death beyond the century-old criterion of cessation of the heartbeat. The tacit consensus seemed to be to view the pronouncement of death as the prerogative of the bedside physician. The transplantation groups needed more flexibility in order to receive timely access to comatose bodies and were actively involved in the creation of the new criteria. For example, clinical criteria were adapted to facilitate organ procurement. Even replacing the term *irreversible coma* with *brain-dead* fit with procurement needs, because only "dead" people can serve as cadaver organ donors. For medical examiners, brain death is insufficient as a definition of death to begin a postmortem investigation, nor are they in a professional position to guarantee the fact of brain death. Yet because they sign death certificates and testify to the cause of death, medical examiners are required to endorse the diagnosis of brain death. At the same time, death investigators are required to monitor physicians' adherence to the use of the brain-death definition to make sure that death is not "sped up" for the purpose of organ or tissue transplantation. Jason, "Role of the Medical Examiner/Coroner."

2. The ambivalence of defining brain death has never completely gone away, however. In October 2004, an elected coroner of Montrose County, Colorado, ruled the death of a man who shot himself through the head a homicide. The coroner argued that the man wasn't fully dead when his heart, liver, pancreas, and kidneys were removed and that the procedures for determining that patients are legally dead are unclear. "Law Should Clearly Define Brain Death," editorial, *Denver Post,* October 7, 2004.

3. Rebecca Voelker, "Can Forensic Medicine and Organ Donation Coexist for the Public Good?" *Journal of the American Medical Association* 271, no. 12 (1994): 891–92.

4. L. Wick et al., "Pediatric Organ Donation: Impact of Medical Examiner Refusal," *Transplantation Proceedings* 27, no. 4 (1995): 2539–44.

5. See, for example, Jason, "Role of the Medical Examiner/Coroner"; and Shafer et al., "Ethical Analysis of Organ Recovery Denials."

6. William Q. Sturner, "Can Baby Organs Be Donated in All Forensic Cases? Proposed Guidelines for Organ Donation from Infants under Medical Examiner Jurisdiction," *American Journal of Forensic Medicine and Pathology* 16, no. 3 (1995): 215.

7. Donald Joralemon, "Shifting Ethics: Debating the Incentive Question in Organ Transplantation," *Journal of Medical Ethics* 27 (2001): 33.

8. See http://www.ustransplant.org for updated figures (accessed September 15, 2005).

9. James L. Luke, "The Shortage of Organs for Transplantation," *New England Journal of Medicine* 325 (1992): 1025.

10. Teresa J. Shafer et al., "Impact of Medical Examiner/Coroner Practices on Organ Recovery in the United States," *Journal of the American Medical Association* 272, no. 20 (1994): 1612; italics in original.

11. Christopher L. Jaynes and James W. Springer, "Decreasing the Organ Donor Shortage by Increasing Communication between Coroners, Medical Examiners, and Organ Procurement Organizations," *American Journal of Forensic Medicine and Pathology* 15, no. 2 (1994): 158.

12. See, for example, Shafer et al., "Ethical Analysis of Organ Recovery Denials"; Aaron Spital, "Ethical and Policy Issues in Altruistic Living and Cadaveric Organ Donation," *Clinics of Transplantation* 11, no. 2 (1997): 77–87.

13. Fox, "Cannibalism"; Lock, *Twice Dead;* Jeffrey Prottas and H. Batten, "The Willingness to Give: The Public and the Supply of Transplantable Organs," *Journal of Health Politics, Policy, and Law* 16 (1991): 121–34.

14. Lock, *Twice Dead.*

15. Renée C. Fox and Judith P. Swazey, *Spare Parts: Organ Replacement in American Society* (Oxford: Oxford University Press, 1992).

16. Sturner, "Can Baby Organs Be Donated in All Forensic Cases?"

17. Nancy G. Kutner, "Issues in the Application of High Cost Medical Technology: The Case of Organ Transplantation," *Journal of Health and Social Behavior* 28 (March 1987): 23–36.

18. Nancy Scheper-Hughes, "The Global Traffic in Human Organs," *Current Anthropology* 41, no. 2 (2000): 194.

19. Fox and Swazey, *Spare Parts,* 206.

20. Diane Vaughan, *The Challenger Launch Decision: Risky Technology, Culture and Deviance at NASA* (Chicago: University of Chicago Press, 1996).

21. Donald Joralemon, "Organ Wars: The Battle for Body Parts," *Medical Anthropology Quarterly* 9, no. 3 (1995): 335–56; Joralemon, "Shifting Ethics."

22. Jason, "Role of the Medical Examiner/Coroner," 193.

23. *Minnesota Statutes* 383B.225.

24. Lauren R. Boglioli and Mark L. Taff, "Religious Objection to Autopsy: An Ethical Dilemma for Medical Examiners," *American Journal of Forensic Medicine and Pathology* 11, no. 1 (1990): 1–8.

25. The National Association of Medical Examiners supported the repeal of religious-exemption laws in 2001, following a similar initiative by the American Academy of Pedi-

atrics and the American Medical Association. See http://www.thename.org/library/Position_
supporting_repealing_religious_exemption_%20Laws.pdf (accessed October 19, 2004); and
American Academy of Pediatrics, "Religious Objections to Medical Care," *Pediatrics* 99, no.
2 (1997): 279–81. Six states have enacted statutes that provide that autopsies can never be
performed against the wishes of the next of kin, absent a compelling public necessity. For a
review of the use of religious objections against autopsies, see Nelkin and Andrews, "Do the
Dead Have Interests?" 285.

26. Wecht, Curriden, and Wecht, *Cause of Death,* 103.

27. Jason, "Role of the Medical Examiner/Coroner."

28. Uniform Anatomical Gift Act (1987), section 8 (a).

29. Jason, "Role of the Medical Examiner/Coroner," 193.

30. Thomas May, Mark P. Aulisio, and Michael A. DeVita, "Patients, Families and Organ
Donation: Who Should Decide?" *Milbank Quarterly* 78, no. 2 (2000): 323–36.

31. Paul P. Lee et al., "Worldwide Legal Requirements for Obtaining Corneas, 1990,"
Cornea 11, no. 2 (1992): 102–7. The Minnesota law allows the medical examiner to keep
the brain without asking for consent. Nelkin and Andrews, "Do the Dead Have Interests?"
289.

32. Eric S. Jaffe, " 'She's Got Bette Davis's Eyes': Assessing the Nonconsensual Removal
of Cadaver Organs under the Takings and Due Process Clauses," *Columbia Law Review* 90,
no. 2 (1990): 528–73.

33. Ralph Frammolino, "Harvest of Corneas at Morgue Questioned: Corneas Taken without Survivor's Permission Are Resold at Huge Markup by Eye Bank, Which Pays Coroner's
Office a Fee," *Los Angeles Times,* November 2, 1997.

34. Ronald Smith, "Doheny Eye Bank," *Los Angeles Times,* November 10, 1997.

35. Sally Squires, "Transplant Tug-of-War," *Washington Post,* November 23, 1993.

36. Jaffe, "She's Got Bette Davis's Eyes."

37. *Minnesota Statutes* 383B 2225 subd. 7.

38. A broad interpretation of the 1987 UAGA would also suggest that the medical examiner
does not need to have the consent of relatives for *any* organ removal after making a reasonable
effort to reach them. Jaffe, "She's Got Bette Davis's Eyes."

39. *Texas Health and Safety Code,* chapter 693.002.

40. New York, County Law, art. 17-a, sec. 674–1, McKinney 1991.

41. Patrick E. Lantz, Donald Jason, and Gregory Davis, "Decreasing the Organ Donor
Shortage," *American Journal of Forensic Medicine and Pathology* 16, no. 3 (1995): 258.

42. Thomas F. Hegert, "Medical Examiners, Coroners, and Organ Recovery in the United
States," *Journal of the American Medical Association* 273, no. 20 (1995): 1578–79.

43. John Sanko, "Senator Ends Push for Bill Limiting Role of Coroner," *Denver Rocky
Mountain News,* April 22, 2000.

44. U.S. Department of Health and Human Services, Secretary's Advisory Committee on
Organ Transplantation, *Interim Report: Recommendations and Appendices,* 2003.

45. Voelker, "Can Forensic Medicine and Organ Donation Coexist for the Public Good?"

46. Shafer et al., "Medical Examiner/Coroner Practices."

47. Prottas and Batten, "The Willingness to Give."

48. Isabelle Durand-Zaleski et al., "Nonprocurement of Transplantable Organs in a Tertiary Care Hospital: A Focus on Sociological Causes," *Transplantation* 62, no. 9 (1996): 1224–
29; Robert C. Mackersie, Oscar Bronsther, and Steven Shackford, "Organ Procurement in
Patients with Fatal Head Injuries: The Fate of the Potential Donor," *Annals of Surgery* 213,
no. 2 (1991): 143–50.

49. Teresa J. Shafer et al., "Vital Role of Medical Examiners and Coroners in Organ Transplantation," *American Journal of Transplantation* 4 (2003): 160.

50. Randy Hanzlick, "Medical Examiners, Coroners, and Organ Recovery in the United States," *Journal of the American Medical Association* 273, no. 20 (1995): 1578.

51. Shafer et al., "Ethical Analysis of Organ Recovery Denials," 236.

52. Here the law seems to supersede ethics after all, because the authors state that medical examiners violate the law and autonomy principle when they refuse organ transfer.

53. Shafer et al., "Ethical Analysis of Organ Recovery Denials," 243, 245; italics in original.

54. Fox, "Cannibalism"; Fox and Swazey, *Spare Parts;* Renée C. Fox and Judith P. Swazey, *The Courage to Fail: A Social View of Organ Transplants and Dialysis,* 2nd ed. (Chicago: University of Chicago Press, 1978); Jack T. Hanford, "Religion, Medical Ethics, and Transplants," *Journal of Medical Humanities* 14, no. 1 (1993): 33–38; Linda Hogle, "Standardization across Non-standard Domains: The Case of Organ Procurement," *Science, Technology, and Human Values* 20, no. 4 (1995): 482–500; Mark Katches, William Heisel, and Ronald Campbell, "The Body Brokers," *Orange County Register* (Santa Ana, CA), April 16, 2000; Kutner, "High Cost Medical Technology"; Margaret Lock, "Reaching Consensus about Death: Heart Transplants and Cultural Identity in Japan," *Society-Société* 13, no. 1 (1989): 15–26; Scheper-Hughes, "Global Traffic"; Lesley A. Sharp, "Organ Transplantation as a Transformative Experience: Anthropological Insights into the Restructuring of the Self," *Medical Anthropology Quarterly* 9, no. 3 (1995): 357–89.

55. Shafer et al., "Ethical Analysis of Organ Recovery Denials," 244.

56. Sharp, "Organ Transplantation."

57. Johnson-McGrath, "Speaking for the Dead."

58. James C. Mohr, *Doctors and the Law: Medical Jurisprudence in the Nineteenth Century* (New York: Oxford University Press, 1993). The ethical principles, for example, are tailored on a medical model.

59. See http://www.unos.org (accessed September 15, 2005).

60. Quoted in Voelker, "Can Forensic Medicine and Organ Donation Coexist for the Public Good?" 891–92.

61. Shafer et al., "Vital Role of Medical Examiners," 165.

62. The figures given for child-abuse cases were 29 percent in 1990–92 and 25 percent in 2000–2001. Shafer et al., "Vital Role of Medical Examiners"; Shafer et al., "Medical Examiner/Coroner Practices."

63. Stephen C. Kurachek et al., "Medical Examiners' Attitudes toward Organ Procurement from Child Abuse/Homicide Victims," *American Journal of Forensic Medicine and Pathology* 16, no. 1 (1995): 1–10; Wick et al., "Pediatric Organ Donation."

64. John A. Morris, Todd R. Wilcox, and William H. Frist, "Pediatric Organ Donation: The Paradox of Organ Shortage despite the Remarkable Willingness of Families to Donate," *Pediatrics* 89, no. 3 (1992): 411–15.

65. Wick et al., "Pediatric Organ Donation."

66. Shafer et al., "Medical Examiner/Coroner Practices," 1612.

67. Ibid.

68. Jason, "Role of the Medical Examiner/Coroner"; Joseph H. Davis and Ronald K. Wright, "Influence of the Medical Examiner on Cadaver Organ Procurement," *Journal of Forensic Sciences* 22, no. 4 (1977): 824–26.

69. Sturner, "Can Baby Organs Be Donated in All Forensic Cases?"

70. Sally Squires, "Two Agencies in a Grim Battle over Bodies," *Washington Post,* November 18, 1993.

71. Joe Stinebaker, "Organ Harvesting Sparks Dispute: DA's Office Says Capital Murder Case May Have Been Jeopardized," *Houston Chronicle*, August 10, 1999.

72. Jasanoff, *Science at the Bar.*

73. Jaynes and Springer, "Decreasing the Organ Donor Shortage."

74. Sturner, "Can Baby Organs Be Donated in All Forensic Cases?"

75. Frank Sheridan, "Pediatric Death Rates and Donor Yield: A Medical Examiner's View," *Journal of Heart and Lung Transplantation* 12, no. 6 (1993): S179–86.

76. Susan E. Duthie et al., "Successful Organ Donation in Victims of Child Abuse," *Clinics of Transplantation* 9, no. 5 (1995): 415–18.

77. Jaynes and Springer, "Decreasing the Organ Donor Shortage."

78. Duthie et al., "Successful Organ Donation"; Frederick T. Zugibe et al., "Model Organ Description Protocols for Completion by Transplant Surgeons Using Organs Procured from Medical Examiner Cases," *Journal of Transplant Coordination* 9, no. 2 (1999): 73–80.

79. Christopher L. Jaynes and James W. Springer, "Evaluating a Successful Coroner Protocol," *Journal of Transplant Coordination* 6, no. 1 (1996): 28–31; Sheridan, "Pediatric Death Rates and Donor Yield: A Medical Examiner's View.."

80. Sheridan, "Pediatric Death Rates"; Zugibe et al., "Model Organ Description Protocols."

81. Jaynes and Springer, "Successful Coroner Protocol."

82. Shafer et al., "Ethical Analysis of Organ Recovery Denials."

83. Abbott, *The System of Professions,* 50–57.

84. The success of these third parties in changing medical practice has been mixed. Timmermans and Berg, *The Gold Standard.*

85. Lundberg, "College of American Pathologists Conference."

86. Lesley A. Sharp, "The Commodification of the Body and Its Parts," *Annual Review of Anthropology* 29 (2000): 304.

87. Tarek Razek, Kim Olthoff, and Patrick M. Reilly, "Issues in Potential Organ Donor Management," *Surgical Clinics of North America* 80, no. 3 (2000): 1021–32.

88. For a review, see Sharp, "Commodification of the Body."

89. Katches, Heisel, and Campbell, "The Body Brokers."

90. Ibid.

91. Ibid.

92. Ibid.

93. In its 2002 annual report, LifeCell included the following warning: "*Negative publicity concerning the use of donated human tissue in reconstructive cosmetic procedures could reduce the demand for our products and negatively impact the supply of available donor tissue.* Although we do not promote the use of our human tissue products for cosmetic applications, clinicians may use our products in applications or procedures that may be considered 'cosmetic.' Negative publicity concerning the use of donated human tissue in cosmetic procedures could reduce the demand for our products or negatively impact the willingness of families of potential donors to agree to donate tissue or tissue banks to provide tissue to us for processing." LifeCell, *2002 Annual Report* (2003), 20, http://www.lifecell.com/downloads/annual/2003%20Annual%20Report%20 with%2010-K.pdf (accessed September 15, 2005); bold in original. In the executive summary of the report, however, LifeCell's chief executive officer, Paul Thomas, writes that "a key component of our improved financial performance is the continued growth of Alloderm in ENT/plastic reconstructive procedures." Ibid., 2. The *Orange County Register* wrote in 2001 that due to its initial reporting, Collagenesis had lost about half its tissue-bank partners. William Heisel, "Skin Firm Finds Solution," *Orange County Register,* March 2, 2001.

94. See the press release at http://www.collagenesis.com/documents/news.htm (accessed February 17, 2004); and Naomi Aoki, "Healing Touch," *Boston Globe*, February 25, 2001.

95. Shafer et al., "Medical Examiner/Coroner Practices," 1612.

96. Jason, "Role of the Medical Examiner/Coroner."

97. Frammolino, "Harvest of Corneas."

98. Ibid.

99. "Lawsuit Accuses Coroner: Says Body Parts Taken without Families OK," *Newsday*, February 1, 1998. A closely related conflict of interest is the issue of patient privacy. Several coroner's or medical examiner's offices routinely give tissue procurers access to patients' medical and other information.

100. *Texas Health and Safety Code*, chapter 693.002.

101. S. Wilkinson, "Commodification Arguments for the Legal Prohibition of Organ Sale," *Health Care Annals* 8, no. 2 (2000): 189–201.

102. Joralemon, "Shifting Ethics."

103. Michael I. Reed, "Expert Power and Control in Late Modernity: An Empirical Review and Theoretical Synthesis," *Organization Studies* 17, no. 4 (1996): 588.

104. Edmund R. Donoghue and Barry D. Lifschultz, "Every Organ, Every Time: Could We Do It?" (paper presented at the National Association of Medical Examiners conference, Orlando, FL, 1999).

105. Victor W. Weedn et al., *National Association of Medical Examiners: Strategic Plan* (National Association of Medical Examiners, 2002), 6.

106. See Abbott, *The System of Professions.*

107. See Abbott, *The System of Professions;* Donald W. Light, "Countervailing Power: The Changing Character of the Medical Profession in the United States," in *The Changing Medical Profession: An International Perspective,* ed. Frederic W. Hafferty and John B. McKinlay, 69–80 (New York: Oxford University Press, 1993); Donald W. Light, "Countervailing Powers: A Framework for Professions in Transition," in *Health Professions and the State in Europe,* ed. Terry Johnson, Gerry Larkin, and Mike Saks, 25–41 (London: Routledge, 1995); and Donald W. Light, "The Medical Profession and Organizational Change: From Professional Dominance to Countervailing Power," in Bird, Conrad, and Fremont, *Handbook of Medical Sociology,* 201–17.

108. Sharp, "Organ Transplantation."

109. Fox and Swazey, *Spare Parts;* Fox and Swazey, *The Courage to Fail.*

CONCLUSION

1. Atkinson, *Discovering Suicide,* 144.

2. Weber, *Economy and Society,* 263.

3. The modification refers to the role of science in establishing authority (see next paragraph).

4. Weber, *Economy and Society,* 215.

5. Robin Stryker, "Rules, Resources, and Legitmacy Processes: Some Implications for Social Conflict, Order, and Change," *American Journal of Sociology* 99, no. 4 (1994): 847–910. Some professionalization scholars make a distinction between bureaucracy and professions. See Freidson, *Professionalism Reborn.*

6. Abbott, *The System of Professions,* 316.

7. Or a "worknet." One of the founders of "actor-network" theory, Bruno Latour, writes, "Really, we should say 'worknet' instead of 'network'. It's the work, and the movement, and the flow, and the changes that should be stressed." Bruno Latour, "A Dialog on Actor Network

Theory," in *The Social Study of Information and Communication Technology: Innovation, Actors, and Contexts,* ed. Chrisanthi Avgerou, Claudio U. Ciborra, and Frank F. Land (Oxford: Oxford University Press, 2004), 69.

8. Hafferty, "Sociology of Medical Education"; Marie R. Haug, "The Deprofessionalization of Everyone?," *Sociological Focus* 8, no. 3 (1975): 197–213; Haug, "Deprofessionalization: An Alternative Hypothesis," in *Professionalisation and Social Change,* ed. Paul Hamos, 195–211 (Keele, UK: University of Keele, 1973); Haug, "A Re-examination of the Hypothesis of Physician Deprofessionalization," *Milbank Quarterly* 66, suppl. 2 (1988): 48–56; Donald W. Light, "Towards a New Sociology of Medical Education," *Journal of Health and Social Behavior* 29 (1988): 307–22; Light, "Professionalism as a Countervailing Power," *Journal of Health Politics, Policy and Law* 16, no. 3 (1991): 499–506; John McKinlay and Lisa D. Marceau, "The End of the Golden Age of Doctoring," *International Journal of Health Services* 32, no. 2 (2002): 379–416; Harold Wilensky, "The Professionalization of Everyone?" *American Journal of Sociology* 60 (1974): 137–58.

9. Freidson, *Professionalism Reborn,* 32.

10. Stefan Timmermans and Emily Kolker, "Evidence-Based Medicine and the Reconfiguration of Medical Knowledge," *Journal of Health and Social Behavior* 45, extra issue (2004), 177–93.

11. Light, "The Medical Profession and Organizational Change"; Light, "Professionalism as a Countervailing Power."

12. Light, "Countervailing Powers."

13. Donald W. Light and Sol Levine, "The Changing Character of the Medical Profession: A Theoretical Overview," *Milbank Quarterly* 66, suppl. 2 (1988): 10–32.

14. Light, "The Medical Profession and Organizational Change," 204.

15. Freidson, *Professional Dominance;* Freidson, *Professionalism Reborn.*

16. Freidson also refers to the market shelter as an "ecological niche." Freidson, *Professional Dominance,* 127.

17. Freidson, *Professionalism Reborn,* 33.

18. Ibid.

19. Frederic W. Hafferty and Donald Light, "Professional Dynamics and the Changing Nature of Medical Work," *Journal of Health and Social Behavior,* extra issue (1995), 132–53.

20. Eliot Freidson, "The Changing Nature of Professional Control," *Annual Review of Sociology* 10 (1984): 8.

21. Most causal chains depend on split-second events, but medical examiners may trace a chronology back over decades. When a man dies from complications due to a gunshot wound suffered years ago, for example, medical examiners may still designate the death a forensic homicide.

22. Diane Vaughan, "Autonomy, Interdependence, and Social Control: NASA and the Space Shuttle Challenger," *Administrative Science Quarterly* 35 (1990): 273–305.

23. Timmermans and Berg, *The Gold Standard.*

24. Freidson uses "dominant" in an ecological and not necessarily a political sense. Dominance refers to the position of the profession in a division of labor. See Eliot Freidson, *Medical Work in America: Essays in Health Care* (New Haven, CT: Yale University Press, 1989); and Freidson, *Professional Dominance.* Also, the question of whether nurses are actually subordinated by physicians is debatable. See Abbott, *The System of Professions;* and David Hughes, "When Nurse Knows Best: Some Observations of Nurse/Doctor Interaction in a Casualty Department," *Sociology of Health and Illness* 10, no. 1 (1988): 1–22.

25. Heather Hartley, "The System of Alignments Challenging Physician Professional

Dominance: An Elaborated Theory of Countervailing Powers," *Sociology of Health and Illness* 24, no. 2 (2002): 178–207; Timmermans and Kolker, "Evidence-Based Medicine."

26. Marc Berg, *Rationalizing Medical Work: Decision Support Techniques and Medical Practices* (Cambridge, MA: MIT Press, 1997).

27. Timmermans and Berg, *The Gold Standard.*

28. Raymond DeVries et al., eds., *Birth by Design: Pregnancy, Maternity Care, and Midwifery in North America and Europe* (London: Routledge, 2001).

29. Patricia M. Barnes et al., "Complementary and Alternative Medicine Use among Adults: United States, 2002," *Advance Data from Vital and Health Statistics* 343 (2004): 1–20; David M. Eisenberg et al., "Trends in Alternative Medicine Use in the United States, 1990–1997: Results of a Follow-up National Survey," *Journal of the American Medical Association* 280, no. 18 (1998): 1569–75.

30. Nancy Worcester and Mariamne Whatley, "The Response of the Health Care System to the Women's Health Movement: The Selling of Women's Health Centers," in *Feminism within the Science and Health Care Profession,* ed. Sue V. Rosser, 89–103 (New York: Pergamon, 1988).

31. Robert Hurley and R. Brent Rawlings, "Who Lost Cost Containment? A Roster for Recrimination," *Managed Care Quarterly* 9, no. 4 (2001): 23–32.

32. Mary-Jo DelVecchio Good, *American Medicine: The Quest for Competence* (Berkeley and Los Angeles: University of California Press, 1998), chap. 8.

33. Freidson elaborates here on the work of Everett Hughes, who noted that professions gain a state monopoly over work. Hughes, *The Sociological Eye.*

34. This dilemma is common in the history of accidents. See Judith Green, *Risk and Misfortune: A Social Construction of Accidents* (London: UCL Press, 1997).

35. Potential suicides may be downgraded to accidental deaths, while potential accidents may be downgraded to undetermined or natural deaths.

36. Abbott, *The System of Professions.*

37. Thomas F. Gieryn, *Cultural Boundaries of Science: Credibility on the Line* (Chicago: University of Chicago Press, 1999); Michele Lamont and Virag Molnar, "The Study of Boundaries across the Social Sciences," *Annual Review of Sociology* 28 (2002): 167–95.

38. Latour, *Science in Action.*

39. Michael J. Thali et al., "Virtopsy, a New Imaging Horizon in Forensic Pathology: Virtual Autopsy by Postmortem Multislice Computed Tomography (MSCT) and Magnetic Resonance Imaging (MRI)—a Feasibility Study," *Journal of Forensic Sciences* 48, no. 2 (2003): 386–403.

40. A leading figure in this field of small-area variation is John Wennberg. See John E. Wennberg and Alan Gittlesohn, "Small Area Variations in Health Care Delivery," *Science* 182 (1973): 1102–8; and John E. Wennberg, *The Dartmouth Atlas of Health Care, 1999* (Chicago: American Hospital Publishing, 1999).

41. Timmermans and Berg, *The Gold Standard.*

42. Institute of Medicine, *Medicolegal Death Investigation System.*

43. Dan Sosin, "The Use of Medical Examiner and Coroner Data for Public Health Surveillance," in Institute of Medicine, *Medicolegal Death Investigation System,* 39.

44. Marcella Fierro, "The Challenge of Terrorism and Mass Disaster," in Institute of Medicine, *Medicolegal Death Investigation System,* 53.

45. Victor Weedn, "The Potential Federal Role in the Death Investigation System," in Institute of Medicine, *Medicolegal Death Investigation System,* 58.

46. Weedn et al., *National Association of Medical Examiners: Strategic Plan,* 5.

47. Institute of Medicine, *Medicolegal Death Investigation System.*

48. For an exception, see Good, *American Medicine.*

49. Mol, *The Body Multiple.*

50. Richard A. Goodman et al., "Forensic Epidemiology: Law at the Intersection of Public Health and Criminal Investigations," *Journal of Law, Medicine, and Ethics* 31 (2003): 684–700.

51. Nolte, "Research Issues."

52. For more information, see http://www.cdc.gov/ncipc/profiles/nvdrs/facts.htm (accessed November 15, 2004).

53. See http://www.thename.org/library/posiiton_NVDRS.pdf (accessed October 11, 2004).

54. Jerome Groopman, *The Anatomy of Hope: How People Prevail in the Face of Illness* (New York: Random House, 2004), 26.

55. Mary-Jo DelVecchio Good et al., "American Oncology and the Discourse on Hope," *Culture, Medicine, and Psychiatry* 14, no. 1 (1990): 59–79.

56. Bass and Jefferson, *Death's Acre,* 275.

POSTSCRIPT

1. Chambliss, *Beyond Caring.*

2. Goffman, *Stigma.*

3. An exception is Kermit A. Crawford and Raymond B. Flannery Jr., "Critical Incident Stress Management and the Office of the Chief Medical Examiner: Preliminary Inquiry," *International Journal of Emergency Mental Health* 4, no. 2 (2002): 97–97.

4. Goffman, *Stigma,* 122.

5. David Sudnow, *Passing On: The Social Organization of Dying* (Englewood Cliffs, NJ: Prentice-Hall, 1967), 58.

BIBLIOGRAPHY

Abbott, Andrew. "Status and Status Strain in the Professions." *American Journal of Sociology* 86, no. 4 (1981): 819–35.

———. *The System of Professions: An Essay on the Division of Expert Labor.* Chicago: University of Chicago Press, 1988.

Abraham, John. "Distributing the Benefit of the Doubt: Scientists, Regulators, and Drug Safety." *Science, Technology, and Human Values* 19, no. 4 (1994): 493–522.

Allen, Breon G., Lawrence G. Calhoun, Arnie Cann, and Richard Tedeschi. "The Effect of Cause of Death on Responses to the Bereaved: Suicide Compared to Accident and Natural Causes." *Omega* 28, no. 1 (1993): 39–48.

Alvarez, A. *The Savage God: A Study of Suicide.* New York: Random House, 1970.

Alvarez, Alexander. "Trends and Patterns of Justifiable Homicide: A Comparative Analysis." *Violence and Victims* 7, no. 4 (1992): 347–56.

American Academy of Pediatrics. "Addendum: Distinguishing Sudden Infant Death Syndrome from Child Abuse Fatalities." *Pediatrics* 108, no. 3 (2001): 812.

———. "Distinguishing Sudden Infant Death Syndrome from Child Abuse Fatalities." *Pediatrics* 107, no. 2 (2001): 437–41.

———. "Investigation and Review of Unexpected Infant and Child Deaths." *Pediatrics* 104, no. 5 (1999): 1158–60.

———. "Religious Objections to Medical Care." *Pediatrics* 99, no. 2 (1997): 279–81.

Anderson, Robert L., and Betty N. Smith. "Deaths: Leading Causes for 2001." *National Vital Statistics Report* 52, no. 9 (2003): 1–86.

Anspach, Renée. *Deciding Who Lives: Fateful Choices in the Intensive Care Nursery.* Berkeley and Los Angeles: University of California Press, 1993.

Aoki, Naomi. "Healing Touch." *Boston Globe*, February 25, 2001.

Ariès, Philippe. *The Hour of Our Death.* London: Allen Lane, 1977.

Armstrong, David. "The Invention of Infant Mortality." *Sociology of Health and Illness* 8, no. 3 (1986): 211–32.

Aronowitz, Robert A. *Making Sense of Illness.* Cambridge: Cambridge University Press, 1998.

Atkinson, M. W., Neil Kessel, and J. B. Dalgaard. "The Comparability of Suicide Rates." *British Journal of Psychiatry* 127 (1975): 247–56.

Atkinson, Maxwell J. *Discovering Suicide: Studies in the Social Organization of Sudden Death.* London: Macmillan, 1978.

———. "Societal Reactions to Suicide: The Role of Coroners' Definitions." In *Images of Deviance,* edited by Stanley Cohen, 165–91. New York: Penguin Books, 1971.

Atkinson, Paul. "Training for Certainty." *Social Science and Medicine* 19, no. 9 (1984): 949–56.

Atrens, Dale M. "The Questionable Wisdom of a Low-Fat Diet and Cholesterol Reduction." *Social Science and Medicine* 39, no. 3 (1994): 433–47.

Baden, Michael M. *Unnatural Death: Confessions of a Medical Examiner.* New York: Random House, 1989.

Bagley, Christopher. "Authoritarianism, Status Integration and Suicide." *Sociology* 6 (1972): 395–404.

Bal, Roland. "How to Kill with a Ballpoint: Credibility in Dutch Forensic Science." *Science, Technology, and Human Values* 30, no. 1 (2005): 52–75.

Barnes, Patricia M., Eve Powell-Griner, Kim McFann, and Richard L. Nahin. "Complementary and Alternative Medicine Use among Adults: United States, 2002." *Advance Data from Vital and Health Statistics* 343 (2004): 1–20.

Barraclough, Brian M. "Poisoning Cases: Suicide or Accident." *British Journal of Psychiatry* 124 (1974): 526–30.

Barraclough, Brian M., Trevor Holding, and Peter Fayers. "Influence of Coroners' Officers and Pathologists on Suicide Verdicts." *British Journal of Psychiatry* 128 (1976): 471–74.

Barzansky, Barbara, and Sylvia I. Etzel. "Educational Programs in US Medical Schools, 2002–2003." *Journal of the American Medical Association* 209, no. 9 (2003): 1190–96.

Baselt, Randall C. *Disposition of Toxic Drugs and Chemicals in Man.* 6th ed. Davis, CA: Chemical Toxicology Institute, 2002.

Bass, Bill, and Jon Jefferson. *Death's Acre: Inside the Legendary Forensic Lab the Body Farm, Where the Dead Do Tell Tales.* New York: Putnam, 2003.

Baszanger, Isabelle. "Entre traitement de la dernière chance et palliatif pur: Les frontières invisibles des innovations thérapeutiques." *Sciences Sociales et Santé* 18, no. 2 (2000): 67–94.

Bauman, Zygmunt. *Mortality, Immortality and Other Life Strategies.* Palo Alto, CA: Stanford University Press, 1992.

Beck, Ulrich. *Risk Society: Towards a New Modernity.* London: SAGE Publications, 1992.

Becker, Howard S. *Outsiders: Studies in the Sociology of Deviance.* New York: Free Press, 1963.

Becker, Howard S., Blanche Geer, Everett C. Hughes, and Anselm L. Strauss. *Boys in White: Student Culture in Medical School.* Chicago: University of Chicago Press, 1961.

Bell, Jarrett. "Grieving Coach Wages Fight for Son." *USA Today,* November 14, 2003.

Belviso, Maura, Antonio De Donno, Leonardo Vitale, and Francesco Introna. "Positional Asphyxia." *American Journal of Forensic Medicine and Pathology* 24, no. 3 (2003): 292–97.

Berg, Marc. "Practices of Reading and Writing: The Constitutive Role of the Patient Record in Medical Work." *Sociology of Health and Illness* 18, no. 4 (1996): 499–562.

———. *Rationalizing Medical Work: Decision Support Techniques and Medical Practices.* Cambridge, MA: MIT Press, 1997.

Berg, Marc, and Geoffrey Bowker. "The Multiple Bodies of the Medical Record: Toward a Sociology of an Artifact." *Sociological Quarterly* 38, no. 3 (1997): 513–37.

Berg, Marc, and Monica Casper. "Constructivist Perspectives on Medical Work: Medical Practices and Science and Technology Studies." *Science, Technology, and Human Values* 20, no. 4 (1995): 395–407.

Bittner, Egon. *The Functions of the Police in Modern Society, Crime and Delinquency Issues.* Washington, DC: U.S. Government Printing Office, 1970.

Blair, Peter. "Re: Why the Danger in Sharing a Sofa?" Electronic letter. *BMJ*, December 20, 1999. http://bmj.bmjjournals.com/cgi/eletters/319/7223/1457 (accessed September 13, 2005).

Blair, Peter S., Peter J. Fleming, Ian J. Smith, Martin Ward Platt, Jeanine Young, Pam Nadin, P. J. Berry, and Jean Golding. "Babies Sleeping with Parents: Case-Control Study of Factors Influencing the Risk of Sudden Infant Death Syndrome." *BMJ* 319 (1999): 1457–62.

Bloom, Samuel. "The Institutionalization of Medical Sociology in the United States, 1920–1980." In *Handbook of Medical Sociology*, edited by Chloe E. Bird, Peter E. Conrad, and Allen M. Fremont, 11–33. Upper Saddle River, NJ: Prentice-Hall, 2000.

Bloor, Michael. "A Minor Office: The Variable and Socially Constructed Character of Death Certification in a Scottish City." *Journal of Health and Social Behavior* 32 (September 1991): 273–87.

Blumstein, Alfred, P. Frederick Rivara, and Richard Rosenfeld. "The Rise and Decline of Homicide—and Why." *Annual Review of Public Health* 21 (2000): 505–41.

Boglioli, Lauren R., and Mark L. Taff. "Religious Objection to Autopsy: An Ethical Dilemma for Medical Examiners." *American Journal of Forensic Medicine and Pathology* 11, no. 1 (1990): 1–8.

Bondeson, Jan. *Buried Alive: The Terrifying History of Our Most Primal Fear.* New York: W. W. Norton & Company, 2001.

Bonnie, Richard. "Closing Remarks." In Institute of Medicine, *Medicolegal Death Investigation System,* 61–64.

———. "Opening Remarks." In Institute of Medicine, *Medicolegal Death Investigation System,* 3–6.

Bosk, Charles L. *Forgive and Remember: Managing Medical Failure.* 2nd ed. Chicago: University of Chicago Press, 2003. First edition published 1979.

Bowker, Geoffrey, and S. Leigh Star. *Sorting Things Out.* Cambridge, MA: MIT Press, 1999.

Bowling, Benjamin. "The Rise and Fall of New York Murder: Zero Tolerance or Crack's Decline?" *British Journal of Criminology* 39, no. 4 (1999): 531–54.

Bradfield, Amy L., and Gary L. Wells. "The Perceived Validity of Eyewitness Identification Testimony: A Test of the Five Biggers Criteria." *Law and Human Behavior* 24, no. 5 (2000): 581–94.

Brannigan, Augustine, and Michael Lynch. "On Bearing False Witness: Credibility as an Interactional Accomplishment." *Journal of Contemporary Ethnography* 16, no. 2 (1987): 115–46.

Bromberg, S., and Christine K. Cassel. "Suicide in the Elderly: The Limits of Paternalism." *Journal of the American Geriatrics Society* 31, no. 11 (1983): 698–703.

Brown, J. H. "Reporting of Suicide: Canadian Statistics." *Suicide* 5, no. 1 (1975): 21–28.

Burney, Ian. *Bodies of Evidence.* Baltimore: Johns Hopkins University Press, 2000.

Callon, Michel. "Some Elements of a Sociology of Translation: Domestication of the Scallops and the Fishermen of St Brieuc Bay." In *Power, Action, and Belief: A New Sociology of Knowledge?* edited by John Law, 196–229. London: Routledge, 1986.

Cantor, Christopher Henry, Antoon A. Leenaars, and David Lester. "Under-Reporting of Suicide in Ireland, 1960–1989." *Archives of Suicide Research* 3, no. 1 (1997): 5–12.

Carter, N., and G. N. Rutty. "Invoking Sudden Infant Death Syndrome in Cosleeping May Be Misleading (Letter to Editor)." *BMJ* 321 (2000): 1019.

Case, Mary E., Michael A. Graham, Tracey Corey Handy, Jeffrey M. Jentzen, and James A. Monteleone. "Position Paper on Fatal Abusive Head Injuries in Infants and Young Children." *American Journal of Forensic Medicine and Pathology* 22, no. 2 (2001): 112–22.

Chadwick, David L., Robert H. Kirschner, Robert M. Reece, and Lawrence R. Ricci. "Shaken Baby Syndrome—a Forensic Pediatric Response." *Pediatrics* 101, no. 2 (1998): 321–23.

Chambliss, Daniel F. *Beyond Caring: Hospitals, Nurses, and the Social Organization of Ethics.* Chicago: University of Chicago Press, 1996.

Chan, Theodore C., Gary M. Vilke, Tom Neuman, and Jack L. Clausen. "Reexamination of Custody Restraint Position and Positional Asphyxia." *American Journal of Forensic Medicine and Pathology* 19, no. 3 (1998): 201–5.

Clarke, Adele. *Disciplining Reproduction: Modernity, American Life Sciences, and "the Problems of Sex."* Berkeley and Los Angeles: University of California Press, 1998.

Clarke, Adele E., Janet K. Shim, Laura Mamo, Jennifer R. Fosket, and Jennifer R. Fishman. "Biomedicalization: Technoscientific Transformations of Health, Illness, and U.S. Biomedicine." *American Sociological Review* 68 (April 2003): 161–94.

Cohle, Stephen D., Anthony Foster, and Sandra L. Cottingham. "Shaken Baby Syndrome." *American Journal of Forensic Medicine and Pathology* 21, no. 2 (2000): 198–99.

Cole, Simon A. "Jackson Pollock, Judge Pollak, and the Dilemma of Fingerprint Expertise." In Edmond, *Expertise in Regulation and Law,* 98–120.

———. *Suspect Identities: A History of Fingerprinting and Criminal Identification.* Cambridge, MA: Harvard University Press, 2001.

———. "Witnessing Identification: Latent Fingerprinting Evidence and Expert Knowledge." *Social Studies of Science* 28, nos. 5–6 (1998): 687–712.

Cole, Stephen. "Merton's Contribution to the Sociology of Science." *Social Studies of Science* 34, no. 6 (2004): 829–44.

Collins, Harry M. *Changing Order: Replication and Induction in Scientific Practice.* London: SAGE, 1985.

———. "The Sociology of Scientific Knowledge: Studies of Contemporary Science." *Annual Review of Sociology* 9 (1983): 265–85.

Collins, Harry M., and Robert Evans. "The Third Wave of Science Studies: Studies of Expertise and Experience." *Social Studies of Science* 32, no. 2 (2002): 235–96.

Collins, Kim A. "Death by Overlaying and Wedging: A 15-Year Retrospective Study." *American Journal of Forensic Medicine and Pathology* 22, no. 2 (2001): 155–59.

———. "SIDS, Overlaying, and Suffocation." Lecture presented at the Third Annual Pediatric Forensic Issues Conference, Orlando, FL, December 2, 1999.

Cooper, P. N., and C. M. Milroy. "The Coroner's System and Under-Reporting of Suicide." *Medicine, Science, and Law* 35, no. 4 (1995): 319–26.

Cowen, Alan R. "In a Bind." *Emergency Medical Services* 24, no. 6 (1995): 54–58.

Crawford, Kermit A., and Raymond B. Flannery Jr. "Critical Incident Stress Management and the Office of the Chief Medical Examiner: Preliminary Inquiry." *International Journal of Emergency Mental Health* 4, no. 2 (2002): 93–97.

Crume, Teresa L., Carolyn DiGuiseppi, Tim Byers, Andrew P. Sirotnak, and Carol J. Garrett. "Underascertainment of Child Maltreatment Fatalities by Death Certificates, 1990–1998." *Pediatrics* 110, no. 2 (2002): 18–23.

Cussins, Charis. "Ontological Choreography: Agency for Women in an Infertility Clinic." In *Differences in Medicine: Unraveling Practices, Techniques and Bodies,* edited by Marc Berg and Annemarie Mol, 166–201. Durham, NC: Duke University Press, 1998.

Daemmrich, Arthur. "The Evidence Does Not Speak for Itself: Expert Witnesses and the Organization of DNA-Typing Companies." *Social Studies of Science* 28, nos. 5–6 (1998): 741–72.

Darbonne, A. "Suicide and Age: A Suicide Note Analysis." *Journal of Consulting and Clinical Psychology* 33 (1969): 46–50.

Davis, Gregory M. "Mind Your Manners, Part I: History of Death Certification and Manner of Death Classification." *American Journal of Forensic Medicine and Pathology* 18, no. 3 (1997): 219–23.

Davis, Joseph H., and Ronald K. Wright. "Influence of the Medical Examiner on Cadaver Organ Procurement." *Journal of Forensic Sciences* 22, no. 4 (1977): 824–26.

"Death of Aide's Son Accidental." *Milwaukee Journal Sentinel,* May 20, 2004.

Deidiker, Russell. "Return of the Killer Fish: Accidental Choking Death on a Bluegill (*Lepomis Macrochirus*)." *American Journal of Forensic Medicine and Pathology* 23, no. 2 (2002): 197–98.

deJong, John L., and Randy Hanzlick. "Level of Agreement between Opinions of Medical Examiner Investigators and Forensic Pathologist Medical Examiners regarding the Manner of Death." *American Journal of Forensic Medicine and Pathology* 21, no. 1 (2000): 11–20.

DeVries, Raymond, Cecilia Benoit, Edward R. Van Teijlingen, and Sirpa Wrede, eds. *Birth by Design: Pregnancy, Maternity Care, and Midwifery in North America and Europe.* London: Routledge, 2001.

Diamond, Timothy. *Making Gray Gold: Narratives of Nursing Home Care.* Chicago: University of Chicago Press, 1992.

DiMaio, Dominick J., and Vincent J. M. DiMaio. *Forensic Pathology.* New York: Elsevier, 1989.

DiMaio, Vincent J. M. "Characteristics of Wounds Produced by Handguns and Rifles." In Froede, *Handbook of Forensic Pathology,* 217–25.

Dingwall, Robert, John Eekelaar, and Topsy Murray. *The Protection of Children.* Oxford: Basil Blackwell, 1983.

Donoghue, Edmund R., and Barry D. Lifschultz. "Every Organ, Every Time: Could We Do It?" Paper presented at the National Association of Medical Examiners conference, Orlando, FL, 1999.

Donohoe, Mark. "Evidence-Based Medicine and Shaken Baby Syndrome, Part 1: Literature Review, 1966–1998." *American Journal of Forensic Medicine and Pathology* 24, no. 3 (2003): 239–42.

Douglas, Jack. *The Social Meanings of Suicide.* Princeton, NJ: Princeton University Press, 1967.

Drago, Dorothy A., and Andrew L. Dannenberg. "Infant Mechanical Suffocation Deaths in the United States, 1980–1997." *Pediatrics* 103, no. 5 (1999): e59.

Draus, Paul. *Consumed in the City: Observing Tuberculosis at Century's End.* Philadelphia: Temple University Press, 2004.

Duneier, Mitchell. *Sidewalk.* New York: Farrar, Straus & Giroux, 1999.

Durand-Zaleski, Isabelle, Renee Waissman, Philippe Lang, Bertrand Weil, Monji Foury, and Francis Bonnet. "Nonprocurement of Transplantable Organs in a Tertiary Care Hospital: A Focus on Sociological Causes." *Transplantation* 62, no. 9 (1996): 1224–29.

Durfee, Michael, Deanne T. Durfee, and M. Patricia West. "Child Fatality Review: An International Movement." *Child Abuse and Neglect* 26, nos. 6–7 (2002): 619–36.

Durkheim, Emile. *Suicide: A Study in Sociology.* Translated by John A. Spaulding and George Simpson. New York: Free Press, 1979. First published 1897.

Duster, Troy. "Medicine: Race and Reification in Science." *Science* 307, no. 5712 (2005): 1050–51.

Duthie, Susan E., Bradley M. Peterson, James Cutler, and Brian Blackbourne. "Successful Organ Donation in Victims of Child Abuse." *Clinics of Transplantation* 9, no. 5 (1995): 415–18.

Eckert, William G. "Medicolegal Investigation in New York City." *American Journal of Forensic Medicine and Pathology* 4, no. 1 (1983): 33–54.

Edmond, Gary. *Expertise in Regulation and Law.* Burlington, VT: Ashgate Publishing Company, 2004.

Edmond, Gary, and David Mercer. "Trashing 'Junk Science.'" *Stanford Technology Law Review* 3 (1998): 1–31.

Eichenwald, Kurt. "Deadly House Calls." *New York Times,* May 13, 2001.

Eid, Michael, and Ed Diener. "Norms for Experiencing Emotions in Different Cultures: Inter- and International Differences." *Journal of Personality and Social Psychology* 81, no. 5 (2001): 869–85.

Eisenberg, David M., Roger B. Davis, Susan L. Ettner, Scott Appel, Sonja Wilkey, Maria Van Rompay, and Ronald C. Kessler. "Trends in Alternative Medicine Use in the United States, 1990–1997: Results of a Follow-up National Survey." *Journal of the American Medical Association* 280, no. 18 (1998): 1569–75.

Elias, Norbert. *The Loneliness of the Dying.* Oxford: Basil Blackwell, 1985.

Emerc, Branko. "Minimizing Mistakes in Clinical Diagnosis." *American Journal of Forensic Medicine and Pathology* 44, no. 4 (1999): 810–13.

Emerson, Robert. *Judging Delinquents.* Chicago: Aldine, 1969.

Evidence-Based Medicine Working Group. "Evidence-Based Medicine: A New Approach to Teaching the Practice of Medicine." *Journal of the American Medical Association* 268, no. 17 (1992): 2420–25.

Fagot-Largeault, Anne. *Les causes de la mort: Histoire naturelle et facteurs de risque.* Paris: L'Institut Interdisciplinaire d'Études Épistémologiques, 1989.

Faigman, David L., David H. Kaye, Michael J. Saks, and Joseph Sanders. *Modern Scientific Evidence: The Law and Science of Expert Testimony.* St. Paul, MN: West, 1997.

Falzon, Andrew L., and Gregory G. Davis. "A 15-Year Retrospective Review of Homicide in the Elderly." *Journal of Forensic Sciences* 43, no. 2 (1998): 371–74.

Fanton, Laurent, Alain Miras, Stephane Tilhet-Coartet, Pierre Achache, and Pierre Malicier. "The Perfect Crime: Myth or Reality?" *American Journal of Forensic Medicine and Pathology* 19, no. 3 (1998): 290–93.

Feifel, Herman, ed. *The Meaning of Death.* New York: McGraw-Hill, 1959.

Fierro, Marcella. "The Challenge of Terrorism and Mass Disaster." In Institute of Medicine, *Medicolegal Death Investigation System,* 52–53.

Fisher, Daniel J. "Equivocal Cases of Teenage Suicide." *Forensic Examiner* 9, nos. 9–10 (2000): 24–27.

Fisher, S. Russell. "History of Forensic Pathology and Related Sciences." In Spitz, *Medicolegal Investigation of Death,* 3–13.

Fleck, Ludwik. *Genesis and Development of a Scientific Fact.* Chicago: University of Chicago Press, 1979. First published 1935.

Fleming, Peter J., Peter S. Blair, Chris Bacon, David Bensley, Iain Smith, Elizabeth Taylor, Jem Berry, Jean Golding, and John Tripp. "Environment of Infants during Sleep and Risk of the Sudden Infant Death Syndrome: Results of 1993–5 Case-Control Study for Confidential Inquiry into Stillbirths and Deaths in Infancy." *BMJ* 313 (1996): 191–95.

Forster, Peter Glover. "Religion, Magic, Witchcraft, and AIDS in Malawi." *Anthropos* 93 (1998): 537–45.

Foucault, Michel. *The Birth of the Clinic.* New York: Vintage Books, 1973.

Fox, Renée C. "An Ignoble Form of Cannibalism: Reflections on the Pittsburgh Protocol for Procuring Organs from Non-Heart-Beating Cadavers." *Kennedy Institute of Ethics Journal* 3, no. 2 (1993): 231–39.

———. "Medical Uncertainty Revisited." In *The Handbook of Social Studies in Health and Medicine,* edited by Gary L. Albrecht, Ray Fitzpatrick, and Susan C. Scrimshaw, 409–25. London: SAGE, 2000.

———. "Training for Uncertainty." In *The Student Physician,* edited by Robert K. Merton, G. Reader, and P. L. Kendall, 207–41. Cambridge, MA: Harvard University Press, 1957.

Fox, Renée C., and Judith P. Swazey. *The Courage to Fail: A Social View of Organ Transplants and Dialysis.* 2nd ed. Chicago: University of Chicago Press, 1978.

———. *Spare Parts: Organ Replacement in American Society.* Oxford: Oxford University Press, 1992.

Frammolino, Ralph. "Harvest of Corneas at Morgue Questioned: Corneas Taken without Survivor's Permission Are Resold at Huge Markup by Eye Bank, Which Pays Coroner's Office a Fee." *Los Angeles Times,* November 2, 1997.

Freidson, Eliot. "The Changing Nature of Professional Control." *Annual Review of Sociology* 10 (1984): 1–20.

———. *Medical Work in America: Essays in Health Care.* New Haven, CT: Yale University Press, 1989.

———. *Professional Dominance: The Social Structure of Medical Care.* New York: Atherton Press, 1970.

———. *Professionalism Reborn: Theory, Prophecy, and Policy.* Chicago: University of Chicago Press, 1994.

———. *Profession of Medicine: A Study of the Sociology of Applied Knowledge.* New York: Harper & Row, 1970.

Freud, Sigmund. *Reflections on War and Death.* New York: Moffat, Yard, 1918.

Froede, Richard C., ed. *Handbook of Forensic Pathology.* Northfield, IL: College of American Pathologists, 1990.

Fuenmayor, Abdel J., and Abdel M. Fuenmayor. "Cardiac Arrest following Holiday Heart Syndrome." *International Journal of Cardiology* 59, no. 1 (1997): 101–3.

Fujimura, Joan. *Crafting Science: A Sociohistory of the Quest for the Genetics of Cancer.* Cambridge, MA: Harvard University Press, 1996.

Gall, Edward A. "The Necropsy as a Tool in Medical Progress." *Bulletin of the New York Academy of Medicine* 44 (1968): 808–29.

Garfinkel, Harold. "Practical Sociological Reasoning: Some Features in the Work of the Los Angeles Suicide Prevention Center." In *Essays in Self-Destruction,* edited by Edwin S. Shneidman, 171–87. New York: Science House, 1967.

———. *Studies in Ethnomethodology.* Englewood Cliffs, NJ: Prentice-Hall, 1967.

Garrety, Karin. "Social Worlds, Actor-Networks and Controversy: The Case of Cholesterol, Dietary Fat and Heart Disease." *Social Studies of Science* 27, no. 5 (1997): 727–73.

Geberth, Vernon J. "Suicide by Cop: Inviting Death from the Hands of a Police Officer." *Law and Order,* July 1993, 105–9.

Gellert, George A., Roberta M. Maxwell, Michael J. Durfee, and Gerald A. Wagner. "Fatalities Assessed by the Orange County Child Death Review Team." *Child Abuse and Neglect* 19, no. 7 (1995): 875–83.

Giacomini, Mita. "A Change of Heart and a Change of Mind? Technology and the Redefinition of Death in 1968." *Social Science and Medicine* 44, no. 10 (1997): 1465–82.

Gibbs, Jack P., and Walter T. Martin. *Status Integration and Suicide.* Eugene, OR: University of Oregon Books, 1964.

Giddens, Anthony. "The Suicide Problem in French Sociology." *British Journal of Sociology* 16 (1965): 276–95.

Giertsen, Jan C., and Inge Morild. "Reliability of Norwegian Suicide Statistics." *Nordisk Medicin* 108, no. 2 (1993): 58–59.

Gieryn, Thomas F. *Cultural Boundaries of Science: Credibility on the Line.* Chicago: University of Chicago Press, 1999.

Gist, Richard, and Q. B. Welch. "Certification Change versus Actual Behavior Change in Teenage Suicide Rates, 1955–1979." *Suicide and Life-Threatening Behavior* 19, no. 3 (1989): 277–88.

Glaser, Barney, and Anselm Strauss. *Awareness of Dying.* Chicago: Aldine, 1965.

———. *The Discovery of Grounded Theory.* New York: Aldine, 1967.

Goff, M. Lee. *A Fly for the Prosecution: How Insect Evidence Helps Solve Crimes.* Cambridge, MA: Harvard University Press, 2000.

Goffman, Erving. *Stigma: Notes on the Management of Spoiled Identity.* New York: Touchstone, 1963.

Golan, Tal. "The Emergence of the Silent Witness: The Legal and Medical Reception of X-Rays in the USA." *Social Studies of Science* 34, no. 4 (2004): 469–99.

Goldsmith, Sara K., Terry C. Pellmar, Arthur M. Kleinman, and William E. Bunney. *Reducing Suicide: A National Imperative.* Washington, DC: National Academies Press, 2002.

Good, Mary-Jo DelVecchio. *American Medicine: The Quest for Competence.* Berkeley and Los Angeles: University of California Press, 1998.

Good, Mary-Jo DelVecchio, Byron J. Good, Cynthia Shaffer, and Stuart E. Lind. "American Oncology and the Discourse on Hope." *Culture, Medicine, and Psychiatry* 14, no. 1 (1990): 59–79.

Goodin, Julia, and Randy Hanzlick. "Mind Your Manners, Part II: General Results from the National Association of Medical Examiners Manner of Death Questionnaire, 1995." *American Journal of Forensic Medicine and Pathology* 18, no. 3 (1997): 224–27.

Goodman, Richard A., Judith W. Munson, Kim Dammers, Zita Lazzarini, and John P. Barkley. "Forensic Epidemiology: Law at the Intersection of Public Health and Criminal Investigations." *Journal of Law, Medicine, and Ethics* 31 (2003): 684–700.

Gorer, Geoffrey. *Death, Grief, and Mourning.* Garden City, NY: Doubleday, 1965.

Green, Judith. "From Accidents to Risk: Public Health and Preventable Injury." *Health, Risk and Society* 1, no. 1 (1999): 25–39.

———. *Risk and Misfortune: A Social Construction of Accidents.* London: UCL Press, 1997.

Gregory, J. Geoff. "Citation Study of a Scientific Revolution: Sudden Infant Death Syndrome." *Scientometrics* 5 (1983): 313–27.

Groopman, Jerome. *The Anatomy of Hope: How People Prevail in the Face of Illness.* New York: Random House, 2004.

Hacking, Ian. *Rewriting the Soul.* Princeton, NJ: Princeton University Press, 1995.

———. *The Taming of Chance.* Cambridge: Cambridge University Press, 1990.

Hafferty, Frederic. *Into the Valley: Death and the Socialization of Medical Students.* New Haven, CT: Yale University Press, 1991.

———. "Reconfiguring the Sociology of Medical Education: Emerging Topics and Pressing Issues." In *Handbook of Medical Sociology,* edited by Chloe E. Bird, Peter E. Conrad, and Allen M. Fremont, 238–57. Upper Saddle River, NJ: Prentice-Hall, 2000.

Hafferty, Frederic W., and Donald Light. "Professional Dynamics and the Changing Nature of Medical Work." *Journal of Health and Social Behavior,* extra issue (1995), 132–53.

Halfon, Saul. "Collecting, Testing and Convincing: Forensic DNA Experts in the Courts." *Social Studies of Science* 28, nos. 5–6 (1998): 801–28.

Hall, Mark A., Ira Mark Ellman, and Danile S. Strouse. *Health Care Law and Ethics in a Nutshell.* 2nd ed. St. Paul, MN: West Group Press, 1998.

Hallam, Elizabeth, Jenny Hockey, and Glennys Howarth. *Beyond the Body: Death and Social Identity.* London: Routledge, 1999.

O'Halloran, Ronald L., and Larry V. Lewman. "Restraint Asphyxiation in Excited Delirium." *American Journal of Forensic Medicine and Pathology* 14, no. 4 (1993): 289–95.

O'Halloran, Ronald L., and Janice G. Frank. "Asphyxial Death during Prone Restraint Revisited." *American Journal of Forensic Medicine and Pathology* 21, no. 1 (2000): 39–52.

Hanford, Jack T. "Religion, Medical Ethics, and Transplants." *Journal of Medical Humanities* 14, no. 1 (1993): 33–38.

Hannan, Michael T., and John Freeman. "The Population Ecology of Organizations." *American Journal of Sociology* 83 (1977): 929–84.

Hansen, Mark. "Why Are Iowa's Babies Dying?" *ABA Journal* 84 (1998): 47–78.

Hanzlick, Randy. "Lawsuits against Medical Examiners or Coroners Arising from Death Certificates." *American Journal of Forensic Medicine and Pathology* 18, no. 2 (1997): 119–23.

———. *The Medical Cause of Death Manual.* Chicago: College of American Pathologists, 1994.

———. "Medical Examiners, Coroners, and Organ Recovery in the United States." *Journal of the American Medical Association* 273, no. 20 (1995): 1578.

———. "On the Need for More Expertise in Death Investigation." *Archives of Pathology and Laboratory Medicine* 120 (1996): 329–32.

———. "Overview of the Medicolegal Death Investigation System in the United States." In Institute of Medicine, *Medicolegal Death Investigation System,* 7–11.

Hanzlick, Randy, and Debra Combs. "Medical Examiner and Coroner Systems: History and Trends." *Journal of the American Medical Association* 279, no. 11 (1998): 870–74.

Hanzlick, Randy, and Julia Goodin. "Mind Your Manners, Part III: Individual Scenario Results and Discussion of the National Association of Medical Examiners Manner of Death Questionnaire." *American Journal of Forensic Medicine and Pathology* 18, no. 3 (1997): 228–45.

Hanzlick, Randy, John C. Hunsaker III, and Gregory J. Davis. *A Guide for Manner of Death Classification.* National Association of Medical Examiners, 2002.

Hanzlick, Randy, and Jesse K. McKenney. "Education of a Pathologist." *Annals of Internal Medicine* 159, no. 9 (1999): 907–8.

Haraway, Donna J. *Simians, Cyborgs, and Women: The Reinvention of Nature.* New York: Routledge, 1991.

Harcourt, Bernard E. *Illusion of Order: The False Promise of Broken Windows Policing.* Cambridge, MA: Harvard University Press, 2001.

Harris, Anthony, Stephen H. Thomas, Gene A. Fisher, and David J. Hirsch. "Murder and Medicine: The Lethality of Criminal Assault, 1960–1999." *Homicide Studies* 6, no. 2 (2002): 128–66.

Harris, Lawrence S. "A Killing of Baby Doe." *Journal of Forensic Sciences* 42, no. 6 (1997): 1180–82.

Hartley, Heather. "The System of Alignments Challenging Physician Professional Dominance: An Elaborated Theory of Countervailing Powers." *Sociology of Health and Illness* 24, no. 2 (2002): 178–207.

Hasson, Jack, and Herbert Schneiderman. "Autopsy Training Programs to Right a Wrong." *Archives of Pathology and Laboratory Medicine* 119 (1995): 289–91.

Hatina, Joseph D. "Shaken Baby Syndrome: Who Are the True Experts?" *Cleveland State Law Review* 46 (1998): 557–83.

Hauck, Fern R., Stanislaw M. Herman, Mark Donovan, Solomon Iyasu, Merrick Cathryn Moore, Edmund Donoghue, Robert H. Kirschner, and Marian Willinger. "Sleep Environment and the Risk of Sudden Infant Death Syndrome in an Urban Population: The Chicago Infant Mortality Study." *Pediatrics* 111, no. 5 (2003): 1207–14.

Haug, Marie R. "Deprofessionalization: An Alternative Hypothesis." In *Professionalisation and Social Change,* edited by Paul Hamos, 195–211. Keele, UK: University of Keele, 1973.

———. "The Deprofessionalization of Everyone?" *Sociological Focus* 8, no. 3 (1975): 197–213.

———. "A Re-examination of the Hypothesis of Physician Deprofessionalization." *Milbank Quarterly* 66, suppl. 2 (1988): 48–56.

Hauser, John E. "The Use of Medical Examiner–Coroner's Cases as Transplant Donors." *Journal of Forensic Sciences* 14, no. 2 (1969): 501–6.

Hegert, Thomas F. "Medical Examiners, Coroners, and Organ Recovery in the United States." *Journal of the American Medical Association* 273, no. 20 (1995): 1578–79.

Heidegger, Martin. *Being and Time.* Translated by Joan Stambaugh. Albany, NY: SUNY Press, 1996. First published 1927.

Heisel, William. "Skin Firm Finds Solution." *Orange County Register* (Santa Ana, CA), March 2, 2001.

Henry, A. F., and J. F. Short. *Suicide and Homicide.* New York: Free Press, 1954.

Hilgartner, Stephen. "The Social Construction of Risk Objects; or, How to Pry Open Networks of Risk." In *Organizations, Uncertainties and Risk,* edited by James F. Short and Lee Clarke, 39–58. Boulder, CO: Westview Press, 1992.

Hill, Rolla B., and Robert E. Anderson. *The Autopsy: Medical Practice and Public Policy.* Boston: Butterworths, 1988.

Hirsch, Charles S. "Restraint Asphyxiation." *American Journal of Forensic Medicine and Pathology* 14, no. 1 (1994): 86.

Hirsch, Charles S., and Vernard I. Adams. "Sudden and Unexpected Death from Natural Causes in Adults." In Spitz, *Spitz and Fisher's Medicolegal Investigation of Death,* 137–74.

Hirsch, Charles S., and Mark A. Flomenbaum. *Forensic Pathology Check Sample FP 95–1: Problem Solving in Death Certification.* Chicago: American Society of Clinical Pathologists, 1995.

Hiss, Jehuda, and Tzipi Kahana. "Trauma and Identification of Victims of Suicidal Terrorism in Israel." *Military Medicine* 165, no. 11 (2000): 889–93.

Hogberg, Ulf, and Eric Bergstrom. "Suffocated Prone: The Iatrogenic Tragedy of SIDS." *American Journal of Public Health* 90, no. 4 (2000): 527–31.

Hogle, Linda. "Standardization across Non-standard Domains: The Case of Organ Procurement." *Science, Technology, and Human Values* 20, no. 4 (1995): 482–500.

Holding, Trevor A., and Brian M. Barraclough. "Undetermined Deaths—Suicide or Accident?" *British Journal of Psychiatry* 133 (1978): 542–49.

Horn, Kevin D., and William A. Devine. "An Approach to Dissecting the Congenitally Malformed Heart in the Forensic Autopsy." *American Journal of Forensic Medicine and Pathology* 22, no. 4 (2001): 405–11.

Hughes, David. "When Nurse Knows Best: Some Observations of Nurse/Doctor Interaction in a Casualty Department." *Sociology of Health and Illness* 10, no. 1 (1988): 1–22.

Hughes, Everett. *The Sociological Eye: Selected Papers.* Chicago: Aldine-Atherton, 1971. First published 1945.

Humphry, Derek. *Final Exit: The Practicalities of Self-Deliverance and Assisted Suicide for the Dying.* 3rd ed. New York: Dell Paperbacks, 2003.

Hunnisett, R. F. *The Medieval Coroner.* Cambridge: Cambridge University Press, 1961.

Hurley, Robert, and R. Brent Rawlings. "Who Lost Cost Containment? A Roster for Recrimination." *Managed Care Quarterly* 9, no. 4 (2001): 23–32.

Hutson, H. Range, Deirdre Anglin, John Yarbrough, Kimberley Hardaway, Marie Russell, Jared Strote, Michael Canter, and Bennett Blum. "Suicide by Cop." *Annals of Emergency Medicine* 32, no. 6 (1998): 665–69.

Illich, Ivan. "The Political Uses of Natural Death." In *Death Inside Out,* edited by Peter Steinfels and Robert M. Veatch, 25–43. New York: Harper & Row, 1974.

Imwinkelried, Edward J. "The Meaning of 'Appropriate Validation' in Daubert v. Merrell Dow Pharmaceuticals, Inc., Interpreted in Light of the Broader Rationalist Tradition, Not the Narrow Scientific Tradition." *Florida State University Law Review* 30 (2003): 735.

Institute of Medicine. *Medicolegal Death Investigation System: Workshop Summary.* Washington, DC: National Academies Press, 2003.

Inwood, M. J., ed. *Hegel Selections.* The Great Philosophers. New York: Macmillan, 1989.

Israel, Robert A., Harry M. Rosenberg, and Lester R. Curtin. "Analytical Potential for Multiple Cause-of-Death Data." *American Journal of Epidemiology* 124, no. 2 (1986): 161–79.

Jacobs, David, and David W. Britt. "Inequality and the Police Use of Deadly Force." *Social Problems* 26 (1979): 403–12.

Jacobs, David, and Robert M. O'Brien. "The Determinants of Deadly Force: A Structural Analysis of Police Violence." *American Journal of Sociology* 103, no. 4 (1998): 837–62.

Jacobson, Solomon, Christopher Bagley, and Ann Rehin. "Clinical and Social Variables Which Differentiate Suicide, Open and Accident Verdicts." *Psychological Medicine* 6 (1976): 417–21.

Jaffe, Eric S. " 'She's Got Bette Davis's Eyes': Assessing the Nonconsensual Removal of Cadaver Organs under the Takings and Due Process Clauses." *Columbia Law Review* 90, no. 2 (1990): 528–73.

Jamison, Kay Redfield. *Night Falls Fast: Understanding Suicide.* New York: Vintage Books, 1999.

Jasanoff, Sheila. "Breaking the Waves in Science Studies: Comment on H. M. Collins and Robert Evans, 'The Third Wave of Science Studies.' " *Social Studies of Science* 33, no. 3 (2003): 389–400.

————. "The Eye of Everyman: Witnessing DNA in the Simpson Trial." *Social Studies of Science* 28, nos. 5–6 (1998): 713–40.

————. "Judicial Fictions: The Supreme Court's Quest for Good Science." *Society* 38, no. 4 (2001): 27–36.

————. *Science at the Bar: Law, Science, and Technology in America.* Cambridge, MA: Harvard University Press, 1995.

Jason, Donald. "The Role of the Medical Examiner/Coroner in Organ and Tissue Procurement for Transplantation." *American Journal of Forensic Medicine and Pathology* 15, no. 3 (1994): 192–202.

Jaynes, Christopher L., and James W. Springer. "Decreasing the Organ Donor Shortage by Increasing Communication between Coroners, Medical Examiners, and Organ Procurement Organizations." *American Journal of Forensic Medicine and Pathology* 15, no. 2 (1994): 156–59.

————. "Evaluating a Successful Coroner Protocol." *Journal of Transplant Coordination* 6, no. 1 (1996): 28–31.

Jennings, C., and Brian Barraclough. "Legal and Administrative Influences on the English Suicide Rate since 1900." *Psychology and Medicine* 10, no. 3 (1980): 407–18.

Jentzen, Jeffrey, George Palermo, Thomas L. Johnson, Khang-Cheng Ho, K. Alan Stormo, and John Teggatz. "Destructive Hostility: The Jeffrey Dahmer Case; A Psychiatric and Forensic Study of a Serial Killer." *American Journal of Forensic Medicine and Pathology* 15, no. 4 (1994): 283–94.

Jobes, David A., Alan L. Berman, and Arnold R. Josselson. "Improving the Validity and Reliability of Medical-Legal Certifications of Suicide." *Suicide and Life-Threatening Behavior* 17, no. 4 (1987): 310–25.

Joffe, Mark, and Stephen Ludwig. "Stairway Injuries in Children." *Pediatrics* 83, no. 3 (1988): 457–61.

Johnson, H. R. M. "The Incidence of Unnatural Deaths Which Have Been Presumed to Be Natural in Coroners' Autopsies." *Medicine, Science, and the Law* 9 (1969): 102–6.

Johnson, Michael P., and Karl Hufbauer. "Sudden Infant Death Syndrome as a Medical Research Problem since 1945." *Social Problems* 30, no. 1 (1982): 65–81.

Johnson-McGrath, Julie. "Speaking for the Dead: Forensic Pathologists and Criminal Justice in the United States." *Science, Technology, and Human Values* 20, no. 4 (1995): 438–59.

Jonasson, Birgitta, Ulf Jonasson, and Tom Saldeen. "Suicides May Be Overreported and Accidents Underreported among Facilities Due to Dextropropoxyphene." *Journal of Forensic Sciences* 44, no. 2 (1999): 334–38.

Joralemon, Donald. "Organ Wars: The Battle for Body Parts." *Medical Anthropology Quarterly* 9, no. 3 (1995): 335–56.

————. "Shifting Ethics: Debating the Incentive Question in Organ Transplantation." *Journal of Medical Ethics* 27 (2001): 30–35.

Jung, Carl. "The Soul and Death." In Feifel, *The Meaning of Death*, 3–16.

Kahn, Jonathan. "How a Drug Becomes "Ethnic": Law, Commerce, and the Production of Racial Categories in Medicine." *Yale Journal of Health Policy and Law Ethics* 4, no. 1 (2004): 1–46.

Karch, Steven B., and Charles V. Wetli. "Agitated Delirium versus Positional Asphyxia." *Annals of Emergency Medicine* 26, no. 6 (1995): 760.

Katches, Mark, William Heisel, and Ronald Campbell. "The Body Brokers." *Orange County Register* (Santa Ana, CA), April 16, 2000.

Katz, Jack. *How Emotions Work.* Chicago: University of Chicago Press, 1999.

Kelleher, Michael J., Paul Corcoran, and Helen S. Keeley. "Suicide in Ireland: Statistical, Social and Clinical Considerations." *Archives of Suicide Research* 3, no. 1 (1997): 13–24.

Kelleher, Michael J., Paul Corcoran, Helen S. Keeley, J. Donnehy, and Ian O'Donnell. "Improving Procedures for Recording Suicide Statistics." *Irish Medical Journal* 89, no. 1 (1996): 14–15.

Kircher, T., J. Nelson, and H. Burdo. "The Autopsy as a Measure of Accuracy of the Death Certificate." *New England Journal of Medicine* 313, no. 20 (1985): 1267–73.

Kirk, Stuart A., and Herb Kutchins. *The Selling of the DSM: The Rhetoric of Science in Psychiatry.* Hawthorne, NY: Aldine de Gruyter, 1992.

Kitsuse, John I., and Aaron V. Cicourel. "A Note on the Uses of Official Statistics." *Social Problems* 11 (1963): 131–39.

Kleck, Gary. "Crime Control through the Private Use of Armed Force." *Social Problems* 35, no. 1 (1988): 163–84.

———. "Miscounting Suicides." *Suicide and Life-Threatening Behavior* 18, no. 3 (1988): 219–36.

Klinenberg, Eric. *Heat Wave: A Social Autopsy of Disaster in Chicago.* Chicago: University of Chicago Press, 2002.

Klockars, Carl B. "A Theory of Excessive Force and Its Control." In *Police Violence*, edited by William A. Geller and Hans Toch, 1–23. New Haven, CT: Yale University Press, 1996.

Knorr-Cetina, Karin. *Epistemic Cultures: How the Sciences Make Knowledge.* Cambridge, MA: Harvard University Press, 1999.

Kochanek, Kenneth D., Sherry L. Murphy, Robert N. Anderson, and Chester Scott. "Deaths: Final Data for 2002." *National Vital Statistics Report* 53, no. 5 (2004): 1–116.

Koehler, Steven A., Hank Weiss, Thomas J. Songer, Leon Rozin, Abdulrezzak Shakir, Shaun Ladham, Bennet Omalu, Joseph Dominick, and Cyril H. Wecht. "Deaths among Criminal Suspects, Law Enforcement Officers, Civilians, and Prison Inmates: A Coroner-Based Study." *American Journal of Forensic Medicine and Pathology* 24, no. 4 (2003): 334–38.

Kohn, Linda T., Janet M. Corrigan, and Molla S. Donaldson, eds. *To Err Is Human: Building a Safer Health System.* Washington, DC: National Academy Press, 2000.

Kramer, Peter. *Against Depression.* New York: Viking, 2005.

Krous, Henry F. "The International Standardized Autopsy Protocol for Sudden Unexpected Infant Death." In *Sudden Infant Death Syndrome: New Trends in the Nineties*, edited by T. O. Rognum, 81–95. Oslo: Scandinavian University Press, 1995.

Kübler-Ross, Elisabeth. *On Death and Dying.* New York: Macmillan, 1969.

Kuhn, Thomas. *The Structure of Scientific Revolutions.* 2nd ed. Chicago: University of Chicago Press, 1962.

Kurachek, Stephen C., Sandra L. Titus, Mike Olesen, and Judson Reaney. "Medical Examiners' Attitudes toward Organ Procurement from Child Abuse/Homicide Victims." *American Journal of Forensic Medicine and Pathology* 16, no. 1 (1995): 1–10.

Kutner, Nancy G. "Issues in the Application of High Cost Medical Technology: The Case of Organ Transplantation." *Journal of Health and Social Behavior* 28 (March 1987): 23–36.

Lakatos, Imre. "Falsification and the Methodology of Research Programmes." In *Criticism and the Growth of Knowledge*, edited by Imre Lakatos and A. Musgrave, 91–195. Cambridge: Cambridge University Press, 1970.

Lamont, Michele, and Virag Molnar. "The Study of Boundaries across the Social Sciences." *Annual Review of Sociology* 28 (2002): 167–95.

Langewische, William. "The Crash of EgyptAir 990." *Atlantic Monthly,* November 2001.

Lantz, Patrick E., Donald Jason, and Gregory Davis. "Decreasing the Organ Donor Shortage." *American Journal of Forensic Medicine and Pathology* 16, no. 3 (1995): 257–59.

Laposata, Elizabeth A. "Positional Asphyxia during Law Enforcement Transport." *American Journal of Forensic Medicine and Pathology* 14, no. 1 (1993): 86–87.

Last, John. *Public Health and Human Ecology.* East Norwalk, CT: Appleton & Lange, 1987.

Latour, Bruno. "A Dialog on Actor Network Theory." In *The Social Study of Information and Communication Technology: Innovation, Actors, and Contexts,* edited by Chrisanthi Avgerou, Claudio U. Ciborra, and Frank F. Land, 65–79. Oxford: Oxford University Press, 2004.

———. *Pandora's Hope: Essays on the Reality of Science Studies.* Cambridge, MA: Harvard University Press, 1999.

———. *The Pasteurization of France.* Cambridge, MA: Harvard University Press, 1988.

———. *Science in Action: How to Follow Scientists and Engineers through Society.* Cambridge, MA: Harvard University Press, 1987.

"Law Should Clearly Define Brain Death." Editorial. *Denver Post,* October 7, 2004.

Lawrence, Christopher. " 'Definite and Material': Coronary Thrombosis and Cardiologists in the 1920s." In *Framing Disease: Studies in Cultural History,* edited by Charles E. Rosenberg and Janet Golden, 50–84. New Brunswick, NJ: Rutgers University Press, 1992.

"Lawsuit Accuses Coroner: Says Body Parts Taken without Families' OK." *Newsday,* February 1, 1998.

LeBrun, George P. *It's Time to Tell; as Told to Edward D. Radin.* New York: William Morrow & Company, 1962.

Lee, Paul P., Joyce C. Yang, Peter J. McDonell, A. Edward Maumenee, and Walter J. Stark. "Worldwide Legal Requirements for Obtaining Corneas, 1990." *Cornea* 11, no. 2 (1992): 102–7.

Leenaars, Antoon A. *Suicide Notes: Predictive Clues and Patterns.* New York: Human Sciences Press, 1988.

Leighton, Alexander C., and Charles C. Hughes. "Notes on Eskimo Patterns of Suicide." *Southwestern Journal of Anthropology* 11 (1955): 327–38.

Levesque, William R. "Medical Examiner Retires." *St. Petersburg Times,* June 29, 2000.

Lie, Reidar K. "The Angina Pectoris Controversy during the 1920s." *Acta Physiologica Scandinavia* 599, suppl. (1991), 135–47.

LifeCell. *2002 Annual Report.* 2003. http://www.lifecell.com/downloads/annual/2003%20Annual%20Report%20with%2010-K.pdf (accessed September 15, 2005).

Light, Donald W. "Countervailing Power: The Changing Character of the Medical Profession in the United States." In *The Changing Medical Profession: An International Perspective,* edited by Frederic W. Hafferty and John B. McKinlay, 69–80. New York: Oxford University Press, 1993.

———. "Countervailing Powers: A Framework for Professions in Transition." In *Health Professions and the State in Europe,* edited by Terry Johnson, Gerry Larkin and Mike Saks, 25–41. London: Routledge, 1995.

———. "The Medical Profession and Organizational Change: From Professional Dominance to Countervailing Power." In *Handbook of Medical Sociology,* edited by Chloe E. Bird, Peter E. Conrad, and Allen M. Fremont, 201–17. Upper Saddle River, NJ: Prentice-Hall, 2000.

―――――. "Professionalism as a Countervailing Power." *Journal of Health Politics, Policy and Law* 16, no. 3 (1991): 499–506.

―――――. "Towards a New Sociology of Medical Education." *Journal of Health and Social Behavior* 29 (1988): 307–22.

―――――. "Uncertainty and Control in Professional Training." *Journal of Health and Social Behavior* 20, no. 4 (1979): 310–22.

Light, Donald W., and Sol Levine. "The Changing Character of the Medical Profession: A Theoretical Overview." *Milbank Quarterly* 66, suppl. 2 (1988): 10–32.

Link, Bruce, and Jo C. Phelan. "Conceptualizing Stigma." *Annual Review of Sociology* 27 (2001): 63–85.

Lock, Margaret. "Contesting the Natural in Japan: Moral Dilemmas and Technologies of Dying." *Culture, Medicine, and Psychiatry* 19, no. 1 (1995): 1–38.

―――――. "Reaching Consensus about Death: Heart Transplants and Cultural Identity in Japan." *Society-Société* 13, no. 1 (1989): 15–26.

―――――. *Twice Dead: Organ Transplants and the Reinvention of Death.* Berkeley and Los Angeles: University of California Press, 2002.

Luckenbill, David F. "Criminal Homicide as a Situated Transaction." *Social Problems* 25, no. 2 (1977): 176–86.

Luke, James L. "The Shortage of Organs for Transplantation." *New England Journal of Medicine* 325 (1992): 1025.

Luke, James L., and Donald T. Reay. "The Perils of Investigating and Certifying Deaths in Police Custody." *American Journal of Forensic Medicine and Pathology* 13, no. 2 (1992): 98–100.

Lundberg, George D. "College of American Pathologists Conference: Restructuring Autopsy Practice for Health Care Reform." *Archives of Pathology and Laboratory Medicine* 120 (1996): 736–39.

―――――. "The Role of the Medicolegal Autopsy in Health Care." In Institute of Medicine, *Medicolegal Death Investigation System,* 44–45.

Lundstrom, Marie, and Rochelle Sharpe. "Getting Away with Murder." *Public Welfare* 49, no. 3 (1991): 18–29.

Lupton, Deborah. *Risk.* London: Routledge, 1999.

Lynch, Michael. "Discipline and the Material Form of Images: An Analysis of Scientific Visibility." *Social Studies of Science* 15, no. 1 (1985): 37–66.

―――――. "The Discursive Production of Uncertainty: The OJ Simpson 'Dream Team' and the Sociology of Knowledge Machine." *Social Studies of Science* 28, nos. 5–6 (1998): 829–68.

―――――. " 'Science above All Else': The Inversion of Credibility between Forensic DNA Profiling and Fingerprint Evidence." In Edmond, *Expertise in Regulation and Law,* 121–35.

―――――. *Scientific Practice and Ordinary Action: Ethnomethodology and Social Studies of Science.* Cambridge: Cambridge University Press, 1993.

Lynch, Michael, and David Boden. *The Spectacle of History: Speech, Text, and Memory at the Iran-Contra Hearings.* Durham, NC: Duke University Press, 1996.

MacDonald, Michael. "The Medicalization of Suicide in England: Laymen, Physicians, and Cultural Change, 1500–1870." *Milbank Quarterly* 67, suppl. 1 (1989): 69–91.

MacDonald, Michael, and Terence R. Murphy. *Sleepless Souls: Suicide in Early Modern England.* Oxford: Clarendon Press, 1990.

Macintyre, Sally. "Some Notes on Record Taking and Making in an Antenatal Clinic." *Sociological Review* 26 (1978): 595–611.

MacKenzie, Donald. *Inventing Accuracy: A Historical Sociology of Nuclear Missile Guidance.* Cambridge, MA: MIT Press, 1993.

————. *Mechanizing Proof: Computing, Risk, and Trust.* Cambridge: MIT Press, 2001.

Mackersie, Robert C., Oscar Bronsther, and Steven Shackford. "Organ Procurement in Patients with Fatal Head Injuries: The Fate of the Potential Donor." *Annals of Surgery* 213, no. 2 (1991): 143–50.

Malla, Ashok, and John Hoenig. "Differences in Suicide Rates: An Examination of Under-Reporting." *Canadian Journal of Psychiatry* 28, no. 4 (1983): 291–93.

Manning, Peter K. *Policing Contingencies.* Chicago: University of Chicago Press, 2003.

Marcuse, Herbert. "The Ideology of Death." In Feifel, *The Meaning of Death,* 64–78.

Martin, Innes. "Organizational Communication and the Symbolic Construction of Police Murder Investigations." *British Journal of Sociology* 53, no. 1 (2002): 67–87.

Martin, Joyce A., Kenneth D. Kochanek, Donna M. Strobino, Bernard Guyer, and Marian F. MacDorman. "Annual Summary of Vital Statistics—2003." *Pediatrics* 115, no. 3 (2005): 619–34.

Marzuk, Peter M., Kenneth Tardiff, Charles S. Hirsch, Andrew C. Leon, Marina Stajic, Nancy Hartwell, and Laura Portera. "Increase in Suicide by Asphyxiation in New York City after the Publication of *Final Exit.*" *Publishing Research Quarterly* 10, no. 4 (1994–95): 62–68.

Massello, William, III. "The Proof in Law of Suicide." *Journal of Forensic Sciences* 31, no. 3 (1985): 1000–1008.

Matza, David. *Becoming Deviant.* Englewood Cliffs, NJ: Prentice-Hall, 1969.

Maulitz, Russell C. *Morbid Appearances: The Anatomy of Pathology in the Early Nineteenth Century.* Cambridge: Cambridge University Press, 1987.

May, Thomas, Mark P. Aulisio, and Michael A. DeVita. "Patients, Families and Organ Donation: Who Should Decide?" *Milbank Quarterly* 78, no. 2 (2000): 323–36.

McKinlay, John, and Lisa D. Marceau. "The End of the Golden Age of Doctoring." *International Journal of Health Services* 32, no. 2 (2002): 379–416.

Meckel, Richard A. *Save the Babies: American Public Health Reform and the Prevention of Infant Mortality, 1850–1929.* Baltimore: Johns Hopkins University Press, 1990.

Merton, Robert K. *On the Shoulders of Giants: A Shandean Postscript.* Chicago: University of Chicago Press, 1993. First published 1965.

————. *Social Theory and Social Structure.* Glencoe, IL: Free Press, 1957.

Mirchandani, Haresh G., Lucy B. Rorke, Adrienne Sekula-Perlman, and Ian C. Hood. "Cocaine-Induced Agitated Delirium, Forceful Struggle, and Minor Head Injury." *American Journal of Forensic Medicine and Pathology* 15, no. 2 (1994): 95–99.

Mishler, Elliot G. *Discourse of Medicine.* Norwood, NJ: Ablex, 1984.

Mitchell, Ed. "Cot Death—the Story So Far." *BMJ* 319 (1999): 1457.

Mitchell, Elizabeth, Henry F. Krous, Terrance Donald, and Roger W. Byard. "An Analysis of the Usefulness of Specific Stages in the Pathologic Investigation of Sudden Infant Death." *American Journal of Forensic Medicine and Pathology* 21, no. 4 (2000): 395–400.

Mitford, Jessica. *The American Way of Death Revisited.* New York: Vintage Books, 2000.

Moens, Guido F. "The Reliability of Reported Suicide Mortality Statistics: An Experience from Belgium." *International Journal of Epidemiology* 14, no. 2 (1985): 272–75.

Mohandie, Kris, and Reid J. Meloy. "Clinical and Forensic Indicators of 'Suicide by Cop.'" *Journal of Forensic Sciences* 45, no. 2 (1999): 384–89.

Mohr, James C. *Doctors and the Law: Medical Jurisprudence in the Nineteenth Century.* New York: Oxford University Press, 1993.

Mol, Annemarie. *The Body Multiple: Ontology in Medical Practice.* Durham, NC: Duke
University Press, 2002.

————. "Wat diagnostische Technieken doen: Het Voorbeeld van de Bloedsuikermeter."
In *Ingebouwde Normen: Medische Technieken Doorgelicht,* edited by Marc Berg and
Annemarie Mol, 143–57. Utrecht: Van der Wees, 2001.

Moller, David Wendell. *Life's End: Technocratic Dying in an Age of Spiritual Yearning.*
Amityville, NY: Baywood Publishing Company, 2000.

Morris, John A., Todd R. Wilcox, and William H. Frist. "Pediatric Organ Donation: The
Paradox of Organ Shortage despite the Remarkable Willingness of Families to Donate."
Pediatrics 89, no. 3 (1992): 411–15.

Nakamura, Suad, Marilyn Wind, and Mary Ann Danello. "Review of Hazards Associated
with Children Placed in Adult Beds." *Archives of Pediatrics and Adolescent Medicine* 153,
no. 10 (1999): 1019–23.

National Research Council. *The Age of Expert Testimony: Science in the Courtroom.*
Washington, DC: National Research Council, 2000.

National Transportation Safety Board. *EgyptAir Flight 990: The Final Report.* Washington,
DC: National Transportation Safety Board, 2002.

Neeleman, Jan, and Simon Wessely. "Changes in Classification of Suicide in England and
Wales: Time Trends and Associations with Coroners' Professional Backgrounds."
Psychology and Medicine 27, no. 2 (1997): 467–72.

Nelkin, Dorothy, and Lori Andrews. "Do the Dead Have Interests? Policy Issues for
Research after Life." *American Journal of Law and Medicine* 24 (1998): 261–91.

Nelson, Franklyn L., Norman L. Farberow, and Douglas R. MacKinnon. "The
Certification of Suicide in Eleven Western States: An Inquiry into the Validity of
Reported Suicide Rates." *Suicide and Life-Threatening Behavior* 8, no. 2 (1978): 75–88.

Newman, Katherine S. *Rampage: The Social Roots of School Shootings.* New York: Basic
Books, 2004.

Noguchi, Thomas T. *Coroner.* With Joseph DiMona. New York: Simon & Schuster, 1983.

————. *Coroner at Large.* With Joseph DiMona. New York: Simon & Schuster, 1985.

Nolte, Kurt. "The Potential Role of Medical Examiners and Coroners in Responding to and
Planning for Bioterrorism and Emerging Infectious Diseases." In Institute of Medicine,
Medicolegal Death Investigation System, 49–52.

————. "Research Issues." In Institute of Medicine, *Medicolegal Death Investigation
System,* 15–18.

Nordenfelt, Lennart. *Causes of Death: A Philosophical Essay.* Göteborg:
Forskningradsnamnden, 1983.

Northcutt, Wendy. *The Darwin Awards II: Unnatural Selection.* New York: Penguin Group,
2001.

O'Carroll, Patrick W. "A Consideration of the Validity and Reliability of Suicide Mortality
Data." *Suicide and Life-Threatening Behavior* 19, no. 1 (1989): 1–16.

Oehmichen, Manfred, Ivana Gerling, and Christoph Meissner. "Petechiae of the Baby's
Skin as Differentiation Symptom of Infanticide versus SIDS." *Journal of Forensic Sciences*
45, no. 3 (2000): 602–7.

Ohberg, Annakatri, and Jouko Lonnqvist. "Suicides Hidden among Undetermined Deaths."
Acta Psychiatrica Scandinavia 98, no. 3 (1998): 214–18.

Oliver, Ronald C., Joel P. Sturtevant, James P. Scheetz, and Mary E. Fallat. "Beneficial
Effects of a Hospital Bereavement Intervention Program after Traumatic Childhood
Death." *Journal of Trauma* 50, no. 4 (2001): 440–48.

O'Neill, Patrick. "Rules Questioned for Assisted Suicide Reports." *Oregonian*, March 21, 1998.

Oteri, Joseph S., Marty S. Weinberg, and Marty S. Pinales. "Cross Examination of Chemists." In *Science in Context: Readings in the History and Philosophy of Science*, edited by Barry Barnes and David Edge, 250–59. Milton Keynes, UK: Open University Press, 1982.

Padosch, Stephan A., Peter H. Schmidt, Lars U. Kroner, and Burkhard Madea. "Death due to Positional Asphyxia under Severe Alcoholisation: Pathophysiologic and Forensic Considerations." *Forensic Science International* 149, no. 1 (2005): 67–73.

Parsons, Talcott. "The Sick Role and the Role of the Physician Reconsidered." *Milbank Memorial Quarterly Fund* 53, no. 3 (1975): 257–78.

Peck, Dennis L., and Kenneth Warner. "Accident or Suicide? Single-Vehicle Car Accidents and the Intent Hypothesis." *Adolescence* 30 (Summer 1995): 463–72.

Peck, Dennis L. " 'Official Documentation' of the Black Suicide Experience." *Omega* 14, no. 1 (1983–84): 21–31.

Perez, Douglas W., and William Ker Muir. "Administrative Review of Alleged Police Brutality." In *Police Violence*, edited by William A. Geller and Hans Toch, 213–33. New Haven, CT: Yale University Press, 1996.

Perez-Pena, Richard, David Kocieniewski, and Jason George. "Death on the Night Shift." *New York Times*, February 29, 2004.

Perrow, Charles. *Normal Accidents: Living with High Risk Technologies.* New York: Basic Books, 1984.

Person, Tiffany L. A., Wendy A. Lavezzi, and Barbara C. Wolf. "Cosleeping and Sudden Unexpected Death in Infancy." *Archives of Pathology and Laboratory Medicine* 126 (2002): 343–45.

Pescosolido, Bernice A., and Robert Mendelsohn. "Social Causation or Social Construction of Suicide? An Investigation into the Social Organization of Official Rates." *American Sociological Review* 51 (1986): 80–101.

Pestaner, Joseph P. "End-of-Life Care: Forensic Medicine v. Palliative Medicine." *Journal of Law, Medicine, and Ethics* 31 (Fall 2003): 365–71.

Phillips, David P., and Todd E. Ruth. "Adequacy of Official Suicide Statistics for Scientific Research and Public Policy." *Suicide and Life-Threatening Behavior* 23, no. 4 (1993): 307–19.

Pickering, Andrew. "Constraints on Controversy: The Case of the Magnetic Monopole." *Social Studies of Science* 11, no. 1 (1981): 63–93.

———. *The Mangle of Practice: Time, Agency, and Science.* Chicago: University of Chicago Press, 1995.

———, ed. *Science as Practice and Culture.* Chicago: University of Chicago Press, 1992.

Plath, Sylvia. *Ariel.* New York: Harper & Row, 1966.

Plunkett, John. "Shaken Baby Syndrome and the Death of Matthew Eappen." *American Journal of Forensic Medicine and Pathology* 20, no. 1 (1999): 17–21.

Pollanen, Michael S., David A. Chiasson, James T. Cairns, and James G. Young. "Unexpected Death Related to Restraint for Excited Delirium: A Retrospective Study of Deaths in Police Custody and in the Community." *Canadian Medical Association Journal* 158, no. 12 (1998): 1603–7.

Pounder, Derrick J. "The Case of Dr. Shipman." *American Journal of Forensic Medicine and Pathology* 24, no. 3 (2003): 219–26.

Preston, Samuel H., and Michael R. Haines. *Fatal Years: Child Mortality in Late Nineteenth-Century America.* Princeton, NJ: Princeton University Press, 1991.

Prior, Lindsay. *The Social Organisation of Death: Medical Discourses and Social Practices in Belfast.* London: Macmillan, 1989.

Prottas, Jeffrey, and H. Batten. "The Willingness to Give: The Public and the Supply of Transplantable Organs." *Journal of Health Politics, Policy, and Law* 16 (1991): 121–34.

Rao, P. Anand. "Keeping the Science Court Out of the Jurybox: Helping the Jury Manage Scientific Evidence." *Social Epistemology* 13, no. 2 (1999): 129–45.

Rapp, Rayna. *Testing Women, Testing the Fetus: The Social Impact of Amniocentesis in America.* New York: Routledge, 2000.

Razek, Tarek, Kim Olthoff, and Patrick M. Reilly. "Issues in Potential Organ Donor Management." *Surgical Clinics of North America* 80, no. 3 (2000): 1021–32.

Reay, Donald T. "Suspect Restraint and Sudden Death." *FBI Law Enforcement Bulletin,* May 1996, 22–25.

Reay, Donald T., and J. W. Eisele. "Deaths from Law Enforcement Neck Holds." *American Journal of Forensic Medicine and Pathology* 3, no. 3 (1982): 253–58.

Reay, Donald T., Corinne L. Fligner, Allan D. Stilwell, and Judy Arnold. "Positional Asphyxia during Law Enforcement Transport." *American Journal of Forensic Medicine and Pathology* 13, no. 2 (1992): 90–97.

Reay, Donald T., and G. A. Holloway. "Changes in Carotid Blood Flow Produced by Neck Compression." *American Journal of Forensic Medicine and Pathology* 3, no. 3 (1982): 199–202.

Reay, Donald T., and John D. Howard. "Restraint Position and Positional Asphyxia." *American Journal of Forensic Medicine and Pathology* 20, no. 3 (1999): 300–301.

Reay, Donald T., John D. Howard, Corinne L. Fligner, and Richard J. Ward. "Effects of Positional Restraint on Oxygen Saturation and Heart Rate following Exercise." *American Journal of Forensic Medicine and Pathology* 9, no. 1 (1988): 16.

Reddy, Sita. "Temporarily Insane: Pathologizing Cultural Difference in American Criminal Courts." *Sociology of Health and Illness* 24, no. 5 (2002): 667–87.

Reed, Michael I. "Expert Power and Control in Late Modernity: An Empirical Review and Theoretical Synthesis." *Organization Studies* 17, no. 4 (1996): 573–97.

Reitan, Albert G. *Specialist's Factual Report of Investigation DCA00MA006.* Washington, DC: National Transportation Safety Board, 1999.

Ressler, Robert A., Ann W. Burgess, and John E. Douglas. *Sexual Homicide: Patterns and Motives.* Lexington, MA: Lexington Books, 1988.

Richard, Christopher, Sarah Mosko, James McKenna, and Sean Drummond. "Sleeping Position, Orientation, and Proximity in Bedsharing Infants and Mothers." *Sleep* 19, no. 9 (1996): 685–90.

Richards, Evelleen. *Vitamin C and Cancer: Medicine or Politics?* London: Macmillan, 1991.

Richardson, Ruth. *Death, Dissection, and the Destitute.* London: Routledge & Kegan Paul, 1987.

Riedel, Marc. "Sources of Homicide Data: A Review and Comparison." In *Homicide: A Sourcebook of Social Research,* edited by M. Dwayne Smith and Margaret A. Zahn, 75–95. Thousand Oaks, CA: SAGE Publications, 1999.

Risinger, Michael D. "Preliminary Thoughts on a Functional Taxonomy of Expertise for the Post-Kumho World." *Seton Hall Law Review* 31 (2000): 508–37.

Roach, Mary. *Stiff: The Curious Lives of Human Cadavers.* New York: W. W. Norton & Company, 2003.

Roeggla, Martin, Andreas Wagner, Markus Muellner, Andreas Bur, Hannelore Roeggla, Michael M. Hirschl, Anton N. Laggner, and Georg Roeggla. "Cardiorespiratory

Consequences to Hobble Restraint." *Wien Klinische Wochenschrift* 109, no. 10 (1996): 359–61.

Rose, Nicolas. *Governing the Soul.* London: Free Association Books, 1989.

Rosenberg, Charles E. "Pathologies of Progress: The Idea of Civilization as Risk." *Bulletin of the History of Medicine* 72, no. 4 (1998): 714–30.

———. "The Tyranny of Diagnosis: Specific Entities and Individual Experience." *Milbank Quarterly* 80, no. 2 (2002): 237–60.

Rosenberg, Mark L., Lucy E. Davidson, Jack C. Smith, Alan L. Berman, Herb Buzbee, George Ganter, George A. Gay, Barbara Moore-Lewis, Don H. Mills, Don Murray, Patrick W. O'Carroll, and David Jobes. "Operational Criteria for the Determination of Suicide." *Journal of Forensic Sciences* 33, no. 6 (1988): 1445–55.

Ross, Darrell L. "Factors Associated with Excited Delirium Deaths in Police Custody." *Modern Pathology* 11, no. 11 (1998): 1127–37.

Roth, Julius. *Timetables: Structuring the Passage of Time in Hospital Treatment and Other Careers.* Indianapolis, IN: Bobbs-Merrill, 1963.

Roth, Randolph. "Child Murder in New England." *Social Science History* 25, no. 1 (2001): 101–47.

Rothman, Sheila M., and David J. Rothman. *The Pursuit of Perfection: The Promise and Perils of Medical Enhancement.* New York: Pantheon Books, 2003.

Ruttenber, James, Janet Lawler-Heavner, Ming Yin, Charles V. Wetli, Lee W. Learn, and Deborah C. Mash. "Fatal Excited Delirium following Cocaine Use: Epidemiologic Findings Provide New Evidence for Mechanisms of Cocaine Toxicity." *Journal of Forensic Sciences* 42, no. 1 (1997): 25–31.

Sachs, Jessica Snyder. *Corpse: Nature, Forensics, and the Struggle to Pinpoint the Time of Death.* Cambridge, MA: Perseus Publishing, 2001.

Sainsbury, Peter. "Validity and Reliability of Trends in Suicide Statistics." *World Health Statistical Quarterly* 36, nos. 3–4 (1983): 339–48.

Saks, Michael. "Banishing Ipse Dixit: The Impact of Kumho Tire on Forensic Identification Sciences." *Washington and Lee University Law Review* 57 (2000): 879–900.

Salib, Emad. "Coroner's Verdicts in the Elderly: A Suicide or an Open Verdict?" *International Journal of Geriatric Psychiatry* 12, no. 4 (1997): 481–83.

Sampson, Robert J., and Stephen W. Raudenbusch. "Systematic Social Observation of Public Spaces: A New Look at Disorder in Neighborhoods." *American Journal of Sociology* 105, no. 3 (1999): 603–51.

Sanko, John. "Senator Ends Push for Bill Limiting Role of Coroner." *Denver Rocky Mountain News,* April 22, 2000.

Sartre, Jean-Paul. *Being and Nothingness: A Phenomenological Essay on Ontology.* New York: Pocket Books, 1966. First published 1943.

Schaechter, Judy, Isis Duran, Jacqueline De Marchena, Glendene Lemard, and Maria E. Vallar. "Are 'Accidental' Gun Deaths as Rare as They Seem? A Comparison of Medical Examiner Manner of Death Coding with an Intent-Based Classification Approach." *Pediatrics* 111, no. 4 (2003): 741–44.

Scheper-Hughes, Nancy. *Death without Weeping.* Berkeley and Los Angeles: University of California Press, 1992.

———. "The Global Traffic in Human Organs." *Current Anthropology* 41, no. 2 (2000): 191–224.

Schmidt, Chester W., John W. Shaffer, Howard I. Zlotowitz, and Russell S. Fisher. "Suicide by Vehicular Crash." *American Journal of Psychiatry* 134, no. 2 (1977): 175–78.

Seale, Clive. *Constructing Death: The Sociology of Dying and Bereavement.* Cambridge: Cambridge University Press, 1998.

Shafer, Teresa J., Lawrence L. Schkade, Roger W. Evans, Kevin J. O'Connor, and William Reitsma. "Vital Role of Medical Examiners and Coroners in Organ Transplantation." *American Journal of Transplantation* 4 (2003): 160–68.

Shafer, Teresa J., Lawrence L. Schkade, Laura A. Siminoff, and Timothy A. Mahoney. "Ethical Analysis of Organ Recovery Denials by Medical Examiners, Coroners, and Justices of the Peace." *Journal of Transplant Coordination* 5, no. 4 (1999): 232–49.

Shafer, Teresa J., Lawrence L. Schkade, Howell E. Warner, Mark Eakin, Kevin O'Connor, Jim Springer, Tim Jankiewicz, William Reitsma, Janet Steele, and Karyn Keen-Denton. "Impact of Medical Examiner/Coroner Practices on Organ Recovery in the United States." *Journal of the American Medical Association* 272, no. 20 (1994): 1607–13.

Shapin, Steven. "Cordelia's Love: Credibility and the Social Studies of Science." *Perspectives on Science* 3, no. 3 (1995): 255–75.

———. "The Politics of Observation: Cerebral Anatomy and Social Interests in the Edinburgh Phrenology Disputes." In *On the Margins of Science: The Social Construction of Rejected Knowledge,* edited by Roy Wallis, 139–78. Keele, UK: Keele University Press, 1979.

———. *A Social History of Truth: Civility and Science in Seventeenth-Century England.* Chicago: University of Chicago Press, 1994.

Shapin, Steven, and Simon Schaffer. *Leviathan and the Air-Pump.* Princeton, NJ: Princeton University Press, 1985.

Sharp, Lesley A. "The Commodification of the Body and Its Parts." *Annual Review of Anthropology* 29 (2000): 287–328.

———. "Organ Transplantation as a Transformative Experience: Anthropological Insights into the Restructuring of the Self." *Medical Anthropology Quarterly* 9, no. 3 (1995): 357–89.

Sheridan, Frank. "Pediatric Death Rates and Donor Yield: A Medical Examiner's View." *Journal of Heart and Lung Transplantation* 12, no. 6 (1993): S179–86.

Shneidman, Edwin S. *Definition of Suicide.* New York: John Wiley & Sons, 1985.

———. *The Suicidal Mind.* Oxford: Oxford University Press, 1996.

———. *Voices of Death.* New York: Harper & Row, 1980.

Shneidman, Edwin S., and Norman L. Farberow, eds. *Clues to Suicide.* New York: McGraw-Hill, 1957.

Shulman, Morton. *Coroner.* Toronto: Fitzhenry & Whiteside, 1975.

Siegel, Barry. "Judging Parents as Murderers on Four Specks of Blood." *Los Angeles Times,* July 11, 1999.

Silverglate, Harvey. "Science and the Au Pair Trial." *Wall Street Journal,* November 11, 1997.

Sirken, Monroe G., Harry M. Rosenberg, Frances M. Chevarley, and Lester R. Curtin. "The Quality of Cause-of-Death Statistics." *Journal of Public Health* 77, no. 2 (1987): 137–39.

Smith, Dorothy E. " 'K Is Mentally Ill': The Anatomy of a Factual Account." *Sociology* 12, no. 1 (1978): 23–53.

Smith, Janet. "Third Report: Death Certification and the Investigation of Deaths by Coroners." In *The Shipman Inquiry,* 530. Norwich, UK, 2003.

Smith, Roger. "Forensic Pathology, Scientific Expertise, and the Criminal Law." In *Expert Evidence: Interpreting Science in the Law,* edited by Roger Smith and Brian Wynne, 56–92. London: Routledge, 1989.

Smith, Roger, and Brian Wynne. "Introduction." In *Expert Evidence: Interpreting Science in the Law,* edited by Roger Smith and Brian Wynne, 1–22. London: Routledge, 1989.

Smith, Ronald. "Doheny Eye Bank." *Los Angeles Times,* November 10, 1997.

Solomon, Shana M., and Edward J. Hackett. "Setting Boundaries between Science and Law: Lessons from *Daubert v. Merrell Dow Pharmaceuticals, Inc.*" *Science, Technology, and Human Values* 21, no. 2 (1996): 131–56.

Sosin, Dan. "The Use of Medical Examiner and Coroner Data for Public Health Surveillance." In Institute of Medicine, *Medicolegal Death Investigation System,* 38–40.

Soslow, Arnold R., and Alan D. Woolf. "Reliability of Data Sources for Poisoning Deaths in Massachusetts." *American Journal of Emergency Services* 10, no. 2 (1992): 124–27.

Speechley, Mark, and Kathleen M. Stavraky. "The Adequacy of Suicide Statistics for Use in Epidemiology and Public Health." *Canadian Journal of Public Health* 82, no. 1 (1991): 38–42.

Spital, Aaron. "Ethical and Policy Issues in Altruistic Living and Cadaveric Organ Donation." *Clinics of Transplantation* 11, no. 2 (1997): 77–87.

Spitz, Werner U. *Spitz and Fisher's Medicolegal Investigation of Death.* 3rd ed. Springfield, IL: Charles C. Thomas, 1993.

Squires, Sally. "Transplant Tug-of-War." *Washington Post,* November 23, 1993.

———. "Two Agencies in a Grim Battle over Bodies." *Washington Post,* November 18, 1993.

Stanistreet, Debbi, Steve Taylor, Victoria Jeffrey, and Mark Gabbay. "Accident or Suicide? Predictors of Coroners' Decisions in Suicide and Accident Verdicts." *Medicine, Science, and Law* 41, no. 2 (2001): 111–15.

Star, S. Leigh. "Power, Technologies, and the Phenomenology of Conventions: On Being Allergic to Onions." In *A Sociology of Monsters: Essays on Power, Technology and Domination,* edited by John Law, 26–56. London: Routledge, 1991.

———. *Regions of the Mind: Brain Research and the Quest for Scientific Certainty.* Stanford, CA: Stanford University Press, 1989.

Starr, Paul. *The Social Transformation of Medicine.* New York: Basic Books, 1982.

Steinhauser, Karen E., Nicholas A. Christakis, Elizabeth C. Clipp, Maya McNeilly, Lauren McIntyre, and James A. Tulsky. "Factors Considered Important at the End of Life by Patients, Family, Physicians, and Other Care Givers." *Journal of the American Medical Association* 284, no. 19 (2000): 2476–82.

Steinhauser, Karen E., Elizabeth C. Clipp, Maya McNeilly, Nicholas A. Christakis, Lauren McIntyre, and James A. Tulsky. "In Search of a Good Death: Observations of Patients, Families and Providers." *Annals of Internal Medicine* 132, no. 10 (2000): 825–32.

Stengel, Erwin, and Norman L. Farberow. "Certification of Suicide around the World." In *Proceedings of the Fourth International Conference on Suicide Prevention,* edited by Norman L. Farberow, 8–15. Los Angeles: Delmar Publishing Company, 1967.

Stewart, James B. *Blind Eye: How the Medical Establishment Let a Doctor Get Away with Murder.* New York: Simon & Schuster, 1999.

Stinebaker, Joe. "Organ Harvesting Sparks Dispute: DA's Office Says Capital Murder Case May Have Been Jeopardized." *Houston Chronicle,* August 10, 1999.

Stratton, Samuel J., Christopher Rogers, and Karen Green. "Sudden Death in Individuals in Hobble Restraints during Paramedic Transport." *Annals of Emergency Medicine* 25, no. 5 (1995): 710–14.

Straus, Robert. "The Nature and Status of Medical Sociology." *American Sociological Review* 22, no. 2 (1957): 200–204.

Strauss, Anselm. *Continual Permutations of Action.* New York: Aldine de Gruyter, 1993.

Strauss, Anselm, Shizuko Fagerhaugh, Barbara Suczek, and Carolyn Wiener. "Sentimental Work in the Technologized Hospital." *Sociology of Health and Illness* 4, no. 3 (1982): 254–78.

———. *The Social Organization of Medical Work.* Chicago: University of Chicago Press, 1985.

Stryker, Robin. "Rules, Resources, and Legitimacy Processes: Some Implications for Social Conflict, Order, and Change." *American Journal of Sociology* 99, no. 4 (1994): 847–910.

Sturner, William Q. "Can Baby Organs Be Donated in All Forensic Cases? Proposed Guidelines for Organ Donation from Infants under Medical Examiner Jurisdiction." *American Journal of Forensic Medicine and Pathology* 16, no. 3 (1995): 215–18.

Sudnow, David. *Passing On: The Social Organization of Dying.* Englewood Cliffs, NJ: Prentice-Hall, 1967.

Sullivan, Frank M., and Susan M. Barlow. "Review of Risk Factors for Sudden Infant Death Syndrome." *Pediatric and Perinatal Epidemiology* 15 (2001): 144–200.

Task Force on Infant Sleep Position and SIDS. "Changing Concepts of Sudden Infant Death Syndrome: Implications for Infant Sleeping Environment and Sleep Position." *Pediatrics* 105, no. 3 (2000): 650–56.

Thali, Michael J., Kathrin Yen, Wolf Schweitzer, Peter Vock, Chris Boesch, Chris Ozdoba, Gerhard Schroth, Michael Ith, Martin Sonnenschein, Tanja Doernhoefer, Eva Scheurer, Thomas Plattner, and Richard Dirnhofer. "Virtopsy, a New Imaging Horizon in Forensic Pathology: Virtual Autopsy by Postmortem Multislice Computed Tomography (MSCT) and Magnetic Resonance Imaging (MRI)—a Feasibility Study." *Journal of Forensic Sciences* 48, no. 2 (2003): 386–403.

Thunder, James M. "Quiet Killings in Medical Facilities: Detection and Prevention." *Issues in Law and Medicine* 18 (2003): 211–37.

Timmermans, Stefan. "Closed-Chest Cardiac Massage: The Emergence of a Discovery Trajectory." *Science, Technology, and Human Values* 24, no. 2 (1999): 213–40.

———. "Resuscitation Technology in the Emergency Department: Towards a Dignified Death." *Sociology of Health and Illness* 20, no. 2 (1998): 144–67.

———. *Sudden Death and the Myth of CPR.* Philadelphia: Temple University Press, 1999.

Timmermans, Stefan, and Alison Angell. "Evidence-Based Medicine, Clinical Uncertainty, and Learning to Doctor." *Journal of Health and Social Behavior* 42, no. 4 (2001): 342–59.

Timmermans, Stefan, and Marc Berg. *The Gold Standard: The Challenge of Evidence-Based Medicine and Standardization in Health Care.* Philadelphia: Temple University Press, 2003.

———. "Standardization in Action: Achieving Local Universality through Medical Protocols." *Social Studies of Science* 26, no. 4 (1997): 769–99.

Timmermans, Stefan, and Emily Kolker. "Evidence-Based Medicine and the Reconfiguration of Medical Knowledge." *Journal of Health and Social Behavior* 45, extra issue (2004), 177–93.

Tullett, Tom. *Clues to Murder.* London: The Bodley Head, 1986.

Turner, Stephen. "What Is the Problem with Experts?" *Social Studies of Science* 31, no. 1 (2001): 123–49.

U.S. Commission on Civil Rights. *Revisiting "Who Is Guarding the Guardians?" A Report on Police Practices and Civil Rights in America.* Washington, DC: U.S. Commission on Civil Rights, 2000.

————. *Who Is Guarding the Guardians?* Washington, DC: U.S. Commission on Civil Rights, 1981.

U. S. Department of Health and Human Services. *Guidelines for Death Scene Investigation of Sudden, Unexplained Infant Deaths: Recommendations of the Interagency Panel on Sudden Infant Death Syndrome.* Washington, DC: National Institutes of Health, 1996.

————. *Medical Examiners' and Coroners' Handbook on Death Registration and Fetal Death Reporting.* Hyattsville, MD: Public Health Service, 1987.

————. Secretary's Advisory Committee on Organ Transplantation. *Interim Report: Recommendations and Appendices.* 2003. http://www.organdonor.gov/acot.html (accessed May 19, 2005).

U.S. Department of Justice. Federal Bureau of Investigation. *Crime in the United States, 2003.* Washington, DC: FBI, 2004.

————. *Uniform Crime Reports Handbook.* 2004 revision. http://www.fbi.gov/ucr/handbook/ucrhandbook04.pdf (accessed September 12, 2005).

Vanatta, Paul R., and Charles S. Petty. "Limitations of the Forensic External Examination in Determining the Cause and Manner of Death." *Human Pathology* 18, no. 2 (1987): 170–74.

Vaughan, Diane. "Autonomy, Interdependence, and Social Control: NASA and the Space Shuttle Challenger." *Administrative Science Quarterly* 35 (1990): 273–305.

————. *The Challenger Launch Decision: Risky Technology, Culture and Deviance at NASA.* Chicago: University of Chicago Press, 1996.

Voelker, Rebecca. "Can Forensic Medicine and Organ Donation Coexist for the Public Good?" *Journal of the American Medical Association* 271, no. 12 (1994): 891–92.

Vovelle, Michel. *La mort et l'occident: De 1300 à nos jours.* Paris: Gallimard, 1983.

Wadee, Shabbir Ahmed. "Forensic Pathology—a Different Perspective: Investigative Medicolegal Systems in the United States." *Medicine and Law* 13 (1994): 519–30.

Walsh, Brendan, Dermot Walsh, and Brendan Whelan. "Suicide in Dublin." *British Journal of Psychiatry* 126 (1975): 309–12.

Warshauer, M. Ellen, and Mary Monk. "Problems in Suicide Statistics for Whites and Blacks." *American Journal of Public Health* 68, no. 4 (1978): 383–88.

Weber, Max. *Economy and Society.* Edited by Guenther Roth and Claus Wittich. Berkeley and Los Angeles: University of California Press, 1978. First published 1914.

Wecht, Cyril H. *Grave Secrets: A Leading Forensic Expert Reveals the Startling Truth about O.J. Simpson, David Koresh, Vincent Foster, and Other Sensational Cases.* New York: Penguin Books, 1996.

————. "Shaken Baby Syndrome." *American Journal of Forensic Medicine and Pathology* 20, no. 3 (1999): 301–2.

Wecht, Cyril H., Mark Curriden, and Benjamin Wecht. *Cause of Death.* New York: Penguin Books, 1993.

Weedn, Victor. "The Potential Federal Role in the Death Investigation System." In Institute of Medicine, *Medicolegal Death Investigation System,* 56–60.

Weedn, Victor W., Michael D. Bell, Mary E. Case, Kim A. Collins, Scott J. Denton, John Edward Gerns, Marie A. Hermann, Donna Hunsaker, Bruce P. Levy, and Kurt Nolte. *National Association of Medical Examiners: Strategic Plan.* National Association of Medical Examiners, 2002.

Weiss, Meira. *The Chosen Body: The Politics of the Body in Israeli Society.* Stanford, CA: Stanford University Press, 2002.

Wells, Gary L. "The Psychology of Line-up Identifications." *Journal of Applied Psychology* 14 (1984): 89–104.

Wennberg, John E. *The Dartmouth Atlas of Health Care, 1999.* Chicago: American Hospital Publishing, 1999.

Wennberg, John E., and Alan Gittlesohn. "Small Area Variations in Health Care Delivery." *Science* 182 (1973): 1102–8.

Westveer, Arthur E., John J. Trestrail, and Anthony J. Pinizotti. "Homicidal Poisonings in the United States: An Analysis of the Uniform Crime Reports from 1980 through 1989." *American Journal of Forensic Medicine and Pathology* 17, no. 4 (1996): 282–88.

Wetli, Charles V. *Laboratory Practice Management LPM-13.* New York: American Society of Clinical Pathologists, 1997.

Wetli, Charles V., and David A. Fishbain. "Cocaine-Induced Psychosis and Sudden Death in Recreational Cocaine Users." *Journal of Forensic Sciences* 30, no. 3 (1985): 873–80.

Wetli, Charles V., Roger E. Mittleman, and Valerie J. Rao. *Practical Forensic Pathology.* New York: Igaku-Shoin, 1988.

Wichita Police Department. *In-Custody Sudden Deaths.* Wichita Police Department Training Bulletin. 1995.

Wick, L., J. Mickell, T. Barnes, and J. Allen. "Pediatric Organ Donation: Impact of Medical Examiner Refusal." *Transplantation Proceedings* 27, no. 4 (1995): 2539–44.

Wilensky, Harold. "The Professionalization of Everyone?" *American Journal of Sociology* 60 (1974): 137–58.

Wilkinson, S. "Commodification Arguments for the Legal Prohibition of Organ Sale." *Health Care Annals* 8, no. 2 (2000): 189–201.

Williams, Fiona L. R., Gillian A. Lang, and David T. Mage. "Sudden Unexpected Infant Deaths in Dundee, 1882–1891: Overlying or SIDS?" *Scottish Medical Journal* 46 (2001): 43–47.

Willinger, Marian. "SIDS Prevention." *Annals of Pediatrics* 24, no. 7 (1995): 358–64.

Wilson, Edward F., Joseph H. Davis, Joseph D. Bloom, Peter J. Batten, and Sheku G. Kamara. "Homicide or Suicide: The Killing of Suicidal Persons by Law Enforcement Officers." *Journal of Forensic Sciences* 43, no. 1 (1997): 46–52.

Wilson, James Q., and George L. Kelling. "Broken Windows." *Atlantic Monthly* 249, no. 3 (1982): 29–38.

———. "Making Neighborhoods Safe." *Atlantic Monthly* 263, no. 2 (1989): 46–52.

Wirthwein, Darren B., Jeffrey J. Barnard, and Joseph A. Prahlow. "Suicide by Drowning: A 20 Year Review." *Journal of Forensic Sciences* 47, no. 1 (2002): 131–36.

Wise, Paul H. "The Anatomy of a Disparity in Infant Mortality." *Annual Review of Public Health* 24 (2003): 341–62.

Woods, R. I., P. A. Watterson, and J. H. Woodward. "The Causes of Rapid Infant Mortality Decline in England and Wales, 1861–1921." Pts. 1 and 2. *Population Studies* 42, no. 3 (1988): 343–66; 43, no. 1 (1989): 113–32.

Worcester, Nancy, and Mariamne Whatley. "The Response of the Health Care System to the Women's Health Movement: The Selling of Women's Health Centers." In *Feminism within the Science and Health Care Profession,* edited by Sue V. Rosser, 89–103. New York: Pergamon, 1988.

World Health Organization. *Prevention of Suicide.* Public Health Paper No. 35. Geneva: World Health Organization, 1968.

Wynne, Brian. "Establishing the Rules of Laws: Constructing Expert Authority." In *Expert Evidence: Interpreting Science in the Law,* edited by Roger Smith and Brian Wynne, 23–55. London: Routledge, 1989.

Zilboorg, Gregory. "Suicide among Civilized and Primitive Races." *American Journal of Psychiatry* 92 (1936): 1347–69.

Zobel, Hiller B. "The Jury on Trial." *American Heritage* 46, no. 4 (1995): 42–52.

Zola, Irving Kenneth. "Medicine as an Institution of Social Control." *Sociological Review* 20 (1972): 487–504.

Zugibe, Frederick T., James Costello, Mark Breithaupt, and Joseph Segelbacher. "Model Organ Description Protocols for Completion by Transplant Surgeons Using Organs Procured from Medical Examiner Cases." *Journal of Transplant Coordination* 9, no. 2 (1999): 73–80.

Zussman, Robert. *Intensive Care: Medical Ethics and the Medical Profession.* Chicago: University of Chicago Press, 1992.